COLOMBO'S CONCISE CANADIAN QUOTATIONS

COLOMBO'S CONCISE CANADIAN QUOTATIONS

Edited by John Robert Colombo

Hurtig Publishers
Edmonton

Hurtig Publishers
10560 105 Street
Edmonton, Alberta

ISBN
0-88830-110-3 (paper)
0-88830-111-1 (case)

Printed and bound
in Canada
by The Hunter Rose Company
Toronto, Ontario

Canada only needs to be known in order to be great.

(J. Castell Hopkins)

Preface

"A dictionary of quotations is a collective composition incorporating the experiences of a vast range of people. In offering the thoughts and sayings of those who call themselves Canadians, or who have had occasion to observe or think about Canada, *Colombo's Canadian Quotations* is really about human experience. It is a celebration of Canada (though it is not entirely concerned with Canada) through the medium of quotation. It is an immense mosaic and a living collage, a repository and an inventory of lore and learning."

With these words I began the preface to *Colombo's Canadian Quotations*, published by Hurtig Publishers in the fall of 1974. They apply equally well to the present book, *Colombo's Concise Canadian Quotations*, which is being published, again by Hurtig Publishers, but this time in the fall of 1976. The new book differs from the old book in many important ways—in length, in arrangement, and in content. It is being published because both the editor and the publisher feel a need exists for a concise, topically arranged collection of familiar and memorable Canadian quotations in both paperback and hardback editions. The present work meets this need.

Colombo's Concise Canadian Quotations presents 2,500 quotations, arranged according to 600 subject categories, with an index of 1,000 authors. The quotations range in time from approximately 400 B.C. to March 31, 1976. (For readers who wish to compare the details of this book with those of the original, *Colombo's Canadian Quotations* presented 6,000 quotations by 2,500 authors, with an index of 20,000 keyword and subject entries; passages ranged in time from approximately 400 B.C. to December 31, 1973.)

This concise edition is not simply a shorter version of the longer book, but a substantially different one. It bears the same relation to the earlier work as a son does to his father. The son issues from the father's body, is recognizably related to the parent, but has many individual features and enjoys a life of his own. Of the 2,500 quotations here, 800 are new and have never before been published in any book of quotations. They come from books, magazines, and newspapers published since the appearance of the earlier book, and from my ongoing research in all areas of Canadiana. For the 1,700 quotations reprinted from CCQ, all the source notes have been revised and all the contributors identified for republication in CCCQ. In some cases, emendations have been made to acknowledge new research. The unpublished material is of a more topical nature than the previously published material, and is much wittier.

The son differs from the father in one other fundamental way. *Colombo's Canadian Quotations* was the first dictionary of Canadian quotations to be arranged alphabetically by author, following in the footsteps of *Bartlett's Familiar Quotations* and *The Oxford Dictionary of Quotations*, whereas CCCQ follows the popular principle of arrangement by subject or category. The six hundred categories are alphabetically arranged, with a consistent system of cross-references that draws the user's attention to topically related subject-areas. This is a major structural shift, for the new arrangement permits the reader immediate access to the subject at hand, an access that is only indirectly possible through the 20,000-entry index to CCQ. But the index to CCCQ is not without interest. It permits the location of a quotation by each of its 1,000 authors and, since it is a detailed index, does not simply list page numbers, but presents a *précis* of each quotation along with its page and column number.

Since CCQ and CCCQ are quite different, semi-independent creations, it was decided to append to them different dedications. Both CCQ and CCCQ bear as their motto, "Canada only needs to be known in order to be great," an affirmation made by J. Castell Hopkins in 1901. CCQ bears a dedication to the Honourable Walter L. Gordon who, it is explained, has done more "to reveal to Canadians that there is such a thing as the national interest, and that its defence is a normal act of national self-respect." CCCQ bears a dedication to George P. Grant, the philosopher and essayist whose moral meditation, *Lament for a Nation* (1965), which I had the privilege of editing for its publishers, has meant so much to an entire generation of Canadians. "We listen to others to discover what we ourselves believe," Professor Grant said on CBC-TV in February 1959, although it is to this man that many Canadians have chosen to listen instead.

This is where the differences end. CCQ and CCCQ have much more in common than the 1,700 quotations they share, for they have a common purpose. Both books attempt to tap the national psyche; to document those words, phrases, and remarks that have become characteristic expressions; and to help to reveal the Canadian spirit through the medium of quotation. To this end, I have regarded breadth as a virtue and inclusiveness as a cardinal principle. The two books include familiar and memorable remarks made by Canadians about any subject under the sun, and amusing or revealing observations made about Canada by foreigners. The result of my "determined browsing," which has now extended over six years, is the publication of books that aim, in the phrases of Marshall McLuhan, "to chart old landmarks" and "to map new terrain," to perpetuate the old and to present the new in a useful and readable way.

Canadians are seldom taken seriously by the editors of books of quotations published in London, New York, and Paris. Wolfe's dying words, Osler's bedside observations, Service's Yukon ballads, Leacock's hyperbole—these may appear. But one searches in vain for the wise observations of Bob Edwards, the wry comments of Sir John A. Macdonald, the clever pronouncements of Marshall McLuhan, or even the utterances of John G. Diefenbaker and Pierre Elliott Trudeau, those two most quotable of Canadians. As often as not, their wit and wisdom go unremarked outside the country (and within the country as well). This nation's contribution to *Bartlett's Familiar Quotations* or *The Oxford Dictionary of Quotations* has remained in the neighbourhood of one-half of one per cent. Are Canadians too taciturn, too unimaginative, to originate memorable remarks? A more convincing reason for the universal neglect of Canadian wit and eloquence might be that this country has lacked lively and wide-ranging collections of quotable material from which native and foreign editors could crib. This is no longer the case. Native and foreign editors, take note!

While it is true that, of the twenty-five hundred quotations in this book, fewer than three hundred are in the instant-recognition class, the majority are notable for being charged with social interest. Most of the quotations here dramatize an important incident in the past; present a popular or unusual point of view; delight or instruct with a pun or an observation that has yet to grow hackneyed with use. For every familiar quotation (like "The twentieth century belongs to Canada") there are perhaps ten that deserve to be familiar—like "The left in Canada is more *gauche* than *sinister*," an observation made by John Paul Harney. It is only through books of quotations that such remarks will reach and remain accessible to a wide public.

The achievements of others made this book possible. A handbook always on my desk is Norah Story's *The Oxford Companion to Canadian History and Literature* (1967). Next to it stands W. Stewart Wallace's *The Macmillan Dictionary of Canadian Biography* (third edition,

1963), *The Canadian Oxford Atlas of the World* (second edition, 1957), William Rose Benét's *The Reader's Encyclopedia* (1948), Walter S. Avis's *A Dictionary of Canadianisms on Historical Principles* (1967), and the ten-volume set of John E. Robbins's *Encyclopedia Canadiana* (edition of 1963). I have consulted, from time to time, *Canadian Quotations and Phrases* (1952), edited by Robert M. Hamilton, whose pioneering work I am pleased to acknowledge, as well as the only other modern collections of Canadian quoted matter, *"Quotations" from English Canadian Literature* (1973) and *Dictionnaire de citations de la littérature québécoise* (1974), both edited by David Strickland.

I wish to acknowledge the assistance I received in the preparation of this concise edition from Philip Singer of the Bathurst Heights Area Branch of the North York Public Library System. The job of mechanically rearranging the entries was done by Stuart Ross, a young poet, and the task of organizing the new material and preparing the typescript was undertaken with enthusiasm, dispatch, and accuracy by Nora Elliott, a librarian now with the North Bay Public Library. Without their dedication, CCCQ would not have been published in 1976.

I am indebted to a whole host of others who responded to the invitation in CCQ (repeated in *Colombo's Little Book of Canadian Proverbs, Graffiti, Limericks, and Other Vital Matters*, published in the fall of 1975, and extended to the users of this book as well) to send in corrections and additional quotations. For specific material I have to thank: J. Patrick Boyer, Margaret Collier, Kirwan H. Cox, Doug Fetherling, Robert I. Fitzhenry, Robert Fulford, J.L. Granatstein, Hugh Hood, Asher Joram, Grace S. Lewis, Martin O'Malley, Janice Patton, Sandy Stewart, Norah Story, Peter Weinrich, and Larry Zolf. For help with CCQ, and indirectly with CCCQ, I remain in the debt of William Toye, the editor of editors. A patron of the arts in his own way is the publisher, Mel Hurtig, whose enthusiasms are contagious. David Shaw, once again, designed the layout and supervised production of the book. While no arts subsidy was requested for the preparation of this concise edition, I must acknowledge the past assistance of the Ontario Arts Council and the Canada Council.

My quote-collecting is an ongoing operation. Readers and users of this volume may help in the preparation of future editions by drawing my attention to errors of omission and commission. If someone's "favourite quotation" is not in this book, let it be in the next one. All communications will be acknowledged.

JOHN ROBERT COLOMBO

42 Dell Park Avenue
Toronto, Ontario
Canada M6B 2T6

Ability

People are always ready to admit a man's ability after he gets there.

> BOB EDWARDS, writer and publisher of the Calgary *Eye Opener*, Jan. 27, 1912.

I looked the sun straight in the eye. He put on dark glasses.

> F.R. SCOTT, Montreal man-of-letters, in "Eclipse" (1964), *Selected Poems* (1966).

Abortion

See also BIRTH CONTROL; WOMEN AND THE LAW.

If men could get pregnant, abortion would be a sacrament.

> LAURA SABIA, head of the National Action Committee on the Status of Women, remark made in 1971.

No one is for abortion. It does damage to the fabric of society and violence to the feelings of self-worth of women.

> *

The biggest baby killers sit in the House of Commons, in all the provincial parliaments and in municipal offices, where budgets are drafted and priorities are established that essentially discard children.

> *

When reverence for life stops at the moment that the umbilical cord is cut, it cannot be taken seriously.

> JUNE CALLWOOD, writer and woman-of-all-causes, in the Toronto *Star*, Aug. 12, 1974.

What's the magic about being able to kill a child just before it's born and not being able to kill it just after?

> OTTO LANG, minister of Justice, on abortion, quoted by John Gray in the Toronto *Star*, Aug. 12, 1974.

I am not pro-abortion any more than I am pro-appendectomy.

HENRY MORGENTALER, Montreal doctor imprisoned for abortion, quoted by Marq de Villiers in *Weekend*, Sept. 14, 1974.

Acadians

Still stands the forest primeval; but under
  the shade of its branches
Dwells another race, with other customs
  and language.
Only along the shore of the mournful and
  misty Atlantic
Linger a few Acadian peasants, whose
  fathers from exile
Wandered back to their native land to die
  in its bosom.
In the fisherman's cot the wheel and the
  loom are still busy;
Maidens still wear their Norman caps and
  their kirtles of homespun,
And by the evening fire repeat
  Evangeline's story,
While from its rocky caverns the deep-
  voiced, neighbouring ocean
Speaks, and in accents disconsolate
  answers the wail of the forest.

> HENRY WADSWORTH LONGFELLOW, American poet, in *Evangeline: A Tale of Acadie* (1847), a moving account of the expulsion of the Acadians in 1775 from "the little village of Grand-Pré" on "the shores of the Basin of Minas."

Achievement

See also SUCCESS.

The biggest things are always the easiest to do because there is no competition.

> SIR W.C. VAN HORNE, railroad builder, about 1890, quoted by Peter C. Newman in *Flame of Power* (1959).

Great deeds are better than great sonnets, and Canada's call to her sons is a stirring one to action; for the poetry of action exists just as does the poetry of words and the great deed that is accomplished is more glorious than the great sonnet.

> SIR ARTHUR CONAN DOYLE, creator of Sherlock Holmes, in "The Future of Canadian Literature," address to the Canadian Club of Montreal, June 4, 1914.

The real value of your life can only be

gauged by what it gives to the world. Life is redeemed by achievement. All its fun is in doing things.

> SIR WILFRED GRENFELL, medical missionary, in *A Labrador Logbook* (1938).

Nobody ever did anything by pussy-footing.

> DONALD GORDON, controversial CNR president, quoted by Peter C. Newman in *Flame of Power* (1959).

If you don't care who gets the credit, you can accomplish anything.

> HARRY "RED" FOSTER, founder of Foster Advertising Ltd., quoted by Maggie Siggins in the Toronto *Telegram*, June 19, 1969.

Man has become what he is through dissatisfaction, which in the end has always made him do everything differently than it was supposed to be done.

> JOSEF SKVORECKY, Czech novelist living in Toronto, in *All the Bright Young Men and Women* (1971).

Actors and Actresses
See also FILM; THEATRE.

Actresses don't have husbands, they have attendants.

> MARGARET ANGLIN, once North America's leading dramatic actress, quoted by Harding Lemay in *Inside, Looking Out* (1971).

What name are you going to use?

> VINCENT MASSEY, future governor general, to his younger brother Raymond who, at the age of twenty-five, announced that he would try his luck on the English stage, 1921.

Son, always give 'em a good show and travel first class.

> WALTER HUSTON, Toronto-born stage and screen personality, to Gregory Peck who asked the character actor why he was so good, quoted by David Shipman in *The Great Movie Stars* (1970).

A diploma can't get you work in the theatre but a part can.

> GENEVIÈVE BUJOLD, Montreal film star now living in Malibu, quoted by Judy Klemesrud in the Montreal *Star*, Nov. 18, 1967.

Actresses never retire. They just raise children.

> WILLIAM SHATNER, Toronto-born television actor married to a former actress, quoted by Sam Solomon in the Toronto *Star*, Dec. 5, 1967.

It is impossible for an actor to pay the telephone bill when the telephone never rings.

> ANDREW ALLAN in *Andrew Allan* (1974), the distinguished director's autobiography.

I've heard there are five stages in a TV star's career.

You can sum up the first stage as: "Who is Lorne Greene?"

Second stage: "Get me Lorne Greene."

Third: "Get me somebody like Lorne Greene."

Fourth: "Get me a young Lorne Greene."

Fifth and last: "Who was Lorne Greene?"

Thank God, they're still saying, "Get me Lorne Greene."

> LORNE GREENE, Ottawa-born television star and actor, quoted by Frank Rasky in the Toronto *Star*, Nov. 12, 1974.

Adultery
See also MARRIAGE; SEX.

Adultery is the same the world over; it's only the method of approach that varies.

> SIR JAMES LOUGHEED, senator from 1889 and chairman of the Senate Divorce Committee, quoted by Robert M. Hamilton in *Canadian Quotations and Phrases* (1952).

Adventure

Adventure is risk with a purpose.

> ROBERT MCCLURE, missionary and former moderator of the United Church of Canada, adapted from a remark in the Toronto *Star*, Aug. 6, 1974.

I don't go where the money is, I go where the adventure is.

> PIERRE BERTON, writer and media personality, interviewed by John Hofsess in *Inner Views* (1975).

Advertising and Slogans
See also BUSINESS.

The good boys die young unless they eat our Graham bread.

> Recipe for Graham Bread published in an Ontario cookbook of 1889, quoted by Madame Jehane Benoit in *The Canadiana Cookbook* (1970).

Advertising is salesmanship in print.

> JOHN E. KENNEDY, creator of the "reason why" advertising concept, to Chicago advertising executive Albert Lasker in 1904. Quoted by John Gunther in *Taken at the Flood: The Story of Albert D. Lasker* (1960).

Goods Satisfactory or Money Refunded.

> TIMOTHY EATON, founder of the T. Eaton Co., evolved the generous guarantee and return policy; it became the company's slogan as early as 1884, but these words first appeared in print in the Eaton's catalogue of 1913.

Advertising may be described as the science of arresting the human intelligence long enough to get money from it.

> STEPHEN LEACOCK, the dean of Canadian humorists, in "The Perfect Salesman," *The Garden of Folly* (1924).

There is a new marvel of science which is already playing an important part in the art of indirect advertising and which is destined to become a still larger factor in the future. It is radio broadcasting. There are certain necessary and proper limitations with respect to the employment of this agency and it is essential that broadcasting be surrounded with such safeguards as will prevent the air becoming what might be described as an atmospheric bill board.

> SIR HENRY THORNTON, broadcasting executive, to the Advertising Clubs of the World, Philadelphia, June 21, 1926. Quoted by E. Austin Weir in *The Struggle for National Broadcasting in Canada* (1965).

It's mainly because of the meat.

> J. SCOTT FEGGANS, advertising chief for Dominion Stores, dreamt up this popular slogan and "came in one morning with the words on the back of the proverbial envelope" in 1955. The Toronto *Star*, Aug. 9, 1975.

COME IN AND GET LOST!

> *

DON'T JUST STAND THERE, BUY SOMETHING!

> *

HONEST ED'S NOT A BAKER . . . BUT HE SAVES YOU "DOUGH"!

> *

IT'S FUN TO SHOP AT . . . HONEST ED'S!

> Signs from Honest Ed's, the well-known discount department store in Toronto, 1960s.

Advertising is a business process that combines the multiplication of message with the modulation of memory.

> GEORGE ELLIOTT, Toronto advertising executive, in "Advertising," *Mass Media in Canada* (1962), edited by John A. Irving.

What is the difference between unethical and ethical advertising? Unethical advertising uses falsehoods to deceive the public; ethical advertising uses truth to deceive the public.

> VILHJALMUR STEFANSSON, outspoken Arctic explorer, in *Discovery: The Autobiography of Vilhjalmur Stefansson* (1964).

Without advertising, it's Russia.

> JOHN STRAITON, vice-chairman of Ogilvy and Mather, quoted by Joanne Strong in the Toronto *Globe and Mail*, May 28, 1973.

Age
See also YOUTH.

Oldest. The greatest authenticated age to which a human has ever lived is 113 years 124 days in the case of Pierre Joubert, a French-Canadian bootmaker. He was born in Charlesbourg, Quebec Province, Canada, on July 15, 1701, and died in Quebec on November 16, 1814. His longevity was the subject of an investigation in 1870 by Dr. Tache, Official Statistician to the Canadian Government, and the proofs published are irrefutable.

> NORRIS and ROSS MCWHIRTER, British encyclopaedists; an "extreme" from the *Guinness Book of World Records* (tenth ed., 1971).

One can always tell when one is getting old and serious by the way that holidays seem to interfere with one's work.

> BOB EDWARDS, writer and publisher of the Calgary *Eye Opener*, Dec. 20, 1913.

When a man reaches forty he usually settles down to make the best of things.

R.D. CUMMING, writer and aphorist, in *Skookum Chuck Fables* (1915).

An excellent recipe for longevity is this: cultivate a minor ailment, and take very good care of it.

SIR WILLIAM OSLER, world-famous physician and medical teacher, quoted by Harvey Cushing in *The Life of Sir William Osler* (1925).

About the only good thing you can say about old age is, it's better than being dead!

STEPHEN LEACOCK, renowned Canadian writer and humorist, in "This Business of Growing Old," *Reader's Digest*, March 1940.

I'm not interested in age. People who tell their ages are silly. You're as young as you feel.

ELIZABETH ARDEN, the Ontario-born cosmetic queen, quoted by Lore and Maurice Cowan in *The Wit of Women* (1969).

Old priests don't make the best bishops.

ALCIDE COURCY, Quebec Liberal party organizer, in reference to the candidacy of the youthful Robert Bourassa in the election of April 29, 1970. Quoted by John Saywell in *Quebec 70* (1971).

While there's snow on the roof, it doesn't mean the fire has gone out in the furnace.

JOHN G. DIEFENBAKER, former prime minister, to those attending his eightieth birthday party, Ottawa, Sept. 17, 1975. Prime Minister Trudeau introduced the octogenarian by greeting him "at eighty, at the midpoint in his political career."

Agriculture
See FARMING.

Alberta

In token of the love which thou hast shown
For this wide land of freedom, I have named
A province vast, and for its beauty famed,
By thy dear name to be hereafter known.
Alberta shall it be! Her fountains thrown
From alps unto three oceans, to all men
Shall vaunt her loveliness e'en now; and when,

Each little hamlet to a city grown,
And numberless as blades of prairie grass,
Or the thick leaves in distant forest bower,
Great peoples hear the giant currents pass,
Still shall the waters, bringing wealth and power,
Speak the loved named—land of silver springs—
Worthy the daughter of our English kings.

MARQUIS OF LORNE, later ninth Duke of Argyle, Governor General of Canada, dedicated this *vers d'occasion* to his wife Princess Louise Caroline Alberta, fourth daughter of Queen Victoria, after he renamed Alberta (formerly the District of Assiniboia) in 1882. From *Yesterday and Today in Canada* (1910).

So farewell to Alberta, farewell to the west,
It's backwards I'll go to the girl I love best.
I'll go back to the east and get me a wife
And never eat cornbread the rest of my life.

Last verse of the traditional song, "The Alberta Homesteader," in *Canada's Story in Song* (1965), edited by Edith Fowke and Alan Mills.

Land of the Second Chance.

HOWARD PALMER, academic, used this phrase in 1972 for the title of a comprehensive study of ethnic groups in southern Alberta.

Drink the Water of the Peace River and You Will Return Again

Sign outside the Administrative Building, Peace River, 1950.

Alcohol
See DRINKING.

American People
See UNITED STATES OF AMERICA.

Anger

. . . for when a man is wrong, and won't admit it, he always gets angry.

THOMAS CHANDLER HALIBURTON, Nova Scotian writer and wit, in *Sam Slick's Wise Saws and Modern Instances* (1853).

Is not anger the cleanest of passions?

GRATTAN O'LEARY, Conservative spokesman in the Senate, quoted by I. Norman Smith in *The Journal Men* (1974).

There is sometimes even an ecstasy in anger.

> DR. JACK BIRNBAUM, Toronto psychiatrist and primal therapist, in *Cry Anger: A Cure for Depression* (1973).

Animals

See also BEAVER, BUFFALO, HORSES, WOLVES.

Have the wild things no moral or legal rights? What right has man to inflict such long and fearful agony on a fellow-creature, simply because that creature does not speak his language?

> ERNEST THOMPSON SETON, artist and naturalist, in "Redruff," *Wild Animals I Have Known* (1895).

Annexation

See also CONTINENTALISM.

The Unanimous Voice of the Continent is Canada must be ours; Quebec must be taken.

> JOHN ADAMS, second president of the United States (1796-1800), made this statement following the death of Brigadier-General Richard Montgomery who fell trying to take Quebec, New Year's Day, 1776.

In the mean time the acquisition *of Canada is not an object with us*, we must make valuable what we have already *acquired* and at the same time take such measures as to *weaken it as a British province*.

> JAMES MUNROE, fifth president of the United States (1817-1825), in a letter written to Thomas Jefferson from Trenton, New Jersey, Nov. 1, 1784. *The Papers of Thomas Jefferson* (1953), edited by Julian P. Boyd.

The conquest of Canada is within your power. I trust I shall not be deemed presumptuous when I state, what I verily believe, that the militia of Kentucky are alone competent to place Montreal and Upper Canada at your feet.

> HENRY CLAY, U.S. senator from Kentucky, an instigator of the War of 1812, speaking in the U.S. Senate in 1810.

I wish the British Government would give you Canada at once. It is fit for nothing but to breed quarrels.

LORD ASHBURTON, British representative in the New Brunswick-Maine boundary dispute, to John Quincy Adams, U.S. ambassador to Britain, 1816.

Fifty-four Forty, or Fight!

> WILLIAM ALLEN, U.S. senator, has been credited with first voicing this rallying cry, which became the slogan of the Democratic party in the 1844 federal election, in a speech on the Oregon boundary question in the Senate in 1844. Allen demanded that the American boundary be extended north to 54° 40′.

Peaceably if possible, forcibly if necessary.

> JAMES GORDON BENNETT, New York publisher and editor expressing the formula the United States should adopt to effect the annexation of Canada, in the New York *Herald*, Feb. 1865.

Now, in that very history we find that it was not such an easy thing to maintain that hundred years of peace . . . when the shibboleth of one of our presidents was "Fifty-four forty or fight," and we didn't get "Fifty-four forty," and we didn't fight.

> WILLIAM HOWARD TAFT, president of the United States (1909-1913), in "Fraternal Relations," address to the Empire Club of Canada, 1919.

Architecture

I believe it will take a thousand years to develop a national style in Canada, but I do see a light in the west over a grain elevator.

> ERIC ARTHUR, Toronto architect and writer, in "Architecture in Canada," *Yearbook of the Arts in Canada: 1928-29* (1929), edited by Bertram Brooker.

. . . you will not find in Canada much of what is commonly considered Great or Original architecture. No Parthenons, no Christopher Wrens, no Westminster Abbeys.

> ALAN GOWANS, Canadian-born professor of architecture, in *Building Canada: An Architectural History of Canadian Life* (1966).

I'm convinced that no one is going to be able to mass-produce a house until the entire process is under a single corporate structure, and probably a single union too.

MOSHE SAFDIE, innovative designer of Expo 67's Habitat, in *Beyond Habitat* (1970).

Architecture is a backdrop for worthwhile human activity.

RAYMOND MORIYAMA, Vancouver-born Toronto architect, quoted in *Time*, July 9, 1973.

In architecture, artistic judgment is a carnival of relativism. One man's horror is another man's Taj Mahal.

CLAUDE T. BISSELL, former president of the University of Toronto, from *Halfway up Parnassus* (1974).

Arctic

See also NORTH, THE.

The whole region I have been describing has excessively hard winter; for eight months in the year the cold is intolerable; the ground is frozen iron-hard, so that to turn earth into mud requires not water but fire . . . . Even apart from the eight month's winter, the remaining four months are cold . . . .

HERODOTUS, ancient Greek historian, in *Herodotus: The Histories* (1954), translated from the Greek by Aubrey de Selincourt. The above passage, written about 430 B.C., in the opinion of some anthropologists refers to the Arctic regions of Canada.

Now we have done better than Bjarni where this country is concerned—we at least have set foot on it. I shall give this country a name and call it *Helluland.*

LEIF THE LUCKY, also known as Leif Ericson, likely landed on Baffin Island in the Eastern Arctic, about 1000 A.D. "Helluland" means "slab-land." *The Vinland Sagas* (1965), translated from the Old Icelandic by Magnus Magnusson and Hermann Palsson.

The lothsome view of the shore, and irksome noyse of the yce was such, as that it bred strange conceits among vs, so that we supposed the place to be wast and voyd of any sensible or vegitable creatures, whereupon I called the same Desolation.

JOHN DAVIS, English explorer searching for the Northwest Passage, in *The Worldes Hydrographical Description* (1595).

Not here; the White North has thy bones,

And thou, heroic sailor soul,
Are passing on thy happier voyage now
Toward no earthly pole.

ALFRED LORD TENNYSON, poet laureate of Great Britain, wrote these lines for the monument erected in 1875 in Westminster Abbey to Sir John Franklin, who perished in the Arctic in 1847 but whose body was never found.

If blood be the price of the Arctic, Lord God we have paid in full.

RUDYARD KIPLING, English author, attributed. "An adaption of two lines from 'The Song of the Dead' by Rudyard Kipling: 'If blood be the price of admiralty, Lord God, we Ha' paid in full.' " Norah Story, *The Oxford Companion to Canadian History and Literature* (1967).

The friendly Arctic.

VILHJALMUR STEFANSSON, outspoken Arctic explorer, in *The Friendly Arctic* (1921). Stefansson's theme is that the North, far from being forbidding, is generally friendly.

The trouble lies in the fact that a Canadian Prime Minister has never been exiled to the Arctic.

VILHJALMUR STEFANSSON, Manitoba-born Arctic explorer, attributed.

It was the borderline between the prosaic world, where things went by rule and rote and where all fitted to the human scale, and the world as God first made it out of chaos, which had no care for humanity.

JOHN BUCHAN, GOVERNOR GENERAL LORD TWEEDSMUIR, writing about northern Quebec in the novel *Sick Heart River* (1941).

There's a dusky, husky maiden in the Arctic,
And she waits for me but it is not in vain,
For some day I'll put my mukluks on and ask her
If she'll wed me when the ice worms nest again.

MONA SYMINGTON, song-writer, the first verse of "When the Ice Worms Nest Again." A version of the song is reproduced by C.E. Gilham in *Raw North* (1947).

Our best defence in the Arctic is the Arctic itself.

W.L. MACKENZIE KING, prime minister, quoted by James Eayrs in *In Defence of Canada:*

Peacemaking and Deterrence (1972).

Nowadays this country has become as remote as Wall Street. If a Canadian wishes to visit the Canadian Arctic, he has to get permission from Washington.

A.Y. JACKSON, member of the Group of Seven, in *A Painter's Country* (1958).

I like Frobisher. But it looks like the moon.

PRINCE CHARLES, on a royal visit to Frobisher Bay, July 5, 1970. Quoted by Pat Carney in *Tiara and Atigi* (1971).

Art

See also CULTURE; ESKIMO ART; PAINTING.

An artist has more than two eyes, that's a fact.

THOMAS CHANDLER HALIBURTON, Nova Scotian writer and wit, in *Sam Slick's Wise Saws and Modern Instances* (1853).

I am having charming audiences, you will be glad to hear; the Canadians are very appreciative people, but it is a great fight in this commercial age to plead the cause of Art. Still the principles which I represent are so broad, so grand, so noble that I have no fear for the future.

OSCAR WILDE, Anglo-Irish playwright, in a letter from Halifax, Oct. 8, 1882. From *The Letters of Oscar Wilde* (1962), edited by Rupert Hart-Davis.

The only positive test of any work of art is the favour of the cultured man.

WILLIAM ARTHUR DEACON, literary editor of the Toronto *Globe and Mail* in the 1940s and 1950s, in "A Theory of Book-Reviewing," *Poteen: A Pot-Pourri of Canadian Essays* (1926).

Have little care that Life is brief,
And less that art is long.
Success is in the silences,
Though fame is in the song.

BLISS CARMAN, New Brunswick-born poet, in "Envoi," *Bliss Carman's Poems* (1929). These lines appear on the poet's tombstone in Poet's Corner, Fredericton.

A work of art . . . must have a beginning and an end and something of an infinitude between the two.

FREDERICK PHILIP GROVE, novelist, in "The Happy Ending," *It Needs To Be Said* (1929).

No greater curse can befall a man than to be afflicted with artistic leanings in Canada.

FREDERICK PHILIP GROVE, novelist, quoted by Stan Obodiac in *My Experiences at a Canadian Authors' Convention* (1957).

It is not hard to say, then, what art should be. Art should be an *awareness*, a sense of *spiritual alertness*, not put on like poetry. The farmer going out to his milking may be aware of its beauty, even though completely inarticulate.

ARTHUR LISMER, member of the Group of Seven, in 1932, quoted by John A.B. McLeish in *September Gale* (1955).

The function of the artist is to disturb. His duty is to arouse the sleeper, to shake the complacent pillars of the world. He reminds the world of its dark ancestry, shows the world its present, and points the way to its new birth. He is at once the product and preceptor of his time. After his passage we are troubled and made unsure of our too-easily accepted realities. He makes uneasy the static, the set and the still. In a world terrified of change, he preaches revolution—the principle of life. He is an agitator, a disturber of the peace—quick, impatient, positive, restless and disquieting. He is the creative spirit of life working in the soul of men.

NORMAN BETHUNE, Ontario-born doctor who died in Mao's China, in a letter to Marion Scott, Madrid, May 5, 1937. Quoted by Roderick Stewart in *Bethune* (1973).

Art is not a mirror but a hammer.

JOHN GRIERSON, founder of the National Film Board in 1939, characteristic remark.

No word meaning "art" occurs in Aivilik, nor does "artist": there are only people. Nor is any distinction made between utilitarian and decorative objects. The Aivilik say simply, "A man should do all things properly."

EDMUND CARPENTER, anthropologist, in *Eskimo* (1959).

More and more we hear people saying

"Don't ask me" or "I am afraid of being wrong" or words to that effect, pointing to a complete surrender of judgment. And where there is no judgment the arts perish.

BARKER FAIRLEY, man-of-letters, in "F.H. Varley," *Our Living Tradition* (1959), edited by Robert L. McDougall.

Great art consists of going beyond reality and not in evading it. One must be able to say, "That is how it is—and something more." Art lies in that "more."

HECTOR GARNEAU, French-Canadian poet, in his journal, April 15, 1935. *The Journal of Saint-Denys-Garneau* (1962), translated by John Glassco.

Art, according to Plato, is a dream for awakened minds, a work of imagination withdrawn from ordinary life, dominated by the same forces that dominate the dream, and yet giving us a perspective and dimension on reality that we don't get from any other approach to reality.

NORTHROP FRYE, literary critic, in "The Keys to Dreamland," *The Educated Imagination* (1963).

No matter how hard you try, there is always going to be someone more underground than you.

ROBERT FULFORD, Toronto columnist, "My Life Underground" (1967), *Marshall Delaney at the Movies* (1974).

Art is anything you can get away with.

MARSHALL MCLUHAN, media pundit, in *The Medium Is the Massage* (1967), with Quentin Fiore.

The Balinese say, "We have no art, we do everything as well as possible."

MARSHALL MCLUHAN, theorist of communications, in *From Cliché to Archetype* (1970), with Wilfred Watson.

There is a difference between art and life and that difference is readability.

MARIAN ENGEL, novelist, the Toronto *Globe and Mail*, Dec. 28, 1974.

Art is anything that people do with distinction.

LOUIS DUDEK, Montreal writer, *Epigrams* (1975).

Atlantic Provinces
See MARITIME PROVINCES.

Automobiles
See DRIVING.

Autumn
See SEASONS.

Aviation

The aeroplane is an invention of the devil and will never play any part in such a serious business as the defence of a nation, my boy!

SIR SAM HUGHES, minister of Militia and Defence, to J.A.D. McCurdy who approached him, in Aug. 1914, to start an air service. Quoted by J.R.K. Main in *Voyageurs of the Air: A History of Civil Aviation in Canada, 1858-1967* (1967).

The whole history of the Canadian North can be divided into two periods—before and after the aeroplane.

HUGH L. KEENLEYSIDE, then deputy minister of Mines and Resources, in the *Canadian Geographical Journal*, Oct. 1949.

I'm proud of the title "bush pilot." It originated in Canada, it relates to men of dedicated interest in flying to the remote regions, and I hope it will never disappear.

C.H. "PUNCH" DICKENS, bush pilot, quoted by Grant McConachie in *Great Canadians* (1965).

Air Canada. That's a good name for a Canadian airline.

JOHNNY CARSON, "The Johnny Carson Show," NBC, Dec. 11, 1974.

Awards
See also TITLES.

I won't win the Leacock Medal for Humour, but I console myself by remembering that Leacock never won the award either.

MAX BRAITHWAITE to John Diefenbaker when the latter predicted the former would win the coveted medal with his book, *Why Shoot the Teacher?* (1965). The prediction came true.

I am dying by honorary degrees.

F.R. SCOTT, professor of law, poet, wit, made

this observation after being awarded an honorary doctorate in 1965.

It's the reward that an opera singer gets. Pop singers get money.

> JAN RUBES, singer, on receiving the Centennial Medal in 1967, quoted by Kaspars Dzeguze in *Maclean's*, Nov. 1968.

The French-speaking film-makers couldn't be here, but they asked me to thank the English-speaking taxpayers.

> GILLES BOIVIN, Quebec director, accepting an Etrog for the musical scoring of *Vertige* at the Canadian Film Awards banquet in Toronto, quoted by Kaspars Dzeguze in the *Globe and Mail*, Oct. 6, 1969.

Thanks. The Maritime mafia has just scratched the surface.

> ANNE MURRAY, popular singer, accepting the 1970 Juno Award of the Canadian music industry as the top female vocalist of the year.

Thanks, I think I deserve this.

> ROD CONEYBEAR, accepting the Nellie for best writer of documentaries on radio, ACTRA Awards, Toronto, April 1974.

Ballet
See DANCE.

Banks
See FINANCE.

Beauty

Ask a Northern Indian, what is beauty? he will answer, a broad flat face, small eyes, high cheek-bones, three or four broad black lines a-cross each cheek, a low forehead, a large broad chin, a clumsy hook-nose, a tawny hide, and breasts hanging down to the belt. Those beauties are greatly heightened, or at least rendered more valuable, when the possessor is capable of dressing all kinds of skins, converting them into the different parts of their clothing, and able to carry eight or ten stone in Summer, or haul a much greater weight in Winter. These, and other similar accomplishments, are all that are sought after, or expected, of a Northern Indian woman.

> SAMUEL HEARNE, explorer, on April 18, 1771, in *A Journey from Prince of Wales's Fort, in Hudson's Bay, to the Northern Ocean* (1795). The text is taken from *A Journey from Prince of Wales's Fort* (1958), edited by Richard Glover.

Canadian girls are so pretty it is a relief to occasionally see a plain one.

> MARK TWAIN, American humorist and writer, quoted by Lena Newman in *An Historical Almanac of Canada* (1967).

All things are beautiful as long as you get them in the proper order.

> JOHN GRIERSON, founder of the National Film Board in 1939, characteristic remark.

There was a time, I guess it was in 1952, when I was doing a lot of paintings that had to do with neon signs. And certainly the neon wasn't pretty but it fascinated me for two or three years. I suddenly realized, walking up that hideous bit of Bay Street from Wellesley Street to Bloor which has mostly showrooms for cars and automobile parts—I suddenly realized these signs were beautiful, all those gorgeous blues, and I realized that if an Egyptian from the time of one of the great Pharaohs were to walk down the street he would have found them a mystery, an overwhelming mystery. There's everything there.

> HAROLD TOWN, Toronto artist, in "Harold Town Talks" (1960), interviewed by Elizabeth Kilbourn, in *Canada: A Guide to the Peaceable Kingdom* (1970), edited by William Kilbourn.

If you're fourteen and reading this, take solace: you probably look a lot better than you think. And *nobody* looks like Miss January.

> MARGO KIDDER, Vancouver-born film actress writing about her thoughts on allowing herself to be photographed for *Playboy*, March 1975.

Beaver
See also ANIMALS; FUR TRADE.

Of the beaver one reads that when it is pursued, knowing this to be on account of the virtue of its testicles for medicinal uses, not being able to flee any farther it stops, and in order to be at peace with its pursuers bites off its testicles with its sharp teeth and leaves them to its enemies.

> LEONARDO DA VINCI, from "Peace," *A Bestiary*, a manuscript unpublished in 1519 when the great Italian artist died. *The Notebooks of Leonardo da Vinci* (1954), edited by Edward MacCurdy.

For his crest, on a wreath argent sable, a beaver proper.

> CHARLES I, King of Great Britain and Ireland, in a royal letter, Newmarket, 1632, granting a coat of arms to Sir William Alexander, Earl of Stirling. This is said to be the first use of the beaver in heraldry associated with Canada. Eleven years earlier, James I had granted Sir William enormous tracts of land in the Maritimes; eleven years later, Sir William would be given the title Viscount Canada.

'Tis a great Pity, Madam, that none of these wonderful Creatures were found in the *Tyber*, or in the Territories of *Parnassus*; what fine Things would the *Greek* and *Roman* Poets have said on this Subject!

> PIERRE-FRANÇOIS-XAVIER DE CHARLEVOIX, French chronicler, in "On Beavers" (1720), *A Voyage to North-America: Undertaken by Command of the Present King of France* (1766).

You know, I'm at last beginning to understand why the beaver is our national emblem. I thought, once, it was due to the industriousness of what had been designated as merely amplified rat. But I was wrong there. For outside its industry the beaver has one peculiar and distinguishing trait. That peculiarity stems from the conviction that its home isn't inhabitable until it has been well damned.

> ARTHUR STRINGER, Chatham-born novelist, in "Canada Finds Her Voice," an address to the Empire Club of Canada, 1949.

The beaver is a good national symbol for Canada. He's so busy chewing he can't see what's going on.

> HOWARD CABLE, orchestra conductor, quoted by Barrie Mason in the Toronto *Star*, July 31, 1971.

Beaverbrook, Lord

I once had youth, and now I have experience.

> LORD BEAVERBROOK, Canadian-born British press lord, in *The Three Keys to Success* (1956).

We were so agreeably placed until he came along to disturb the waters of tranquillity.

> LORD BEAVERBROOK'S opinion of Roy Thomson, who had just become Lord Thomson of Fleet, quoted by Russell Braddon in *Roy Thomson of Fleet Street* (1965).

Here I must say, in my eighty-sixth year, I do not feel greatly different from when I was eighty-five. This is my final word. It is time for me to become an apprentice once more. I have not settled in which direction. But somewhere, sometime soon.

> LORD BEAVERBROOK'S parting words at a gala banquet in London held by Lord Thomson of Fleet on May 25, 1964, to celebrate "the Beaver's" eighty-fifth birthday. It was Beaverbrook's last public appearance; within two weeks, he was dead.

Belief
See also CHRISTIANITY.

Take everything you like seriously, except yourselves.

> RUDYARD KIPLING, English writer, advice to the faculty and students of McGill University where Kipling was awarded his first honorary degree, Montreal, 1907.

We listen to others to discover what we ourselves believe.

> GEORGE P. GRANT, philosopher, introducing a series of interviews with prominent thinkers, on CBC-TV. *CBC Times*, Feb. 28, 1959.

Needing to believe, therefore I may choose.

> ABRAHAM L. FEINBERG, Toronto rabbi, in *Storm the Gates of Jericho* (1964).

The world is my country
The human race is my race
The spirit of man is my God
The future of man is my heaven

> F.R. SCOTT, Montreal man-of-letters, in "Creed" (1964), *Selected Poems* (1966).

Today, rather than pretend to an atheism that can no more be proved than can the existence of God, I prefer to think that agnosticism is the only *modest* faith.

VILHJALMUR STEFANSSON, outspoken Arctic explorer, in *Discovery: The Autobiography of Vilhjalmur Stefansson* (1964).

It is far too much to claim for *Home Country* that it's the chronicle of a time. But it is the chronicle of a political education, my own. And what I've learned is not to believe in magical leaders any more; that character and compassion are more important than ideology; and that even if it's absurd to think you can change things, it's even more absurd to think that it's foolish and unimportant to try.

PETER C. NEWMAN, journalist and author, in *Home Country: People, Places, and Power Politics* (1973).

Bennett, R.B.

[I urge] men and women to put the iron heel ruthlessly on propaganda of that kind.

R.B. BENNETT, prime minister, addressing the Ontario Conservative Association, Nov. 1932. Bennett's stand on leftist and communist agitation earned him the sobriquet, "Iron-Heel Bennett."

Bennett, W.A.C.

I'm plugged into God.

W.A.C. BENNETT's most characteristic remark during his premiership of British Columbia from 1952 to 1972.

Bethune, Norman

Give my everlasting love to . . . all my Canadian and American friends. Tell them I have been very happy. My only regret is that I shall now be unable to do more.

NORMAN BETHUNE, medical doctor born in Gravenhurst, Ontario, and hero of Mao's China, in his last letter written in northern China, Nov. 13, 1939. Quoted by Ted Allan and Sydney Gordon in *The Scalpel, the Sword: The Story of Dr. Norman Bethune* (1952).

Comrade Bethune's spirit, his utter devotion to others without any thought of self,

was shown in his boundless sense of responsibility to his work and his boundless warm-heartedness towards all comrades and the people. Every Communist must learn from him. . . .

MAO TSE-TUNG, chairman of the People's Republic of China, "In Memory of Norman Bethune," tribute to Norman Bethune written on Dec. 21, 1939, in *Quotations from Chairman Mao Tse-tung* (1966), edited by Lin Piao.

If Canada does not often produce great artists, scientists, and professional men, it is not because the material is not amongst us, but because we do not know how to handle it. The characteristics of genius too often arouse our suspicion and distrust, whence it comes that our prophets are so often without honour in their own country. Perhaps if Canada had been a little different, Norman Bethune would not have died in China.

B.K. SANDWELL, editor of *Saturday Night*, Dec. 1939.

Suddenly I realize there are many Bethunes.
From many candidates, fate chooses
Both its victims and its heroes
Often one and the same . . .
Another necessity, another Canuck, and
there could have been another Bethune.

So many of us live in anguish
Because we were spared his anguish . . . .

MILTON ACORN, leftist poet, from "Bethuniverse," *More Poems for People* (1972).

Bilingualism

See also CANADA: FRENCH AND ENGLISH; LANGUAGE.

I didn't know at first that there were two languages in Canada. I just thought that there was one way to speak to my father and another to talk to my mother.

LOUIS ST. LAURENT, prime minister, quoted by Dale Thomson in *Louis St. Laurent: Canadian* (1967).

I am in favour of equal rights for Canadians of French and English speech throughout Canada, within the limits of the practicable. I am not in favour of insisting that every postal clerk in Vancouver should speak French, or every postal clerk in Chicoutimi English. They don't need to: there are not enough French-speaking people in Vancouver or English-speaking people in Chicoutimi.

EUGENE FORSEY, labour advocate, address to the Congress on Canadian Affairs, Laval University, 1961, in *The Canadian Experiment, Success or Failure* (1962).

It is a paradox of French-Canadian life: the more bilingual we become, the less need there is to be bilingual.

MARCEL CHAPUT, separatist, in *Why I am a Separatist* (1962), translated by Robert A. Taylor.

English was good enough for Jesus Christ.

RALPH MELNYK, Saskatchewan farmer, when asked by Ed Ogle of *Time* his views on the Bi & Bi Commission, which he felt was created to force him to learn French.

My passport is bilingual, though my heart is not.

GILLES VIGNEAULT, Quebec chansonnier, quoted in *Time*, Jan. 24, 1972.

What language do you listen to music in?

GÉRARD PELLETIER, secretary of State, replying to criticism that he authorized all-French narration for an outdoor concert on Parliament Hill, July 1, 1972.

Absolutely no more than five years would be required for all Canadians to become fully and totally bilingual.

RÉAL CAOUETTE, leader of the Créditiste party, in the House of Commons, Nov. 21, 1974.

Lack of communication has held Canada together for one hundred years. Once we can speak each other's language, the mystique of being what we are is gone.

DAVE BROADFOOT, as "The Honourable Member for Kicking Horse Pass," in *Sex and Security* (1974).

On our street Monsieur Lévesque was the man who spoke exquisite English.

LARRY ZOLF, zany broadcaster, who grew up in Winnipeg, quoted by James Quig in *Weekend*, April 5, 1975.

All pro athletes are bilingual. They speak English and profanity.

GORDIE HOWE, hockey star, quoted by George Gamester in the Toronto *Star*, May 27, 1975.

I will not leave Ottawa until the country and the government are irreversibly bilingual.

PIERRE ELLIOTT TRUDEAU, prime minister, addressing a Liberal fund-raising dinner in Montreal, Nov. 31, 1975.

Birds

I know of no bird or animal that can equal the Canada Goose for getting well after being wounded. It is said that a cat has nine lives; if that is true, the Canada Goose has at least eighteen, nine on each side of the border.

JACK MINER, pioneer naturalist who, until his death in 1944, banded wildlife at his famous bird sanctuary at Kingsville, Ontario.

It is said that Canada Geese, unlike wild ducks and most other birds, usually mate for life. Their marriage is a contract entered into and faithfully preserved "until death do us part." It is even claimed that the partnership, in effect, remains binding beyond death and that when either member of it dies the survivor does not pair again.

MALCOLM MACDONALD, British high commissioner in Ottawa from 1941 to 1945 and amateur ornithologist, *The Birds of Brewery Creek* (1947).

The national bird of Canada is the grouse.

STUART KEATE, publisher of the Vancouver *Sun*, from an address delivered in 1971.

Nobody has asked me but if I were to choose a national bird for Canada, it would be the starling. He struts self-reliantly, asks no favours of anybody, and never puts out his claw for relief.

GORDON SINCLAIR, newspaperman, radio and TV personality, in the Toronto *Globe and Mail*, Jan. 10, 1972.

Birth Control
See also ABORTION.

I'm a Roman Catholic and I take a dim view of 2,500 celibates shuffling back and forth to Rome to discuss birth control and not one woman to raise a voice.

> LAURA SABIA, chairwoman of the Ontario Advisory Council on the Status of Women, quoted in 1975.

If women had been running the world back when the wheel was invented, they would have invented the pill instead.

> DORIS ANDERSON, editor of *Chatelaine*, in conversation, Feb. 1976.

Bluenose
See SHIPS AND SAILING for *Bluenose I* and *Bluenose II*.

The Nova Scotian . . . is the gentleman known throughout America as Mr. Blue Nose, a *sobriquet* acquired from a superior potato of that name, for the good qualities of which he is never tired of talking, being anxious, like most men of small property, to exhibit to the best advantage the little he had.

> THOMAS CHANDLER HALIBURTON, Nova Scotian writer and wit, in *The Old Judge; or, Life in a Colony* (1849).

Books
See also BOOKS: CANADIAN; CENSORSHIP; LIBRARIES.

Truly we have tarried long enough with the Senators—let us look abroad and see what other classes are achieving. We have beside us a mountain of Books, Magazines, Pamphlets and Newspapers, that have been accumulating for the last two months, unopened and unread. Like a Turk, in the dim twilight of his Harem, we scarcely know which to choose, but, we shall commence at the apex of the pyramid, and dig downwards.

> JOSEPH HOWE, editor and statesman, in an editorial in the *Novascotian*, May 2, 1833.

A good book has no ending.

> R.D. CUMMING, writer, in *Skookum Chuck Fables* (1915).

It is easier to buy books than to read them and easier to read them than to absorb them.

> SIR WILLIAM OSLER, physician and medical teacher, from *Sir William Osler: Aphorisms from*

His Bedside Teachings and Writings (1950), edited by W.B. Bean.

Yet how many people there are who read as though some prize awaited them when they turned the last page! They do not wish *to read* a book; they want *to have read* it—no matter how.

> ROBERTSON DAVIES, man-of-letters, in *A Voice from the Attic* (1960).

Books: Canadian
See also BOOKS.

The bold truth is that Canada has the money, but would rather spend it on whiskey than on books. It prefers to inflame its stomach, rather than inform its brain.

> ROBERT BARR, writer, in "Literature in Canada," the *Canadian*, Nov. 1889.

. . . there is no spiritual gratification to be found simply in the sale of any book, no matter what kind of tripe, in Canada, any more than there is in the sale of a package of tea . . . the problem with Canada is not that Canadians don't buy books as well as the people of other countries—in terms of comparative population Canadians do buy books: the trouble is that there is not much sense of adventure in reading in our people: they go for the books that have a big sale in other countries.

> MORLEY CALLAGHAN, novelist, in "The Plight of Canadian Fiction," *University of Toronto Quarterly*, Jan. 1938.

"Who reads a Canadian book," it was asked some years ago, "except by mistake?"

> A.R.M. LOWER, historian, in "The Social Sciences in the Post-War World," *Canadian Historical Review*, Mar. 1941.

. . . Canada is a small and backward country: the tongue of half of it is French. The English half is probably the dumbest English-speaking population anywhere. It reads less per capita than any other known civilised population.

> WYNDHAM LEWIS, British writer and artist, in a letter, Nov. 9, 1941, *The Letters of Wyndham Lewis* (1963), edited by W.K. Rose.

Any Canadian who turns up his nose at a

Canadian book because it is a Canadian book, is a foule byrd.

> LAWRENCE J. BURPEE, editor and author, in "Quotable Quotes," *Canadian Author and Bookman*, March 1943.

If the old scornful question were ever asked in our day, "Who reads an American book?" the answer would be shouted, "Canadians."

> MIRIAM CHAPIN, Montreal journalist, in *Contemporary Canada* (1959).

To my colleagues in the public service with the sincere hope that they will find this book too long to have it Xeroxed by their secretaries and distributed free.

> RONALD F. HAYES, academic, in the dedication to *The Chaining of Prometheus* (1973).

I want this country to have a reputation for making beautiful books. It's a dream I have, that when people around the world pick up a beautiful book, they'll know it's from Canada.

> LORRAINE MONK, head of the NFB's still-photography division and editor of collections of photographs, quoted by Roy MacSkimming in the Toronto *Star*, June 7, 1975.

Border: Canada–U.S.

The meat of the buffalo tastes the same on both sides of the border.

> SITTING BULL, who crossed the border after the battle of Little Big Horn in 1876, attributed.

Thank God, we are once more on British soil.

> SIR WINSTON CHURCHILL's first words as he stepped from a Boston train at Windsor Station, Montreal, Dec. 23, 1900, when the British M.P. was twenty-six.

That long frontier from the Atlantic to the Pacific oceans, guarded only by neighbourly respect and honourable obligations, is an example to every country and a pattern for the future of the world.

> SIR WINSTON CHURCHILL, British war-time leader and statesman, in a speech in honour of R.B. Bennett, Canada Club, London, England, April 20, 1939.

The boundary between Canada and the U.S. is a typically human creation; it is physically invisible, geographically illogical, militarily indefensible, and emotionally inescapable.

> HUGH L. KEENLEYSIDE, External Affairs officer, adapted from the introduction to his study, *Canada and the United States* (1929).

There is therefore little need for eulogy of the "undefended frontier." (Orators differ as to its length; it extends, apart from the Canada-Alaska boundary, for 3,986 miles.) Our frontier has long been immune from conflict, it is true, but it has suffered grievously from the effects of rhetoric. As a matter of fact, some of the realities have been obscured by the clouds of oratory which hang above this famous border. It has long been undefended, but realists have observed that the disparity of population has made armaments for one country futile and for the other superfluous.

> VINCENT MASSEY, first native-born governor general of Canada, in *On Being Canadian* (1948).

Natural frontiers exist between nations, but the border between Canada and the United States is not one of them. Birds fly over it, fish swim through it, ore bodies lie under it, stands of timber straddle it, rivers traverse it. As in the movement of trade, so in the disposition of resources. The continent is an economic unit. Its bisection is political, not geographic. What nature joined together, Canadians have sought to sunder.

> JAMES EAYRS, political scientist and defence critic, in "Sharing a Continent: The Hard Issues," *The United States and Canada: The American Assembly* (1964), edited by John Sloan Dickey.

CLOSE THE 49TH PARALLEL, ETC.

> GREG CURNOE, pop artist from London, Ontario, message stencilled on his canvasses. Quoted by Dennis Reid in *Greg Curnoe: Canada X Biennial, Sao Paulo* (1969).

And by midnight or so
While the fires of her manifest destiny smoulder
You'll be all ready to slip across
The world's longest undefended border.

> GEORGE JONAS, poet and TV producer, in

"American Girl: A Canadian View," *The Happy Hungry Man* (1970).

British Columbia

Her Majesty hopes that this new colony on the Pacific may be but one step in the career of steady progress by which Her Majesty's dominions in North America may ultimately be peopled, in an unbroken chain from the Atlantic to the Pacific, by a loyal and industrious population of subjects of the British Crown.

> QUEEN VICTORIA, address to the British House of Commons in 1871, quoted by Alexander Morris in *Nova Britannia; of Our New Canadian Dominion Foreshadowed* (1884).

British Columbia is a barren, cold, mountain country that is not worth keeping. It would never have been inhabited at all, unless by trappers of the Hudson's Bay Company, had the "gold fever" not taken a party of mining adventurers there, and ever since that fever died down the place has been going from bad to worse. Fifty railroads would not galvanise it into prosperity.

> HENRY LABOUCHÈRE, British editor, in "The Canadian Dominion Bubble," *Truth*, Sept. 1, 1881.

Were I an intending immigrant I would risk a good deal of discomfort to get on to the land in British Columbia; and were I rich, with no attachments outside England, I would swiftly buy me a farm or a house in that country for the mere joy of it.

> RUDYARD KIPLING, English author, in *Letters to the Family: Notes on a Recent Trip to Canada* (1908), reprinted in *Letters of Travel, 1892-1913* (1920).

The first almighty fact about British Columbia is mountains.

> RODERICK HAIG-BROWN, British Columbia magistrate and naturalist, in "With Its Face to the West," *The Face of Canada* (1959).

Here we lead a privileged life; we are able to golf, ski, sail, climb mountains, garden, ten months every year. Philosophical discussion is not popular in B.C.

> PADDY SHERMAN, editor of the Vancouver

Province, quoted by Solange Chaput Rolland in *My Country, Canada or Quebec?* (1966).

British Empire and Commonwealth

See also CANADA: UNITED KINGDOM RELATIONS; COLONIALISM.

Travel a thousand miles up a great river; more than another thousand along great lakes and a succession of smaller lakes; a thousand miles across rolling prairies; and another thousand through woods and over three great ranges of mountains, and you have travelled from Ocean to Ocean through Canada. All this Country is a single Colony of the British Empire; and this Colony is dreaming magnificent dreams of a future when it shall be the "Greater Britain," and the highway across which the fabrics and products of Asia shall be carried, to the Eastern as well as the Western sides of the Atlantic.

> GEORGE MUNRO GRANT, principal of Queen's University, in *Ocean to Ocean: Sandford Fleming's Expedition through Canada in 1872* (1873).

Make us the half-way house of the Empire.

> GEORGE MUNRO GRANT, imperialist, in a letter to Sir Wilfrid Laurier, Feb. 25, 1899, with specific reference to the Pacific cable project.

Those who dislike the colonial connection speak of it as a chain, but it is a golden chain, and I for one, am glad to wear the fetters.

> SIR JOHN A. MACDONALD, first prime minister of Canada, paraphrase of a statement in the House of Commons, March 30, 1875.

"WE HOLD A VASTER EMPIRE THAN HAS BEEN."

> SIR WILLIAM MULOCK, postmaster-general under Laurier, arranged the issue of Canada's first commemorative stamp in 1898 to honour the "Imperial penny postage." The two-cent stamp, the first printed in multiple colours, bore the above legend in English only. The phrase earlier appeared in "Song of Empire," a poem written by Sir Lewis Morris to celebrate Queen Victoria's Jubilee, June 20, 1887.

One Flag, One Throne, One Empire.

> MARGARET MURRAY, founder of the Imperial Order Daughters of the Empire, Feb. 13, 1900; this is the IODE motto.

The proper basis of the British Empire was that it was to be composed of a galaxy of nations under the British Crown.

> SIR WILFRID LAURIER, prime minister, in the House of Commons, Dec. 2, 1907. According to Robert M. Hamilton in *Canadian Quotations and Phrases* (1952), Sir Wilfrid first used the phrase, "a galaxy of free nations," in the Guildhall, London, England, July 11, 1902.

I look forward to a development in the future along the line of an increasingly equal status between the Dominions and the mother country.

> SIR ROBERT BORDEN, prime minister of Canada during the First World War, statement made at the Imperial War Conference in London, April 16, 1917. Sir Robert presented a resolution favouring "a full recognition of the Dominions as autonomous nations of an Imperial Conference." With the help of Prime Minister Smuts of the Union of South Africa, the resolution was passed. *Robert Laird Borden: His Memoirs* (1938), edited by Henry Borden.

You and I have transformed the structure of the British Empire.

> JAN CHRISTIAN SMUTS, prime minister of the Union of South Africa, to Sir Robert Borden at the Imperial War Conference in London, April 16, 1917. Smuts also recommended that the term *British Empire* be replaced by the term *British Commonwealth of Nations. Robert Laird Borden: His Memoirs* (1938), edited by Henry Borden.

Equal Status!

> W.L. MACKENZIE KING, prime minister, throwing a British half-penny and a Canadian one-cent piece into the molten metal of the bells for the Peace Tower carillon, Croyden, England, while attending the Imperial Conference in 1926. Quoted by Robert M. Hamilton in *Canadian Quotations and Phrases* (1952).

They [the Dominions] are autonomous Communities within the British Empire, equal in status, in no way subordinate one to another in any aspect of their domestic or external affairs, though united by a common allegiance to the Crown, and freely associated as members of the British Commonwealth of Nations.

> From the Report of Inter-Imperial Relations Committee, Imperial Conference, Nov. 18,

1926, called the Balfour Declaration after A.J. Balfour. Reproduced in *Historical Documents of Canada: Volume V: The Arts of War and Peace, 1914-1945* (1972), edited by C.P. Stacey.

Canada First, then the Empire.

> R.B. BENNETT, leader of the Conservative party and later prime minister, campaign slogan, 1930.

3. It is hereby declared and enacted that the Parliament of a Dominion has full power to make laws having extra-territorial operation.

4. No Act of Parliament of the United Kingdom passed after the commencement of this Act shall extend or be deemed to extend, to a Dominion as part of the law of that Dominion, unless it is expressly declared in that Act that that Dominion has requested, and consented to, the enactment thereof.

> Historic sections from the Statute of Westminster, 1931, *British North America Acts and Selected Statutes: 1867-1962* (1962), edited by Maurice Ollivier.

There may come a higher citizenship some day, when all frontiers will be abolished and a man shall owe allegiance only to humanity. Until that time arrives it is no mean thing to have been a citizen of the British Empire.

> BEVERLY BAXTER, Toronto-born journalist and British M.P., contributor of a fortnightly, "London Letter" to *Maclean's*, in *Strange Street* (1935).

His lectures were crowded. Adam Smith, John Stuart Mill, and Malthus would come to life. He, before Winston Churchill, saved the British Empire every Monday, Wednesday, and Friday, at three o'clock, in Room 20.

> JOHN T. CULLITON, recalling Stephen Leacock who taught at McGill between 1903 and 1936. Quoted by Barbara Nimmo in her edition of Stephen Leacock's *Last Leaves* (1945).

British North America Act
See CONFEDERATION.

British Subject

As for myself, my course is clear. A British

subject I was born—a British subject I will die.

SIR JOHN A. MACDONALD, first prime minister of Canada. This most memorable of expressions of faith may be found in many forms, two of which follow. Macdonald's maxim was adopted as the slogan of the Conservative party in the election of 1891, Macdonald's last campaign.

The cardinal point in our policy is connection with Great Britain. I am a British subject, and British born, and a British subject I hope to die.

SIR JOHN A. MACDONALD, address at the Thomas White dinner in Montreal, Nov. 1875, quoted by Donald Creighton in *John A. Macdonald: The Old Chieftain* (1955).

I commend these issues to your determination, and to the judgment of the whole people of Canada, with an unclouded confidence that you will proclaim to the world your resolve to show yourselves not unworthy of the proud distinction you enjoy—of being numbered among the most dutiful and loyal subjects of our beloved Queen. As for myself, my course is clear. A British subject I was born—a British subject I will die.

SIR JOHN A. MACDONALD's last address in the House of Commons, Feb. 7, 1891.

I see no reason why the people of Canada should not look forward to Canada becoming a sovereign and independent State. The right hon. gentleman stated that he was born a British subject and hoped to die one. Sir, I was born a British colonist, but do not wish to die a tadpole British colonist. I do not wish to die without having all the rights, privileges and immunities of the citizen of a nation.

AMOR DE COSMOS, prime minister of British Columbia (1872–1874) and federal M.P., in the House of Commons, April 21, 1882.

For myself I am a true Briton. I love the old land dearly. I am glad that I was born a British subject; a British subject I have lived for three score years and something more. I hope to live and die a British subject. I trust and hope that my children and my grand-children who have also been born British subjects will live their lives as

British subjects, and as British subjects die.

SIR OLIVER MOWAT, prime minister of Ontario, in an address in Toronto, Feb. 18, 1891, quoted by C.R.W. Biggar in *Sir Oliver Mowat* (1905).

Broadcasting

See also COMMUNICATION; NEWS; RADIO; TELEVISION.

The policy which guides operations of the CBC National News Service is based on the primary conception that this service is in the nature of a public trust; to present all significant news of the day's happenings in Canada and abroad, factually, without bias or distortion, without tendentious comment, and in clear and unambiguous style.

DAN MCARTHUR, first supervisor of CBC Radio's news service, formulation of news policy for the first network news broadcast, Jan. 1, 1941.

Canadian content.

ANDREW STEWART, chairman of the Board of Broadcast Governors. The Broadcasting Act of 1958 required the BBG to ensure that all radio and TV be "basically Canadian in content and character." The BBG ruled that all TV stations would be required to telecast a minimum of "45% Canadian content" as of April 1, 1961, and "55% Canadian content" as of April 1, 1962.

The only thing that really matters in broadcasting is program content; all the rest is housekeeping.

ROBERT M. FOWLER, business executive, first sentence of *The Royal Commission Report of the Committee on Broadcasting* (the Fowler Report), 1965, by Robert M. Fowler, Marc Lalonde, and G.C.E. Steele.

The CBC is nothing more than an enormous party line.

JIMMY JAMES, CBC producer, quoted by Scott Young in the Toronto *Globe and Mail*, March 3, 1975.

Brock, Sir Isaac

Most of the people have lost all confidence—I however speak loud and look big . . . .

SIR ISAAC BROCK, brigadier-general in Upper Canada during the War of 1812, to Sir George Prevost, July 20, 1812, quoted by J. Mackay Hitsman in *The Incredible War of 1812* (1965).

Push on, brave York Volunteers!
Sir Isaac Brock's most famous words. This command was once popularly believed to have been his dying order, issued immediately before he fell during the Battle of Queenston Heights, Oct. 13, 1812. Scholars now claim it was Brock's rallying cry to the York (Toronto) Militia as he galloped past Brown's Point, more than a mile from where he was mortally wounded.

Upon the Heights of Queenston one dark October day,
Invading foes were marshalled in battle's dread array.
Brave Brock looked up the rugged steep and planned a bold attack;
"No foreign flag shall float," said he, "above the Union Jack."
                    *
Each true Canadian soldier laments the death of Brock;
His country told its sorrow in monumental rock;
And if a foe should e'er invade our land in future years,
His dying words will guide us still: "Push on, brave Volunteers!"
First and last verses of "The Battle of Queenston Heights," *Canada's Story in Song* (1965), edited by Edith Fowke and Alan Mills.

Brown, George

I know enough of the feeling of this meeting to know that you would rather have John A. drunk than George Brown sober.
SIR JOHN A. MACDONALD, first prime minister of Canada, opinion on George Brown, a fellow Father of Confederation and a political opponent. Quoted by C.B. Biggar in *Anecdotal Life of Sir John A. Macdonald* (1891).

The great reason why I have always been able to beat Brown is that I have been able to look a little ahead, while he could on no occasion forego the temptation of a temporary triumph.
SIR JOHN A. MACDONALD in a letter to M.C. Cameron, Ottawa, Jan. 3, 1873, quoted by Sir

Joseph Pope in *Memoirs of The Right Honourable Sir John Macdonald* (1894).

Buffalo
See also ANIMALS.

Thus it continues till you leave ye. woods behind
And then you have beast of severall kind
The one is a black a Buffillo great
Another is an outgrown Bear wch. is good meat
His skin to gett I have used all ye. means I can
He is mans food & he makes food of man
His hid they would not let me it preserve
But said it was a god & they should Starve
HENRY KELSEY, an agent for the Hudson's Bay Company and the first white man to see the prairies and to describe the buffalo, which he spotted on Aug. 20, 1690, in his *Journal* of 1691, first published in *The Kelsey Papers* (1929), edited by A.G. Doughty and Chester Martin.

Business
See also ADVERTISING AND SLOGANS; CAPITALISM; MULTINATIONAL CORPORATION.

The greatest good to the greatest number.
TIMOTHY EATON, founder of the T. Eaton Company in 1869. Quoted by George G. Nasmith in *Timothy Eaton* (1923).

Every successful enterprise requires three men—a dreamer, a businessman, and a son-of-a-bitch.
PETER MCARTHUR, columnist who wrote about farm life in western Ontario, a favourite epigram coined about 1904, with the failure of the humorist's newspaper.

The business leaders who clamour for government to "let business alone" would die of fright if any government took them at their word. For it is not only factory acts, workmen's compensation, old age pensions, minimum wage laws and public utility commissions which would disappear; it is also tariff protection, loans, guarantees, subsidies and bounties and half a hundred other government services and aids to business. Laissez-faire is dead.
EUGENE FORSEY, labour advocate, in "The Economic Problem," *Towards the Christian*

Revolution (1936), edited by R.B.Y. Scott and Gregory Vlastos.

We make more money out of men than we ever make out of things.
> GARFIELD WESTON, the largest bread manufacturer in the world, quoted by Matthew Halton in *Big Dough in Bread*, *Maclean's*, Aug. 15, 1948.

I hold no brief for private enterprise. But I have unshakeable faith in individual enterprise.
> C.L. BURTON, chairman of the Robert Simpson Company, *A Sense of Urgency* (1952).

The most important question facing Canada today is not bilingualism, nor is it cultural growth: it is the problem of economic backwardness which leaves us increasingly weak in competition with other nations.
> J.J. BROWN, Montreal writer, in *The Inventors: Great Ideas in Canadian Enterprise* (1967).

The more good decisions made in boardrooms . . . the fewer will have to be made in cabinet chambers.
> ROBERT H. WINTERS, industrialist and federal Cabinet minister, quoted by Peter C. Newman in *The Distemper of Our Times* (1968).

Corporate welfare bums.
> DAVID LEWIS, leader of the New Democratic Party, in his speech in New Glasgow, Nova Scotia, Aug. 3, 1972. Quoted by Walter Stewart in *Divide and Con* (1973).

Canada, in its essentials, is a public enterprise country, always has been, and probably always will be. Americans have, or at least had, a genius for private enterprise; Canadians have a genius for public enterprise. As long as we describe Canada in terms of the American model, we will continue to see ourselves as second-rate Americans, because we *are* second-rate Americans, not being Americans at all.
> HERSCHEL HARDIN, Vancouver playwright and nationalist, *A Nation Unaware* (1974).

Fill a need, keep things simple, buck the trend, messy sells better than neat.
> EDWIN MIRVISH, founder of Honest Ed's, the world's first discount department store, quoted by Ethel A. Starbird in *National Geographic*, Aug. 1975.

Life at the top is financially rewarding, spiritually draining, physically exhausting, and short.
> PETER C. NEWMAN in *The Canadian Establishment: Volume One* (1975).

Canada

See also BORDER: CANADA–U.S.; BRITISH EMPIRE AND COMMONWEALTH; CANADA: ANGLO–AMERICAN RELATIONS; CANADA: FRENCH AND ENGLISH; CANADA: INTERNATIONAL RELATIONS; CANADA: UNITED KINGDOM RELATIONS; CANADA: UNITED STATES RELATIONS; CANADIANS; CONTINENTALISM; FEDERAL–PROVINCIAL RELATIONS; FRANCE; FRENCH CANADA; UNITY, NATIONAL.

Some are for keeping Canada, some Guadaloupe. Who will tell me what I shall be hanged for not keeping?
> WILLIAM PITT the Elder, prime minister of Great Britain when Quebec was taken in 1759, question supposedly asked in the British House of Commons. Quoted by Hilda Neatby in *Quebec: The Revolutionary Age 1760-1791* (1966).

England would be better off without Canada; it keeps her in a prepared state for war at a great expense and constant irritation.
> NAPOLEON BONAPARTE, French dictator, in *Diary of Pulteney Malcolm at St. Helena*, Jan. 11, 1817, quoted by H.L. Mencken in *A New Dictionary of Quotations on Historical Principles* (1942).

I am not one of those who believe that the destiny of Canada must inevitably be annexation with the United States. Canada possesses all the elements of a great independent country. It is destined, I sometimes say to myself, to become the Russia of the New World.

> BENJAMIN DISRAELI, later British prime minister, in the British House of Commons in 1846.

I fear that I have not got much to say about Canada, not having seen much; what I got by going to Canada was a cold.

> HENRY DAVID THOREAU, New England writer, in *A Yankee in Canada* (1866).

I believe that the day will come, and that many now present will live to see it, when a portion at least of the lands on the other side of the Rocky Mountains, being also brought into colonization and guarded by free institutions, one direct line of railway communication will unite the Pacific and the Atlantic.

> SIR EDWARD BULWER LYTTON, colonial secretary, in an address to the British Parliament, quoted by Alexander Morris in "The Hudson's Bay and Pacific Territories" (1858), in *Nova Britannia* (1884).

This Canada of ours.
  Fair Canada,
  Dear Canada,
This Canada of ours!

> JAMES D. EDGAR, a founder of Canada First and future Speaker of the House of Commons, from *This Canada of Ours and Other Poems* (1893). The title poem was published as early as 1870.

The hills all round, as seen from our celebrated platform [Dufferin Gate, Quebec Citadel], are of the most lovely autumn colours, and covered, as they are with red and orange trees, they really look like flames in the distance, or like gigantic flower-gardens; for our *trees* are quite as brilliant as your best *flowers*, and if you can imagine your conservatory magnified a million times, and spread over miles and miles of hill and dale, you will begin to understand how we do things in this Canada of ours.

> LADY DUFFERIN, wife of the governor general, entry for Sept. 21, 1872, in *My Canadian Journal* (1891). *My Canadian Journal: 1872-1878* (1969).

Awake, my country, the hour is great with change!

Under this gloom which yet obscures the land,
From ice-blue strait and stern Laurentian range
  To where giant peaks our western bounds command,
A deep voice stirs, vibrating in men's ears
  . . . .

> SIR CHARLES G.D. ROBERTS, poet and writer, lines from "An Ode for the Canadian Confederacy" (1882), *Selected Poems* (1939).

O Child of Nations, giant-limbed,
  Who stand'st among the nations now
Unheeded, unadorned, unhymned,
  With unanointed brow,—

How long the ignoble sloth, how long
  The trust in greatness not thine own?
Surely the lion's brood is strong
  To front the world alone!

> SIR CHARLES G.D. ROBERTS, poet and writer, from "Canada" (1882), *Selected Poems* (1939).

Canada is bounded on the north by gold; on the west by the East; on the east by history; and on the south by friends.

> FRANCES SHELLEY WEES, Oregon-born detective-story writer who has lived in Canada for many years; aphorism, from a prose poem, "Geography Lesson," which has appeared in textbooks since 1937.

No one knows my country, neither the stranger nor its own sons. My country is hidden in the dark and teeming brain of youth upon the eve of its manhood. My country has not found itself nor felt its power nor learned its true place. It is all visions and doubts and hopes and dreams. It is strength and weakness, despair and joy, and the wild confusions and restless strivings of a boy who has passed his boyhood but is not yet a man.

> BRUCE HUTCHISON, journalist and author, *The Unknown Country* (1942).

Parents unmarried and living apart
relatives keen to bag the estate

schizophrenia not excluded—
will he learn to grow up before it's too late?

> EARLE BIRNEY, leading poet, from "Canada: Case History" (1945), *Selected Poems 1940-1966* (1966).

What are you . . . ? they ask.
And she replies: I am the wind that wants
    a flag.
I am the mirror of your picture
until you make me the marvel of your life.
Yes, I am one and none, pin and pine,
    snow and slow,
America's attic, an empty room,
a something possible, a chance, a dance
that is not danced. A cold kingdom.

> PATRICK ANDERSON, poet, from "Poem on Canada," *The White Centre* (1946).

In every generation Canadians have had to rework the miracle of their political existence. Canada has been created because there has existed within the hearts of its people a determination to build for themselves an enduring home. Canada is a supreme act of faith.

> A.R.M. LOWER, distinguished historian, in *Colony to Nation* (1946, 1964).

Canada is a country whose major problems are never solved.

> A.R.M. LOWER, historian, in *My First Seventy-Five Years* (1975).

To strive, even dimly, to foresee the wonders of Canada's next generation is to summon the utmost powers of the imagination.

> DWIGHT D. EISENHOWER, president of the United States, before a joint sitting of the Canadian Senate and the House of Commons on Nov. 14, 1953.

The line which marks off the frontier and the farmstead, the wilderness from the baseline, the hinterland from the metropolis, runs through every Canadian psyche.

> W.L. MORTON, historian, in *The Canadian Identity* (1961).

Nor is it very difficult to understand why a Canadian passport should be so popular. Part of the explanation is that with it one can travel easily almost anywhere. Another reason for the popularity of the little blue booklet stamped in gold is that one can speak English or French or Ukrainian or Polish or Chinese and still be a Canadian. One can, in fact, be almost anyone and still be a Canadian; and to be a Canadian is to have a passport to the whole world.

> DOUGLAS LePAN, poet and essayist, from "In Frock Coat and Moccasins" (1964), *Canada: A Guide to the Peaceable Kingdom* (1970), edited by William Kilbourn.

Canada could have enjoyed:
  English government,
    French culture,
      and American know-how.

Instead it ended up with:
  English know-how,
    French government,
      and American culture.

> JOHN ROBERT COLOMBO, poet and editor, in "O Canada" (1965), *The New Romans* (1968), edited by Al Purdy.

One of the derivations proposed for the word Canada is a Portuguese phrase meaning "nobody here." The etymology of the word Utopia is very similar, and perhaps the real Canada is an ideal with nobody in it. The Canada to which we really do owe loyalty is the Canada that we have failed to create . . . our identity, like the real identity of all nations, is the one that we have failed to achieve . . . . The uncreated identity of Canada may be after all not so bad a heritage to take with us.

> NORTHROP FRYE, literary scholar, in *The Modern Century* (1967).

Canada has no identity and never has had an identity. Any sense of identity we have is our sense of density. So far we have had the advantage of dabbling in identities.

*

Canada is a Distant Early Warning System for the American experience.

*

Canada is the only country in the world that knows how to live without an identity.

*

You can be a French Canadian or an English Canadian but not a "Canadian." We know how to live without an identity, and this is one of our marvellous resources.

> MARSHALL McLUHAN, media pundit, in "Canada: A Borderline Case," CBC Radio, May 29, 1967.

What always amuses me is talk of the "emerging nationhood of Canada" and poppycock of that kind. Canada is not a country: it is the northern fringe of the United States. It looks huge on the map, but when you get there you find that the country is five thousand miles long and only two hundred miles wide. The rest is uninhabited desert.

CECIL HARMSWORTH KING, British press lord, in *Strictly Personal* (1969).

Yet it is true that this land has a group of cranky losers. Again and again they surface, as they did last year, to complain that Canada is not the British America of their grandfathers' time. Yet how could it be so? If only they would look at the country in all its wild grandeur with all its new people and see that such a land must always be changing and becoming something new, and always with a new beauty in its changing face!

MORLEY CALLAGHAN, Toronto novelist, in "Canada: 'Always a New Beauty in Its Changing Face,' " the Toronto *Star*, Dec. 30, 1972.

Canada has never been a melting pot; more like a tossed salad.

ARNOLD EDINBOROUGH, Toronto writer, in an address at Chautauqua, New York, on Aug. 3, 1973.

Canada is so far away it hardly exists.

JORGE LUIS BORGES, the Argentine author, to broadcaster Robert Zend in Buenos Aires, Oct. 4, 1974.

Canada: Anglo-American Relations

You are at once struck with the difference between the English and the American population, system and ideas. On the other side of the lake, you have much more apparent property, but much less real solidarity and security. The houses and stores of Toronto are not to be compared with those of the American towns opposite. But the Englishman has built according to his means—the American according to his expectations.

FREDERICK MARRYAT, popular novelist and sea captain, in *Diary in America, with Remarks on Its Institutions* (1839).

Canada . . . is a magnet exercising a double attraction, drawing both Great Britain and the United States towards herself and thus drawing them closer to each other. She is the only surviving bond which stretches from Europe across the Atlantic Ocean.

SIR WINSTON CHURCHILL, British statesman, in the *Saturday Evening Post*, Feb. 15, 1930.

Canada is the linchpin of the English-speaking world.

SIR WINSTON CHURCHILL, British prime minister, at Mansion House, London, England, Sept. 4, 1941.

Canada: French and English
See also BILINGUALISM; CANADIANS; FRENCH CANADA; "TWO SOLITUDES."

Let me hear no more of the invidious distinction of French and English. You are all his Britannic Majesty's beloved Canadian subjects.

EDWARD AUGUSTUS, Duke of Kent, fourth son of George III of England, who served in Quebec, Nova Scotia, and New Brunswick from 1791 to 1800, and was commander-in-chief of the British forces in North America; address upon the passage of the Constitutional Act in 1791.

That the two tribes of men, French and English, do not assimilate is no new discovery; it is nothing more than Nature herself did when she deliberately created the British Channel.

SIR FRANCIS BOND HEAD, ebullient lieutenant-governor of Upper Canada during the Rebellion of 1837, in "Memorandum on the Present Political State of the Canadas," Oct. 18, 1836.

I expected to find a contest between a government and a people: I found two nations warring in the bosom of a single state: I found a struggle, not of principles, but of races; and I perceived that it would be idle to attempt any amelioration of laws or institutions until we could first succeed in terminating the deadly animosity that now separates the inhabitants of Lower Canada into the hostile divisions of French and English.

LORD DURHAM, "Radical Jack," in *Lord Durham's Report on the Affairs of British North America* (1912), edited by Sir Charles P. Lucas. The *Report* appeared in 1839.

English and French, we climb by a double flight of stairs toward the destinies reserved for us on this continent, without knowing each other, without meeting each other, and without even seeing each other, except on the landing of politics. In social and literary terms, we are far more foreign to each other than the English and French of Europe.

PIERRE-JOSEPH-OLIVER CHAUVEAU, first premier of Quebec after Confederation, in *L'Instruction publique au Canada* (1876), quoted by Mason Wade in the introduction to his *Canadian Dualism* (1960).

For us, sons of France, political sentiment is a passion; while, for the Englishman, politics are a question of business.

*

While the Frenchman wants you to have his opinion, the Englishman wants you to have opinions of your own.

*

The Englishman respects your opinions; but he never thinks of your feelings.

SIR WILFRID LAURIER, future prime minister, in a Montreal address, May 14, 1884, *Wilfrid Laurier on the Platform* (1890).

And I will say this, that we are all Canadians. Below the island of Montreal the water that comes from the north from Ottawa unites with the waters that come from the western lakes, but uniting they do not mix. There they run parallel, separate, distinguishable, and yet are one stream, flowing within the same banks, the mighty St. Lawrence, and rolling on toward the sea bearing the commerce of a nation upon its bosom—a perfect image of our nation. We may not assimilate, we may not blend, but for all that we are still the component parts of the same country.

SIR WILFRID LAURIER, future prime minister, in a Toronto address, Dec. 10, 1886, reproduced in the Toronto *Globe* the following day.

A free Anglo-French Confederacy, in the northern part of America, united by bonds of amity and kinship with Great Britain and France, of two great nations from which it had derived its races, its civilization and its thoughts, and offering to the trade and the intellectuality of the world a friendly rival and counterpoise to the expanding civilization of the United States, would become one of the greatest contributions to humanity.

HENRI BOURASSA, French-Canadian nationalist, in "Imperialism and Nationalism," an address to the Canadian Club of Ottawa, Dec. 18, 1912.

. . . the relationship which exists between the French and English Canadians . . . is a *modus vivendi* without cordiality.

*

I remember having breakfasted with a French Canadian in Montreal and having dined with an English Canadian family in Toronto on the same day. The contrast was quite a shock to my senses. It was like experiencing the different pressures in a diving bell. Involuntarily I thought of the uncompromising formula of Maurice Barrès: "Prayers that do not mingle."

ANDRÉ SIEGFRIED, French writer, in *Canada: An International Power* (1937), translated by H.H. and Doris Hemming.

Then, even as the two race-legends woke again remembering ancient enmities, there woke with them also the felt knowledge that together they had fought and survived one great war 'they had never made, and that now they had entered another; that for nearly a hundred years the nation had been spread out on the top half of the continent over the powerhouse of the United States and still was there; that even if the legends were like oil and alcohol in the same bottle, the bottle had not broken yet. And, almost grudgingly, out of the instinct to do what was necessary, the country took the first irrevocable steps towards becoming herself, knowing against her will that she was not unique but like all the others, alone with history, with science, and the future.

HUGH MACLENNAN, Montreal novelist, in *Two Solitudes* (1945).

The advantages of living with two cultures
Strike one at every turn,
Especially when one finds a notice in an

office building:

"This elevator will not run on Ascension Day";

Or reads in the *Montreal Star*:

"Tomorrow being the Feast of the Immaculate Conception,

There will be no collection of garbage in the city";

Or sees on the restaurant menu the bilingual dish:

DEEP APPLE PIE

TARTE AUX POMMES PROFONDES

F.R. SCOTT, Montreal man-of-letters, in "Bonne Entente" (1954), *Selected Poems* (1966).

We French, we English, never lost our civil war,

endure it still, a bloodless civil bore;

no wounded lying about, no Whitman wanted.

It's only by our lack of ghosts we're haunted.

EARLE BIRNEY, poet, from "Can.Lit." (1962), *Selected Poems 1940-1966* (1966).

It may be that our persistent unilingualism is to be related to the narrowness of our view of human nature. More generally, it may be that our failure to understand Quebec is the result of almost metaphysical inadequacy.

DOUGLAS LEPAN, poet and essayist, remark made in 1968, quoted in *Saturday Night*, Jan. 1972.

Tomorrow, as today, Montreal will be only 350 miles from Toronto. Thus we will have French and English existing side by side, exchanging goods, services and ideas, depending on each other in many ways.

CLAUDE RYAN, Montreal editor, in "Claude Ryan's Answer," *Maclean's*, May 1971.

Canada: International Relations

See also EXTERNAL AFFAIRS.

When the grown Canada shakes the world with his strength, will it be for evil or for good? The answer to that question depends upon yourselves—upon you, the young men of the Canadian Club, who have it in your power to shape for good or for evil the character of your country.

EARL GREY, governor general from 1904 to 1911, in an address to the Canadian Club of Toronto, Nov. 26, 1906.

A small power is in a sense by its very smallness relieved from much of the responsibility which participation in decisions involves, and which the implementation of such decisions requires. At the other extreme the great powers can protect their positions with the veto. A "middle power" such as Canada, however, is in a different position. Its economic strength and political influence are of importance, and its prestige is high. The material and moral contribution which Canada can make to collective action, as the last two wars have shown, is significant.

LOUIS ST. LAURENT, Liberal secretary of State, in the House of Commons, April 29, 1948. This is an early use of the phrase *middle power* to rank Canada's world influence, made in connection with Canada's seat on the Security Council of the United Nations.

Greece is a sort of American vassal; the Netherlands is the country of American bases that grow like tulip bulbs; Cuba is the main sugar plantation of the American monopolies; Turkey is prepared to kowtow before any United States proconsul and Canada is the boring second fiddle in the American symphony.

ANDREI GROMYKO, Soviet delegate to the United Nations, quoted in the New York *Herald Tribune*, June 30, 1953.

By the accident of geography and history we find ourselves squarely between the two greatest powers on earth. We have no fortresses facing either. We want to live at peace with our northern neighbours, as we have lived so long at peace with our southern neighbours.

JOHN G. DIEFENBAKER, prime minister, in an address at the United Nations, New York, Sept. 26, 1960.

It is a truism that one person who wants something is a hundred times stronger than a hundred who want to be left alone. A Canada prepared to pioneer with lucidity and daring the role of the first "international nation" in history would not only have an immense impact on its fellow states. It might also transform its

33

own political life. It could, conceivably, turn the present rather bored citizen acquiescence in modern politics into something more exciting and active, into participation, into enjoyment, into purpose, even into fun.

> BARBARA WARD, British writer, in "The First International Nation" (1969), *Canada: A Guide to the Peaceable Kingdom* (1970), edited by William Kilbourn.

I don't know why people take exception to me. A few weeks ago in Toronto a Canadian said that it was an awful black eye for the Yanks that the Russians had put a spaceman up before the Americans. I said to him, "My friend, Ireland will put a shillelagh into orbit, Israel will put a matzo ball into orbit, and Liechtenstein will put a postage stamp into orbit before you Canadians ever put up a mouse." Do you know, he hit me.

> BRENDAN BEHAN, Irish playwright, quoted by Ulick O'Connor in *Brendan* (1970).

Canada: United Kingdom Relations

See also BRITISH EMPIRE AND COMMONWEALTH.

Now you ought to make it your business to get rid of the Dominion.

> LORD SHERBROOKE, British statesman, to Lord Dufferin after his appointment as governor general in 1872, quoted by Herbert Paul in *The Life of Froude* (1905).

A Nation spoke to a Nation,
 A Throne sent word to a Throne:
"Daughter am I in my mother's house,
 But mistress in my own.
The gates are mine to open,
 As the gates are mine to close.
And I abide by my Mother's House,"
 Said our Lady of the Snows.

> RUDYARD KIPLING, British man-of-letters, final verse of "Our Lady of the Snows," subtitled "Canadian Preferential Tariff, 1897," published in the London *Times*, April 27, 1897. The tariff was denounced as an impediment to tourism and immigration. Until World War I, the third and fourth lines were widely quoted to symbolize Canada's relation to Great Britain.

It is far more to Canada's advantage than

ours to be on good terms with us. Lord Salisbury, in a private conversation the other day, compared her to a coquettish girl with two suitors, playing off one against the other. I should think a closer analogy would be to call her a married flirt, ready to betray John Bull on any occasion, but holding him responsible for all her follies.

> JOHN HAY, U.S. ambassador to the Court of St. James, in a letter to General John Watson Foster, Dec. 27, 1897. Quoted by John Bartlett Brebner in "The North Atlantic Triangle," *Canada* (1954), edited by George W. Brown.

Canada for the British and Why Not!

> ISAAC M. BARR, British colonist, from the "Barr Pamphlet," *British Settlements in North Western Canada* (1902), reproduced by J. Hanna McCormick in *Lloydminster* (1922).

Scarcely had I landed in Great Britain when I made a speech. In that very first speech I stated the question fairly to the British people. I told them that we had a preference which we intended to give them, I stated the obstacles, and I asked them to help us to have those treaties removed. I did it in these words: "Either England must advance or Canada must recede." These words were quoted the following day in all the press of Great Britain. They were repeated day after day and week after week, and the consequence was that some two months afterwards the treaties, the obnoxious treaties, were denounced by the British Government.

> SIR WILFRID LAURIER, leader of the Liberal party, in a campaign address, Massey Hall, Toronto, Oct. 14, 1904, published in the *Globe* the following day. In London for the Diamond Jubilee of Queen Victoria in 1897, Sir Wilfrid had spoken against the trade treaties Britain had concluded with Germany and Belgium.

When I lived in England, one heard of a certain type of ladies who lived in some parts of London under the protection of certain gentlemen. Theirs was a profession considered to be more lucrative than honourable, and I have no desire that this country of mine should be either the kept woman of the United States, or the harlot of the Empire.

> WILLIAM LAWSON GRANT, headmaster of Upper Canada College, in "The Fallacy of

Nationalism" (1912), an address to the Empire Club of Canada in 1912.

Vaster Britain.

WILLIAM WILFRED CAMPBELL, poet who aspired to become the first poet laureate of the British Empire, evolved this conception of Canada as a "Vaster Britain," in *Sagas of Vaster Britain: Poems of the Race, the Empire, and the Divinity of Man* (1914).

There, I say, British, yes, but Canadian first; if necessary secession from Britain rather than sacrifice of Canada; Canada alongside of Britain so long as it is possible, but Canada first and forever.

HENRI BOURASSA, French-Canadian nationalist, quoted by A.G. Dewey in *The Dominions and Diplomacy* (1929).

It does not matter what the surface civilization may be in Canada; it is from this great country overseas that you got the source of your civilization. There in the little winding lanes which lead around to the Red Lion and the Crown and Anchor; there in the little villages scattered all over, and there along the muddy banks of the Thames lie the germs of our civilization here.

BEVERLEY BAXTER, Toronto-born journalist and British M.P., who contributed a fortnightly "London Letter" to *Maclean's*, in "Behind the Scenes," an address to the Empire Club of Canada in 1932.

All aid short of help.

HAROLD WILSON, president of the Board of Trade and future prime minister of Great Britain, summing up the Canadian attitude on his tour of the country, quoted by Blair Fraser in "Canada and Britain's Economy," the *Listener*, March 26, 1953.

Canada: United States Relations

See also BORDER: CANADA-U.S.; CONTINENTALISM; UNITED STATES OF AMERICA.

I have another and a far brighter vision before me. It may be but a vision, but I will cherish it. I see one vast confederation, stretching from the frozen north in unbroken lines to the glowing south, and from the wild billows of the Atlantic westward to the calmer waters of the Pacific main,

and I see one people, and one language, and one law, and one faith, and over all that wide continent the home of freedom and the refuge of the oppressed of every race and every clime.

JOHN BRIGHT, English orator and member of Parliament, in an address at Birmingham, England, 1862.

It is possible, I wish I could say it is probable, that the evil may cure itself through internal purgation; but Canadian vigilance must sleep no more except upon its arms.

THOMAS D'ARCY MCGEE, future Father of Confederation, in the House of Assembly, Quebec, March 27, 1862, from *Speeches and Addresses Chiefly on the Subject of British-American Union* (1865).

I must confess that in going from the States into Canada, an Englishman is struck by the feeling that he is going from a richer country into one that is poorer, and from a greater country into one that is less.

ANTHONY TROLLOPE, British novelist, in *North America* (1862).

Canada is a live country, live, but not, like the States, kicking.

RUPERT BROOKE, English poet, on his visit to North America in 1913, from *Letters from America* (1916).

The Swiss make no distinction between Canadians and citizens of the United States. I wondered about this, and asked a hotelkeeper if he didn't notice any difference between the people from the two countries.

"Monsieur," he said, "Canadians speak English and always stay two days longer at any place than Americans do." So there you are.

ERNEST HEMINGWAY, American writer then a *Star* writer, in "The Hotels in Switzerland," the Toronto *Star Weekly*, March 4, 1922. *Byline: Ernest Hemingway* (1967), edited by William White.

An honest attempt to enumerate the points in which our Canadian civilization differs from that of the United States is apt to be almost as brief as the famous essay upon snakes in Ireland.

FRANK H. UNDERHILL, socialist and later reluctant Liberal, in "O Canada," the *Canadian Forum*, Dec. 1929.

I accept now with equanimity the question so constantly addressed to me, "Are you an American?" and merely return the accurate answer, "Yes, I am a Canadian."

LESTER B. PEARSON, future prime minister, in "Canada and the United States," Jan. 31, 1941, from *Words and Occasions* (1970).

Americans are benevolently ignorant about Canada, while Canadians are malevolently well informed about the United States.

J. BARTLET BREBNER, historian, attributed, about 1945.

Canada and the United States have reached the point where we no longer think of each other as "foreign" countries. We think of each other as friends, as peaceful and co-operative neighbours on a spacious and fruitful continent.

HARRY S. TRUMAN, American president, addressing a joint meeting of the Senate and the House of Commons, June 11, 1947.

If we could get off by ourselves on a continent island, far away from the wicked Americans, all we should achieve would be to become a people like the Australians. (And even then the American goblin would get us in the end, as he is getting the Australians.) Let us be thankful, then, that we live next door to the Americans. But if we allow ourselves to be obsessed by the danger of American cultural annexation, so that the thought preys on us day and night, we shall only become a slightly bigger Ulster.

FRANK H. UNDERHILL, writer and teacher, in "Notes on the Massey Report" (1951), *In Search of Canadian Liberalism* (1960).

In Canada's capital, the city of Ottawa, there is an old canal which winds through the town. Weeping willows grow beside it and arch over it and not one Canadian in ten thousand knows when or why it was built. It was built more than a century ago by a British engineer to help defend Canada against the United States; and the fact

that today this old canal is but a museum piece, its origin unknown or unremembered, tells the blessed thing that has come between these two countries and which today has roots deeper than before.

GRATTAN O'LEARY, Conservative spokesman and senator, in "Canada's Political Philosophy," *Canada: Nation on the March* (1953), introduction by H.L. Enman.

Defensively, as well as geographically, we are joined beyond any possibility of separation.

DWIGHT D. EISENHOWER, president of the United States, before a joint sitting of the Senate and the House of Commons, Nov. 14, 1953.

Today I assure you once more of the pride and gratification that we of the United States feel in our long and friendly association with you, our sturdy northern neighbour.

DWIGHT D. EISENHOWER, president of the United States, before a joint sitting of the Senate and the House of Commons, July 9, 1958.

This stone bears witness to the common purpose of two nations whose frontiers are the frontiers of friendship, whose ways are the ways of freedom, and whose works are the works of peace.

Inscription, St. Lawrence Seaway, Prescott, Ont., June 26, 1959.

Perhaps the most striking thing about Canada is that it is not part of the United States.

J. BARTLET BREBNER, historian, made this the opening sentence of *Canada: A Modern History* (1960).

We share common values from the past, a common defence line at present, and common aspirations for the future, and indeed the future of all mankind.

Geography has made us neighbours. History has made us friends. Economics has made us partners. And necessity has made us allies. Those whom nature hath so joined together, let no man put asunder.

What unites us is far greater than what divides us.

JOHN F. KENNEDY, president of the United States, in an address at a joint sitting of the

Canadian Senate and the House of Commons, May 17, 1961.

Not life, liberty, and the pursuit of happiness, but peace, order, and good government are what the national government of Canada guarantees. Under these, it is assumed, life, liberty, and happiness may be achieved, but by each according to his taste. For the society of allegiance admits of a diversity the society of compact does not, and one of the blessings of Canadian life is that there is no Canadian way of life, much less two, but a unity under the Crown admitting of a thousand diversities.

W.L. Morton, historian, in *The Canadian Identity* (1961).

Ours is a sovereign nation
Bows to no foreign will
But whenever they cough in Washington
They spit on Parliament Hill.

Joe Wallace, leftist versifier, from "A Sovereign Nation," *A Radiant Sphere* (1964).

It is in the abiding interest of both countries that, whenever possible, divergent views between the two governments should be expressed and if possible resolved in private through diplomatic channels. Only a firm mutual resolve and the necessary practical arrangements to keep the totality of the relationship in good and friendly working order can enable our countries to avoid needless frictions and minimize the consequences of disagreement.

A.D.P. Heeney, Canadian diplomat, in "Canada and the United States: Principles for Partnership" (June 1965), by A.D.P. Heeney and Livingston T. Merchant, former U.S. ambassador to Canada.

Canadians are generally indistinguishable from the Americans, and the surest way of telling the two apart is to make the observation to a Canadian.

Richard Starnes, Scripps-Howard columnist, quoted by Gerald Clark in *Canada: The Uneasy Neighbour* (1965).

Canadians are much more likely to be respected in the United States if they fight for their interests and their independence, than if they give in silently and without protest every time Uncle Sam looks cross.

Walter L. Gordon, minister of finance and economic nationalist, in *A Choice for Canada* (1966).

In Canada we talk a lot about cultural protectionism; we don't do it much. Among Canadians you will find a major difference of opinion as to whether that last sentence amounts to bragging or complaining.

Robert Fulford, Toronto columnist, from "Pro-Canadians and Anti-Americans" (1966), *Crisis at the Victory Burlesk* (1968).

Canada, I have long believed, is fighting a rearguard action against the inevitable—substantial integration which will require for its full realization a progressively expanding area of common political decision . . . . I wonder, for example, if the Canadian people will be prepared indefinitely to accept, for the psychic satisfaction of maintaining a separate national and political identity, a per capita income less than three-fourths of ours. The struggle is bound to be a difficult one—and I suspect, over the years, a losing one . . . .

George Ball, U.S. under-secretary of State in the administrations of presidents Kennedy and Johnson, in *The Discipline of Power* (1968).

To think of the U.S. is to think of ourselves—almost.

George P. Grant, professor of Religion at McMaster University, in "From Roosevelt to L.B.J.," *The New Romans* (1968), edited by Al Purdy.

However, if I still feel the longest unmanned frontier is an artificial one, I no longer look forward, as I once did, to the day when it might disappear and we would join fully in the American adventure. Vietnam and Ronald Reagan, among other things, have tempered my enthusiasm. Looked at another way, yes, we *are* nicer. And suddenly that's important.

Mordecai Richler, Montreal novelist, in "The North American Pattern," *The New Romans* (1968), edited by Al Purdy.

Americans should never underestimate the constant pressure on Canada which the mere presence of the United States has produced. We're a different people from you and we're a different people partly because of you.

*

Living next to you is in some ways like sleeping with an elephant. No matter how friendly and even-tempered is the beast, if I can call it that, one is affected by every twitch and grunt . . . .

PIERRE ELLIOTT TRUDEAU, prime minister, in an address to the National Press Club, Washington, March 26, 1969.

We're not going to move away from the U.S. We're going to be friends willy-nilly, and probably more willy than nilly.

PIERRE ELLIOTT TRUDEAU, prime minister, in an interview, Dec. 21, 1971.

Our relationship with you is too complex to be described, too involved to be understood fully, too deeply entrenched to be disregarded. We are no more capable of living in isolation from you than we are desirous of doing so.

PIERRE ELLIOTT TRUDEAU, prime minister, introducing Richard M. Nixon, U.S. president, before a joint sitting of the Canadian Senate and the House of Commons, April 14, 1972.

I'm an old Canadian—I don't want to be a new American.

HUGH GARNER, Toronto novelist, appearing as part of a delegation of ACTRA performers and writers before the CRTC in Ottawa, 1970.

We must also build a new spirit of partnership within the Western hemisphere that we share together. It has been said that Canada is bounded "on the north by gold, on the west by the East, on the east by history, and on the south by friends."

Hon. Members: Hear, hear!

Mr. Nixon: We hope that this will always be the case.

RICHARD M. NIXON, U.S. president, in an address before a joint sitting of the Canadian Senate and the House of Commons, April 14, 1972.

First let me get something out of the way. While the distinction seems terribly difficult for some to make, and while it has had to be repeated in Canada at least a thousand times too often, it nevertheless appears mandatory to repeat again and

38

again: "It's not necessary to be anti-American to be pro-Canadian."

MEL HURTIG, Edmonton publisher and economic nationalist, in an address to the World Federalists, Kingston, June 8, 1973.

The distance between Canada and the United States is much wider than the St. Lawrence River which forms the boundary, and the Thousand Islands Bridge connects the two nations by leaps of the imagination.

JOHN KEATS, American social critic, in *Of Time and an Island* (1974).

Canada First Movement
See also NATIONALISM.

Canada First.

JAMES D. EDGAR, a founder of Canada First and future Speaker of the House of Commons, helped choose the name of the nationalist movement in 1870.

Several names were mentioned, and someone said that Edgar had made a suggestion. I walked across the hall into Edgar's office, and asked him what he had suggested. He seemed to have forgotten the exact words, but said, "Canada before all, or Canada first of all." I said, "That will do: Canada First," and went back to my room and proposed it to the others, and after some discussion it was unanimously decided that we should call ourselves the "Canada First" Party, meaning that we should put Canada first, before every other consideration.

GEORGE TAYLOR DENISON, senior police magistrate in Toronto from 1877 to 1923, and a founder of Canada First, recalled coining the phrase in 1870 with Sir James D. Edgar, in *The Struggle for Imperial Unity* (1909). A year later, on publication of William Foster's address, *Canada First* (1871), the phrase achieved currency as a slogan.

To those, sir, who have life before them, let my prayer be this: Remember from this day forth never to look simply at the horizon as it may be limited by the limits of the Province, but look abroad over all the continent, wherever the British flag floats, and let your motto be, "Canada first, Canada last, and Canada always."

SIR WILFRID LAURIER, leader of the Liberal party, in a campaign address at Massey Hall, Toronto, Oct. 14, 1904, published in the *Globe* the following day.

Canada Goose

See BIRDS.

Canadian Boat Song

See also MUSIC.

Faintly as tolls the evening chime
Our voices keep tune and our oars keep
    time.
Soon as the woods on shore look dim,
We'll sing at St. Ann's our parting hymn.
Row, brothers, row, the stream runs fast,
The Rapids are near and the daylight's
    past.

Why should we yet our sail unfurl?
Why is not a breath the blue wave to curl;
But when the wind blows off the shore,
Oh! sweetly we'll rest our weary oar.
Blow, breezes, blow, the stream runs fast,
The Rapids are near and the daylight's
    past.

Utawas' tide! this trembling moon
Shall see us float over thy surges soon.
Saint of this green isle! hear our prayers,
Oh, grant us cool heaven and favouring
    airs.
Blow, breezes, blow, the stream runs fast,
The Rapids are near and the daylight's
    past.

> THOMAS MOORE, the Irish poet, wrote his lyric, "A Canadian Boat Song: Written on the River St. Lawrence," in 1804 at Ste. Anne de Bellevue, while visiting with the explorer Simon Fraser; the poem was first published in *Epistles, Odes and Other Poems* (1806).

Listen to me, as when ye heard our father
    Sing long ago the song of our shores—
Listen to me, and then in chorus gather
    All your deep voices, as ye pull your
        oars:
    *Fair these broad meads—these hoary woods are
        grand;*
    But we are exiles from our fathers' land.

From the lone shieling of the mistry island
    Mountains divide us, and the waste of
        seas—
Yet still the blood is strong, the heart is

Highland,
And we in dreams behold the Hebrides:
    *Fair these broad meads—these hoary woods are
        grand;*
    But we are exiles from our fathers' land.

> DAVID MACBETH MOIR, Scottish versifier who had never visited North America but had corresponded with the novelist John Galt, might have written these stanzas from "Canadian Boat-Song (from the Gaelic)" which appeared anonymously in *Blackwood's*, Sept. 1829. Reproduced from G.H. Needler's *The Lone Shieling* (1941).

Canadian Pacific Railway

See also PACIFIC SCANDAL; RAILROADS.

Stand fast, Craigellachie!

> GEORGE STEPHEN, president of the CPR, raised last-minute capital in Nov. 1884 in London, England, when the railway company was all but bankrupt, by selling his own bonds and those of his cousin, Donald Smith, Lord Strathcona. He then sent this cablegram to Smith. Quoted by Pierre Berton in *The National Dream: 1871-1881* (1970). Craigellachie is Gaelic for "the rock of alarm." Lord Strathcona was given the honour of driving in the "last spike" at Craigellachie, Eagle Pass, B.C., Nov. 7, 1885. A plaque marking the spot includes this inscription: "Here on November 7, 1885, a plain iron spike welded East to West."

Building that railroad would have made a Canadian out of the German Emperor.

> SIR W.C. VAN HORNE, engineer and railway-builder, on renouncing his American citizenship in the 1880s.

The last spike will be just as good an iron one as there is between Montreal and Vancouver, and anyone who wants to see it driven will have to pay full fare.

> SIR W.C. VAN HORNE, who drove the CPR through the Rockies, quoted by Walter Vaughan in *Sir William Van Horne* (1926).

All I can say is that the work has been done well in every way.

> SIR W.C. VAN HORNE, engineer, impromptu remark at the "last spike" ceremony, Craigellachie, B.C., Nov. 7, 1885.

Who is going to ride on that railway, Indians and buffalos?

> SIR WILFRID LAURIER, prime minister, remark during the construction of the CPR, attributed by Alvin Hamilton and reported by Peter Stursberg in *Diefenbaker: Leadership Gained* (1975).

Take good care of the Canadian Pacific Railway.

> BARON SHAUGHNESSY, who succeeded Van Horne as president of the CPR, to Edward Beatty, future CPR president, in 1923. Quoted by R.G. MacBeth in *The Romance of the Canadian Pacific Railway* (1924).

Any horse that can't outrun the CPR deserves to die.

> PADDY NOWLAN, Calgary lawyer, refusing to take the case of a farmer whose horses were being run over by the railroad. Quoted by Robert E. Gard in *Johnny Chinook* (1945).

Canada's greatest need is a moral equivalent of the CPR.

> FRANK H. UNDERHILL, historian and writer, attributed, about 1950.

The National Dream.

> PIERRE BERTON, writer and broadcaster, encouraged Canadians to regard the construction of the CPR in 1885 as the realization of "the national dream." *The National Dream: 1871-1881* (1970) is the title of the first volume of his two-volume history, *The Great Railway*; the second volume is *The Last Spike: 1881-1885* (1971).

There has to be something wrong with a country whose National Dream is a railroad.

> BERNARD SLADE, Ontario-born, California-based playwright, quoted by Tom Hedley in the *Canadian*, July 26, 1975.

Canadian Shield

The Canadian Shield is fascinating country of enormous wealth but there is too much of it. In Canada there is too much of everything. Too much rock, too much prairie, too much tundra, too much mountain, too much forest. Above all, too much forest. Even the man who passionately believes that he shall never see a poem as lovely as a tree will be disposed to give po-
40

etry another try after he has driven the Trans-Canada Highway.

> EDWARD MCCOURT, prairie writer, in *The Road Across Canada* (1965).

The Shield! The Canadian Shield!
Come, Muse of rockbound nationalists, for whom our stammering typing engine waits smiling with teeth of alphabets. You who inflate the eloquence of Northern laureates, come, let us celebrate the real estate. Sing, Learned Dame—as so often before—not of men, not of poor flesh and blood, but of rocks, stones, mud, bogs, fens, muskegs, permafrost, tundra!

> KILDARE DOBBS, essayist, in *The Great Fur Opera* (1970), with illustrations by Ronald Searle.

Canadiana

Canadiana, Canadiana,
Mens sana in corpore sana,
Other nations are top banana,
But we'll still take Canadiana.

> TIM PORTEOUS and JAMES DOMVILLE, lyrics from "Culturality Squad," written by the two talented undergraduates for *My Fur Lady*, the McGill musical that opened in Montreal on Feb. 7, 1957.

Canadians

See also CANADA: FRENCH AND ENGLISH; CANUCK; CITIZENSHIP; FRENCH CANADIANS.

I am branded in Quebec as a traitor to the French, and in Ontario as a traitor to the English. In Quebec I am branded as a Jingoist, and in Ontario as a Separatist. In Quebec I am attacked as an Imperialist, and in Ontario as an anti-Imperialist. I am neither. I am a Canadian.

> SIR WILFRID LAURIER, leader of the Liberal party, in a campaign speech, St. John, Quebec, 1911, from *Life and Letters of Sir Wilfrid Laurier* (1921), by O.D. Skelton.

There are indeed people who lack a developed persona—"Canadians who know not Europe's sham politeness"—blundering from one social solecism to the next, perfectly harmless and innocent, soulful bores or appealing children, or, if they are women, spectral Cassandras dreaded for their tactlessness, eternally misunderstood, never knowing what they are about, always taking forgiveness for granted, blind to the world, hopeless dreamers. From them we can see how a neglected persona works, and what one must do to remedy the evil.

> CARL GUSTAV JUNG, Swiss psychoanalyst, in "The Relations between the Ego and the Unconscious" (1916), in *Two Essays on Analytic Psychology* (1966), translated by R.F.C. Hull. The quoted words come from a poem about life among the Indians published in 1839 by the German poet Johann Gottfried Seume.

"And bring your friend," said Mrs. Braddocks laughing. She was a Canadian and had all their easy social graces.

> ERNEST HEMINGWAY, American writer, in *The Sun Also Rises* (1926).

If I were English, Canada
Should love me like the deuce.
But I was born in Canada
So what the hell's the use!

> WILSON MACDONALD, Toronto poet, last stanza of "The Song of a Bloody Canuck," from *Open House* (1931), edited by William Arthur Deacon and Wilfred Reeves.

This sound sense of the possible.

> EDGAR MCINNIS, historian, defining the Canadian spirit which seeks "moderation" and "cooperation" to enable Canada to "surmount each successive crisis," in *Canada: A Political and Social History* (1947).

A Canadian is a fellow who has become a North American without becoming an American.

> ARTHUR L. PHELPS, broadcaster, adapted from his address at the University of New Brunswick, Feb. 18, 1947.

The Canadian is often a baffled man because he feels different from his British kindred and his American neighbours, sharply refuses to be lumped together with either of them, yet cannot make plain his difference.

> J.B. PRIESTLEY, British playwright, in the introduction to *The Bodley Head Leacock* (1957), edited by J.B. Priestley.

A Canadian is someone who knows he is going somewhere, but isn't sure where.

> W.L. MORTON, historian, quoted by Gerald Clark in *Canada: The Uneasy Neighbour* (1965).

So to each of you, I say I believe in a Canada—a Canada undivided. A Canadian I was born, a Canadian I will die.

> JOHN G. DIEFENBAKER, former prime minister, in an address at the annual convention of the Progressive Conservative party, Toronto, Sept. 7, 1967.

Imagine a Canadian Dream, which implied that everybody in the world ought to share it! Imagine a Committee on Un-Canadian Activities! You can't. Un-Canadianism is almost the very definition of *Canadianism*.

> HUGH HOOD, Montreal novelist, in "Moral Imagination: Canadian Thing" (1968), *The Governor's Bridge Is Closed* (1973).

I admire and covet not only American styles and achievements but also the American's generosity of spirit and willingness to take total responsibility for himself and his actions. A Canadian, by contrast, has been called someone who doesn't play for keeps.

> WILLIAM KILBOURN, Toronto historian, in "Some Feelings about the United States," *The New Romans* (1968), edited by Al Purdy.

But being a Canadian
By conscious and considered choice
I have to remember no one & nothing
Which in this 1969th year of grace
Suits me just fine

> GEORGE JONAS, Toronto poet, "On the Virtues of Being a Canadian" in *The Happy Hungry Man* (1970).

Canadians represent, as it were, the least militant North American minority group. The white, Protestant, heterosexual ghetto of the north.

> MORDECAI RICHLER, Montreal novelist, in the introduction to *Canadian Writing Today* (1970).

Canadians are, after all, simply romantics who lost the courage of their hopes.

> SCOTT SYMONS, novelist, in *Heritage* (1971).

A Canadian is someone who drinks Brazilian coffee from an English teacup, and munches a French pastry while sitting on his Danish furniture, having just come home from an Italian movie in his German car. He picks up his Japanese pen and writes to his member of Parliament to complain about the American takeover of the Canadian publishing business.

CAMPBELL HUGHES, head of an American multinational publishing firm in Toronto, adapted the definition, quoted by *Time*, March 1, 1971.

A Canadian is somebody who knows how to make love in a canoe.

PIERRE BERTON, writer and broadcaster, attributed by Dick Brown in the *Canadian*, Dec. 22, 1973.

A Canadian is a North American who does not owe allegiance to the United States or Mexico.

GEORGE WOODCOCK, Vancouver man-of-letters, quoted by Paul Gresco in the *Canadian*, May 17, 1975.

The trouble with Canadians—and if you've ever met one you will surely agree—is they suffer from an underdeveloped sense of the absurd.

GEOFFREY STEVENS, columnist, in the Toronto *Globe and Mail*, Aug. 27, 1975.

Canoe

"Now, I think that it much better that, as we all go along together, that every man paddle his own canoe. That my thought."

FREDERICK MARRYAT, popular novelist and sea captain, in *The Settlers in Canada* (1844). The Indian's remark is frequently cited as the earliest appearance in print of the idiom "every man must paddle his own canoe."

And up on the hills against the sky,
A fir tree rocking its lullaby,
Swings, swings,
Its emerald wings,
Swelling the song that my paddle sings.

PAULINE JOHNSON, Mohawk poet, last lines of "The Song My Paddle Sings," *The White Wampum* (1895). The text is taken from *Flint and Feather* (1912).

What the camel is to desert tribes, what the horse is to the Arab, what the ship is to the colonizing Briton, what all modern means of locomotion are to the civilized world today, that, and more than that, the canoe was to the Indian who lived beside the innumerable waterways of Canada.

WILLIAM WOOD, historian, in *All Afloat* (1920).

Yes, a canoe is an incomparable companion in the Canadian spring and summer and autumn. But in winter it is helpless. When the lakes and rivers freeze life flees from its limbs. Its body grows paralyzed and its spirit dies. Like many animals then, it must hide itself away. Since it cannot migrate like a Swallow, it hibernates like a Bear.

MALCOLM MCDONALD, British high commissioner in Ottawa from 1941 to 1945, in *The Birds of Brewery Creek* (1947).

What sets a canoeing expedition apart is that it purifies you more rapidly and inescapably than any other. Travel a thousand miles by train and you are a brute; pedal five hundred on a bicycle and you remain basically a bourgeois; paddle a hundred in a canoe and you are already a child of nature.

PIERRE ELLIOTT TRUDEAU, future prime minister, in "Exhaustion and Fulfilment: The Ascetic in a Canoe" (1944), from *Wilderness Canada* (1970), edited by Borden Spears.

Canuck

See also CANADIANS.

"Come boys and have some grog, I'm what you call a canuck;" (a Canadian).

SIR JAMES E. ALEXANDER, Scots author, quoting "a lusty fellow," *L'Acadie* (1849). This is the earliest appearance in print of "Canuck" for Canadian. By the turn of the century, Johnny Canuck personified Canada.

They had better start making stronger rope—if they want to hold Canadians captive!

LEO BACHLE, the artist who created Johnny Canuck, the eponymous strongman hero of Dime Comics in 1941. From Michael Hirsch and Patrick Loubert's *The Great Canadian Comic Books* (1971).

Capital Punishment

See also CRIME.

We know how to hang in Canada.

PIERRE BOUCHER, governor of Trois-Rivières in the 1650s, attributed by Agnes Repplier in *Mère Marie of the Ursulines* (1931).

What a pity public hangings were ever done away with! Had they continued a few years longer, the horrible practice of hanging men would have passed away under the pressure of public opinion.

> PATRICK SLATER, pseudonym of Toronto lawyer and author John Mitchell, in *The Yellow Briar* (1933).

In carrying out the extreme sentence of the law, I am the last wheel and the smallest wheel. The judge sanctions the execution; I merely perform it. I take it very religiously.

> ARTHUR BARTHOLOMEW ENGLISH, Canada's official executioner, quoted by Frederick Griffin in *Variety Show* (1936).

The death penalty degraded society, glamourized murder, and raised the killer to be an aristocrat among criminals.

> BEVERLEY BAXTER, Toronto-born journalist and British M.P., who contributed a fortnightly "London Letter" to *Maclean's* magazine. Quoted by Louis Blake Duff in *The County Kerchief* (1949).

Capitalism
See also BUSINESS; LABOUR.

Labour is just as much interested in the maintenance of capitalism, that is to say, the supremacy of capital, as the slave was in the perpetuation of the slave power.

> PHILLIPS THOMPSON, labour reporter who covered the police court for the Toronto *Telegram*, in *The Politics of Labour* (1887).

Dear Sorge:

We arrived here yesterday, after having had to turn about between Toronto and Kingston because of a storm (it was quite a nasty breeze) and tie up in Port Hope. Thus the two days from Toronto to here turned into *three*. The St. Lawrence and the rapids are very pretty. Canada is richer in ruined houses than any other country but Ireland. We are trying to understand the Canadian French here—that language beats *Yankee English holler* [in English in the original]. This evening we leave for Plattsburg and then into the Adirondacks and possibly to the Catskills, so that we can hardly be back in New York by Sunday

. . . .

It is a strange transition from the States to Canada. First one imagines that one is in Europe again, and then one thinks one is in a positively retrogressing and decaying country. Here one sees how necessary the feverish speculative spirit of the Americans is for the rapid development of a new country (presupposing capitalist production as a basis); and in ten years this sleepy Canada will be ripe for annexation—the farmers in Manitoba, etc., will demand it themselves. Besides, the country is half-annexed already socially—hotels, newspapers, advertising, etc., all on the American pattern. And they may tug and resist as much as they like; the economic necessity of an infusion of Yankee blood will have its way and abolish this ridiculous boundary line—and when the time comes, John Bull will say "Yea and Amen" to it.

> Yours
> F.E.
> FRIEDRICH ENGELS, friend of Karl Marx, in a letter written in Montreal on Sept. 10, 1888, to Victor Sorge, *Letters to Americans: 1848-1895* (1953), edited by Alexander Trachtenberg.

The only difference between jail and a job is that here I am separated from my wife and family. Under capitalism all the workers are in jail all the time. And lots of them haven't got the security of shelter and food that is offered in a penitentiary.

> J.B. McLACHLAN, Cape Breton unionist, in the *Maritime Labour Herald*, Nov. 17, 1923. Quoted by Paul MacEwan in "Labour and Politics in Cape Breton," the *Cape Breton Highlander*, April 17, 1968.

One of the great problems before Canada today is not to save capitalism from socialism or communism, but to save capitalism from certain capitalists.

> GRATTAN O'LEARY, editor and future senator, in "The Public and the Politician," an address to the Empire Club of Canada in 1933.

To those who object that capitalism is "rooted in human nature," we answer: Possibly, but so was cannibalism. We no longer eat each other. A civilization is within our reach in which we shall no longer exploit each other.

> EUGENE FORSEY, research director and future

senator, in "The Nature of the Canadian Economy," *Social Planning for Canada* (1935), by the Research Committee of the League for Social Reconstruction.

Only in times of peace can the wastes of capitalism be tolerated
F.R. SCOTT, Montreal man-of-letters, in "The Efficiency of Socialism," *Queen's Quarterly*, summer 1935.

It is unlikely Canada will ever have a Labour government because every Canadian working man considers himself a potential capitalist.
M.J. COLDWELL, national president of the CCF, attributed when he was asked privately by a newspaperman when labour would come to power in Canada, following Labour's victory under Clement Attlee in Britain in 1945.

I have seen the face of capitalism, and it is fascism!
MICHEL CHARTRAND, leader of the left wing of the Quebec labour movement and president of the Montreal Central Council of the CNTU. Quoted by Ken Sobel in the *Village Voice*, May 27, 1971.

Customs Inspector: Why are you entering the country?
Buckley: To desocialize Canada.
Customs Inspector: How long do you intend to remain?
Buckley: Twenty-four hours.
WILLIAM F. BUCKLEY JR., spokesman for American conservatism, answering a Canadian customs inspector when entering the country to debate with David Lewis, the NDP leader, in 1973.

I just followed the same business principles that worked in Timmins and North Bay. I did the same things in Edinburgh and London as I did back here, except I added a few zeroes at the end.
ROY THOMSON, Canadian-born British press lord, explaining his business practices, which took him from ownership of the Timmins *Press* to the London *Times*. Quoted by Roy Mac-Skimming in the Toronto *Star*, July 16, 1975.

A civilization shaped by market transactions is a civilization responsive to the common appetites, preferences and aspirations of common people.
EDGAR BURTON, vice-president of Simpsons Ltd., address to the Board of Trade, Toronto *Globe and Mail*, Feb. 3, 1976.

Cartier, Jacques

In fine I am rather inclined to believe that this is the land God gave to Cain.
JACQUES CARTIER, French navigator and explorer, had this reaction to the bleak shore of the Gulf of St. Lawrence, today's Labrador and Quebec, discovered and described during the summer of 1534 in his *Première relation*, from *The Voyages of Jacques Cartier* (1924), translated by H.P. Biggar.

The sayd men did moreover certify unto us, that there was the way and beginning of the great river of Hochelaga and ready way to Canada, which river the further it went the narrower it came, even into Canada, and that there was fresh water, which went so farre upwards, that they had never heard of any man who had gone to the head of it, and that there is no other passage but with small boats.
JACQUES CARTIER, French navigator and explorer, on July 26, 1535, in "A Shorte and Briefe Narration" (1535), reproduced by Richard Hakluyt in *The Principal Navigations, Voyages, Traffiques, and Discoveries of the English Nation* (1589). This is the earliest recorded use of the word "Canada."

We have decided to again send Cartier to Canada and Hochelaga, and as far as the lands of Saguenay . . . with a goodly number of ships and men of all rank, skills, and trades . . . so that we may better fulfil our intention and to do actions agreeable to God our creator and redeemer.
FRANÇOIS I, king of France, thus commissioned Jacques Cartier to undertake his third voyage, dated Oct. 17, 1540, in *A Collection of Documents Relating to Jacques Cartier and the Sieur de Roberval* (1930), edited by H.P. Biggar.

In the seaport of Saint Malo, 'twas a smiling morn, in May,
When the Commodore Jacques Cartier to the westward sail'd away;

In the crowded old cathedral all the town
were on their knees,
For the safe return of kinsmen from the
undiscovered seas;
And every autumn blast that swept o'er
pinnacle and pier,
Fill'd manly hearts with sorrow and gentle
hearts with fear.

> THOMAS D'ARCY MCGEE, a Father of Confederation, in "Jacques Cartier," *The Poems of Thomas D'Arcy McGee* (1869), edited by Mrs. J. Sadlier.

Catholicism
See also CHRISTIANITY.

For Instance, when the Jesuits Preach up the Incarnation of *Jesus Christ*, they'l answer, *That's Wonderful*: When the Question is put to them, whether they'l turn Christians, they reply, that *they'l consider of it* . . . . Such, Sir, is the Obstinacy and prepossession of this People.

> BARON DE LA HONTAN, unorthodox French officer who spent ten years in North America, writing in 1703 of the Huron Indians, from *New Voyages to North-America* (1905), translated by Reuben Gold Thwaites.

Behold the Pope of Canada and the English Sot.

> THOMAS WALKER, pro-American merchant, thus defaced the statue of King George in Place d'Armes on May 1, 1775, when the Quebec Act was passed in Montreal. From W.A.D. Styles's *Unusual Facts of Canadian History* (1947).

Let each say in his heart, "I hear my *curé*, my *curé* hears the bishop, the bishop hears the Pope, and the Pope hears Our Lord Jesus Christ."

> BISHOP IGNACE BOURGET of Montreal, in a circular letter, Feb. 1, 1867, quoted by Mason Wade in *The French Canadians* (1968).

What is this great work of which the Canadian people is to be the instrument? The Canadians will answer us with one voice, and alike from pulpit and from tribune we shall hear these words given forth: "Our mission is to fulfil in America, we who are a people of French blood, the part that France herself fulfilled in Europe . . . .

There is a divine mission which they must fulfil. A Catholic people, one of those that have remained most faithful to the Church, they must win over the whole of North America to Catholicism."

> CHARLES GAILLY DE TAURINES, French writer, in *La nation canadienne* (1894), quoted by André Siegfried in *The Race Question in Canada* (1907).

Do the French lilies reign
Over Mont Royal and Stadacona still?

*

Whither I go I know not, nor the way,
Dark with strange passions, vexed with
heathen charms,
Holding I know not what of life or death;
Only be Thou beside me day by day,
Thy rod my guide and comfort, underneath
Thy everlasting arms.

> MARJORIE PICKTHALL, poet, lines from "Père Lalemant," *The Selected Poems of Marjorie Pickthall* (1957), edited by Lorne Pierce.

Where was the source
Of his strength . . . not in these the
source—
But in the sound of invisible trumpets
blowing
Around two slabs of board, right-angled,
hammered
By Roman nails and hung on a Jewish hill.

> E.J. PRATT, epic poet, from "Brébeuf and His Brethren" (1940), *The Collected Poems of E.J. Pratt* (second ed., 1958), edited by Northrop Frye.

When Lalemant and de Brébeuf, brave
souls,
Were dying by the slow and dreadful coals,
Their brother Jesuits in France and Spain
Were burning heretics with equal pain.
For both the human torture made a feast:
Then is priest savage, or Red Indian
priest?

> F.R. SCOTT, Montreal man-of-letters, in "Brébeuf and His Brethren" (1957), from *Selected Poems* (1966).

The church always arrives on the scene a little breathless and a little late.

> BERNARD J.E. LONERGAN, Jesuit theologian, attributed about 1963.

45

CCF
See NEW DEMOCRATIC PARTY.

Censorship
See also BOOKS; NEWS.

Let your readers here pause and marvel.
And by and by when their astonishment is
surmounted, I may enlarge upon the works
and untimely end of the great Censor, who
soared beyond Parnassus, and died in a
dung heap.

THOMAS McCULLOCH, Maritime satirist, in
Letter 18 of the "Letters of Mephibosheth
Stepsure," published in the *Acadian Recorder* in
1821 and 1822, from *The Stepsure Letters* (1960),
edited by Douglas Lochhead.

Your verdict will be the most important in
its consequences, ever delivered before this
tribunal; and I conjure you to judge me by
the principles of English law, and to leave
an unshackled press as a legacy to your
children. You remember the press in your
hours of conviviality and mirth—oh! do
not desert it in this its day of trial.
*
Yes, gentlemen, come what will, while I
live, Nova Scotia shall have the blessing of
an open and unshackled press.

JOSEPH HOWE, Nova Scotian editor and statesman, excerpts from his two-day "Address to
the Jury," May 1835. Howe, tried for publishing a libellous letter in the *Novascotian*, was ac-
quitted. From *The Speeches and Public Letters of
the Hon. Joseph Howe* (1858), edited by William
Annand.

If I can be proscribed today, for defending
myself and my friends in the newspapers,
another Nova Scotian may be rejected tomorrow because the Governor likes not the
colour of his hair.

JOSEPH HOWE, Halifax editor, in an address at
a public dinner, Cumberland County, fall
1844, from *The Speeches and Public Letters of the
Hon. Joseph Howe* (1858), edited by William
Annand.

The subject who is truly loyal to the Chief
Magistrate will neither advise nor submit
to arbitrary measures.—JUNIUS.

JUNIUS, identified as Laughlin Maclearne, a
surgeon in the British army and secretary to
the Earl of Shelburne, from one of the "Junius

Letters," published anonymously in the *London
Public Advertiser* between 1769 and 1772. No issue of the Toronto *Globe and Mail* (or of the
Globe before it) has appeared without these
words. The motto was chosen by its publisher
George Brown, and appeared in the first issue
of March 5, 1844.

Over two-thirds of the book, or 250 pages,
deal with filthy, obscene descriptions that
are offensive to decency and utterly unnecessary for what we have been told is the
purpose of the book.

ROBERT TASCHEREAU, justice of the Supreme
Court of Canada, in 1959, part of the dissent-
ing opinion on the merits of *Lady Chatterley's
Lover* (1928).

I went to bat for the Lady Chatte
  Dressed in my bib and gown.
The judges three glared down at me
  The priests patrolled the town.

F.R. SCOTT, member of the faculty of Law of
McGill University, who successfully defended
D.H. Lawrence's novel, *Lady Chatterley's Lover*,
against a charge of obscenity in 1959, in "A
Lass in Wonderland" (1964), from *Selected
Poems* (1966).

It's such an honour being banned in Italy,
the mother of sensuality. It's like being
asked to straighten your tie in a bordello.
*
It is ironic that the pictures were removed
on the complaint of a cardinal. I regard
censorship as a cardinal sin.

HAROLD TOWN, when the Toronto artist
learned his drawings had been removed from
an exhibition in Italy, the *Globe and Mail*, June
29, 1964.

Centennial
See also CONFEDERATION.

We all, I'm sure, have many hopes for
Canada on this Centennial day—that she
may grow, thrive, prosper in all things. To
these I would add one hope more: that
Canada will not so greatly grow, and not
so grossly thrive, as to destroy this heritage
of solitude which makes us what we are
and which our children will know perhaps
better than we how to value.

BLAIR FRASER, well-known journalist, in "A
Centennial Sermon," at the Church of the

Messiah, Montreal, July 2, 1967. From *"Blair Fraser Reports"* (1969), edited by John Fraser and Graham Fraser.

Children
See also MOTHERS.

Cow's milk is for calves.

*

It moves direct from producer to consumer. The cats can't get at it. It doesn't have to be warmed up on a picnic. It comes in such cute containers. [List of reasons why mother's milk is superior to the cow's.]

DR. ALAN BROWN, pioneer pediatrician, remarks frequently made, quoted by Dorothy Sangster in *Maclean's*, Aug. 1, 1952.

The first half of our lives is ruined by our parents, and the second half by our children.

RICHARD J. NEEDHAM, Toronto columnist, in *A Friend in Needham, or a Writer's Notebook* (1969).

There are no lobbyists for children.

MARY VAN STOLK, writer, in *The Battered Child in Canada* (1972).

Alligator pie, alligator pie,
If I don't get some I think I'm gonna die.

DENNIS LEE, poet and editor, from *Alligator Pie* (1974).

Nicholas Knock was a venturesome boy.
　He lived at Number Eight.
He went for walks in the universe
　And generally got home late.

DENNIS LEE, poet and editor, from *Nicholas Knock and Other People* (1974).

I'm the proud father of two half-Jewish, half-Newfie kids who are very bright but fall down a lot.

LARRY ZOLF, zany broadcaster, quoted by James Quig in *Weekend*, April 5, 1975.

Christianity
See also BELIEF; CATHOLICISM; CHURCH; GOD; RELIGION.

The letter is badly written and quite soiled, because, in addition to other inconveniences, he who writes it has only one whole finger on his right hand; and it is difficult to avoid staining the paper with the blood which flows from his wounds, not yet healed; he uses arquebus powder for ink, and the earth for a table.

FRANCESCO GIUSEPPE BRESSANI, Jesuit missionary, in a letter to the general of the Jesuits, written on July 15, 1644, while a captive of the Iroquois, quoted by Albert Tessier in "François-Joseph Bressani," *Dictionary of Canadian Biography: Volume I: 1000-1700* (1965).

Once, when he was among the Neutral Nation, in the winter of 1640, he beheld the ominous apparition of a great cross slowly approaching from the quarter where lay the country of the Iroquois. He told the vision to his comrades.
"What was it like? How large was it?" they eagerly demanded. "Large enough," replied the priest, "to crucify us all." To explain such phenomena is the province of psychology, and not of history.

FRANCIS PARKMAN, Boston historian, on Jean de Brébeuf, Jesuit missionary and martyr, quoted by Parkman in *The Jesuits in North America in the Seventeenth Century* (1867).

Are there any Christian nations left? There remain Portugal, Spain since the restoration of Franco, France under the regime of Pétain. And, I would add, Italy under the reign of Mussolini.

HENRI BOURASSA, French-Canadian nationalist, in a Montreal address, Nov. 5, 1942. Quoted by Stanley B. Ryerson in *French Canada* (1943).

Like human culture as a whole, Christianity in the future may become more of a do-it-yourself affair than at any previous time.

LESLIE DEWART, leading Catholic thinker, in *The Foundations of Belief* (1969).

I think it's a long time since any Christian clergyman had anything to do with carpenters.

HARRY BROWN, CBC Radio broadcaster, after interviewing a churchman who refused to endorse a carpenter's strike, in June 1975.

Christmas

Chrétiens, prenez courage,
Jésus Saveur est né!
Du malin les ouvrages

A jamais sont ruinés.
Quand il chante merveille,
A ces troublants appas
Ne prêtez pas l'oreille:
Jésus est né: In excelsis gloria!

'Twas in the moon of wintertime
When all the birds had fled,
That Mighty Gitchi Manitou
Sent angel choirs instead.
Before their light the stars grew dim,
And wand'ring hunters heard the hymn:
"Jesus, your King, is born;
Jesus is born; in excelsis gloria!"

> JEAN DE BRÉBEUF, Jesuit missionary and martyr, wrote the first Canadian Christmas carol in the Huron tongue in 1641; it was translated by an unknown Quebec Jesuit before 1800 and first printed in Ernest Myrand's *Noëls anciens de la Nouvelle-France* (1899). The English version, an interpretation by Jesse Edgar Middleton, is from Robert E. Oliver's *Jesous Ahatonhia* (1967).

I once asked a Christmas Eve group of children if they believed in Santa Claus. The very smallest ones answered without hesitation, "Why, of course!" The older ones shook their heads. The little girls smiled sadly but said nothing. One future scientist asserted boldly, "I know who it is"; and a little make-strong with his eye on gain said: "I believe in it all; I can believe in anything." That boy, I realized, would one day be a bishop.

> STEPHEN LEACOCK, renowned Canadian writer and humorist, in "Wartime Santa Claus," *My Remarkable Uncle and Other Sketches* (1942).

Telling lies to a child does permanent damage to his mind. A child who believes in Santa Claus, who really and literally believes, because his daddy told him so, that Santa comes down all the chimneys in the world on the same night has had his thinking ability permanently impaired if not destroyed.

> BROCK CHISHOLM, Toronto psychiatrist and first director-general of the World Health Organization from 1948 to 1953, in "Tell Them the Truth," *Maclean's*, Jan. 15, 1946.

Church
See also CHRISTIANITY.

I am an outside pillar of the Church.

> JOHN SANDFIELD MACDONALD, Ontario premier in the late nineteenth century, quoted by Bruce W. Hodgins in *John Sandfield Macdonald* (1971).

My mother's a Catholic. My father was an Orangeman. Where does that leave me? Right in the Anglican Church.

> CHARLOTTE WHITTON, first woman mayor of Ottawa, quoted by Eva-Lis Wuorio in *Maclean's*, March 1, 1951.

Chinese Marxists are like Quebec collegians. On questions of religion and sex, they lose their sang-froid.

> PIERRE ELLIOTT TRUDEAU, future prime minister in *Two Innocents in Red China* (1968), by Jacques Hébert and Pierre Elliott Trudeau, translated by I.M. Owen from the original 1961 edition.

I believe the United Church should be a uniting church.

> JAMES RALPH MUTCHMORE, former moderator of the United Church of Canada, in *Mutchmore* (1965).

Cities and Towns
See also CITIES AND TOWNS: INDIVIDUAL.

Again, as always, it was the dignity of the cities that impressed—an austere Northern dignity of outline, grouping, and perspective, aloof from the rush of traffic in the streets. Montreal, of the black-frocked priests and the French novices, had it; and Ottawa, of the gray stone palaces and the St. Petersburg-like shining water frontages; and Toronto, consumingly commercial, carried the same power in the same repose. Men are always building better than they know . . . .

> RUDYARD KIPLING, British man-of-letters, in *Letters to the Family* (1908), reprinted in *Letters of Travel 1892-1913* (1920).

Mariposa is not a real town. On the contrary, it is about seventy or eighty of them. You may find them all the way from Lake Superior to the sea, with the same square streets and the same maple trees and the same churches and hotels, and everywhere the sunshine of the land of hope.

> STEPHEN LEACOCK, the dean of Canadian hu-

morists, in the preface to *Sunshine Sketches of a Little Town* (1912).

Never shall I forget those naked, clean-swept little Canadian towns, one just like the other. Before I was twelve years old, I must have lived in fifty of them.
MARIE DRESSLER, Canadian-born stage and film comedienne, from *My Own Story* (1934), as told to Mildred Harrington, foreword by Will Rogers.

City dwellers are the only majority group I know that allow themselves to be over-governed, under-represented and ignored.
DAVID CROMBIE, mayor of Toronto, in an address to the annual convention of the Manitoba Progressive Conservative party, Winnipeg, quoted by the Toronto *Globe and Mail*, March 8, 1975.

Cities and Towns: Individual
See also MONTREAL; OTTAWA; QUEBEC CITY; TORONTO; VANCOUVER; WINNIPEG.

Bassano
BEST IN THE WEST BY A DAM SITE.
Highway sign outside Bassano, a town of 861 which is eighty miles east of Calgary. The proud town, named after the Marquis de Bassano, a CPR shareholder (the town is built on the CPR line), boasts the Bassano Dam, the first irrigation dam built in Alberta and still in use.

Biggar
NEW YORK IS BIG, BUT THIS IS BIGGAR.
Roadsign outside Biggar, west of Saskatoon, Sask., 1960s.

Charlottetown
I found Charlottetown to be wicked enough for a far larger place.
Opinion of an anonymous visitor in the nineteenth century.

Edmonton
Edmonton is as big as Chicago, but it isn't all built up yet.
Anonymous remark, quoted by Lena Newman in *An Historical Almanac of Canada* (1967).

Halifax
Into the mist my guardian prows put forth,
Behind the mist my virgin ramparts lie,

The Warden of the Honour of the North,
Sleepless and veiled am I.
RUDYARD KIPLING, British man-of-letters, from "The Song of the Cities" in *The Seven Seas* (1896).

Iroquois
The Best Dam Town on the Seaway.
Highway sign at the entrance to Iroquois, Ont., a town on the St. Lawrence Seaway, 1957.

Kingston
Indeed, it may be said of Kingston, that one half of it appears to be burnt down, and the other half not to be built up.
CHARLES DICKENS, British novelist, who first visited eastern Canada in 1842, in *American Notes for General Circulation and Pictures from Italy* (1905).

Medicine Hat
You people in this district seem to have all Hell for a basement.
RUDYARD KIPLING, British man-of-letters, writing in 1892 to the townsfolk, alluding to the natural gas in that area of Alberta.

Believe me, the very name is an asset, and as years go on will become more and more of an asset. It has no duplicate in the world; it makes men ask questions.
RUDYARD KIPLING, British writer and "Father Confessor of the Empire," excerpt from a letter to Francis F. Fatt, postmaster and leader of the retentionists, on Dec. 9, 1910, when there was agitation in Medicine Hat to change the town's name. The full letter appears in a brochure published by the Medicine Hat *News*.

Moose Jaw
There was a young man of Moose Jaw
Who wanted to meet Bernard Shaw;
    When they questioned him, "Why?"
    He made no reply,
But sharpened an ax and a saw.
Anonymous limerick on the Saskatchewan city, 1950s.

Regina
If you had a lit-tle more wood, and a lit-tle more water, and here and there a hill, I think the prospect would be improved.
SIR JOHN A. MACDONALD, prime minister, remark in Regina in 1886, quoted by E.B. Big-

gar in *Anecdotal Life of Sir John A. Macdonald* (1891).

Saint-Louis-du-Ha! Ha!
Saint-Louis-du-Ha! Ha!
Amusingly named Quebec village in Rivière du Loup County on the south shore of the St. Lawrence. On the north shore there is a tributary of the Saguenay River named Ha Ha River which has a Ha Ha Bay.

Victoria
Canada possesses two pillars of Strength and Beauty in Quebec and Victoria. The former ranks by herself among those Mother-cities of whom none can say "This reminds me." To realize Victoria you must take all that the eye admires most in Bournemouth, Torquay, the Isle of Wight, the Happy Valley of Hong Kong, the Doon, Sorrento, and Camps Bay; add reminiscences of the Thousand Islands, and arrange the whole round the Bay of Naples, with some Himalayas for the background.
RUDYARD KIPLING, British man-of-letters, in *Letters to the Family* (1908), reprinted in *Letters of Travel 1892-1913* (1920).

Windsor
Is there anybody here from Windsor?
PAUL MARTIN, member of Parliament for the Windsor, Ont., area from 1935 to 1974, then high commissioner to the United Kingdom, characteristic remark.

Citizenship
See also CANADIANS.

Water cannot rise above its source, neither can social progress rise higher than the level of the citizenship of the people.
HENRY WISE WOOD, president of the United Farmers of Alberta from 1916 to 1931, in the *Western Independent*, Feb. 18, 1920.

I am the first prime minister of this country of neither altogether English nor French origin. So I determined to bring about a Canadian citizenship that knew no hyphenated consideration . . . . Well, I never deviated from this purpose. It's the reason I went into public life. I'm very happy to be able to say that in the House of Commons today in my party we have members of Italian, Dutch, German, Scandinavian, Chinese and Ukrainian origin—and they are all Canadians.
JOHN G. DIEFENBAKER, prime minister, interviewed by Jeannine Locke, in *Maclean's*, March 29, 1958.

I, ——, swear that I will be faithful and bear true allegiance to Her Majesty Queen Elizabeth the Second, her Heirs and Successors, according to law, and that I will faithfully observe the laws of Canada and fulfil my duties as a Canadian citizen.
So help me God.
The Oath of Allegiance as administered at the citizenship ceremony, from *Guide to Canadian Citizenship* (1971), published by the Department of the Secretary of State.

My hands tremble
As I sign my naturalization papers
Making me a Canadian citizen
And Canada my final resting place.
TAKEO NAKANO, a Japanese-born Canadian, wrote this *waka*, translated from the Japanese by Robert Y. Kadoguchi in *Volvox: Poetry from the Unofficial Languages of Canada* (1971), edited by J. Michael Yates.

Civil Rights

A Loyal British Subject
Who Objects to be trodden upon
By any man except
Her Gracious Majesty Queen Victoria
DANIEL "NIGGER DAN" WILLIAMS, eccentric Fort St. John settler, warning erected where the property he squatted on met that of the Hudson's Bay Company, April 12, 1873. Quoted by A.C. Garrioch in *A Hatchet Mark in Duplicate* (1929).

In Canada we don't ban demonstrations, we re-route them.
ALAN BOROVOY, head of the Canadian Civil Liberties Association, in the *Canadian*, April 29, 1972.

With every civil right there has to be a corresponding civil obligation.
EDSON HAINES, judge of the Supreme Court of Ontario, addressing the Ontario Psychiatric Association, in Toronto, Jan. 27, 1973.

Civilization

You ask me, then, whether in my opinion civilization is favourable to human happiness? In answer to the question, it may be answered, but there are degrees of civilization, from Cannibals to the most polite of European nations. The question is not, then, whether a degree of refinement is not conducive to happiness; but whether you, or the natives of this land, have obtained this medium. On this subject we are at present, I presume, of very different opinions.

JOSEPH BRANT, Mohawk leader, quoted by William L. Stone in *Life of Joseph Brant–Thayendanegea* (1838).

If we as a nation are concerned with the problem of defence, what, may we ask ourselves, are we defending? We are defending civilization, our share of it, our contribution to it. The things with which our inquiry deals are the elements which give civilization its character and meaning. It would be paradoxical to defend something which we are unwilling to strengthen and enrich, and which we even allow to decline.

VINCENT MASSEY, future governor general, from the *Royal Commission on National Development in the Arts, Letters, and Sciences* (1951), commonly called the Massey Report.

We're born princes and the civilizing process turns us into frogs.

ERIC BERNE, Montreal-born, California-based psychiatrist and organizer of Transactional Analysis, in *Games People Play* (1964).

Modern civilization makes all local cultures anachronistic. Where modern science has achieved its mastery, there is no place for local cultures.

GEORGE P. GRANT, a leading spokesman for conservatism, in *Lament for a Nation* (1965).

Classes, Social
See also SOCIETY.

We have no aristocracy but of virtue and talent, which is the only true aristocracy, and is the old and true meaning of the term.

THOMAS D'ARCY MCGEE, future Father of Confederation, in an address to the Legislative Assembly, in Quebec, Feb. 9, 1865. From

Parliamentary Debates on the Subject of Confederation of the British North American Provinces (1865).

The fight is not between hand workers and brain workers. It is not between industrial workers and agricultural workers. The fight is essentially between producers and the parasites.

J.S. WOODSWORTH, future leader of the CCF, on July 25, 1919; in *Records Relating to the Winnipeg General Strike, 1919,* quoted by Margaret Fairley in *Spirit of Canadian Democracy* (1945).

Class organization is the only road along which civilization can travel to safety. I believe in that as I believe in God.

HENRY WISE WOOD, "Wise Old Henry," president of the United Farmers of Alberta from 1916 to 1931, in the *Grain Grower's Guide,* Nov. 5, 1919, quoted by William Kirby Rolph in *Henry Wise Wood of Alberta* (1950).

Let the Old World, where rank's yet vital,
Part those who have and have not title.
Toronto has no social classes—
Only the Masseys and the masses.

B.K. SANDWELL, influential editor of *Saturday Night* from 1932 to 1951, from "On the Appointment of Governor-General Vincent Massey, 1952," in F.R. Scott and A.J.M. Smith's *The Blasted Pine* (1957).

Classless society is a dream of people with no class.

ROBERT ZEND, Hungarian-born Toronto writer, in the 1960s.

The bourgeoisie has been the only revolutionary class in history. That thought crucifies me.

IRVING LAYTON, outspoken poet, in *The Whole Bloody Bird* (1969).

Climate
See WEATHER.

Colleges and Universities
See also EDUCATION.

A university has as its main aim to supplement the weakness of the individual by the strength of the race.

JOHN WATSON, influential Kant scholar and professor of Philosophy at Queen's University from 1872 to 1924, quoted by John A. Irving in "The Development of Philosophy in Central Canada from 1850 to 1900," *Canadian Historical Review*, Sept. 1950.

If I were founding a university—and I say it with all the seriousness of which I am capable—I would found first a smoking room; then when I had a little more money in hand I would found a dormitory; then after that, or more probably with it, a decent reading room and a library. After that, if I still had money over that I couldn't use, I would hire a professor and get some text books.

STEPHEN LEACOCK, humorist and professor of Economics at McGill, in "Oxford as I See It," *My Discovery of England* (1922).

Speaking in a general way one may say that in the West McGill predominates in medicine, Queen's in the Church and Toronto at (not behind) the Bar. Thus McGill attends the sick and when McGill has done its work, Queen's buries them and when they're buried Toronto divides up their estates among the three. It is what Adam Smith so happily called the Division of Labour.

STEPHEN LEACOCK, humorist and professor of Economics at McGill, in "No Vote of Thanks," *My Discovery of the West* (1937).

A good deal of what you say and do here will be ephemeral, and will be caught up and dissolved in the stream of experience. But much else that you do will remain with you and will determine your future. One thinks of the words of Goethe: "Be careful what you wish for in your youth, for you will get it in your middle age."

CLAUDE T. BISSELL, then president of the University of Toronto, from an address to the staff and students, Sept. 1958, in *The Strength of the University* (1968).

If Canada is to be more than a geographical expression, her nationhood will be born in her Universities. And if her Universities are to discover any merit or mission, then students will educate the educators into that discovery—and salvation. May they come to it before it is too late.

JOHN R. SEELEY, sociologist, in "The 'Berkeley Issue' in Time and Place," *The University Game*

(1968), edited by Howard Adelman and Dennis Lee.

Colonialism

See also BRITISH EMPIRE AND COMMONWEALTH.

The *loss* of Canada I should deem a gain, though it is worth to us a thousand empires in the east; that is to say, it is not a thousandth part as mischievous to us.

WILLIAM COBBETT, British journalist, in letter five, *Letters on the Late War between the United States and Great Britain* (1815).

The baneful domination of the mother country.

JOSEPH HUME, British politician and "philosophical radical," in a letter to William Lyon Mackenzie of March 29, 1834, which Mackenzie published in the *Colonial Advocate* on May 22, only to find himself accused of treason.

These wretched colonies will all be independent, too, in a few years, and are a millstone round our necks.

BENJAMIN DISRAELI, prime minister of Great Britain, in a letter concerning the Newfoundland fisheries, on Aug. 13, 1852, from *The Life of Benjamin Disraeli, Earl of Beaconsfield* (1910-1920), by W.F. Monypenny and G.E. Buckle.

Colonists are the pariahs of the Empire.

THOMAS CHANDLER HALIBURTON, Nova Scotian writer and wit, in *Sam Slick's Wise Saws and Modern Instances* (1853).

I am no more against Colonies than I am against the solar system. I am against dependencies, when nations are fit to be independent.

GOLDWIN SMITH, British-born journalist, in *The Empire* (1863).

The greatest colony of the greatest Empire the world has ever seen.

Canada as described by the colonial delegates attending the International Conference at Ottawa in 1894.

A colony, yet a nation—words never before in the history of the world associated together.

SIR WILFRID LAURIER, prime minister, in his

address at Queen Victoria's Jubilee, in London, England, 1897.

I, that write these lines, am an Independent, because I will not be a Colonial. This Colonial status is a worn-out, by-gone thing.

STEPHEN LEACOCK, economist and humorist, in *Great Canada* (1907).

An Imperialist, to me, means a man who accepts gladly and bears proudly the responsibilities of his race and breed. [Applause] If that be so, what a trust is ours, what a trust is ours!

R.B. BENNETT, future prime minister, in an Empire Day address to the Empire Club of Toronto, 1914, quoted by Carl Berger in *The Sense of Power* (1970).

Canadian nationalism was systematically encouraged and exploited by American capital. Canada moved from colony to nation to colony.

HAROLD ADAMS INNIS, economist and historian, from "Great Britain, the United States and Canada" (1948), *Essays in Canadian Economic History* (1956), edited by Mary Quayle Innis.

Imperialism was one form of Canadian nationalism.

CARL BERGER, historian, in *The Sense of Power* (1970).

Canada, with its empty spaces, its largely unknown lakes and rivers and islands, its division of language, its dependence on immense railways to hold it physically together, has had this peculiar problem of an obliterated environment throughout most of its history. The effects of this are clear in the curiously abortive cultural developments of Canada . . . . They are shown even more clearly in its present lack of will to resist its own disintegration, in the fact that it is practically the only country left in the world which is a pure colony, colonial in psychology as well as in mercantile economics.

NORTHROP FRYE, literary scholar, in the preface to *The Bush Garden* (1971).

Communication
See also BROADCASTING.

The medium is the message.

MARSHALL MCLUHAN, media pundit, first used this now-famous aphorism in Vancouver, July 30, 1959, at a reception following a symposium at the University of British Columbia on the subject of music and the mass media. The remark was first published in book form in *Understanding Media* (1964).

The new electronic independence recreates the world in the image of a global village.

MARSHALL MCLUHAN, media pundit, in *The Gutenberg Galaxy* (1962).

Owing to Canada's size, communications have always meant more to us than to most other countries. We have proceeded, and still proceed, less by settlement than by communications. Very little of Canada has really been settled. The great gaps of northern Quebec and Ontario and the British Columbia mountains amaze most transcontinental travellers. Even more astonishing are the vast emptinesses of our immense northern hinterlands. The emergence of the electronic mass media offers Canada the best prospect it has ever had of becoming a genuine national community.

JOHN A. IRVING, philosopher, in "The Problems of the Mass Media" from *Mass Media in Canada* (1962), edited by John A. Irving.

If we fail to communicate, the country will fall into parishes.

ROBERT WEAVER, writer and CBC executive, quoted by *CBC Times*, March 30, 1963.

We wish media owners, as an industry, would think again about the policy of maximizing profits by skimping on the quality of the product. The maximizing is their business. The skimping is everybody's business.

*

Above all, maintain a healthy skepticism vis-à-vis the media. We don't mean cynicism. The media are human institutions, humanly fallible. But in our observation they're in the hands of people pretty generally devoted to doing an honest job of information. Don't expect the moon from them, but don't settle for moonshine either.

KEITH DAVEY, outspoken senator, in the *Report of the Special Senate Committee on Mass Media, Volume I: The Uncertain Mirror* (1971).

Without communication, there is no socie-
ty, whether it be a hive of bees, a troop of
Boy Scouts, a bar association, or a nation.
GRAHAM SPRY, early advocate of national
broadcasting, quoted by Harry J. Boyle in
Content, March 1972.

Communism

When this thing is over the British flag will
still be on the City Hall, and not the Red
flag!
CHARLES F. GRAY, mayor of Winnipeg, in an
address to anti-strike war veterans at Winnipeg City Hall, June 4, 1919. *Winnipeg 1919*
(1973), edited by Norman Penner.

If the Communists wouldn't organize demonstrations, it wouldn't be necessary for the
police to break them up.
JIMMY SIMPSON, mayor of Toronto in the
1930s, quoted by Tom McEwen in *He Wrote for
Us* (1951).

I have been tried and found guilty in this
court. I hope you will not think it bravado
if I say that I only hope that I will not be
found wanting by the organizations and
the works that I have tried to represent. I
will try to take whatever sentence you give
me in the same spirit I have tried to do the
work I have done.
TIM BUCK, Communist labour leader, to the
judge and jury in Toronto that found him
guilty of seditious conspiracy, Nov. 1931,
quoted by Oscar Ryan in *Tim Buck* (1975).

I was shot at —
TIM BUCK, Communist leader, opening words
at the trial of A.E. Smith in Toronto, Nov.
1933. The words, which referred to an incident
on Oct. 20, 1932, when rifle bullets were shot
into his cell at Kingston Penitentiary, were
striken from the court's record.

If it's good enough for Moscow, it's good
enough for me.
TIM BUCK, long-time leader of the Communist
Party of Canada, to Joseph Salsberg, who had
just returned from the Soviet Union with
doubts about the official explanation of the
purge of Jewish writers in the 1950s, quoted by
Philip Sykes in the Toronto *Star*, Nov. 10,
1972.

Communism is Canadian because it shows
that there is a way out of the conditions of
hatred, crime, disease, poverty, unemployment and war.
A.E. SMITH, Methodist minister turned Communist leader, in *All My Life* (1949).

You don't know the difference between
communism and rheumatism!
HARVEY MURPHY, sometime vice-president of
the Union of Mine, Mill and Smelter Workers,
reply to charges that the union was communist
dominated, at the Mine-Mill Convention at
the Royal York Hotel, Toronto, in 1959.

For the communist . . . his first moral duty
is to recognize the truth: the truth that human differences are not a matter of blood
and skin; the truth that private ownership
of land and resources has come about
through theft; the truth that whether he
wills it or not each man is dependent on
the past and on the present labour of all
men.
MARGARET FAIRLEY, socialist and writer, in
"Moral Responsibility of the Communist,"
Marxist Quarterly, winter 1965.

Flying over Canada, I saw small fields.
Flying over the Soviet Union, you will see
enormous fields.
ALEXEI KOSYGIN, Soviet leader, quoted by
Bruce West in the Toronto *Globe and Mail*, Oct.
26, 1971.

Composers
See also MUSIC.

Will *nobody* write a few songs for Canada?
THOMAS MACQUEEN, founder of the *Huron
Signal* in 1848, quoted by Henry J. Morgan in
Bibliotheca Canadensis (1867).

Folk songs, to mean something really vital
in the art of a nation, must lead to larger
forms—rhapsodies, concertos, quartets,
symphonies, cantatas, ballets or operas.
Not until these issue freely from the hand
of our composers and grace the great audi-
toriums of the world will our expectation
be fulfilled.
MARIUS BARBEAU, Quebec folklorist, in
"French and Indian Motifs in Our Music,"
Yearbook of the Arts in Canada: 1928-29 (1929),
edited by Bertram Brooker.

Canada has enough unpublished music manuscripts to make a line of the treble clef from Montreal to Winnipeg.

AUGUSTUS BRIDLE, Toronto critic, in "Composers Among Us," *Yearbook of the Arts in Canada: 1928-29* (1929), edited by Bertram Brooker.

From about age eight I had the idea I wanted to be a composer—mainly, at that time, in order to become very, very famous.

JOHN BECKWITH, composer and teacher, interviewed by *Musicanada*, Nov. 1967.

Question: Is there a distinctive Canadian music?
Answer: Show me a distinctive Canadian!

GODFREY RIDOUT, composer, interviewed by *Musicanada*, June–July 1968.

There are songs yet to be found in Sioux Lookout, Kamloops, Oromocto, Lévis, Corner Brook—wherever there are people.

PIERRE JUNEAU, as chairman of the CRTC, in the introduction to Ritchie York's *Axes, Chops & Hot Licks* (1971).

Confederation
See also CANADA; CENTENNIAL; DOMINION.

No, Sir, these provinces should be united, and they from their territorial extent, their commercial enterprise, their mineral wealth, their wonderful agricultural productions, and above all, their intelligent, industrious, and still loyal population, in time form a nation second to none on earth; until then I prefer to be a citizen of the world.
    *
Now, take these facts and see what an empire is here, surely the best in climate, soil, mineral, and other productions in the world, and peopled by such a race, as no other country under heaven can produce. No, Sir, here are *the bundle of sticks* [;] all they want is to be well united.

THOMAS CHANDLER HALIBURTON, Nova Scotian writer and wit, in *Nature and Human Nature* (1855).

A new nationality.

ALEXANDER MORRIS, lawyer and future lieu-tenant-governor of Manitoba, in a lecture in Montreal in 1858, published as *The Hudson's Bay and Pacific Territories* (1859).

I conclude, Sir, as I began, by entreating the House to believe that I have spoken without respect of persons, and with a sole single desire for the increase, prosperity, freedom, and honour of this incipient Northern nation. I call it a Northern nation—for such it must become if all of us do but do our duty to the last.
    *
I look to the future of my adopted country with hope, though not without anxiety; I see in the not remote distance, one great nationality bound, like the shield of Achilles, by the blue rim of ocean—I see it quartered into many communities—each disposing of its internal affairs—but all bound together by free institutions, free intercourse, and free commerce; I see within the ground of that shield, the peaks of the Western mountains and the crests of the Eastern waves—the winding Assiniboine, the five-fold lakes, the St. Lawrence, the Ottawa, the Saguenay, the St. John, and the Basin of Minas—by all these flowing waters, in all the valleys they fertilise, in all the cities they visit in their courses, I see a generation of industrious, contented, moral men, free in name and in fact, men capable of maintaining, in peace and in war, a Constitution worthy of such a country.

THOMAS D'ARCY MCGEE, future Father of Confederation, Legislative Assembly, Quebec, May 2, 1860, *Speeches and Addresses Chiefly on the Subject of British-American Union* (1865).

Who will oppose—who are now opposed to the union? Only those who have a vested interest in their own insignificance.

THOMAS D'ARCY MCGEE, future Father of Confederation, Halifax address, Aug. 14, 1864, *Speeches and Addresses Chiefly on the Subject of British-American Union* (1865).

The Fathers of Confederation.

This sobriquet is applied to those thirty-six delegates from the British North American colonies who attended one or more of the three conferences in Charlottetown (September 1, 1864), Quebec City (October 10-29, 1864), and London, England (December 4, 1866), that led to Confederation (July 1, 1867). The

Fathers are named by John Robert Colombo in *Colombo's Canadian References* (1976).

A careful consideration of the general position of British North America induced the conviction that the circumstances of the times afforded the opportunity, not merely for the settlement of a question of personal politics, but also for the simultaneous creation of a new nationality.

LORD MONCK, future governor general, in the throne speech, Parliament of Canada, Quebec, Jan. 19, 1865, reported in the Toronto *Globe*, Jan. 20, 1865.

The Honorable Mr. *Dorion (Hochelaga)* moved, in amendment thereto, seconded by the Honorable Mr. *Laframboise*, That the words, "But this House deems it a duty respectfully to express to Your Excellency its firm conviction that the people of this Province, fully appreciating the blessings of their existing political relations with the Great Empire of which they form a part, neither wish nor seek to create a new nationality," be added at the end thereof.

SIR ANTOINE-AIMÉ DORION, leader of the Opposition for the Province of Canada, when Governor General Lord Monck urged the creation "of a new Nationality" in the throne speech and moved the above amendment which, while popular with the Quebec members, was defeated sixty-four to twenty-five, Jan. 23, 1865. From *Journals of the Legislative Assembly of the Province of Canada* (1865).

My hon. friend, the member for Hochelaga, thought he did a very clever thing the other evening when he disentombed an old newspaper article of mine, entitled "A New Nationality," and endeavoured to fix on me the paternity of the phrase—destined to become prophetic—which was employed by a very distinguished personage in the Speech from the Throne at the opening of the session. I do not happen to remember the article alluded to as one of my first essays in political writing in Canada; but I am quite sure that the almost forgotten publication in which it appeared was never known, even by name, to the illustrious person who delivered the speech on that occasion.

*

Events stronger than advocacy, events stronger than men, have come in at last like the fire behind the invisible writing to bring out the truth of these writings and to impress them upon the mind of every thoughtful man who has considered the position and probable future of these scattered provinces.

*

One individual chooses Tuponia and another Hochelaga, as a suitable name for the new nationality. Now I would ask any hon. member of this House how he would feel if he woke up some fine morning and found himself, instead of a Canadian, a Tuponian or a Hochelagander. I think, sir, we may safely leave for the present the discussion of the name as well as the origin of the new system proposed . . . .

THOMAS D'ARCY MCGEE, future Father of Confederation, Legislative Assembly, Quebec, Feb. 9, 1865, in *Parliamentary Debates on the Subject of the Confederation of the British North American Provinces* (1865). McGee coined the expression "a new Nationality" in an article he wrote, about 1857, when he arrived in Montreal and founded *New Era*.

Since we cannot find a comparison on this poor earth emblematic of our future greatness, let us borrow one from the heavens at the risk of losing ourselves in the clouds with the advocates of Confederation; I propose the adoption of the rainbow as our emblem. By the endless variety of its tints the rainbow will give an excellent idea of the diversity of races, religions, sentiments and interests of the different parts of the Confederation. By its slender and elongated form, the rainbow would afford a perfect representation of the geographical configuration of the Confederation. By its lack of consistence—an image without substance—the rainbow would represent aptly the solidity of our Confederation. An emblem we must have, for every great empire has one; let us adopt the rainbow.

SIR HENRI-GUSTAVE JOLY DE LOTBINIÈRE, politician and writer, in the Legislative Assembly, Quebec, on Feb. 20, 1865, from *Parliamentary Debates on the Subject of the Confederation of the British North American Provinces* (1865).

. . . the Botheration Scheme was ventilated in every part of the Province, and, so far as Nova Scotia is concerned, may now be considered as dead as Julius Caesar.

> JOSEPH HOWE, Nova Scotian editor and statesman and opponent of Confederation, in "Botheration Letter, No. 12," Halifax *Morning Chronicle*, March 2, 1865. "An epithet for the plan of federal union of the British North American colonies, it was taken from Barney Rooney's *Letters on Confederation, Botheration and Political Transmogrification* (Halifax, 1865), "an amusing satire on the Quebec Conference by William Garvie," according to Norah Story in *The Oxford Companion to Canadian History and Literature* (1967).

It shall be lawful for the Queen, by and with the Advice and Consent of the Senate and House of Commons, to make Laws for the Peace, Order, and good Government of Canada . . . . [Article 91]

> The British North America Act, 1867; commonly called the BNA Act. The full title of the act is "The Confederation Act, 1867; An Act for the Union of Canada, Nova Scotia, and New Brunswick, and the Government thereof; and for purposes connected therewith." The BNA Act was passed March 29, 1867, and became effective July 1, 1867.

What has Confederation done for Canada? What has Confederation not done for Canada?

> EARL GREY, governor general from 1904 to 1911, an address to the Canadian Club of Ottawa on April 21, 1909.

The union of the Canadian Provinces resembles, as a wit said in the debate, not that of a bundle of rods, gaining strength by their union, to which a confederationist had complacently compared it, but that of seven fishing-rods tied together by the ends.

> GOLDWIN SMITH, British-born journalist, in *Reminiscences* (1910), edited by Arnold Haultain.

After establishing facts like these, can we keep from crying out: "Confederation, the graveyard of minorities!"

> MARCEL CHAPUT, civil servant in Ottawa who espoused separatist views, in *Why I am a Separatist* (1962), translated by Robert A. Taylor.

The Fathers wrought well, and laid our

foundations deep and strong. But the building is still unfinished, and parts of it have suffered some damage through the years. It does not need a bombing squad or a wrecking crew. But it does need alterations, repairs, additions, the expansion of certain rooms; and all of us must be made to feel at home in it.

> EUGENE FORSEY, historian and future senator, in "Canada: Two Nations or One?" *Canadian Journal of Economics and Political Science*, Nov. 1962.

I used to say to my classes in constitutional law, "We have a *rendez-vous* with the BNA Act. It's going to come some day!"

> F.R. SCOTT, Montreal man-of-letters, from "Address" (1964), *The Future of Canadian Federalism* (1965), edited by P.A. Crépeau and C.B. Macpherson.

The Only Living Father of Confederation.

> JOEY SMALLWOOD, first premier of Newfoundland when it joined Confederation in 1949, devised this title for himself, but Ray Guy, through repeated references to it in his column in the St. John's *Telegram* in 1965, made it stick.

Confederation is a genocide without end.

> ANDRÉ D'ALLEMAGNE, Quebec writer, in *Le colonialisme au Québec* (1966), quoted by Marcel Rioux in *Quebec in Question* (1971).

Confederation has been like a mail-order bra: intended to contain and uplift, it has instead drawn attention to the cleavage.

> ERIC NICOL, Vancouver humorist, in *100 Years of What?* (1959), illustrated by Peter Whalley.

Confederation had been a political union of several provinces, not a cultural compact between two ethnic communities, English and French.

> DONALD CREIGHTON, distinguished historian, in *Canada's First Century* (1970).

The Canadian Confederation was nothing more than a vast financial transaction carried out by the bourgeoisie at the expense of the workers of the country, and more especially the workers of Quebec.

> PIERRE VALLIÈRES, Quebec writer and former separatist, in *White Niggers of America* (1971), translated by Joan Pinkham.

Conquest of 1759

See also FRENCH CANADA; MONTCALM, MARQUIS DE; QUEBEC; WOLFE, JAMES.

Quebec is impregnable.

LE MARQUIS DE VAUDREUIL-CAVAGNAL, PIERRE DE RIGAUD, the last governor of New France, made this vain boast in 1759. Quoted by Christopher Hibbert in *Wolfe at Quebec* (1959).

We need not suppose that the enemy have wings.

MARQUIS DE MONTCALM, leader of the French troops at Quebec City, in a letter to the Marquis de Vaudreuil-Cavagnal, last governor of New France, who dismissed Montcalm's recommendation that a battalion be stationed at Anse au Foulon. The letter was written on Sept. 12, 1759, hours before Wolfe's troops scaled the cliff and took Quebec.

Now that Montcalm is dead, the King will have some peace!
*

It makes little difference; Canada is useful only to provide me with furs.
*

Now the King can sleep.
*

We can be happy without Canada.

MADAME DE POMPADOUR, mistress of Louis XV of France, sentiments on learning of the fall of Quebec in 1759, attributed.

Tell M. de Vaudreuil I have come to take Canada and I will take nothing less.

JEFFREY AMHERST, commander-in-chief of the British forces in America, to Chevalier Louis-Antoine de Bougainville who, on Sept. 7, 1760, approached Amherst at Lachine, on behalf of the Marquis de Vaudreuil, governor of New France, to come to terms. Quoted by J.C. Long in *Lord Jeffrey Amherst, A Soldier of the King* (1933).

I much prefer peace to Canada; and I believe that France can do very well without Quebec.

VOLTAIRE, French satirist, in a letter to Etienne-François, Duc de Choiseul, on Sept. 6, 1762, reproduced in *A Pageant of Canada* (1967), prepared by Roy Strong.

MORTEM VIRTUS COMMUNEM
FAMAM HISTORIA
MONUMENTUM POSTERITAS DEDIT

JOHN CHARLTON FISHER, Quebec journalist, inscription for the Wolfe and Montcalm monument which stands in the Governor's Garden adjoining the Château Frontenac, Quebec City, on Sept. 8, 1828. The Latin words translate: "Valour gave them a common death; history a common fame; posterity a common monument."

One will be convinced that the Conquest has not been a misfortune for us, but that it has been the providential means which God used to save us as a people.

LOUIS-FRANÇOIS-RICHER LAFLÈCHE, Bishop of Trois-Rivières from 1870 to 1898, writing in 1866, quoted by Ramsay Cook in *Canada and the French-Canadian Question* (1966).

A happier calamity never befell a people than the conquest of Canada by the British arms.

FRANCIS PARKMAN, historian and chronicler of the fall of New France, in *The Old Régime in Canada* (1874).

In truth, the funeral of Montcalm was the funeral of New France.

FRANCIS PARKMAN, distinguished Boston historian, in *Montcalm and Wolfe* (1884).

Would it have been a Good Thing if Wolfe had succeeded in writing Gray's Elegy instead of taking Quebec?

WALTER CARRUTHERS SELLAR and ROBERT JULIAN YEATMAN, English humorists, in "Test Paper V," *1066 and All That* (1930).

Conscience

Your conscience is what your mother told you before you were six years old.

BROCK CHISHOLM, psychiatrist and first director-general of the World Health Organization, in "Tell Them the Truth," *Maclean's*, Jan. 15, 1946, as told to Blair Fraser.

Conscience is that within us that tells us when our neighbours are going wrong.

PETER MCARTHUR, columnist who wrote about farm life in western Ontario, in *The Best of Peter McArthur* (1967), edited by Alec Lucas.

Conscription

See also WAR.

Of course, I am met here by the "no precedent" clause contained in the order in council. I am free to say that this clause is the only thing which I can approve in the whole course of the government; but I am afraid it is a frail barrier to oppose to the current of noisy militarism which is carrying us all over British possessions. It is this fear which I expressed in my letter to the Prime Minister when I said: "The precedent, Sir, is the accomplished fact."

> HENRI BOURASSA, French-Canadian nationalist, in the House of Commons, March 13, 1900.

Continuous consultation leading to concerted action.

> SIR ROBERT BORDEN, prime minister, World War One conscription formula, attributed.

Your armaments, cannons, rifles, bombs, and battleships, what kind of Christmas tree decorations are those?

> CAMILLIEN HOUDE, long-time mayor of Montreal, in an anti-conscription address, at Saint-Henri, winter, 1938. Quoted by André Laurendeau in "The Conscription Crisis, 1942," *André Laurendeau: Witness for Quebec* (1973), translated by Philip Stratford.

If I were under the impression that conscription was the last way to win the war, I would be for conscription.

> JOSEPH-ADÉLARD GODBOUT, twice premier of Quebec during the 1930s and 1940s, widely quoted anti-conscription remark made in Jan. 1942.

Not necessarily conscription but conscription if necessary.

> W.L. MACKENZIE KING, prime minister, enunciation of the government's policy regarding conscription and the war effort, in the House of Commons, June 10, 1942.

Conservation

See also NATURE.

What is conservation? About a year and a half ago practical people said: The thing is pure con*ver*sation . . . . It is like the heading in the copybook, "Be Good and You will be Happy."

> AGNES LAUT, popular pioneer author, in

"Conservation," an address to the Canadian Club of Ottawa, Feb. 11, 1910.

I have been often asked what my work consists of. It begins to be rather ambiguous, I think. It is this . . . I want to arouse in Canadian people a sense of responsibility, the great responsibility they have for that north country and its inhabitants, human and animal.

> GREY OWL, assumed name of George Belaney, pioneer naturalist, in "A Plea for the Canadian Northland" (1936), an address to the Empire Club of Canada in 1936.

If we go on as we are, we will destroy in the next century everything that poets have been singing about for the past two thousand years.

> FRED BODSWORTH, novelist and ornithologist, in "Wilderness Canada: Our Threatened Heritage," from *Wilderness Canada* (1970), edited by Borden Spears.

In fact, the biblical promise has come true at last. Man has dominion over the earth. God grant that he may now learn to have dominion over himself.

> DONALD A. CHANT, founder of Pollution Probe, and RALPH O. BRINKHURST, writer, the concluding sentence of *This Good, Good Earth* (1971).

"Scratch a Canadian and you find a phony pioneer," I used to say to myself in warning. But all the same it is true, I think, that we are not yet totally alienated from physical earth, and let us only pray we do not become so.

> MARGARET LAURENCE, novelist, in *Maclean's*, Dec. 1972.

Conservatism

I need not remind you that there may be as much originality in applying an accepted creed to novel conditions as in inventing a new one.

> JOHN BUCHAN, LORD TWEEDSMUIR, governor general, in "Lord Durham," *Canadian Historical Review*, March 1939.

The whole world is burdened with young fogies. Old men with ossified minds are easily dealt with. But men who look young, act young, and everlastingly harp on the fact that they are young, but who nevertheless think and act with a degree of caution which would be excessive in their grandfathers, are the curses of the world. We have a good many young fogies in Canada—fellows who, at thirty, are well content with beaten paths and reach-me-down opinions. Their very conservatism is second-hand, and they don't know what they are conserving.

ROBERTSON DAVIES, man-of-letters, in *The Table Talk of Samuel Marchbanks* (1949).

Conservative Party
See also POLITICS.

Seriously, you would make a decent Conservative, if you gave your own judgement a fair chance and cut loose from Holton and Dorion and those other beggars. So pray do become true blue at once: it is a good standing colour and bears washing.

SIR JOHN A. MACDONALD, prime minister, in a letter to Alexander Tilloch Galt, Nov. 2, 1857, quoted by O.D. Skelton in *The Life and Times of Sir Alexander Tilloch Galt* (1920).

Mr. Mackenzie (commenting on a clause in a new bill)—"If that is considered an improvement, it is certainly one of a Tory character."
Sir John—"A satisfac-Tory character."

SIR JOHN A. MACDONALD, prime minister, quoted by E.B. Biggar in *Anecdotal Life of Sir John A. Macdonald* (1891).

There are times when it requires more courage to stand still than to go forward.

JOHN OLIVER, the incorruptible, self-educated premier of British Columbia from 1918 to 1927, quoted by James Morton in *Honest John Oliver* (1933).

He is the true Conservative who lops the mouldered branch away.

R.B. BENNETT, prime minister, characteristic remark based on the couplet from Tennyson's "Hands All Round," which runs: "That man's the true Conservative / Who lops the moulder'd branch away." *Canadian Problems as Seen by Twenty Outstanding Men of Canada* (1933), edited by W.R. Herridge and Richard B. Coates.

I am not a Progressive Conservative, I am a continuing Conservative.

CHARLES H. CAHAN, secretary of State from 1930 to 1935 in the R.B. Bennett government, when the Conservative party became the Progressive Conservative party in 1942.

This is the first time in my life that I have spoken from a Tory platform.

MITCHELL HEPBURN, premier of Ontario from 1934 to 1942, speaking from a manure-spreader to a group of farmers, one of whom roared: "Throw her in high gear, Mitch, she's never had a bigger load on." *Mitch Hepburn* (1967), by Neil McKenty.

Whether now judged right or wrong, whatever I have said, whatever I have done, is going to remain unrevised and unrepented. As it is, it will await whatever verdict may come.

ARTHUR MEIGHEN, leader of the Conservative Opposition, in "The CBC—A Party Instrument," a speech to the Conservative convention in Winnipeg, Dec. 9, 1942, from *Unrevised and Unrepented* (1949).

Conservative. If I could only find the conservative party.

CHARLOTTE WHITTON, first woman mayor of Ottawa, answering a question about her political allegiance, quoted by Eva-Lis Wuorio in *Maclean's*, March 1, 1951.

The impossibility of conservatism in our era is the impossibility of Canada. As Canadians we attempted a ridiculous task in trying to build a conservative nation in the age of progress, on a continent we share with the most dynamic nation on earth.

GEORGE P. GRANT, professor of Religion at McMaster University and a leading spokesman for conservatism, in *Lament for a Nation* (1965).

The real trouble with the Conservative party is that basically it has been a party of Anglo-Saxon racists. They really don't believe in the equality of all Canadians. They really don't believe the French have any right in this country, unless they act like a conquered people.

J.W. PICKERSGILL, Liberal Cabinet minister and Mackenzie King's chief adviser, quoted by Peter C. Newman in "Jack Pickersgill"

(1973), *Home Country* (1973).

The Big Blue Machine.
CLAIRE HOY, Toronto *Star* reporter, coined this phrase to describe the political apparatus of the Conservative party in Ontario, in power for more than thirty years. He first used it in April 1971, applying the nickname of the Cincinnati Reds (the baseball team was called the Big Red Machine) to the Conservatives. "It implies of course a big, slick, arrogant organization, which it is, and which explains why the party has never liked it," he wrote in 1975.

I can't recall anyone ever leaving the Tory party because there is nothing in terms of a central philosophy to leave.
JAMES GILLIES, Conservative financial critic, addressing the Kiwanis Club of Toronto, quoted by Jonathan Manthorpe in the *Globe and Mail*, Sept. 3, 1975.

Continentalism
See also ANNEXATION; CANADA: UNITED STATES RELATIONS; ECONOMIC NATIONALISM.

So I look upon Prince Rupert's Land and Canada, and see how an ingenious people, and a capable, enlightened government, are occupied with bridging rivers and making railroads and telegraphs to develop, organize and create and preserve the great British provinces of the north; by the Great Lakes, the St. Lawrence and around the shores of Hudson's Bay, and I am able to say, "It is very well; you are building excellent states to be hereafter admitted to the American Union."
WILLIAM H. SEWARD, Republican politician and future U.S. secretary of State, in a campaign speech at St. Paul, Minnesota, reported in the New York *Herald*, Jan. 25, 1861.

When the experiment of the "dominion" shall have failed—as fail it must—a process of peaceful absorption will give Canada her proper place in the great North American Republic.
HORACE GREELEY, New York editor, who counselled his generation to "Go West, young man, go West," in the New York *Tribune*, May 10, 1867, quoted by P.B. Waite in *The Life and Times of Confederation* (1962).

Canadian nationality being a lost cause,

the ultimate union of Canada with the United States appears now to be morally certain; so that nothing is left for Canadian patriotism but to provide that it shall be a union indeed, and not an annexation ....
GOLDWIN SMITH, British-born journalist, in *The Political Destiny of Canada* (1878).

Canada is like an apple on a tree just beyond reach. We may strive to grasp it, but the bough recedes from our hold just in proportion to our effort to catch it. Let it alone, and in due time it will fall into our hands.
JAMES G. BLAINE, U.S. secretary of State, in 1889, quoted by W.E. Harris in *Canada's Last Chance* (1970).

I am for it, because I hope to see the day when the American flag will float over every square foot of the British-North American possessions clear to the North Pole. They are people of our blood. They speak our language. Their institutions are much like ours. They are trained in the difficult art of self-government ....
CHAMP CLARK, Missouri representative, speaking in Congress in favour of reciprocity, in *The Congressional Record*, Feb. 14, 1911.

The only way to get away from the influence of the American economy would be to float our half of the continent off somewhere else.
JOHN KENNETH GALBRAITH, well-known Ontario-born economist, attributed, 1960s.

Maybe the American will be happy to have us. True, we aren't as picturesque as Crackers, ebullient as Californians or greedy as Texans, but we're reliable. We could staff a civil service nicely, we're the kind of folks who could be trusted to make the change in a gas station without knocking down the owner for too much. What more could Canada want?
DENNIS DUFFY, American-born Toronto academic, in the Toronto *Globe and Mail*, June 10, 1972.

Cooking
See FOOD.

Co-operative Movement

Practise self-help.

FATHER JAMES TOMPKINS, a founder of the co-operative Antigonish Movement at St. Francis Xavier University in the 1920s, characteristic maxim, quoted by J.R. Kidd in his *Adult Education in Canada* (1950).

There's no such thing as a Catholic co-operative store, a Methodist store, or a pious store . . . two plus two makes four in the accounts no matter what religion you have.

FATHER JAMES TOMPKINS, priest and Nova Scotia-born educator, quoted by E.A. Corbett in "Dr. James Tompkins," *Pioneers in Adult Education in Canada* (1955), edited by Harriet Rouillard.

Corruption

See also CRIME; PATRONAGE.

The only thing on the level is mountain-climbing.

EDDIE QUINN, Montreal wrestling promoter during the 1920s and 1930s, characteristic remark, quoted by Tim Burke in the Montreal *Gazette*, March 17, 1973.

. . . he thought that a contribution would be in order to the Ontario Conservative Party because we would probably be having a lot more dealings with the Ontario people, and that gratefulness was always regarded as an important factor in dealing with democratic governments.

R.O. SWEEZEY, business executive, in a statement regarding large business contributions to political parties, before the Special Committee on the Beauharnois Power Project, Ottawa, July 15, 1931. From *Appendix to the Sixty-Ninth Volume of the Journals of the House of Commons, Session 1931* (1931).

I used to look down on the world for being corrupt, but now I adore it for the utter magnificence of that corruption.

RICHARD J. NEEDHAM, Toronto columnist, in *A Friend in Needham, or a Writer's Notebook* (1969).

The thing which amazes me is that I know perfectly well, as a historian, that there is corruption in any government—there's always corruption. It's bad when it's more than fifteen percent.

MICHEL BRUNET, Quebec historian, inter-

viewed by Ramsay Cook in *The Craft of History* (1973), edited by Eleanor Cook.

Courage

If there were no cowards there would be no bullies.

GEORGE ILES, scientific writer, in *Canadian Stories* (1918).

It is courage the world needs, not infallibility . . . courage is always the surest wisdom.

SIR WILFRED GRENFELL, pioneer medical doctor and missionary to Newfoundland, in *A Labrador Logbook* (1938).

Today, when it takes little courage to be extreme, I am grateful that Canada has the courage to remain moderate . . . . As long as she remains aggressively moderate, Canada will survive.

GEORGE JONAS, poet and playwright, from "In Praise of Moderation," *Maclean's*, Nov. 1974.

Coureur de bois

See also FUR TRADE; NEW FRANCE.

It is difficult, almost impossible, for all the French still unused to this Indian country to make long trips and *courir les bois et forêts*.

GABRIEL SAGARD-THÉODAT, Recollet missionary to New France, in his *Histoire du Canada* (1636). The italicized phrase means "to get about in the woods and forests"; according to R.M. Saunders in "Coureur de Bois: A Definition," *Canadian Historical Review*, June 1940, this is the first use in print of the phrase that later became *coureur de bois*.

We were Caesars, being nobody to contradict us.

PIERRE-ESPRIT RADISSON, French explorer, in "Lake Superior Voyage" (1661), *The Explorations of Pierre Esprit Radisson* (1961), edited by Arthur T. Adams.

One day while in a jocular mood the old man began to talk over his past life. It was full of adventure, and may appear amusing to others as it did to us. I shall give it as nearly as I can in his own words. "I have now," said he, "been forty-two years in this country. For twenty-four I was a light canoeman. I required but little sleep, but sometimes got less than I required.

I have had twenty wives in the country; and was once possessed of fifty horses and six running dogs trimmed in the first style. I was then like a *bourgeois*, rich and happy.

*

I wanted for nothing; and I spent all my earnings in the enjoyment of pleasure. Five hundred pounds twice told have passed through my hands, although now I have not a spare shirt to my back nor a penny to buy one.

*

There is no life so happy as a *voyageur's* life; none so independent; no place where a man enjoys so much variety and freedom as in the Indian country. *Huzza, huzza pour le pays sauvage!"*

ALEXANDER ROSS, Hudson's Bay Company historian, quoting an anonymous *coureur de bois* in *The Fur Hunters of the Far West* (1855).

You hesitate. The trees are entangled with menace.
The voyage is perilous into the dark interior.
But then your hands go to the thwarts. You smile. And so
I watch you vanish in a wood of heroes,
Wild Hamlet with the features of Horatio.

DOUGLAS LEPAN, poet and essayist, last lines of "Coureur de Bois," *The Wounded Prince and Other Poems* (1948).

C'est l'aviron qui nous mèm', qui nous mont',
C'est l'aviron qui nous monte en haut.

Refrain of "C'est l'aviron qui nous mème" (Coming Back Home), quoted by Marius Barbeau in *Jongleur Songs of Old Quebec* (1962) who writes: "It has come to enjoy the reputation of being one of the gayest voyageur songs." The two lines translate: "It is the paddle that drives the canoe, / It is the paddle that moves us on."

Crime

See also CAPITAL PUNISHMENT; CORRUPTION; JUSTICE; LAW.

Dear Friend
My partner Will Geary got to putting on airs and I shot him and he is dead the potatoes is looking well. Yours truly

SNOOKUM JIM, a resident of Fort Whoop-Up in the 1870s, in a letter to the RCMP at Benton, Alta., quoted by T. Morris Longstreth in *The Silent Force* (1927).

I don't even know what street Canada is on.

AL CAPONE, Chicago gangster, quoted in 1931 by Roy Greenaway in *The News Game* (1966).

You've got me, boys. I've had enough.

RED RYAN, notorious bank robber, dying whisper after a gun battle with the Sarnia police, May 23, 1936. Quoted by Harold Dingman in the Toronto *Globe*, May 25, 1936.

I'm going out to flood the rink.

LUCIEN RIVARD, convicted Montreal drug peddler, with words to this effect gained access to the prison yard and leapt over the wall of Bordeaux Jail at 6:30 p.m., March 2, 1965. Rivard, nicknamed "the Gallic Pimpernel," was recaptured July 16, and extradited to the United States. From *The Shape of Scandal* (1965), by Richard Gwyn.

Against the Montreal underworld, even the King of England is powerless!

PACIFIQUE "PAX" PLANTE, Quebec's leading crime fighter, quoted by Alain Stanké in *Pax, lutte à finir avec la pègre* (1972).

All the great crimes of history are committed by collective sin, that is, collective blindness, collective egoism, which dehumanize and destroy others.

GREGORY BAUM, ecumenically minded Catholic priest, quoted by June Callwood in the Toronto *Globe and Mail*, Aug. 5, 1974.

The man who holds the responsibility for my tragedy is free . . . living off the avails of prosecution.

PETER DEMETER, Mississauga businessman, address to the jury after being found guilty of arranging the murder of his wife. This is a reference to a former friend, then unemployed but supported by the police while acting as a witness for the Crown, in London, Ont., Dec. 5, 1974.

To read the Toronto papers, you'd think this was Italy or something.

ROBERT BOURASSA, premier of Quebec, on the reaction of Toronto newspapers to the Cliche Report, which found widespread corruption in Quebec's construction industry. Quoted the following day in the Toronto *Globe and Mail*, May 10, 1975.

If the Mafia exists in Montreal, it's proba- bly like the Knights of Columbus.
ARMAND COURVILLE, Montreal meat-whole- saler and witness at the Quebec Police Com- mission Inquiry into organized crime, quoted in the Toronto *Globe and Mail*, May 27, 1975.

Critics

See also LITERATURE; THEATRE: CANADIAN.

A satirist is a man who discovers unpleas- ant things about himself and then says them about other people.
PETER MCARTHUR, columnist who wrote about farm life in western Ontario, in *The Best of Peter McArthur* (1967), edited by Alec Lucas.

The critic who discovers a flaw in Cana- dian literature is considered very clever; but the critic who discovers genius in our poetry or prose is immediately taunted with nationalistic prejudice.
WILSON MACDONALD, Toronto poet, in "The Stigma of Colonialism," *Open House* (1931), edited by William Arthur Deacon and Wilfred Reeves.

The critics condemn my books because of what they call my lack of realism. My re- ply to them is that sunsets are just as real as pigstyes and I prefer writing about sun- sets.
L.M. MONTGOMERY, novelist and author of *Anne of Green Gables* (1908), in an address to the Toronto Women's Press Club about 1936.

I am, in fact, the *only* drama critic in Cana- da. The rest are reviewers.
*
There are three things wrong with *Love in Albania*: the play, the direction and the casting.
NATHAN COHEN, well-known Toronto drama critic, quoted by Barbara Moon in *Maclean's*, June 18, 1957.

After all, the Old Vic is just another stock company.
NATHAN COHEN, outspoken columnist for the Toronto *Star*, refusing to recant after writing a critical review of a production staged by

Britain's leading theatrical company, in the 1960s.

The beauty of being a critic
is that one can write as if one were infalli- ble
and be forever wrong.
LOUIS DUDEK, Montreal poet, from "A Coro- net for Critics," *Collected Poetry* (1971).

Pessimism is a form of intellectual laziness.
JEAN DRAPEAU, mayor of Montreal, on the critics of the Montreal Olympics, in July 1975.

Cultural Protectionism

What would happen in Canada if full sov- ereignty were invoked and the southern border were sealed tight against American mass culture—if the airwaves were jam- med, if all our comic books were embar- goed, if only the purest and most uplifting of American cultural commodities were al- lowed entry? Native industries would take over obviously. Cut off from American junk, Canada would have to produce her own.
RICHARD H. ROVERE, American political writ- er, in *Maclean's*, Nov. 5, 1960.

If I were still a practising as distinct from an advisory Canadian I would be much more concerned about maintaining the cultural integrity of the broadcasting sys- tem and with making sure Canada has an active, independent theatre, book-publish- ing industry, newspapers, magazines and schools of poets and painters.
I would be very much concerned that the widest possible support was given by all levels of government to the preservation of the cultural traditions associated with the particular ethnic groups in Canada, and with French Canada. Also, to make sure that Canadian theatre and artists re- ceived encouragement. And that people weren't totally dependent on American magazines.
These are the things that are important for the maintenance of cultural autonomy. I wouldn't worry for a moment about the difference between Canadian or American corporations.
JOHN KENNETH GALBRAITH, Ontario-born economist and author, in an interview con-

ducted by Robert McKeown, in *Weekend*, March 25, 1967.

When I return to Canada from time to time, what I always find most tiresome is the cultural protectionism, the anti-Americanism. No heritage is worth preserving unless it can survive the sun, the mixed marriage, or the foreign periodical. Culture cannot be legislated or budgeted or protected with tariffs. Like potatoes.

MORDECAI RICHLER, Montreal novelist, in "The North American Pattern," from *The New Romans* (1968), edited by Al Purdy.

Support your fellow Canadians. We should buy lousy Canadian novels instead of importing lousy American novels.

JOHNNY WAYNE, one-half of the Wayne and Shuster comedy team, quoted by H.R.W. Morrison in *Star Week*, April 20, 1968.

Culture

See also ART; DANCE; FILM; LITERATURE; MULTICULTURALISM; MUSIC; THEATRE.

I must venture to Quebec tomorrow, or have company at home: amusements are here necessary to life; we must be jovial, or the blood will freeze in our veins.

I no longer wonder the elegant arts are unknown here; the rigour of the climate suspends the very powers of the understanding: what then must become of those of the imagination? Those who expect to see

"A new Athens rising near the pole,"

will find themselves extremely disappointed. Genius will never mount high, where the faculties of the mind are benumbed half the year.

FRANCES BROOKE, pioneer author of "the first Canadian novel," *The History of Emily Montague* (1769).

We Canadians, of course, have had to get used to being told we don't amount to much. The late lamented Kaiser, when he concocted his cultural map of the world, marked Canada off as a blank. Sarah Bernhardt, when last in this country on one of her repetitious farewells, complained that we had no poets and no poetry. Robert Barr said we spent more money on our

booze than on our books. When a group from the Canadian Authors' Association journeyed to England and visited George Bernard Shaw, that Chesterfieldian Irishman announced that he was under the impression Canada *had* no authors. Much of Shaw's eminence, of course, has been achieved through his rudeness and his tendency to stand Truth on her head. For when this same association of authors invited him to Canada his gracious response was that he had no intention of visiting an outlandish country of savages where a man of Shavian alertness would promptly die of intellectual starvation.

ARTHUR STRINGER, Chatham-born American novelist, in "Canada Finds Her Voice" (1949), an address to the Empire Club of Canada in 1949.

Canadian achievement in every field depends mainly on the quality of the Canadian mind and spirit. This quality is determined by what Canadians think, and think about; by the books they read, the pictures they see and the programmes they hear. These things, whether we call them arts and letters or use other words to describe them, we believe to lie at the roots of our life as a nation.

VINCENT MASSEY, future governor general, in the *Royal Commission on National Development in the Arts, Letters and Sciences, 1949-51* (1951), commonly called the Massey Report.

In an age of mass audiences it is the minorities who stand firm, and their loyalties are international.

ROBERT WEAVER, CBC executive, in "Books," *Mass Media in Canada* (1962), edited by John A. Irving.

I have no desire to bolster the sagging cultural economy of this country.

BRENDAN BEHAN, Irish playwright, after being hospitalized in Toronto, in *The Wit of Brendan Behan* (1968), compiled by Sean McCann.

France has culture but no civilization. England has civilization but no culture. The United States has neither. Canada has both.

ROBIN MATHEWS, Ottawa academic, in an address to the Women Teachers' Association of Ontario, Toronto, spring 1973.

Twenty-five hundred years of rational culture are in the process of dissolution.

> MARSHALL MCLUHAN, media pundit, in *Take Today* (1972), with Barrington Nevitt.

If the Chinese dare to make their alphabet phonetic, Chinese culture will dissolve in ten years.

> MARSHALL MCLUHAN, media pundit, at the Montreal International Book Fair, quoted by Christie McCormick in the Montreal *Gazette*, May 16, 1975.

Curiosity

No great literature or art is possible without a great people, a people ripened by experience, stirred by curiosity, and alive to wonder—a people with the daring capacity to expect the wonderful and then attempt to realize it.

> LORNE PIERCE, long-time editor of the Ryerson Press, in *An Editor's Creed* (1960).

Someone once said that the two most important things in developing taste were sensitivity and intelligence. I don't think this is so; I'd rather call them curiosity and courage. Curiosity to look for the new and the hidden; courage to develop your own tastes regardless of what others may say or think.

> R. MURRAY SCHAFER, Vancouver composer and teacher, in *The Composer in the Classroom* (1965).

And I say to you that if you bring curiosity to your work it will cease to be merely a job and become a door through which you enter the best that life has to give you.

> ROBERTSON DAVIES, man-of-letters, in his acceptance speech on receiving an honorary doctorate from Trent University, the Toronto *Star*, Nov. 9, 1974.

Dance

See also CULTURE.

Surely Canadians have taken to ballet as happily as the Russians have taken to hockey.

> MALCOLM ROSS, academic, in "Editor's Introduction," *The Arts in Canada: A Stock-Taking at Mid-Century* (1958).

A nation's character and soul is typified by its dances.

> BORIS VOLKOFF, the Russian-born "father of Canadian ballet," favourite adage, quoted by the Toronto *Globe and Mail*, March 12, 1974.

To dance good it hurts very much.

> BORIS VOLKOFF, the ballet master who died in 1973, quoted by John Fraser in the *Globe and Mail*, Dec. 28, 1974.

Fishing is my profession, dancing is my hobby.

> MIKHAIL BARYSHNIKOV, a leading Soviet dancer who defected from the Bolshoi Ballet troupe performing in Toronto on June 29, 1974. The remark was made the following day at a secluded farm in the Caledon Hills, north of Toronto. Quoted by Nalini Stewart in *Maclean's*, Jan. 1975.

Dancing isn't a tournament. The only competition you have is yourself and your expectations.

> KAREN KAIN, the young ballerina who won the International Ballet Competition in the summer of 1973 for a *pas de deux* with Frank Augustyn. Quoted by Alan Edmonds in the *Canadian*, Feb. 16, 1975.

Death

Every day in which I have neglected to prepare myself to die, was a day of mental alienation.

> LOUIS RIEL, Métis leader, quoted by Nicholas Flood Davin, "Interview with Riel," the Regina *Leader*, Nov. 16, 1885.

A little while and I will be gone from among you, whither I cannot tell. From nowhere we came, into nowhere we go. What is life? It is a flash of a firefly in the night. It is a breath of a buffalo in the winter time. It is as the little shadow that runs across the grass and loses itself in the sunset.

> CROWFOOT, Blackfoot chief, dying words, uttered overlooking the Bow River, April 25, 1890, quoted by John Peter Turner in *The North-West Mounted Police: 1873-1893* (1950).

A man called on me the other day with the idea of insuring my life. Now, I detest life-insurance agents; they always argue that I shall some day die, which is not so.

> STEPHEN LEACOCK, dean of Canadian humorists, in "Insurance up to Date," *Literary Lapses* (1910).

Movement is the essence of being. When a thing stands still and says, "Finished," then it dies. There isn't such a thing as completion in this world, for that would mean Stop!

> EMILY CARR, West Coast painter and writer, May 3, 1934, in *Hundreds and Thousands: The Journals of Emily Carr* (1966).

Just say I was born and that I am not dead yet.

> A.M. KLEIN, Montreal poet, reply to James Laughlin of New Directions when the publishers asked him for a blurb for *The Hitleriad* (1944). Quoted by Miriam Waddington in the *Canadian Forum*, Oct.-Nov. 1972.

I doubt that death is real. One always runs the risk of a resurrection.

> ANDRÉ LAURENDEAU, editor of *Le Devoir*, Nov. 1963, from *André Laurendeau: Witness for Quebec* (1973), translated by Philip Stratford.

The cost of living is seeing others die.

> ABRAHAM L. FEINBERG, Toronto rabbi, in *Storm the Gates of Jericho* (1964).

Oh, a man's got to die of something!

> ADAM SHORTT, political economist, quoted by Arthur R.M. Lower in *My First Seventy-Five Years* (1967).

No new graves
Congregation gone
Religion gone

I stare at the chance-taking dead

> R.G. EVERSON, Montreal poet, last stanza of "The Chance-Taking Dead," *Selected Poems: 1920-1970* (1970).

Death is a name for beauty not in use.

> IRVING LAYTON, poet, from "Composition in Late Spring," *The Collected Poems of Irving Layton* (1971).

I will see you again in Spence Bay, or in Heaven.

> DAVID KOOTOOK, fourteen-year-old Eskimo lad, in a letter written to his family on Nov. 12, 1972, four days after the crash of the mercy flight taking him from Cambridge Bay to Yellowknife.

Well, I'm all packed and ready to go. I'm an aged agnostic, unafraid of death and undeluded with thoughts of a life hereafter.

> GREGORY CLARK, newspaperman, at eighty-two, quoted by Frank Rasky in the Toronto *Star*, June 7, 1975.

I'll be standing on a bandstand till I die. Hopefully, it'll be when they're ringing in the year 1993, and I'll be standing up there leading them in Auld Lang Syne, while everybody's dancing and having a ball.

> GUY LOMBARDO, popular band leader born in London, Ont., quoted by Frank Rasky in the Toronto *Star*, Sept. 15, 1975.

Defeat

See FAILURE.

Democracy

The Kingdom of Heaven and perfect democracy are synonymous terms. [December 11, 1918]

*

Democracy may be simply defined as the people in action. [July 2, 1919]

> HENRY WISE WOOD, president of the United Farmers of Alberta and chairman of the Alberta Wheat Pool Board, in the *Grain Growers' Guide*, quoted by William Kirby Rolph in *Henry Wise Wood of Alberta* (1950).

There is no greater farce than to talk of democracy. To begin with, it is a lie; it has never existed in any great country.

> HENRI BOURASSA, French-Canadian politician and nationalist, in his address at Atwater Market Hall, Montreal, Feb. 10, 1943.

Historically, French Canadians have not really believed in democracy for themselves; and English Canadians have not really wanted it for others. Such are the foundations upon which our two ethnic groups have absurdly pretended to be building democratic forms of government. No matter the ensuing structure has turned out to be rather flimsy.

> PIERRE ELLIOTT TRUDEAU, prime minister of Canada, in *Federalism and the French Canadians* (1968).

I do not see how America can find its identity, much less avoid chaos, unless a massive citizens' resistance develops which is opposed to exploitation and imperialism on the one hand, and to jack-booted radicalism on the other. It would not be a new movement, but simply the will of the people, the people as a genuine society strong enough to contain and dissolve all mobs. It would be based on a conception of freedom as the social expression of tolerance, and on the understanding that violence and lying cannot produce anything except more violence and more lies. It would be politically active, because democracy has to do with majority rule and not merely with enduring the tyranny of organized minorities. It would not be conservative or radical in its direction, but both at once.

> NORTHROP FRYE, literary critic, in "America: True or False?" in *Notes for a Native Land: A New Encounter with Canada* (1969), edited by Andy Wainwright.

We have a political democracy in Canada, i.e., the right to vote for or against political parties and a wide range of civil liberties, but emphatically we do not have a democratic society, i.e., a society in which there is roughly equal access to power and wealth.

> ED BROADBENT, leader of the NDP, quoted in the Toronto *Globe and Mail*, April 9, 1975.

Depression, The Great

FOR SALE: Eight hundred acres highly improved stock farm, located on Pelletier Creek. Would sell on cash instalment basis. If interested write Fred Hearsey, Duncairn, Sask. N.B. I might be tempted to trade this farm for something really useful, say some white mice or goldfish, or even a playful little mouse. F.H.

> FRED HEARSEY, Saskatchewan farmer, is said to have placed this classified advertisement in a newspaper during the Depression. Quoted by James H. Gray in *The Winter Years* (1966).

The essence of being in your twenties in the Thirties was that no matter how well tuned up you were, you stayed on the ground, or just above it, for ten years.

> HUGH MACLENNAN, Montreal novelist, in "What It Was Like To Be in Your Twenties in the Thirties," *The Great Depression* (1969).

Do you want to know something? I don't think I'd have wanted to miss the Great Depression for the world.

> HUGH GARNER, Toronto novelist, in "On the Road through the Thirties" (1971), quoted by Michiel Horn in *The Dirty Thirties: Canadians in the Great Depression* (1972).

When the Depression came, our world stopped and we got off.

> JAMES H. GRAY, Calgary writer, quoted by Barry Broadfoot in *Ten Lost Years 1929-1939: Memoirs of Canadians Who Survived the Depression* (1973).

Destiny
See FUTURE.

Diefenbaker, John G.

My fellow Canadians . . . .

> JOHN G. DIEFENBAKER, member of Parliament for Prince Albert, Saskatchewan, and prime minister of Canada, characteristic salutation in the late 1950s and early 1960s.

I couldn't have called him an s.o.b., I didn't know he was one—at that time.

> JOHN F. KENNEDY, American president, in a reference to Prime Minister John Diefenbaker at a meeting in Ottawa, May 1961. "Kennedy had inadvertently left behind one of the staff papers he had been using. Diefenbaker not only expropriated the paper but threatened to

expose it publicly, claiming that it referred to him as an s.o.b. (Apparently this was a typically illegible reference to the OAS, which the president was urging Canada to join.) Kennedy denied the charge . . . ." Quoted by Theodore G. Sorenson in *Kennedy* (1965).

When John Diefenbaker enters the room, Arthur Maloney stands up.
ARTHUR MALONEY, Toronto Conservative, at the party's annual meeting in Ottawa, 1966, quoted by Thomas Van Dusen in *The Chief* (1968).

I was criticized for being too much concerned with the average Canadian. I can't help that; I'm one of them.
JOHN G. DIEFENBAKER, address at the annual convention of the Progressive Conservative party, Toronto, Sept. 7, 1967.

Flora MacDonald is the finest woman to have walked the streets of Kingston since Confederation.
JOHN G. DIEFENBAKER, attributed by Larry Zolf, Jan. 1975, about the Conservative M.P. for Kingston and the Islands.

Disappointment

No age, no age is called golden until it is long past. Any age is merely foot-slogging and twenty-four-hour days. To survive you need a good capacity to absorb disappointments.
ANDREW ALLAN, CBC producer, quoted by Harry J. Boyle in his introduction to *Andrew Allan* (1974).

There's this much to be said for sour grapes; you'll never get fat on them.
RICHARD J. NEEDHAM, Toronto columnist, in the Toronto *Globe and Mail*, Nov. 29, 1974.

Disasters

They say that Winnipeg was saved from complete disaster by a miracle. It was—a miracle of guts and hard work. The miracle of one hundred thousand multiplied by ten. A million fingers in the dikes.
WILLIAM HURST, Winnipeg city engineer, describing the efforts of the volunteer dike-builders who stopped the flooding waters when the

Red River overflowed its banks on May 5, 1950. Quoted by Frank Rasky in *Great Canadian Disasters* (1961).

I think this calls for a bottle of 7-Up!
DOUGLAS JEWKES, imprisoned Nova Scotian miner rescued nine days after the Springhill coal mine caved in. These were his first words to his rescuers in Nov. 1958. He explained that a vision of 7-Up had sustained him; he was hired by the soft-drink company as a warehouseman. Quoted by Frank Rasky in *Great Canadian Disasters* (1961).

We have to choose between collapse and ruin.
ALLAN LAMPORT, former Toronto mayor and malapropist, attributed.

Discovery
See also EXPLORATION.

Discovery begins by finding the discoverer.
GEORGE ILES, scientific popularizer, in *Canadian Stories* (1918).

How wonderful it must be to be young in an age which stands on the very verge of space travel. Yes, it is thrilling indeed to realize that among the children of today some will become the men and women who will reach out into space in their beautifully built rocket ships to charter many routes to distant points which beckon so enticingly in the vast spread of the universe.
FRANK H. ELLIS, pilot who flew the first commercial flight in the Canadian North and landed his Avro biplane at Le Pas, Manitoba, Oct. 18, 1920, in Ellis's *In Canadian Skies* (1959).

A land may be said to be discovered the first time a European, preferably an Englishman, sets foot on it.
VILHJALMUR STEFANSSON, outspoken Arctic explorer, in *Discovery: The Autobiography of Vilhjalmur Stefansson* (1964).

I have heard there is someone—not a human being but a spirit—in the moon. When I heard that the two men had landed on the moon I wondered what the spirit thought of these two men landing on his land.

PITSEOLAK, Cape Dorset artist, in *Pitseolak: Pictures Out of My Life* (1971), edited by Dorothy Eber.

I am an explorer. I adventure into the present. I make startling discoveries.
MARSHALL MCLUHAN, media pundit, interviewed by Linda Sandler, *Miss Chatelaine*, Sept. 3, 1974.

Disease
See also MEDICINE.

Care more particularly for the individual patient than for the special features of the disease.
SIR WILLIAM OSLER, physician and medical teacher, quoted by Harvey Cushing in *The Life of Sir William Osler* (1925).

"There is a rich man's tuberculosis and a poor man's tuberculosis." The rich man recovers and the poor man dies . . . .
NORMAN BETHUNE, Gravenhurst-born medical doctor and hero in Mao's China, in "A Plea for Early Compression," *Canadian Medical Association Journal*, July 1932.

Divorce
See also MARRIAGE.

A divorce is like an amputation; you survive, but there's less of you.
MARGARET ATWOOD, woman-of-letters, in *Time*, March 19, 1973.

What causes ninety-nine per cent of all Canadian divorces? A stalemate.
PAUL GOTLIEB, Montreal ad man and novelist, 1975.

Doctors
See also MEDICINE.

A physician who treats himself has a fool for a patient.
*
It cannot be denied that in dealings with the public just a little touch of humbug is immensely effective, but it is not necessary.
*
One of the first duties of the physician is to educate the masses not to take medicine.
SIR WILLIAM OSLER, physician and medical teacher, *Sir William Osler: Aphorisms from His*

Bedside Teachings and Writings (1950), edited by W.B. Bean.

But the hardest lesson I learned [on repatriation to this country some three years ago] was that it was far easier to get a bookie on the phone, and place a bet at the track, than it was to reach a doctor, many of whom actually come to your house only for a party.
MORDECAI RICHLER, Montreal novelist, *Saturday Night*, Sept. 1975.

Dominion
See also CONFEDERATION.

In the hearts and minds of the
delegates who assembled
in this room on September 1, 1864
was born the Dominion of Canada.

Providence being their guide
They built better than they knew.
Inscription on a bronze plaque erected in 1917 but unveiled July 1, 1927, in the Legislative Chamber, Province House, Charlottetown, the room in which the basis was established for a confederation of the British North American colonies.

The Kingdom of Canada.
SIR JOHN BEVERLEY ROBINSON, chief justice of early Ontario, on a proposed union of the colonies of Upper and Lower Canada under the monarchy, in *Letters from Mr. Commissioner Robinson on the Canada Trade and Canada Union Bills* (1822). Sir John A. Macdonald incorporated the phrase in the first draft of the BNA Act, but in later drafts "Kingdom" was discarded in favour of "Dominion."

His Dominion shall be from sea to sea.
SIR SAMUEL LEONARD TILLEY, New Brunswick statesman and a Father of Confederation, at the London Conference in Dec. 1866. It was felt that the working title of the country, the Kingdom of Canada, would offend the Americans, and at Tilley's suggestion "Kingdom" was replaced by "Dominion." Tilley was inspired by the Bible (Zechariah 9:10).

The N. American delegates have expressed a strong wish that the Confederate Province sd. not only have a common name but also a certain rank and they wish that it sd.

be known as the "Dominion of Canada." They wd. have preferred to call it a Viceroyalty. This in my opinion wd. be open to grave objection but I see no harm in the concession to them of the term "dominion." It is a tribute on their part to the monarchical principle and if somewhat in opposition to the institutions on the other side of the border, not in any offensive opposition.

LORD CARNARVON, British colonial secretary, in a letter to the Earl of Derby, Feb. 6, 1867, quoted by W.L. Morton in *The Critical Years: The Union of British North America 1853-1873* (1964).

It shall be lawful for the Queen, by and with the Advice of Her Majesty's Most Honourable Privy Council, to declare by Proclamation that, on and after a Day therein appointed, not being more than Six Months after the passing of this Act, the Provinces of Canada, of Nova Scotia, and New Brunswick shall form and be One Dominion under the name of Canada; and on and after that Day those Three Provinces shall form and be One Dominion under that Name accordingly.

Article 3 of the British North America Act, 1867, commonly called the BNA Act. The BNA Act was passed in the British Parliament on March 29, 1867, and became effective July 1, 1867.

. . . We, therefore, by and with the advice of Our Privy Council, have thought fit to issue this Our Royal Proclamation, and we do ordain, declare and command that, on and after the first day of July, 1867, the Provinces of Canada, Nova Scotia and New Brunswick, shall form and be One Dominion, under the name of Canada . . . . Given at Our Court at *Windsor Castle*, this twenty-second day of May, in the year of our Lord one thousand and eight hundred and sixty-seven, in the thirtieth year of Our Reign. *God save the Queen.*

Queen Victoria, in "A Proclamation . . . by the Queen," *Journals of the House of Commons of the Dominion of Canada, 1st session, 1st Parliament* (1868).

What is the difference between Dominion Day and Independence Day, between the First of July and the Glorious Fourth? . . . Not much—only forty-eight hours.

JAMES EAYRS, Toronto political scientist, "Canadianism," the Toronto *Star*, July 3, 1975.

Doukhobors

Mr. Esling: My references were to the religious fanatics who today are offending the public by exhibitions of absolute nakedness. In order to bring this right home I would like to know what the Prime Minister would think if he went into his garden in the morning to pick pansies or violets and was confronted by six naked Doukhobors.

Mr. King: I would send for my honourable friend the Leader of the Opposition and the leader of the Progressive Party.

Mr. Bennett: There would be a riot if you overlooked your own supporters.

R.B. BENNETT to Prime Minister W.L. Mackenzie King; overheard in the House of Commons in 1928.

Philip: This is Doukhobor country, you know.
Elizabeth: Really?
Philip: Yes, if you look over on the edge of the crowd, I think you'll see one of them.
Elizabeth: Naked?

QUEEN ELIZABETH II, in Calgary, 1951, quoted by Pierre Berton in *The Royal Family* (1954).

Drapeau, Jean
See OLYMPICS.

Dreams

Morning and noon and midnight
    exquisitely,
  Rapt with your voices, this alone we
    knew,
Cities might change and fall, and men
    might die,
  Secure were we, content to dream with
    you
    That change and pain are shadows
  faint and fleet,
    And dreams are real, and life is only
    sweet.

ARCHIBALD LAMPMAN, Ottawa poet, in the final stanza of "Frogs," *The Poems of Archibald Lampman* (1900), edited by Duncan Campbell Scott.

It is great good fortune that we still have

our frontier land in which pioneers may struggle and build, where they may dream their dreams of empire, and eventually write upon pages now blank the story of those realized dreams.

VILHJALMUR STEFANSSON, outspoken Arctic explorer, in *The Northward Course of Empire* (1922).

If you dream of Canada: You will have good business.

If you dream of seeing Canada on the map: You will have a vigorous mind.

If you dream of going to Canada from abroad: You have many loyal friends.

If you dream of going abroad from Canada: Happiness is assured.

ZOLAR, American astrologer, adapted from *Zolar's Encyclopaedia and Dictionary of Dreams* (1963).

If our dreams aren't to be fulfilled they should at least be splendid.

STEPHEN VIZINCZEY, the Budapest-born Canadian author, in *The Rules of Chaos* (1969).

It's funny how you tire of yesterday's dreams.

RANDY BACHMAN, millionaire leader of the Winnipeg rock group, Bachman-Turner Overdrive, quoted by Alan Edmonds in *Weekend*, Jan. 4, 1975.

Drinking

See also PROHIBITION; VIRTUES AND VICES.

The climate is infinitely more healthy than most of England. Indeed, it may be pronounced the most healthy country under the sun, considering that whiskey can be procured for about one shilling sterling per gallon.

WILLIAM "TIGER" DUNLOP, eccentric colonist, in *Statistical Sketches of Upper Canada, for the Use of Emigrants* (1832).

There is nothing that the new settler complains more feelingly of, than the want of good beer and ale.

CATHARINE PARR TRAILL, pioneer and author, in *The Female Emigrant's Guide* (1854).

Don't let the Indians whoop you up.

Unknown Fort Benton merchant to J.J. Healy and Alfred B. Hamilton, who subsequently

named their whiskey post Fort Whoop-Up in the fall of 1869. Quoted by James G. MacGregor in *A History of Alberta* (1972).

Look here, McGee, this Government can't afford two drunkards, and you've got to stop.

SIR JOHN A. MACDONALD, first prime minister, to Thomas D'Arcy McGee, quoted by E.B. Biggar in *Anecdotal Life of Sir John A. Macdonald* (1891).

Give me the five iron . . . no, on second thought, give me that other club . . . no, no give me that one I bought up in Toronto. Ah yes, that Canadian Club.

W.C. FIELDS, the American satirist, used this in one of his routines in the 1930s.

Ontario's such a respectable place;
Drinking's no crime, but it's still a disgrace,
So hide us away behind curtain and screen
While we stealthily go through the motions obscene
In a manner genteel, correctly genteel,
Secret and stuffy, but always genteel.

L.A. MACKAY, poet, in "Frankie Went Down to the Corner" (1936), *The Ill-Tempered Lover and Other Poems* (1948).

Two weeks ago, I had a lake named after me. They never named one after Sir John because he wasn't addicted that way.

JOHN G. DIEFENBAKER, address at the annual convention of the Progressive Conservative party, Toronto, Sept. 7, 1967.

No, Agnes, a Bordeaux is not a house of ill-repute.

GEORGE BAIN, Toronto columnist and wine-fancier, in *Champagne is for Breakfast* (1972).

Driving

I wasn't driving too fast, I was flying too low.

PHILLIP A. GAGLARDI, "Flying Phil," B.C. Cabinet minister from 1952 to 1972. Gaglardi made the remark to a patrol officer who stopped him for speeding. From Paddy Sherman's *Bennett* (1966).

An expressway is a bit like a mythical beast. You have to kill it three times.

JANE JACOBS, Toronto-based American urbanologist who helped stop the Spadina (Allen) Expressway in Toronto in 1971. Quoted by Jon Caulfield in *The Tiny Perfect Mayor* (1973).

Duplessis, Maurice

L'Union Nationale, c'est moi!

*

Colleague: I hope you are well.
Duplessis: Je suis dangereusement bien.
[I am dangerously well]

MAURICE DUPLESSIS, premier of Quebec intermittently between 1936 and his death in 1959, adapted from Leslie Roberts's *The Chief: A Political Biography of Maurice Duplessis* (1963).

The bishops eat out of my hand.

MAURICE DUPLESSIS, characteristic expression, quoted by Pierre Laporte in *The True Face of Duplessis* (1961).

Ottawa gives to foreigners, Duplessis gives to his province.

Slogan of the Union Nationale in the Quebec election of July 28, 1948. Quoted by J.W. Pickersgill in *My Years with Louis St. Laurent* (1975).

I never married because I have a mistress, a most demanding, but a wonderful mistress—my Province of Quebec.

MAURICE DUPLESSIS, adapted from Pierre Sévigny's *This Game of Politics* (1965).

You have got to make him a combination of Churchill, de Gaulle, Moses, God, and maybe the Devil, because he has got a bit of that in him. This combination usually wins votes. Do that.

Duplessis telling Pierre Sévigny how to create an image for John G. Diefenbaker that would be successful in Quebec in 1957. Quoted by Peter Stursberg in *Diefenbaker: Leadership Gained* (1975).

Easter

This Man of April walks again—
Such marvel does the time allow—
With laughter in His blesséd bones,
And lilies on His brow.

LEO KENNEDY, poet, last verse from "Words for a Resurrection," from *The Shrouding* (1933).

Ecology
See CONSERVATION.

Economic Nationalism
See also CONTINENTALISM; MULTINATIONAL CORPORATION; NATIONALISM; TRADE.

There are two things that are not desirable for Canada, extreme economic nationalism and abject political colonialism.

JOHN W. DAFOE, editor of the Winnipeg *Free Press*, May 4, 1926, quoted by Ramsay Cook in *The Politics of John W. Dafoe and the Press* (1963).

On the whole, however, the most substantial Canadian nationalism in times of peace has been economic nationalism.

J. BARTLET BREBNER, well-known historian, in "Canadianism," Presidential Address, *Report of the Canadian Historical Association* (1940).

Instead of being owners ourselves of our resources we will wake up some day to find we are owers . . . the "n" is gone. Owners . . . owers . . . note the difference.

JOHN FISHER, broadcaster and public speaker, known as "Mr. Canada" throughout the 1940s and 1950s, in "John Fisher Reports," address to the Empire Club of Canada, 1950.

Thus, far from contributing to the growth of a stronger, more independent, and identity-conscious nation, Canadian nationalism as it has developed in recent years has been diverting Canada into a narrow and garbage-cluttered cul-de-sac.

HARRY G. JOHNSON, Toronto-born economist

at the University of Chicago, in "Problems of Canadian Nationalism" (1961), *The Canadian Quandary* (1963).

Much will have to change in Canada if the country is to stay the same.

ABRAHAM ROTSTEIN, influential political economist in 1961, from *The Precarious Homestead* (1973).

The extent of foreign control of Canadian industry is unique among the industrialized nations of the world.

MELVILLE H. WATKINS, political economist and chairman of the Task Force on the Structure of Canadian Industry; opening sentence of *Foreign Ownership and the Structure of Canadian Industry* (1968), known as the Watkins Report.

If there is one thing that worries Canadians more than economic domination, it is that someone, sometime, will try to do something about it.

GEORGE BAIN, columnist, in the Toronto *Globe and Mail*, Nov. 4, 1969.

Capital has no nationality.

ROBERT W. BONNER, chairman of the board of MacMillan Bloedel Limited, in "Capital Has No Nationality," address to the Empire Club of Canada, Dec. 10, 1970.

If America's conquest of Canada is based on America's strength, Canada's surrender is based on Canadian weakness.

PETER C. NEWMAN, journalist and author, quoted in the Toronto *Star*, June 14, 1975.

Economics

See also FINANCE; INFLATION.

Democracy will defeat the economist at every turn at its own game.

HAROLD ADAMS INNIS, political economist, in "Government Ownership and the Canadian Scene" (1933), *Essays in Canadian Economic History* (1956), edited by Mary Quayle Innis.

If we cared less about wealth, perhaps it would be easier to effect a more even distribution of it. Perhaps if we gave a little more unhurried thought to the purpose of life, we would better understand the place of the economic system in it.

W.H. HERRIDGE, brother-in-law of Prime

Minister R.B. Bennett, in an address to the Canadian Club of Ottawa, Dec. 15, 1934. Quoted by Michiel Horn in *The Dirty Thirties* (1971).

There were warnings of apprehension from economists. There always are; apprehension is their business.

*

The subject is called political economy because it has nothing to do with politics and nothing to do with economy.

STEPHEN LEACOCK, humorist and political economist, attributed.

Education

See also COLLEGES AND UNIVERSITIES; SCIENCE AND SCIENTISTS; TEACHERS.

Genius may require to be breathed into the soul, but it must be fanned by the domestic hearth; and therefore, boys, let not your hours be wasted—let every house be a school house.

JOSEPH HOWE, editor and future statesman, in "Winter Evenings," the *Novascotian*, Nov. 27, 1828. Quoted in *Joseph Howe: Voice of Nova Scotia* (1964), edited by J. Murray Beck.

A great many children go to school to learn to read novels.

R.D. CUMMING, writer, *Skookum Chuck Fables* (1915).

Whoever ceases to be a student has never been a student.

GEORGE ILES, scientific popularizer, in *Canadian Stories* (1918).

Outside of the asylum there are also the two great types, the student-lark who loves to see the sun rise, who comes to breakfast with a cheerful morning face and in hilarious spirits . . . the student-owl with his saturnine morning face, thoroughly unhappy, cheated by the wretched breakfast-bell of the two best hours of the day for sleep . . . .

SIR WILLIAM OSLER, world-famous physician and medical teacher, from *Sir William Osler: Aphorisms from His Bedside Teachings and Writings* (1950), edited by W.B. Bean.

Get all the education you can; then add the learning.

JACK MINER, pioneer naturalist who banded

wildlife at his famous bird sanctuary at Kingsville, Ontario, a "Minerism."

A little learning is a dangerous thing but a lot of ignorance is just as bad.
> BOB EDWARDS, "Eye Opener Bob," publisher of the Calgary *Eye Opener*, Aug. 20, 1921.

The man who has ceased to learn ought not to be allowed to wander around loose in these dangerous days.
> M.M. COADY, educator, quoted by J.R. Kidd in *How Adults Learn* (1959).

"The advantages of a classical education are two-fold; it enables us to look with contempt upon those who have not shared its advantages, and it fits us for places of emolument, both in this world and in the next . . . ."
> E.W. STEACIE, former director of the National Research Council, quoting with disapproval "the Prebendary of Durham" in an address in 1959. From *Science in Canada* (1965), edited by J.D. Babbitt.

Curiosity is the very basis of education and if you tell me that curiosity killed the cat, I say only the cat died nobly.

*

A university should provide you with one thing at least—a reading list for the rest of your life.
> ARNOLD EDINBOROUGH, columnist and public speaker, in the convocation address, University of Ottawa, Oct. 1962.

Education is impossible without love, without loving a few of the great men of the past.
> JEAN-PAUL DESBIENS, "Brother Anonymous," in *For Pity's Sake* (1965), translated by Frédéric Côté.

Good intentions and sentimentalism are not enough. At the first meeting of the Canadian Association for Adult Education in 1935 there was coined a slogan that, while somewhat vulgar, is worth some consideration, "Now and then forget your bleeding heart and use your bloody head!"
> J. ROBY KIDD, adult educator, in *Education for Perspective* (1969).

Education is not something to make a man

a lawyer, a doctor, an engineer or priest. It is something to make him a man. The true education is not to give a man a standard of living, but a standard of life.
> GRATTAN O'LEARY, Conservative spokesman, quoted by I. Norman Smith in *The Journal Men* (1974).

Youngsters today're educated until it comes out of their ears, and they don't know a darn thing!
> MARGARET "MA" MURRAY, pioneer newspaperwoman, CBC-TV, June 3, 1975.

They told me A equalled B, but I knew it wasn't so. A doesn't equal B and it never has.
> GREGORY CLARK's reason for failing freshman mathematics two years running at the University of Toronto in 1912; on accepting an honorary doctorate from the same university in 1975. *Weekend*, June 7, 1975.

Efficiency

One trouble with being efficient is that it makes everybody hate you so.
> BOB EDWARDS, publisher of the Calgary *Eye Opener*, March 18, 1916.

An efficient organization is one in which the accounting department knows the exact cost of every useless administrative procedure which they themselves have initiated.
> E.W.R. STEACIE, former director of the National Research Council, in *Science in Canada* (1965), edited by J.D. Babbitt.

The Peter Principle—In a hierarchy, every employee tends to rise to his level of incompetence.
> DR. LAURENCE J. PETER, native of British Columbia who teaches psychology at the University of Southern California, in *The Peter Principle* (1969), by Dr. Peter and Raymond Hull.

Man cannot live by incompetence alone.
> DR. LAURENCE J. PETER, in *The Peter Prescription* (1972).

If it works, it's obsolete.
> MARSHALL MCLUHAN, media pundit, quoted by A. Alvarez in *The Savage God* (1971).

Elections

See also POLITICS; VOTE.

Nobody would ask for the vote by ballot but from gross ignorance; it is the most corrupt way of using the franchise.

JOHN STRACHAN, influential Anglican minister and politician in Upper Canada, in *The Seventh Report from the Select Committee of the House of Assembly of Upper Canada on Grievances . . . W.L. Mackenzie, Chairman* (1835). Reproduced by J.L.H. Henderson, editor of *John Strachan* (1969).

Elections are not won by prayers alone.

ISRAEL TARTE, Sir Wilfrid Laurier's Quebec lieutenant and a Liberal party bagman. The notorious remark was made in 1896 when Sir Wilfrid Laurier and Tarte both won re-election.

Well, I told them the truth. They say the truth shall set you free. It's certainly set me free.

AGNES MACPHAIL, first woman elected to the House of Commons (1921-1940). The remark was made in 1940, when she was defeated at the polls. Quoted by Miriam Chapin in *Contemporary Canada* (1959).

As Prince Albert goes, so goes the nation.

JOHN G. DIEFENBAKER, long-time member of Parliament from Prince Albert, Saskatchewan, and prime minister of Canada, in Prince Albert, April 7, 1963.

I never campaign. I just visit with the people.

JOHN G. DIEFENBAKER, at a campaign picnic, 1965.

At times I have to hold my nose while marking the ballot.

FRANK H. UNDERHILL, socialist and later a reluctant Liberal. The remark was made at a Liberal party gathering in 1967. Quoted by Peter C. Newman in "Frank Underhill" (1970), *Home Country* (1973).

The biggest trouble with political promises is that they go in one year and out the other.

AL BOLISKA, Toronto radio personality, in *The Mahareeshi Says* (1968).

But when polling day came, I was defeated by large and enthusiastic majorities . . . .

GRAHAM SPRY, proponent of national radio broadcasting, in "The CCF Party in Its Formative Years," *The Great Depression* (1969), edited by Victor Hoar.

I represent help for the helpless, hope for the hopeless, and bras for the bra-lass.

ROBERT L. STANFIELD, Conservative leader, at a Christmas party in 1971. Quoted by Geoffrey Stevens in *Stanfield* (1973).

Emigration

See also IMMIGRATION.

And now the winter's over, it's homeward we are bound,

And in this cursed country we'll never more be found.

Go back to your wives and sweethearts, tell others not to go

To that God-forsaken country called Canaday-I-O.

Last verse of "Canaday-I-O," said to be written by Ephraim Braley, New England lumberjack working in the Maritimes in 1853, from *Folk Songs of Canada* (1954), edited by Edith Fowke and Richard Johnston.

Those who stay at home will build up the country, and those who go abroad will save us from parochialism.

GEORGE MUNRO GRANT, educator, in "Our National Objects and Aims," *Maple Leaves* (1891).

The Dominion that had begun in Lamentations seemed to be ending in Exodus.

Sir Richard Cartwright, appointed a senator in 1904, attributed.

As a member of those melancholy expatriates who have been dubbed the League of Fallen Maple Leaves, I have learned to tread lightly when I venture back to the land of my birth.

ARTHUR STRINGER, Canadian-born American writer, in "Canada Finds Her Voice," an address to the Empire Club of Canada in 1949.

Emotions

See HEART.

Empire Day

See also VICTORIA DAY.

Among the titles suggested were the following:—"Flag Day," "Britannia Day," "Patriotic Day" and "Empire Day." None of these titles, except the last, seems to me to be acceptable . . . . "Empire Day" suggests that larger British sentiment which I think now prevails throughout the Empire, and to which Canada has for many years contributed not a little . . . . As to the time most convenient for the celebration of such a day, from suggestions received, and from a careful consideration of the whole question, I would respectfully advise that the school day immediately preceding the 24th of May be the day selected . . . . For this and the next generation or two, the recollection of her illustrious reign will on reflection quicken the pulse of the many hundreds of thousands of school children as they remember the greatness of the Empire over which she [Queen Victoria] reigned so long.

> GEORGE W. ROSS, Ontario minister of Education, responding to a series of letters written by Mrs. Clementina Fessenden, a Hamilton school teacher, in a memorandum to the Dominion Teacher's Association, July 23, 1898. Empire Day outlasted the empire itself, at least in Toronto where it was being observed a half-century later. Quoted by J. Castell Hopkins in *The Origin and History of Empire Day* (1910).

I want you boys to remember what Empire Day means. Empire Day is the festival on which every British subject should reverently remember that the British Empire stands out before the whole world as the fearless champion of freedom, fair play and equal rights; that its watchwords are responsibility, duty, sympathy and self-sacrifice; and that a special responsibility rests with you individually to be true to the traditions and to the mission of your race.

> EARL GREY, governor general, in an address to Toronto school cadets, May 1909, quoted by Robert M. Stamp in "Empire Day in the Schools of Ontario," *Journal of Canadian Studies*, Aug. 1973.

Enemies

Humanity has but three great enemies: fever, famine and war; of these by far the greatest, by far the most terrible, is fever.

> SIR WILLIAM OSLER, physician and medical teacher, quoted by Harvey Cushing in *The Life of Sir William Osler* (1925).

Having a hearty enemy adds to the zest of life.

> ARCHIBALD MacMECHAN, writer, quoted by M.G. Parks in his introduction to the 1974 edition of MacMechan's *Headwaters of Canadian Literature* (1924).

What do these enemies of the human race look like? Do they wear on their foreheads a sign so that they may be told, shunned and condemned as criminals? No. On the contrary, they are the respectable ones. They are honoured. They call themselves, and are called, gentlemen. What a travesty on the name, Gentlemen! . . . These men make the wounds.

> NORMAN BETHUNE, medical doctor who died in northern China in 1939, in "Wounds," the *Canadian Tribune*, June 15, 1940; reprinted in *New Frontiers*, fall 1952.

The greatest enemies of even the best things are toadies.

> JOSEF SKVORECKY, Czech novelist resident in Toronto, in *All the Bright Young Men and Women* (1971), translated by Michael Schonberg.

Energy Crisis

See also OIL.

There is one thing Canadians should always remember. In many parts of the world including much of the southern United States people will be uncomfortable if heating fuel is cut off, but in Canada many people would die. We need our energy fuels just to stay alive in our rigorous climate and fuel for our future is essential. We cannot return to the use of wood and coal, and nuclear power has not yet been developed to be an adequate alternative to fossil fuels.

> J. TUZO WILSON, Toronto geophysicist, in "Selling Today What We'll Need Tomorrow," *Maclean's*, March 1973.

That "Eastern Bastard" is My Brother!
ROD SYKES, mayor of Calgary, promoted the above bumper sticker to oppose one that had appeared on Alberta cars during the oil crisis of Nov. 1973: "Let the Eastern Bastards Freeze in the Dark." Quoted by James H. Gray in the Toronto *Star*, Dec. 15, 1973.

Epitaphs
See also LAST WORDS.

Here Lies
Ezekial Aikle
Age 102
The Good
Die Young
Epitaph from a cemetery near East Dalhousie, Nova Scotia.

In memory of Robert Randell, Esq., M.P.P., the victim of Colonial Misrule, who died May 21st, 1831, aged 68 years.
Epitaph of the reformer who tried in vain to redress the personal injustices done him; inscription on his tombstone in Drummond Hill Cemetery, Niagara Falls.

Ye weak beware, here lies the strong,
A Victim of his strength,
He lifted sixteen hundred pounds,
And here he lies at length.
Epitaph of Daniel MacDonald, who died Oct. 27, 1871, at age thirty-three, after winning a strong-man contest in Montreal, from Little Lake Cemetery, Peterborough.

H.F. Davis,
Born Vermont, 1820,
Died, Slave Lake, 1893.
Pathfinder, Pioneer, Miner, Trader.
"He was everyman's friend
and never locked his cabin door."
Epitaph of Henry Fuller "Twelve-Foot" Davis, well-loved pioneer prospector and trader, on his gravestone overlooking the town of Peace River, Alberta. Davis once staked a claim between two others only twelve feet apart, from which he took $15,000 in gold and his nickname.

SACRED OF KATIE—IPOO
SAM BOYAN HE DIDE—IPOO
RIP JULIE YECTION—IPOO
JOSEPH'S ROSIE DI—IPOO

West-coast Indian grave markings on wooden crosses. "Time was marked by centuries in this cemetery. Years—little years—what are they? As insignificant as the fact that reversing the figure nine turns it into the letter P." Emily Carr in *Klee Wyck* (1941).

Born a man—Died a grocer
Epitaph of John Smith, 1852-1914, in a New Brunswick cemetery.

HAINE HAINT
ARTHUR HAINE, Vancouver atheist, ordered that the above inscription be included on his tombstone. Quoted by Robert L. Ripley in *Ripley's Believe It or Not!* (second series, 1934).

Lest We Forget. Murdered, Estevan, Sept. 29, 1931, by the RCMP.
Inscription on the headstone raised at Bienfait, near Estevan, by the Mine Workers of Canada to mark the common grave of three young workers killed by rifle fire during the Estevan coal-miner's strike. A short time after the monument was erected, the words "the RCMP" were erased.

I am yesterday and I know tomorrow.
Epitaph of Reginald Fessenden, Quebec-born broadcasting pioneer, who died in 1932. The words (in Egyptian hieroglyphics) appear on his stone memorial in Bermuda. Quoted by Ormond Raby in *Radio's First Voice* (1970).

Remember, Henry, none of this Sir "stuff" at the cemetery, just plain "Robert Laird Borden, born Grand Pré, N.S.—1854; died Ottawa, Ont.—1937."
SIR ROBERT L. BORDEN, on his deathbed, to his nephew, regarding the wording on the headstone that would mark his grave in Beechwood Cemetery, Ottawa. From the foreword by Henry Borden, his nephew and editor, to *Letters to Limbo* (1971).

He loved the simple things,
He hated war,
But when his call came,
He gave his all.
Inscribed on the marker of an unidentified Canadian soldier buried at Normandy, June 6, 1944.

God give me work
Till my life shall end

And life
Till my work is done.

> Lines inscribed on the tombstone of Margaret McWilliams, founder and president of the Canadian Federation of University Women, buried in Winnipeg in 1952. Quoted by Betty Jane Wylie in *The Clear Spirit* (1966), edited by Mary Quayle Innis.

Eskimo Art
See also ART; ESKIMOS.

These arctic carvings are not the cold sculptures of a frozen world. Instead, they reveal to us the passionate feelings of a vital people well aware of all the joys, terrors, tranquility, and wildness of life around them.

> JAMES HOUSTON, founder of the Eskimo art movement in 1952, quoted by George Swinton in *Sculpture of the Inuit* (1971).

I am going to keep on doing them [making prints and drawings] until they tell me to stop. If no one tells me to stop, I shall make them as long as I am well. If I can, I'll make them even after I am dead.

> PITSEOLAK, Cape Dorset artist, quoted by George Swinton in *Sculpture of the Eskimo* (1972).

In a life where neither reason nor strength prevail, where cunning counts for little and pity least of all, the Eskimo sings of life, for only art avails, and even then, not always.

> EDMUND CARPENTER, anthropologist, in *Eskimo Realities* (1973).

Eskimos
See also ESKIMO ART; INDIANS.

Chimo.

> A mixed Indian and Eskimo word of salutation, pronounced either "chy-mo" or "cheemo," according to Walter S. Avis's *A Dictionary of Canadianisms on Historical Principles* (1967).

They first pointed to the ships, eagerly asking, "What great creatures those were?" "Do they come from the sun or the moon?" "Do they give us light by night or by day?" Sacheuse told them that he was a man, that he had a father and mother like themselves; and, pointing to the south, said that he came from a distant country in that direction. To this they answered, "That cannot be, there is nothing but ice there."

> SIR JOHN ROSS, explorer and captain of the *Sabine*, who sailed into Melville Bay and was thus greeted by the polar Eskimos, Aug. 10, 1818, from *A Voyage of Discovery Made under the Orders of the Admiralty* (1819).

And yet, there is only
One great thing,
The only thing:
To live to see, in huts and on journeys
The great day that dawns
And the light that fills the world.

> From "a little nameless Eskimo song" sung at Kent Peninsula, reported by Knud Rasmussen, on the Fifth Thule Expedition in 1921-24, in *The Mackenzie Eskimos* (1942), edited by H. Ostermann.

I took possession of Baffin Island for Canada in the presence of several Eskimo, and after firing nineteen shots I instructed an Eskimo to fire the twentieth, telling him that he was now a Canadian.

> CAPTAIN J.E. BERNIER, who claimed the Arctic archipelago for Canada on July 1, 1909, in "Our Northern Heritage," an address to the Empire Club of Canada in 1926.

The Eskimo, on the other hand, simply accepts things as they are, and lets them go at that. If they do not work out for him, he will dismiss misfortune with one word: "*Ayorama*"—"That's destiny, that's life, there isn't anything I can do about it."

> RAYMOND DE COCCOLA, Oblate priest, and PAUL KING, writer, in *Ayorama* (1955).

Here were a people with less resources than any other people on earth, and yet they were the happiest people I have ever known.

> ROBERT FLAHERTY, documentary filmmaker, quoted by Frances Flaherty in "Introducing *Man of Aran*," Robert Hughes's *Film: Book 1: The Audience and the Filmmaker* (1959). Flaherty is describing the Eskimo of the Hudson Bay area, among whom he lived for ten years while prospecting for iron ore.

Espionage

Spies rarely look the part.

IGOR GOUZENKO, Ukrainian cipher clerk who defected from the Soviet embassy in Ottawa on Sept. 5, 1945, taking with him the West's first proof of widespread Soviet espionage. Quoted by Frank Rasky in *Gay Canadian Rogues* (1958).

A loyal ally does not spy; he simply exchanges information.
JAMES STEELE, academic, from "Canada's Vietnam Policy," in *An Independent Foreign Policy for Canada?* (1968), edited by Stephen Clarkson.

Ethics
See also GOOD AND EVIL.

The way of the transgressor is very popular. [May 8, 1915]
*
Meanwhile, the meek are a long time inheriting the earth. [September 16, 1916]
BOB EDWARDS, writer and publisher of the Calgary *Eye Opener* from 1902 to 1922.

Ethics are merely a form of collective bargaining at the professional level.
JOHN C. PARKIN, Toronto architect, in an address to the Saskatchewan Symposium on Architecture, Regina, Oct. 21, 1961.

If you live by your principles and are true to them, you can't fail.
M.J. COLDWELL, NDP founder and parliamentarian, quoted by Pierre Elliott Trudeau in a memorial tribute in the House of Commons, Sept. 30, 1974.

Science presented us first with normative ethics, then with relativistic ethics, and at last with no ethics at all.
GEORGE FALUDY, Hungarian-born, Toronto-based poet and humanist, 1974.

A man should preserve his integrity, though he must sell his soul to do it.
ERIC NICOL, Vancouver humorist, in *Letters to My Son* (1974).

Exploration
See also DISCOVERY.

These Indians were of a different tribe from those which I had already seen, as our guide did not understand their language. I now mixed up some vermilion in melted grease, and inscribed, in large characters, on the South-East face of the rock on which we had slept last night, this brief memorial—"Alexander Mackenzie, from Canada, by land, the twenty-second of July, one thousand seven hundred and ninety-three."
SIR ALEXANDER MACKENZIE, first explorer to cross the American continent north of Mexico, on the shore of Dean Channel, Bella Coola River, British Columbia. *Voyages from Montreal on the River St. Laurence, through the Continent of North America, to the Frozen and Pacific Oceans* (1801). The text is taken from *The Journals and Letters of Sir Alexander Mackenzie* (1970), edited by W. Kaye Lamb.

A Norseman died in Ontario 900 years ago.
J.W. CURRAN, publisher of the Sault Ste. Marie *Daily Star*, used this as the title of a talk to the Empire Club of Canada in 1938. Curran wrote *Here Was Vinland* (1939) about the Sault Ste. Marie area.

A.D. one thousand was the year
That Norsemen crossed the sea;
Just where they went, and when they left
Is history's mystery.
MARSH JEANNERET, poetaster and publisher, first verse of *History's Mystery* (1961), illustrated by J.L. Patterson.

Expo 67

Terre des Hommes
ANTOINE DE SAINT-EXUPÉRY, French aviator-author who provided Expo 67 with its theme, "Terre des Hommes/Man and His World." Saint-Exupéry published a book of lyrical reflections, *Terre des Hommes* (1939), which included the passage: "To be a man is to feel that through one's own contribution, one helps to build the world." The book was translated into English and published as *Wind, Sand and Stars* (1939).

Enough of this educational stuff. Let's go to La Ronde and have some fun.
SENATOR ROBERT KENNEDY to his wife and six children at Expo 67, La Ronde being the large amusement park. Quoted by Robert Fulford in *This Was Expo* (1968).

VISIT/EZ EXPO?
VISIT/EZ LES SLUMS!
Graffiti in Montreal in 1967.

Habitat is in the tradition of spontaneous self-made environments, the beginnings of a contemporary vernacular.

MOSHE SAFDIE, the Israeli-born architect responsible for the innovative dwelling, in *Beyond Habitat* (1970).

External Affairs

See also CANADA: INTERNATIONAL RELATIONS; INTERNATIONALISM; ISOLATIONISM.

We should not be here at all, as our instructions should be summarized as: say nothing and do nothing unless you can undo something of what was done at Geneva . . . . Dining alone this evening I developed a plan for the perfect representation of Canada at Conferences. Our delegate would have a name, even a photograph; a distinguished record, even an actual secretary—but he would have no corporeal existence and no one would ever notice that he was not there.

HUME WRONG, leading member of the Department of External Affairs and resident representative to the League of Nations; his reflections in 1937, quoted by Vincent Massey in *What's Past Is Prologue* (1963).

Members of the Canadian Foreign Service do not feel—they think.

HUME WRONG, counsellor of the Canadian legation in Washington, quoted by Charles Ritchie in *The Siren Years* (1974), Dec. 15, 1938.

No interest in Ethiopia, of any nature whatever, is worth the life of a single Canadian citizen.

ERNEST LAPOINTE, minister of Justice, in a speech in Quebec City, 1939, quoted by James Eayrs in *Diplomacy and Its Discontents* (1971).

Without sacrificing the universality of the United Nations, it is possible for the free nations of the world to form their own closer association for collective self-defence under article 51 of the charter of the United Nations . . . the formation of such a defensive group of free states would not be a counsel of despair but a message of hope.

LOUIS ST. LAURENT, secretary of State and future prime minister, in the House of Commons, April 29, 1948. The speech led to the formation of the North Atlantic Treaty Organization (NATO).

To be influential with modest means one needs to be modest in demeanour . . . let us tread softly and carry a bulging briefcase of bright ideas.

PEYTON V. LYON, international affairs specialist, in "Canada Is Becoming a Mouse that Roars" (1960), *The Policy Question: A Critical Appraisal of Canada's Role in World Affairs* (1963).

Reporter: Does it mean, Sir, that if Canada does not accept nuclear weapons for these airplanes that she is not actually fulfilling her NATO commitments?

Norstad: I believe that's right. She would be meeting it in force but not under the terms of the requirements that have been established by NATO.

GENERAL LAURIS NORSTAD, supreme commander of NATO, reply at an Ottawa press conference, Jan. 3, 1963; this statement helped to bring down the Diefenbaker administration. Quoted by Peyton V. Lyon in *Canada in World Affairs: 1961-1963* (1963).

Diplomacy would not be diplomacy if it was not quiet.

PAUL MARTIN, long-time Cabinet minister, adapted from a remark quoted in the Toronto *Globe and Mail*, Sept. 14, 1974.

Failure

See also SUCCESS.

One of the worst stings of defeat is the sympathy that goes with it.

BOB EDWARDS, writer and publisher of the Calgary *Eye Opener*, June 8, 1912.

You may do all you can for the other fellow, but it is a failure unless he, himself, is willing to get up in the morning.

JACK MINER, pioneer naturalist who banded

wildlife at his famous bird sanctuary at Kingsville, Ontario, in *Wild Goose Jack* (1969).

I'm not afraid of failure. I've had it.
> SUZANNE PLESHETTE, Canadian-born Hollywood actress, quoted by Jack Hirschenberg in the Toronto *Star*, March 24, 1963.

Statistics are for losers.
> HARRY HAYES, minister of Agriculture, in the House of Commons, Oct. 14, 1963.

This above all, to refuse to be a victim.
> MARGARET ATWOOD, woman-of-letters, from *Surfacing* (1972).

Faith
See BELIEF.

Fame

To have done this is to have lived, though fame
Remember us with no familiar name.
> ARCHIBALD LAMPMAN, poet, from "The Largest Life," *The Poems of Archibald Lampman* (1900), edited by Duncan Campbell Scott.

Fame, from a literary point of view, consists in having people know you have written a lot of stuff they haven't read.
> BOB EDWARDS, writer and publisher of the Calgary *Eye Opener*, summer 1920.

Imagine you, Gladys Smith, of Toronto, Canada, with the Queen of Siam in your bathtub.
> MARY PICKFORD, Toronto-born film actress and "America's Sweetheart," to herself when the King and Queen of Siam were guests of Pickford and Douglas Fairbanks at Pickfair, their Hollywood home, in the late 20s. Quoted by Robert Windeler in *Sweetheart* (1973).

"I'm world-famous," Dr. Parks said, "all over Canada."
> MORDECAI RICHLER, Montreal novelist, in *The Incomparable Atuk* (1963).

For the first thirty years of my life I made the headlines; now I'm lucky to make the footnotes.
> F.R. SCOTT, Montreal poet and lawyer, in 1974.

Fame—the privilege of being pestered by strangers.
*
Reputation is better than fame.
> LOUIS DUDEK, Montreal man-of-letters, in *Epigrams* (1975).

Family Compact

I shall be happy to consult with yourself and Mr. Rolf on the measures to be adopted to relieve this province from the evils which a family compact have brought upon it.
> MARSHALL SPRING BIDWELL, lawyer, in a letter to William Warren Baldwin in 1828. This is the earliest use of the term "family compact" to describe the ultra-conservative Loyalist group that governed Upper Canada in the early nineteenth century. From *A Dictionary of Canadianisms on Historical Principles* (1967), edited by Walter S. Avis.

The *"family compact"* of Upper Canada is composed of those members of its society who, either by their abilities and character have been honoured by the confidence of the executive government, or who, by their industry and intelligence, have amassed wealth. The party, I owe, is comparatively a small one; but to put the multitude at the top and the few at the bottom is a radical reversion of the pyramid of society which every reflecting man must foresee can end only in its downfall.
> FRANCIS BOND HEAD, or "Galloping Head," the ebullient lieutenant-governor of Upper Canada during the Rebellion of 1837, in *A Narrative* (1839).

Farming
See also WHEAT.

Up! be stirring, be alive,
Get upon a farm and thrive!
He's a king upon a throne
Who has acres of his own!
> ALEXANDER McLACHLAN, folk poet, in the refrain from "Acres of Your Own," included by William Douw Lighthall in *Songs of the Great Dominion* (1889).

Everything a farmer does is done in his spare time.
> SIR ANDREW MACPHAIL, writer and teacher, in

"The Farmer," an address to the Empire Club of Canada in 1920.

Prosperity follows the cow.
> H.H. DEAN, teacher, from "Dairying in Canada," *Handbook of Canada* (1924).

To be born on a farm is the greatest good that can befall a human being. To live on a farm and enjoy all that it has to offer is the greatest good that can be attained by a poet or a philosopher.
> PETER MCARTHUR, columnist who wrote about farm life in western Ontario, in *Around Home* (1925).

A farmer makes his money in the country and spends it in the city, while an agriculturist makes his money in the city and spends it in the country.
> JOHN MITCHELL, novelist who published pseudonymously as Patrick Slater, to Max Braithwaite in 1946, from *Braithwaite's Ontario* (1974).

The farmer is king, oh, the farmer is king,
And except for his wife and daughter,
Who boss him around, he runs the thing,
Come drought, come hell or high water.
> PAUL HIEBERT, humorist, last stanza of a poem supposedly composed by Sarah Binks, the Sweet Songstress of Saskatchewan, in *Sarah Binks* (1947).

For all Westerners, even city people, the farmer is the touchstone, our fertility symbol, the core of our mythology. He is the grass roots, the salt of the earth, the moral fibre of the nation: he is The People. His gradual disappearance shakes our sense of identity and makes us question the validity of our history. Those of us who remain in the West feel a small chill, as if the farmer's flight from the land has blighted our own hopes and brought on us a sense of attenuation and decay. Is that all there is? The farmer is the guardian of the western dream; without him, the West is just the East.
> HEATHER ROBERTSON, writer, in *Grass Roots* (1973).

Fear

I confess I was afraid of nothing.
> GABRIEL DUMONT, Riel's adjutant-general

during the Northwest Rebellion of 1885, quotation translated by George F.G. Stanley in "Gabriel Dumont's Account of the North West Rebellion, 1885," *Canadian Historical Review*, Sept. 1949.

I am afraid of the worst, but I am not sure what that is.
> ABRAHAM ROTSTEIN, influential political economist, in an aphorism dating from 1972.

Federal-Provincial Relations
See also CANADA; UNITY, NATIONAL.

As between the various Provinces comprising the Dominion, we need some cement more binding than geographical contact; some bond more uniting than a shiftless expediency; some lodestar more potent than a mere community of profit. Temporizing makeshifts may suit a futureless people.
> WILLIAM A. FOSTER, leading nationalist, in *Canada First* (1871).

You have perhaps heard the story of the four students—British, French, American, Canadian—who were asked to write an essay on elephants. The British student entitled his essay "Elephants and the Empire." The French student called his "Love and the Elephant." The title of the American student's essay was "Bigger and Better Elephants," and the Canadian student called his "Elephants: A Federal or a Provincial Responsibility?"
> ROBERT H. WINTERS, former minister of Trade, adapted from an address delivered in 1966.

Feelings
See HEART.

Feminism
See also WOMEN.

All mass movements have a lunatic fringe, but women's lib seems to have a lunatic centre.
> DR. JOHN RICH, Toronto marriage counsellor, in *Chatelaine*, April 1971.

You know, Women's Lib is really a takeover of the abandoned business world . . . . I mean that men have dropped out of management and women are taking over.

MARSHALL MCLUHAN, media pundit, interviewed by Linda Sandler in *Miss Chatelaine*, Sept. 3, 1974.

WHY NOT?
Theme of Canada's participation in International Women's Year, launched Jan. 27, 1975. Authorship of the phrase, which has appeared on buttons and posters, is claimed by Dalton Camp.

Fenians

Tramp, tramp, tramp our boys are marching,
Cheer up, let the Fenians come!
For beneath the Union Jack we'll drive the rabble back,
And we'll fight for our belov'd Canadian home.

Anti-Fenian marching song, authorship of which has been attributed to Lachlan McGoun, a Scottish-born housepainter living in Napanee while serving with the artillery during the Fenian raids of 1866.

We are a Fenian Brotherhood, skilled in the arts of war,
And we're going to fight for Ireland, the land that we adore.
Many battles we have won, along with the boys in blue,
And we'll go aid capture Canada, for we've nothing else to do.

"Song of the Fenian Brotherhood" (1866), quoted by John Murray Gibbon in *Canadian Mosaic* (1938).

They may tak' Montreal, and they may tak' Toronto, and they may tak' Woodstock, but they'll no tak' Zorra!

The good citizens of East and West Zorra, Oxford County townships, defied the invading Fenians in 1866, as quoted by W.E. Elliott in *Politics Is Funny* (1952).

As to the propriety of invading Canada, I have always had but one opinion: Canada is a province of Great Britain; the British flag floats over it and English soldiers protect it, and, I think, wherever the English flag and English soldiers are found, Irishmen have a right to attack. In striking at

England through Canada we attempted no more than was done by the American Republic in the war of the Revolution.

"GENERAL" JOHN O'NEILL, president of the Fenian Brotherhood, in *Official Report of Gen. John O'Neill, President of the Fenian Brotherhood; on the Attempt to Invade Canada, May 25, 1870* (1870).

Film
See also ACTORS AND ACTRESSES; AWARDS; CULTURE.

I knew nothing whatsoever about films. I had no one to speak to. But here in the North I discovered primitive man, people in the midst of life who are always so close to death that they live in the moment nobly.

ROBERT FLAHERTY, well-known documentary filmmaker, quoted by Arthur Calder-Marshall in *The Innocent Eye* (1963).

You in Canada should not be dependent either on the United States or on Great Britain. You should have your own films and exchange them with those of other countries. You can make them just as well in Toronto as in New York City.

D.W. GRIFFITH, pioneer movie director, in an interview, the Toronto *Star*, Dec. 15, 1925.

Hollywood has never had a shortage of the sort of person who, in the midst of a burning house, will sit down to write a speech explaining how he, personally, always chose non-combustible materials when they were reasonably priced and acceptable to his associates.

ROBERT FULFORD, Toronto columnist, in 1968, from *Marshall Delaney at the Movies* (1974).

I know a whole lot of people here are pushing hard to make Hollywood Establishment films. The trouble is, of course, that they won't be nearly as good as Hollywood Establishment films. So why the hell bother?

DON SHEBIB, director of *Goin' Down the Road*, quoted by Betty Lee in the Toronto *Globe and Mail*, Oct. 31, 1970.

The purpose of my films is to give the intellect a rest.

NORMAN MCLAREN, animator with the NFB, in "Eye Hears, Ear Sees," CBC-TV, winter 1971.

To create a Canadian film industry, we first have to create Canada. Whatever happens to Canada's film culture will be symptomatic of Canada as a whole. The struggle goes on and everyone—including the apathetic—is determining the outcome.

JOHN HOFSESS, film critic, in *Inner Views* (1975).

I'm the off-white hope of the Canadian cinema.

TED KOTCHEFF, Toronto-born film director of Bulgarian ancestry, on the TV show, "The Education of Mike McManus," Aug. 5, 1975.

Finance
See also ECONOMICS; MONEY; TAXES.

When I go into a bank I get rattled.

STEPHEN LEACOCK, humorist and economist, in "My Financial Career," *Literary Lapses* (1910).

My hon. friend is getting very indignant. Something evidently has got under his skin. May I repeat what I have said? With respect to giving moneys out of the federal treasury to any Tory government in this country for these alleged unemployment purposes, with these governments situated as they are today, with policies diametrically opposed to those of this government, I would not give them a five-cent piece.

W.L. MACKENZIE KING, prime minister, in the House of Commons, April 3, 1930. This is his famous "five-cent piece" speech.

Having asked for $20,000,000 at the special session my right hon. friend, finding conditions worse than ever, began to experience difficulty in fixing the amount for the last year. Facing this situation he found it necessary, in order to do what he thought would satisfy the unemployed, to ask not for $20,000,000, $40,000,000, $60,000,000, $80,000,000 or $100,000,000, but to ask this parliament to give a blank cheque which he might fill in for as much as he wished to draw.

W.L. MACKENZIE KING, leader of the Opposition, accusing Prime Minister R.B. Bennett of demanding a "blank cheque" from Parliament during the Depression, in the House of Commons, Feb. 8, 1932.

A buck is a buck.

KENNETH CARTER, chairman of the Carter Commission on Tax Reform, whose report was released on Feb. 24, 1967.

Statistical tables are like skeletons. Perhaps that is the reason so many people view them with awe.

JOHN PORTER, political economist, in *Canadian Social Structure* (1967).

Fish and Fishing

How could one be expected to show an interest in a country like Canada, demanded Lord Melbourne the Prime Minister, where a salmon would not rise to a fly?

LORD MELBOURNE, prime minister of Great Britain between 1834 and 1841, paraphrased by James Morris in *Heaven's Command* (1973).

Some people may care to discuss this case from the point of view of England, others from the point of view of the United States, but I shall discuss it from the point of view of the fish.

ROBERT BENCHLEY, American humorist about 1905. A Harvard undergraduate, he was speaking extemporaneously on the Newfoundland–United States cod-fisheries dispute.

Per angler per day, perdition. My good man, I ask you what is the sense of me being Governor of this widespread, far-flung, sea-to-sea Dominion if I cannot catch all the fish I have a mind to?

DUKE OF CONNAUGHT, governor general and sportsman, to a park warden at Consolation Lake near Banff who warned him that the limit was "fifteen fish per angler per day," some time between 1911 and 1916.

The weather for catching fish is that weather, and no other, in which fish are caught.

W.H. BLAKE, essayist and translator of *Marie Chapdelaine*, in *Brown Waters and Other Sketches* (1925).

I have examined all the arguments in favour of no life in the Arctic Sea, and it seems to me that they are the kind of arguments that would appeal to a philosopher but would *not* appeal to fish.

VILHJALMUR STEFANSSON, outspoken Arctic explorer, in *Discovery* (1964).

Flag

One School, One Flag, One Language.

OGLE ROBERT GOWAN, Irish-born politician and journalist who founded the Orange Association of British America in Brockville, Ontario, in 1830, and gave it this motto.

For the sake of my flag, I come here to die.

OCTAVE CRÉMAZIE, Quebec man-of-letters, from the poem, "Le drapeau de Carillon," written in 1858 to recall the centenary of Montcalm's valiant defence of Fort Carillon, in *Les Oeuvres complètes d'Octave Crémazie* (1882), edited by Abbé H.-R. Casgrain.

Men of Canada, keep both hands on the Union Jack!

LORD DUNDONALD, general officer commanding the militia, on his departure from Ottawa, July 26, 1904, after his dismissal from office for protesting political interference, quoted by J. Castell Hopkins in *The Canadian Annual Review of Public Affairs, 1904* (1905).

One Fleet, One Flag, One Throne.

SIR ROBERT BORDEN, leader of the Conservative party, slogan in the general election of Sept. 21, 1911.

Nationalist: Do you realize that this country hasn't even got a flag?
Comedian: That's a start.

MORT SAHL, Montreal-born nightclub satirist, in an exchange in Toronto in 1961.

The flag has been made a party emblem, the Pearson pennant.

JOHN G. DIEFENBAKER, leader of the Opposition, coined the epithet, "the Pearson pennant," in an address at Winnipeg, June 16, 1964.

This is the flag of the future, but it does not dishonour the past.

LESTER B. PEARSON, prime minister, in the House of Commons, Dec. 15, 1964. Canada acquired its own flag at 2:30 a.m., Dec. 16,

1964. The "Maple Leaf" was officially raised and flown for the first time on Feb. 15, 1965.

F.L.Q.
See SEPARATISM.

Food

There, amid the snows of the north, under an Eskimo's hospitable roof, for the first time I shared with them in that cheering, invigorating emblem of civilization—tea!

CHARLES FRANCIS HALL, American Arctic explorer, in *Arctic Researches and Life among the Esquimaux* (1865).

We have seen thee, queen of cheese,
Lying quietly at your ease,
Gently fanned by evening breeze,
Thy fair form no flies dare seize.

JAMES MCINTYRE, an Ingersoll coffin-maker and poetaster, in "Ode on the Mammoth Cheese," written to celebrate an immense round of cheese weighing over seven thousand pounds, the largest ever moulded by man, in McIntyre's *Musings on the Banks of the Canadian Thames* (1884).

If a man goes without food for one day, he will lie. If he goes without food for two days, he will steal. If he goes without food for four days, he will riot and kill. The food business is the most essential in the world, and the largest.

NATHAN STEINBERG, supermarket magnate, quoted by Peter C. Newman in *Flame of Power* (1959).

If you're interested in cooking, you're also just naturally interested in art, in love and in culture.

MADAME JEHANE BENOÎT, well-known Quebec chef, quoted by Tom Alderman in the *Canadian*, Dec. 28, 1974.

Football
See also SPORTS.

The Canadian superfan comes to the Grey Cup to get out of himself and reach out for all those things he has been promised all week, all the vicarious plastic things. He is there with his ticket waiting for it to happen to him.

LaVerne Barnes, wife of a football player, in *The Plastic Orgasm* (1971).

The first person I'd like to thank is God. The second person is John Bassett.

Tom Wilkinson, quarterback for the Edmonton Eskimos, accepting the Schenley Award in Vancouver, quoted by Al Sokol in the *Toronto Star*, Nov. 22, 1974. (Bassett's role had been a negative one: he arranged for the quarterback to be fired from the Toronto Argonauts in 1970.)

Foreign Investment
See ECONOMIC NATIONALISM.

France

Let us endeavour, then, rather to improve Old France, than strive to found a New France in the most unpromising regions of the West.

Pierre-François-Xavier de Charlevoix, French chronicler, quoted by François-Xavier Garneau in *History of Canada from the Time of Its Discovery till the Union Year 1840-41* (1862), translated by Andrew Bell.

Everything which is French comes to us from France, but everything which comes to us from France is not always French.

Canon Lionel Groulx, influential priest and historian, in *Dix ans d'Action française* (1926).

Voice in the crowd: Vive la France!
Trudeau: Si vous voulez. Vive la France, et vive les Anglais, aussi. Et vive la république des patates frites.

Pierre Elliott Trudeau, leader of the Liberal party, in Chatham, Ontario, June 11, 1968.

Freedom
See also LIBERTY.

I cannot dismiss you without earnestly desiring you to promote by precept and example, among your respective counties, the regular habits of piety and morality, the surest foundations of all private and public felicity; and at this juncture, I particularly recommend to you to explain, that this province is singularly blest, not with a mutilated constitution, but with a constitution which has stood the test of experience, and which is the very image and transcript of that of Great Britain; by which she has long established and secured to her subjects as much freedom and happiness as is possible to be enjoyed under the subordination necessary to civilized society.

John Graves Simcoe, governor of Upper Canada, in an address at the closing of the first session of the first Parliament of Upper Canada, Oct. 15, 1792, from *Letters to Sir Joseph Banks* (1890).

Farewell, old master, this is enough for me.
I'm going straight to Canada where coloured men are free.

Couplet from "The Voice of the Fugitive" (1851), in *Canada's Story in Song* (1965), edited by Edith Fowke and Alan Mills.

. . . the time will come when that national spirit which has been spoken of will be truly felt among us, when we shall realize that we are four million Britons who are not free, when we shall be ready to take up that freedom, and to ask what the late prime minister of England assured us we should not be denied—our share of national rights.

Edward Blake, Liberal politician, at Aurora, Ontario, Oct. 3, 1873. The "Aurora Speech" was edited and published by W. Stewart Wallace in *Canadian Historical Review*, Sept. 1921.

Then let us ever hope and pray,
In this our own progressive day,
    May freedom spread her pinion
O'er heads that think and hearts that feel,
And labour for the common weal
    In this our dear dominion.

Alexander McLachlan, folk poet, in the last stanza of "The Men of the Dominion," *The Poetical Works* (1900), edited by E. Margaret Fulton (1974).

With glowing hearts we see thee rise,
The True North, strong and free,
And stand on guard, O Canada,
We stand on guard for thee.

R. Stanley Weir, jurist and author, from "O Canada," written in 1908.

The real division in the world today is not between socialism and capitalism, it is between freedom and totalitarianism.

> FRANK H. UNDERHILL, socialist thinker, in "Random Remarks on Socialism and Freedom" (1947), *In Search of Canadian Liberalism* (1960).

Freedom wears a crown.

> JOHN COLBORNE FARTHING, political scientist at Bishop's College, Lennoxville, used the monarchical metaphor as the title of his only book, published in 1957, edited by Judith Robinson.

Freedom is not a gift but something that must be won. The only freedom is that which has been torn from authority.

> GÉRARD FILION, editor of *Le Devoir*, quoted by Pierre Elliott Trudeau in "Some Obstacles to Democracy in Quebec" (1958), *Federalism and the French Canadians* (1968).

We live a hundred times better than a commissar. We live in air that is perfumed with freedom.

> SVETLANA GOUZENKO, wife of the Soviet cipher clerk who defected to the West, quoted by Frank Rasky in *Gay Canadian Rogues* (1958).

Freedom is the right to be wrong, not the right to do wrong.

> JOHN G. DIEFENBAKER, prime minister, on March 11, 1958.

I can assure you that as long as there is a drop of blood in my body they won't stop me from talking about freedom.

> JOHN G. DIEFENBAKER, long-time parliamentarian, in Sudbury, June 3, 1962.

It's ironical that the first people to demand free speech are the first people to deny it to others.

> CLAUDE T. BISSELL, president of the University of Toronto, to student protesters who were interrupting an address by Clark Kerr, former president of Berkeley, Royal Ontario Museum, Feb. 5, 1969. *Halfway up Parnassus* (1974).

Only the tiniest fraction of mankind want freedom. All the rest want someone to tell them they are free.

> IRVING LAYTON, outspoken poet, in *The Whole Bloody Bird* (1969).

To those who think that the law of gravity

interferes with their freedom, there is nothing to say.

> LIONEL TIGER, McGill-educated anthropologist, in *The Imperial Animal* (1971).

Freedom for Hungary! Freedom for all!

> GEZA MATRAI, Hungarian-born Canadian who assaulted Alexei Kosygin while the Soviet premier was strolling with Prime Minister Trudeau across Parliament Hill, Oct. 19, 1971.

French Canada

See also CANADA: FRENCH AND ENGLISH; CONQUEST OF 1759; FRENCH CANADIANS; NEW FRANCE; QUEBEC.

Nos institutions, notre langue, nos lois.

> ETIENNE PARENT, editor of the Quebec City newspaper, *Le Canadien*, chose this motto when the paper was revived on May 7, 1831.

The most enlightened, patriotic and humane men in Canada make extraordinary efforts to render people dissatisfied with the simple happiness that still contents them.

> ALEXIS DE TOCQUEVILLE, French historian, in *Democracy in America* (1835), translated by George Lawrence, edited by J.P. Mayer and Max Lerner (1966).

Our people don't want english capital nor english people here,—they have no ambition beyond their present possessions, & never want to go beyond the sound of their own Church Bells.

> LOUIS-JOSEPH PAPINEAU, leader of the Rebellion of 1837 in Lower Canada, quoted by Stewart Derbishire in "Report to Lord Durham on Lower Canada, 1837," edited by Norah Story, *Canadian Historical Review*, March 1937.

Their nationality is, after all, an inheritance; and they must be not too severely punished, because they have dreamed of maintaining on the distant banks of the St. Lawrence, and transmitting to their posterity, the language, the manners, and the institutions of that great nation, that for two centuries gave the tone of thought to the European Continent.

*

There can hardly be conceived a nationality more destitute of all that can invigorate and elevate a people, than that which is exhibited by the descendants of the French in Lower Canada, owing to their retaining their peculiar language and manners. They are a people with no history, and no literature.

LORD DURHAM, British statesman, in *Lord Durham's Report on the Affairs of British North America* (1912), edited by Sir Charles P. Lucas; the report first appeared in 1839.

A million of inhabitants may seem a small affair to the mind of a philosopher who sits down to write out a constitution. He may think it would be better that there should be but one religion, one language, and one system of laws, and he goes to work to frame institutions that will bring all to that desired state; but I can tell honourable gentlemen that the history of every country goes to show that not even by the power of the sword can such changes be accomplished.

SIR ANTOINE-AIMÉ DORION, leader of the Opposition and member for Hochelaga, in an address, Feb. 16, 1865, from *Parliamentary Debates on the Subject of the Confederation of the British North American Provinces* (1865).

French Canada is a relic of the historical past preserved by isolation, as Siberian mammoths are preserved in ice.

GOLDWIN SMITH, British-born journalist living in Toronto, in *The Political Destiny of Canada* (1878).

Quebec does not have opinions, only sentiments.

SIR WILFRID LAURIER, prime minister, quoted by Mason Wade in *The French Canadians: 1760-1967* (1968).

We are not only a civilized race, we are the pioneers of civilization; we are not only a religious people, we are the messengers of the religious idea; we are not only submissive sons of the Church, we are, we ought to be, numbered among its zealots, its defenders, and its apostles. Our mission is less to manipulate capital than to change ideas; it consists less in lighting the fires of factories than in maintaining and radiating afar the hearthlight of religion and thought.

MONSEIGNOR LOUIS-ADOLPHE PAQUET, professor of theology at Laval, in a Quebec City address, on St. Jean-Baptiste Day, 1902, quoted in another version by Mason Wade in *The French Canadians: 1760-1967* (1968).

"Do you know anything about French Canada?"

"I once knew a little—a long time ago."

"Well, they are a remarkable race there. They ought to have made a bigger show in the world than they have."

JOHN BUCHAN, LORD TWEEDSMUIR, governor general, in his novel *Sick Heart River* (1941).

Whatever the future of mankind in North America, I feel pretty confident that these French-speaking Canadians, at any rate, will be there at the end of the story.

ARNOLD J. TOYNBEE, eminent British historian, in *Civilization on Trial* (1948).

We will do our best to spread the wealth of Ontario across our country.

ROBERT BOURASSA, Quebec premier, quoted by Richard Cleroux in the Toronto *Globe and Mail*, May 1, 1972.

All America is riddled, like Swiss cheese, with pockets of French. The *ancien régime*, refusing to die.

CLARK BLAISE, Montreal novelist, in "The March," *Tribal Justice* (1974).

French Canadians

See also CANADIANS; FRENCH CANADA; QUEBEC.

Barring Catastrophe shocking to think of, this Country must, to the end of Time, be populated by the Canadian Race.

SIR GUY CARLETON, LORD DORCHESTER, governor-in-chief of British North America, in a letter written in 1767, quoted by W. Stewart Wallace in "The Beginnings of British Rule in Canada," *Canadian Historical Review*, Sept. 1925.

As to my opinion of the Canadians, I think there is nothing to fear from them, while we are in a state of prosperity, and nothing to hope from when in distress; I speak of the people at large; there are some among them who are guided by sentiments of honour, but the multitude is influenced only by hopes of gain, or fear of punishment.

SIR GUY CARLETON, LORD DORCHESTER, in a letter of 1776 concerning the French of Quebec, from *Documents Relating to a Constitutional History of Canada: 1759-1828* (1907-35), edited by Adam Shortt and Sir Arthur Doughty.

A Frenchman is naturally noisy; but the Canadian Charioteers! Heaven defend me from *them*! I have heard the jackalls in the woods of Hindostan,—I have witnessed the chattering herds of monkies on the coast of Malay,—but their howlings and chatterings were *music* to the sounds which now assailed my ears.

JEREMY COCKLOFT, British traveller, in *Cursory Observations Made in Quebec, Province of Lower Canada, in the Year 1811* (1960), edited by William Toye.

Be satisfied we will never forget our allegiance till the last cannon which is shot on this continent in defence of Great Britain is fired by the hand of a French Canadian.

SIR ETIENNE-PASCAL TACHÉ, a Father of Confederation, in an address to the Quebec Assembly, April 24, 1846, quoted by Jacques Monet in *The Last Cannon Shot* (1969).

I must moreover confess that I for one am deeply convinced of the impolicy of all such attempts to denationalize the French. Generally speaking they produce the opposite effect from that intended, causing the flame of national prejudice and animosity to burn more fiercely.—But suppose them to be successful what wd. be the result? You may perhaps *americanise*, but, depend upon it, by methods of this description, you will never *anglicise* the French inhabitants of the Province.—Let them feel on the other hand that their religion, their habits, their prepossessions, their prejudices if you will, are more considered and respected here than in other portions of this vast continent which is being overrun by the most reckless, self-sufficient and dictatorial section of the Anglo Saxon race, and who will venture to say that the last hand which waves the British flag on American ground may not be that of a French Canadian?

LORD ELGIN, governor general, in a letter to Earl Grey, May 4, 1848, from *The Elgin-Grey*

Papers: 1846-1852 (1937), edited by A.G. Doughty.

Johnnie Courteau of de mountain
Johnnie Courteau of de hill
Dat was de boy can shoot de gun
Dat was de boy can jomp an' run
An' it's not very often you ketch heem still
    Johnnie Courteau!

WILLIAM HENRY DRUMMOND, dialect poet, first verse of "Johnny Courteau," a personification of the habitant that dates back to 1901, in *Dr. W.H. Drummond's Complete Poems* (1926).

The young French Canadian is perhaps the only child in America who has what could be called an ideal, and whose dream is not merely to become an Astor or a Vanderbilt!

EDMOND DE NEVERS, French-Canadian author, 1890s, attributed by Abbé Groulx, quoted by Susan Mann Trofimenkoff in *Abbé Groulx* (1973).

It is not necessary that we possess industry and money. We will no longer be French Canadians but Americans almost like the others. Our mission is to possess the earth and spread ideas. To cling to the soil, to raise large families, to maintain the hearths of intellectual and spiritual life, that must be our role in America.

JULES-PAUL TARDIVEL, Kentucky-born Quebec nationalist, declaration of faith made in 1902, quoted by Ramsay Cook in "Quebec: The Ideology of Survival," in *The Prospect of Change* (1965), edited by Abraham Rotstein.

Our special task, as French Canadians, is to insert into America the spirit of Christian France. It is to defend against all comers, perhaps even against France herself, our religious and national heritage. This heritage does not belong to us alone. It belongs to all Catholic America. It is the inspiring and shining hearth of that America. It belongs to the whole Church, and it is the basic foundation of the Church in this part of the world. It belongs to all French civilization of which it is the refuge and anchor amid the immense sea of saxonizing Americanism.

HENRI BOURASSA, French-Canadian nationalist, in *La langue, gardienne de la foi* (1918), quoted by George Grant in *Lament for a Nation* (1965).

The "revenge of the cradle" should naturally lead to thinking about "the protection of the cradle."

*

There are so many among us who turn through vanity and ambition towards the stronger side, towards an opulence which they mistake for elegance. Even if it were only to protect these weaklings, Ladies and Gentlemen, let us make it *chic* to be French Canadian.

> CANON LIONEL GROULX, influential priest and historian at the Université de Montréal, in "Pour l'action française," an address before the Monument National, Montreal, April 10, 1918, *Dix ans d'action française* (1926), reproduced by Susan Mann Trofimenkoff in *Abbé Groulx* (1973).

You know, we French Canadians are improved Frenchmen.

> MAURICE DUPLESSIS, premier of Quebec intermittently between 1936 and 1959, quoted by Pierre Laporte in *The True Face of Duplessis* (1961).

You may trace to its lair the soft Chinook,
And the North Wind trail to the Barrens' floor;
But you'll always find, or I'm much mistook,
That some old Frenchman's done it before.

> JOHN BUCHAN, LORD TWEEDSMUIR, governor general, in "The Forerunners," from *The Long Traverse* (1941).

In politics, French Canadians have always thought with their feet.

> PIERRE ELLIOTT TRUDEAU, Montreal lawyer, later prime minister, in the introduction to *The Asbestos Strike* (1956), translated by James Boake in 1974.

French Canadians are perhaps the only people in the world who "enjoy" democracy without having had to fight for it.

> PIERRE ELLIOTT TRUDEAU, Montreal thinker, later prime minister, in "Some Obstacles to Democracy in Quebec" (1958), in *Federalism and the French Canadians* (1968).

The interesting thing about me is that I speak French and I breathe American air.

> ROBERT CHARLEBOIS, Quebec rock singer, quoted by *Time*, Dec. 18, 1972.

Friends and Friendship

In the chambers of our hearts there is room and verge for many friends. Their avenues are guarded by no state, no ceremonial; no introduction is needed to gain admission there, and those who once enter need never take their leave.

> LORD DUFFERIN, governor general, in Quebec City, Sept. 23, 1872, quoted by Gladys Chantler Walker in her edition of Lady Dufferin's *My Canadian Journal: 1872-1878* (1969).

No one who has a friend can be altogether at war with the world.

> NELLIE L. MCCLUNG, pioneer feminist, in *Sowing Seeds in Danny* (1908).

A friend who knows your secret holds a mortgage on your peace of mind. [Dec. 25, 1920]

*

The difference between a friend and an acquaintance is that a friend helps where an acquaintance merely advises. [Aug. 20, 1921]

> Bob Edwards, writer and publisher of the Calgary *Eye Opener* from 1902 to 1922.

Plato taught me.
Tu Fu accompanied me.
Goethe instructed me.
Mozart enlightened me.
With Marx I quarrelled.
Georges Braque gave me happiness.
With my friends I live.

> WALTER BAUER, German-born man-of-letters living in Toronto, in his own translation of an unpublished poem, "Companions," June 1975.

Front de libération du Québec
See SEPARATISM.

Fuddle-Duddle

Fuddle-duddle.

> PIERRE ELLIOTT TRUDEAU, prime minister, responding to a question in the House of Commons, Feb. 16, 1971: "Mr. Speaker, the hon. member has accused me of uttering a four-letter word in this House. That is an absolute untruth . . . . " Later, outside the House, Trudeau explained to George Bain and other reporters that the words he mouthed were "fuddle-duddle."

Fur Trade
See also BEAVER; COUREUR DE BOIS.

Most of the merchants and young men of
Montreal spend the greatest part of their
time in trading with the Indians, at an
amazing distance from Canada; and it often happens that they are three years together absent from home.

> J. HECTOR ST. JOHN CRÈVECOEUR, French
> writer and North American farmer, in *Letters
> from an American Farmer* (1782).

... it has occurred to me however that Phil-
anthropy is not the exclusive object of our
visits to these Northern Regions, but that
to it are coupled interested motives, and
that Beaver is the grand bone of conten-
tion.

> SIR GEORGE SIMPSON, "the Little Emperor" of
> the Hudson's Bay Company, in a letter from
> Fort Wedderburn, on May 18, 1821, in the
> *Journal of Occurrences in the Athabasca Department
> by George Simpson, 1820 and 1821 and Report*
> (1931), edited by E.E. Rich.

I was at an age when imagination lends its
colouring to everything, and the stories of
these Sindbads of the wilderness made the
life of a trapper and fur-trader perfect romance to me.
*
Such was the Northwest Company in its
powerful and prosperous days, when it
held a kind of feudal sway over a vast domain of lake and forest. We are dwelling
too long, perhaps, upon these individual
pictures, endeared to us by the associations
of early life, when, as yet a stripling youth,
we have sat at the hospitable boards of the
"mighty Northwesters," the lords of the as-
cendant at Montreal, and gazed with wondering and inexperienced eye at the baro-
nial wassailing, and listened with
astonished ear to their tales of hardships
and adventures. It is one object of our task,
however, to present scenes of the rough life
of the wilderness, and we are tempted to
fix these few memorials of a transient
state of things fast passing into oblivion; for
the feudal state of Fort William is at an
end; its council chamber is silent and de-
serted; its banquet-hall no longer echoes to
the burst of loyalty, or the "auld world"
ditty; the lords of the lakes and forests have

passed away; and the hospitable magnates
of Montreal—where are they?

> WASHINGTON IRVING, American author, in
> *Astoria; or Anecdotes of an Enterprise Beyond the
> Rocky Mountains* (1836).

Future
See also PRESENT.

How mysterious are the ways of
providence—how dark, crooked, and per-
verse the ways of man.

> EGERTON RYERSON, Upper Canadian educa-
> tor and clergyman, in *The Story of My Life*
> (1883), edited by J.G. Hodgins.

Be Canadians and the future is yours.

> LOUIS-HONORÉ FRÉCHETTE, distinguished
> Quebec poet, quoted by G.M. Fairchild, editor
> of *Canadian Leaves* (1887).

We should try to arrange ourselves so that
we will appear as plausible as possible to
posterity.

> R.D. CUMMING, writer and aphorist, in
> *Skookum Chuck Fables* (1915).

I have not the least fear of the future. I regard it as certain as sunrise.

> SIR W.C. VAN HORNE, railroad builder,
> quoted by Walter Vaughan in *Sir William Van
> Horne* (1926).

In Europe the poor man is tolerated if he
can look upon a great past; in America, if
he looks to a future.

> FREDERICK PHILIP GROVE, novelist, in *A Search
> for America* (1927).

I have seen the future and it doesn't work.

> ROBERT FULFORD, Toronto cultural journalist,
> created this aphorism in the Toronto *Star*, Jan.
> 25, 1967. It is an inverted version of the re-
> mark made by Lincoln Steffens in 1919 on his
> return from the Soviet Union: "I have seen the
> future, and it works."

I have long considered it one of God's
greatest mercies that the future is hidden
from us. If it were not, life would surely be
unbearable.

> EUGENE FORSEY, research director, now sena-
> tor, in "Trade Unions in 2020?" *Visions 2020*
> (1970), edited by Stephen Clarkson.

Geography

Again, Lord D. has made the subject of the construction route and requirements of the Canadian Pacific Railway his especial study. Until this great work is completed, our Dominion is little more than a "geographical expression." We have as much interest in B. Columbia as in Australia, and no more. The railway once finished, we become one great united country with a large interprovincial trade, and a common interest.

> SIR JOHN A. MACDONALD, first prime minister of Canada, in a letter to Sir Stafford Northcote, chancellor of the exchequer in Disraeli's cabinet, referring to Governor General Lord Dufferin, May 1, 1878, in *The Correspondence of Sir John Macdonald* (1921), edited by Sir Joseph Pope.

You cannot legislate against geography.

> SIR WILFRID LAURIER, Liberal leader and future prime minister of Canada, in a speech at Somerset, Quebec, Aug. 2, 1887.

In the beginning was geography.

> W. STEWART WALLACE, historian, in "The Growth of National Feeling," *Canadian Historical Review*, June 1920.

It is equally true, I should add, that if some countries have too much history, we have too much geography . . . .

> W. L. MACKENZIE KING, prime minister, in the House of Commons, June 18, 1936.

The present Dominion emerged not in spite of geography but because of it.

> HAROLD ADAMS INNIS, distinguished historian and economist, quoted by Donald Creighton in *Harold Adams Innis: Portrait of a Scholar* (1957).

The Niagara Escarpment is Canada's own fault.

> DON CULLEN, writer and performer at the Bohemian Embassy in Toronto, 1960.

Geography even more than religion has made us puritans, although ours is a puritanism tempered by orgy.

> WILLIAM KILBOURN, Toronto historian, in *Canada: A Guide to the Peaceable Kingdom* (1970).

We look
like a geography but
just scratch us
and we bleed
history.

> MIRIAM WADDINGTON, poet, in "Canadians," *Driving Home* (1972).

God

See also CHRISTIANITY.

Unto the hills around do I lift up
My longing eyes,
O whence for me shall my salvation come,
From whence arise?
From God the Lord doth come my certain
aid,
From God the Lord, who heaven and
earth have made.

> THE MARQUIS OF LORNE, governor general of Canada from 1878 to 1883, is credited with adapting the words of Psalm 121, for the popular Protestant hymn, "Unto the Hills."

God has many bests.

> JOHN MARK KING, moderator of the General Assembly of the Presbyterian Church in 1883, and principal of Manitoba College. The aphorism was often quoted by J.S. Woodsworth, leader of the CCF.

Who starts the nations? The very same one who creates them, God. God is the master of the universe, our planet is his land, and the nations, the tribes are members of his family, and as a good Father he gives a portion of his lands to that nation, to that tribe, to everyone, that is his heritage, that is his share of the inheritance, of the people, or nation or tribe.

> LOUIS RIEL, leader of the Métis, address to the jury, Regina, July 31, 1885, from *The Queen vs. Louis Riel* (1886).

I took a day to search for God,
And found Him not. But as I trod
By rocky ledge, through woods untamed,
Just where one scarlet lily flamed,
I saw His footprint in the sod.

BLISS CARMAN, poet, in "Vestigia" (1921), *Bliss Carman's Poems* (1929).

The legend arose that a green correspondent [covering the Winnipeg flood in May 1950] cabled his London editor: GOD LOOKED DOWN FROM THE PEMBINA HILLS NEAR WINNIPEG TODAY ON AN AWESOME SCENE OF DESTRUCTION . . . . The editor wired back: FORGET FLOOD. INTERVIEW GOD.

FRANK RASKY, journalist, in *Great Canadian Disasters* (1961).

God is alive. Magic is afoot. God is alive. Magic is afoot. God is afoot. Magic is alive. Alive is afoot. Magic never died.

LEONARD COHEN, Montreal poet and singer, in *Beautiful Losers* (1966).

Without God we have no rights, only such privileges as may be granted us by the state.

ALDEN NOWLAN, poet and author, *Between Tears and Laughter* (1971).

Man makes art because God forgets.

LOUIS DUDEK, Montreal man-of-letters, *Epigrams* (1975).

Gold Rush

TO WHOM IT MAY CONCERN

I do, this day, locate and claim, by right of discovery, five hundred feet, running up stream from this notice. Located this 17th day of August, 1896.

G.W. Carmack

G.W. CARMACK, the prospector who made the first gold strike in the Yukon. "Carmack blazed a small spruce tree with his hand axe, and on the upstream side wrote with a pencil . . . ." Quoted by Pierre Berton in *Klondike* (1958).

A bunch of the boys were whooping it up in the Malamute saloon;
The kid that handles the music-box was hitting a rag-time tune;
Back of the bar, in a solo game, sat Dangerous Dan McGrew,
And watching his luck was his light-o-love, the lady that's known as Lou.

ROBERT W. SERVICE, "The Poet of the Yukon," first verse of "The Shooting of Dan McGrew" (1907), *The Complete Poems of Robert Service* (1944).

There are strange things done in the midnight sun
By the men who moil for gold;
The Arctic trails have their secret tales
That would make your blood run cold;
The Northern Lights have seen queer sights,
But the queerest they ever did see
Was that night on the marge of Lake Lebarge
I cremated Sam McGee.

ROBERT W. SERVICE, refrain of "The Cremation of Sam McGee" (1907), *The Complete Poems of Robert Service* (1944).

The Klondike experience had taught all these men that they were capable of a kind of achievement they had never dreamed possible. It was this, perhaps more than anything else, that set them apart from their fellows. In the years that followed, they tended to run their lives as if they were scaling a perpetual Chilkoot, secure in the knowledge that any obstacle, real or imagined, can be conquered by a determined man. For each had come to realize that the great stampede, with all its searchings and its yearnings, with all its bitter surprises, its thorny impediments, and its unexpected fulfillments, was, in a way, a rough approximation to life itself.

PIERRE BERTON, author and TV personality, in *Klondike* (1958)

Golden Dog

Je suis un chien qui ronge lo
En le rongeant je prends mon repos
Un temps viendra qui n'est pas venu
Que je morderay qui maura mordu

I am a dog that gnaws his bone
I crouch and gnaw it all alone
The time will come which is not yet
When I'll bite him by whom I'm bit

WILLIAM KIRBY, publisher of the *Niagara Mail*, saw this "Golden Dog" inscription in 1839 over the lintel of a house on the Rue Baude, Quebec City. His translation appeared in *The Golden Dog (Le chien d'or)* (1877, 1896). The carved stone, with a gilded figure of a dog gnawing a bone and the French rhyme, now adorns the entrance-way to the Quebec City Post Office and recalls a tale of vengeance dating back to 1737.

Good and Evil
See also ETHICS.

All philosophy and all religions teach us this one solemn truth, that in this life the evil surpasses the good.

JAMES DE MILLE, writer and teacher, *A Strange Manuscript Found in a Copper Cylinder* (1888).

Some men are good because they find it cheaper than being wicked. [May 22, 1915]

*

A good man who goes wrong is just a bad man who has been found out. [Sept. 22, 1917]

BOB EDWARDS, writer and publisher of the Calgary *Eye Opener* from 1902 to 1922.

I ask for your prayers. I ask for your assistance and your cooperation. I will make mistakes, but I hope it will be said of me when I give up the highest honour that you can confer on any man, as was said of another in public service: "He wasn't always right; sometimes he was on the wrong side, but never on the side of wrong." That is my dedication; that is my humble declaration.

JOHN G. DIEFENBAKER, member of Parliament for Prince Albert, Saskatchewan, at the conclusion of his acceptance speech, Dec. 10, 1955, succeeding George Drew as leader of the Conservative party.

Government
See also PARLIAMENT.

You must place the Government in advance of public opinion, you must give those in whom the people have confidence an interest in preserving the *system* of your Government, and maintaining the connection with the Mother Country, and then you will hear no more grievances because real ones will be redressed, imaginary ones will be forgotten . . . .

ROBERT BALDWIN, a moderate reformer in Upper Canada who recommended responsible

government, in a letter to Lord Durham, Toronto, Aug. 23, 1828, quoted by P.B. Waite in *Pre-Confederation* (1965).

There are those doubtless who fear the ignorance of the people of Upper Canada; I, on the other hand, stand more in dread of rulers like ours who are virtually independent of them. The people have an interest in good government, but the rulers have a gain by misrule.

WILLIAM LYON MACKENZIE, publisher and ardent reformer, in the *Colonial Advocate*, July 14, 1831, reproduced by Margaret Fairley in her edition of *The Selected Writings of William Lyon Mackenzie* (1960).

The happiness of every country depends upon the character of its people, rather than the form of its government.

*

You may change constitutions for ever, but you cannot change man.

*

There's no tyranny on airth equal to the tyranny of a majority.

THOMAS CHANDLER HALIBURTON, Nova Scotian writer and wit, attributed.

. . . but I may incidentally remark that, while we speak in England of "Her Majesty's Opposition," the Conservatives of Ontario have attempted to better the phrase, and style themselves "Her Majesty's Loyal Opposition."

SIR CHARLES W. DILKE, British imperialist, in *Problems of Greater Britain* (1866–67, 1890).

Phipps, if you had a secretary you could govern the universe.

NICHOLAS FLOOD DAVIN, journalist and M.P., regarding R.W. Phipps, a Toronto pamphleteer and protectionist who helped formulate Macdonald's National Policy, quoted by Sir John Willison in *Reminiscences Political and Personal* (1919).

This is a difficult country to govern.

SIR WILFRID LAURIER, prime minister, in a letter to Sir John Willison, March 7, 1905. This is an echo of Sir John A. Macdonald's observation, "Canada is a hard country to govern," and an anticipation of Lester B. Pearson's statement on March 26, 1965: "It has been said that Canada is the most difficult country in the world to govern. I am perhaps more aware of that than I used to be."

It may not be realized abroad, but it is recognized in this country that a great deal of our political corruption has arisen in the first place in the local legislatures. We are

"A people for high dreaming meant,
But damned by too much government."

WILLIAM WILFRED CAMPBELL, poet, in *Canada* (1907), illustrated by T. Mower Martin.

He once remarked, with the sombre wisdom of experience, that there were only two kinds of government, the "scarcely tolerable" and the "absolutely unbearable," and it was in that spirit that he faced the future.

JOHN W. DAFOE, editor of the Winnipeg *Free Press* until his death in 1944, quoted by George V. Ferguson in *John W. Dafoe* (1948).

You can have too much dignity in government.

MITCH HEPBURN, controversial premier of Ontario from 1934 to 1942, characteristic saying. Quoted by Gordon Donaldson in *Grandeur, Ghosts and Gargoyles* (1974).

Governments propose, and oppositions dispose.

JOHN G. DIEFENBAKER, prime minister, in the House of Commons, Nov. 2, 1962.

The duty of the Opposition is to turn out the government.

JOHN G. DIEFENBAKER, leader of the Opposition, Ottawa, March 13, 1964.

Those people in Ottawa couldn't run a peanut stand.

W.A.C. BENNETT, premier of British Columbia in the 1950s and 1960s, attributed in 1967.

Canadians do not want to escape from the tyranny of big business only to fall into the clutches of big government.

T.C. DOUGLAS, leader of the New Democratic Party, in his farewell address at the Ottawa convention, April 21, 1971.

If nothing else, Rideau Hall has saved us from having a White House.

HUGH L. KEENLEYSIDE, former External Affairs officer, at the conference of the Canadian Broadcasting League in Ottawa, March 23, 1973.

Governor General
See also MONARCHY; PARLIAMENT.

I long for September, beyond which I will not stay If they were to make me Duke of Canada and Prince of Regiopolis as this place is called.

LORD SYDENHAM, the autocratic governor general of the Canadas who was thrown by his horse and died fifteen days later, on Sept. 19, 1841; in a letter to Lord John Russell, June 5, 1841, quoted by John Charles Dent in *The Last Forty Years: Canada Since the Union of 1841* (1881).

It is quite true that after I had been appointed to Canada (1872) Bob Lowe (Lord Sherbrooke) came up to me in a club and said, "Now you ought to make it your business to get rid of the Dominion." To which I replied that I certainly did not intend to be handed down to history as the Governor General who had lost Canada.

LORD DUFFERIN, governor general of Canada from 1872 to 1878, quoted by George W. Ross in "Shall Canada Be Always a Dependency of the Empire?" address before the National Club, Ottawa, Oct. 28, 1908.

A Governor General resembles the humble functionary we see superintending the working of some complicated mass of chain-driven machinery. This personage merely walks about with a little tin vessel of oil in his hand and he pours in a drop here and a drop there, as occasion or the creaking of a joint may require, while his utmost vigilance is directed to no higher aim than the preservation of his wheels and cogs from the intrusion of dust, grits, or other foreign bodies.

LORD DUFFERIN in an address to the National Club, Toronto, Jan. 12, 1877.

It is no easy thing to be a governor-general of Canada. You must have the patience of a saint, the smile of a cherub, the generosity of an Indian prince, and the back of a camel.

LORD LORNE, governor general from 1878 to 1883, quoted by W. Stewart MacNutt in *Days of Lorne* (1955).

I shall expect to hear on arrival that I am in the habit of enforcing seignorial rights after the manner of the old French nobles.

LORD LANSDOWNE, governor general from 1883 to 1888, to a friend in the Colonial Office just prior to his appointment, quoted by Lord Newton in *Lord Lansdowne* (1929).

I cannot go, I have no message for you yet.

EARL GREY, governor general from 1904 to 1911, declining an invitation to address the Canadian Club of Toronto upon his appointment.

For nearly five years I have, quite conscious of my constitutional limitations, walked the tight-rope of platitudinous generalities and I am not aware of having made any serious slip.

EARL GREY, governor general from 1904 to 1911, in a Winnipeg address, Oct. 13, 1909, quoted by R. MacGregor Dawson in *The Government of Canada* (1952).

You know, the Governor-General cannot escape the word "constitutional." You people may say that the government is all right if it votes to your way of thinking but I must say it is all right no matter how it votes.

LORD BYNG, governor general from 1921 to 1926, quoted by John Cowan in *Canada's Governors-General: 1867-1952* (1952).

We don't want any more Mintos. We don't want any more Byngs. I sometimes wonder if we want any more of 'em at all, but we really do.

JOHN W. DAFOE, editor of the Winnipeg *Free Press* until his death in 1944, quoted by George V. Ferguson in *John W. Dafoe* (1948).

Man, according to Aristotle, is a political animal, but there is an exception in the case of a Governor-General. His views on public policy can only be the views of his Ministers. If he touches on the subject he must confine himself to what may be called Governor-Generalities.

JOHN BUCHAN, LORD TWEEDSMUIR, governor general from 1935 to 1940, in *Canadian Occasions: Addresses* (1940).

Nothing touched me quite so much as this comment in a Canadian newspaper: "He made the Crown Canadian." It was too generous a tribute; but that was what I had tried to do.

VINCENT MASSEY, first native-born governor general, from 1952 to 1959, in *What's Past Is Prologue* (1963).

Great Lakes

And His Royal Highness agrees, that all other armed vessels, on these lakes shall be forthwith dismantled, and that no other vessels of war shall be there built or armed.

SIR CHARLES BAGOT, British envoy extraordinary and minister plenipotentiary to the U.S., in the "arms-limitation" clause of the Rush-Bagot Agreement between Great Britain and the United States, Washington, April 28–9, 1817.

It is slightly uncanny; like everything in these great lakes. I have a perpetual feeling that a lake ought not to be this size. A river and a little lake and an ocean are natural; but not these creatures. They are too big, and too smooth, and too sunny; like an American business man.

RUPERT BROOKE, English poet, in a letter to Edmund Gosse, July 27, 1913, written while sailing Lake Superior, from *The Letters of Rupert Brooke* (1968), edited by Geoffrey Keynes.

Grits, The

See also LIBERAL PARTY.

We want only men who are *Clear Grit*.

DAVID CHRISTIE, the farmer who became Speaker of the Senate, coined the term "clear Grit" in 1849 in Toronto. A Grit is a member of the Liberal party; a clear Grit is "an out-and-out purist, and so a thorough-going radical" (in J.M.S. Careless's phrase). The noun *grit* implies something firm, the adjective *clear* something positive and unspotted. Quoted by J.C. Dent in *The Last Forty Years: Canada Since the Union of 1841* (1881).

Hiving the Grits.

SIR JOHN A. MACDONALD, first prime minister, summing up the effect of the Redistribution Act, April 1882, on Ontario constituencies where the Grit vote was strong, quoted by Norah Story in *The Oxford Companion to Canadian History and Literature* (1967).

Group of Seven
See also PAINTING.

All their pictures look pretty much alike, the net result being more like a gargle or a gob of porridge than a work of art . . . the Hot Mush madness . . . .

H.F. GADSBY, art critic who coined the term *the Hot Mush School* in an early attack on the Group of Seven, from "The Hot Mush School," the Toronto *Star*, Dec. 12, 1913.

To the Memory of Tom Thomson Artist Woodsman and Guide who was drowned in Canoe Lake July 8th 1917. He lived humbly but passionately with the wild. It made him brother to all untamed things of nature. It drew him apart and revealed itself wonderfully to him. It sent him out from the woods only to show these revelations through his art. And it took him to itself at last. His fellow artists and other friends and admirers join gladly in this tribute to his character and genius. His body is buried at Owen Sound, Ontario, near where he was born August 1877.

TOM THOMSON, painter and inspiration to the Group of Seven, inscription on his cairn, Canoe Lake, Algonquin Park, reproduced by Ottelyn Addison and Elizabeth Harwood in *Tom Thomson: The Algonquin Years* (1969). The inscription was the work of J.E.H. MacDonald; the memorial was erected Sept. 27, 1917.

Take everything as it comes; the wave passes, deal with the next one.

TOM THOMSON, painter, a saying recalled by Arthur Lismer from their Algoma days when they had gone canoeing in rough water, quoted by John A.B. McLeish in *September Gale* (1955).

If the walls of the Canadian section of the British Empire Exhibition are to be covered with crude cartoons of the Canadian Wilds, devoid of perspective, atmospheric feeling and sense of texture, it is going to be a bad advertisement for this country. We should advise the Department of Immigration and Colonization to intervene to prevent such a catastrophe.

HECTOR CHARLESWORTH, British-born Toronto critic, reaction to paintings of the Group of Seven, in *Saturday Night*, Sept. 15, 1923.

A school-teacher asked her class to name a member of the Group of Seven. One little hand shot up and the boy replied, "Well, I know that one of them was called Jack Pine."

ARTHUR LISMER, teacher and painter, entertained his students with this story during the 1940s. *Jack Pine* is a well-known canvas by Tom Thomson.

When I laid in the painting, it suddenly struck me that it could express Tom Thomson, and thereafter it was Tom I had in mind—his remoteness, his genius, his reticence.

LAWREN HARRIS, member of the Group of Seven, from "In Memoriam to a Canadian Artist" (1950), in *Lawren Harris* (1969), edited by Bess Harris and R.C.P. Colgrove.

I guess I'm like a compass, always heading north. I really do belong to the caribou country, not to the cow country.

A.Y. JACKSON, member of the Group of Seven, to Naomi Jackson Groves, quoted by her in *A.Y.'s Canada* (1969).

I'd like to get down and look at them pictures of barns and outbuildings done by them fellas that used to paint by numbers—what they call yer grope of seven. Tom Thomson, Jack Jackson, John Johnson and Jim Jimson. Now that'd be the kinda culture I could take.

DON HARRON, entertainer, as Charlie Farquharson in an award-winning radio commercial for the opening of the new Art Gallery of Ontario, broadcast Oct. 26, 1974.

Happiness

Let no man imagine that he knows what a present is worth till he has found what happiness can be produced by a blue bead, a yellow button, a needle, or a piece of an old iron hoop.

SIR JOHN ROSS, Arctic explorer, in *Narrative of a Second Voyage in Search of a Northwest Passage* (1835).

Happiness is when the toothache stops.

ROBERT ZEND, Hungarian-born Toronto writer, in the 1960s.

Just remember, baby, there's more to life than happiness.

FRANK SHUSTER, one-half of the Wayne and Shuster comedy team, quoted by Susan Kastner in the Toronto *Star*, Dec. 30, 1965.

We envy the happiness of other people mainly because we believe in it.

IRVING LAYTON, outspoken poet, in *The Whole Bloody Bird* (1969).

Happiness is a moral question, not a question of wealth and property. On the mountain, we have more unhappy people than there are in the slums.

JEAN DRAPEAU, mayor of Montreal, on Olympic spending, quoted by Carl Dow in the *Canadian*, Sept. 19, 1970.

Happiness is always a by-product. It is probably a matter of temperament, and for anything I know it may be glandular. But it is not something that can be demanded from life, and if you are not happy you had better stop worrying about it and see what treasures you can pluck from your own brand of unhappiness.

ROBERTSON DAVIES, man-of-letters, in "The Master's Voice: The Table Talk of Robertson Davies," quoted by Peter C. Newman in *Maclean's*, Sept. 1972.

"You know, Roy, it's happiness that really counts."

"Ah, yes, but happiness cannot buy money."

ROY THOMSON, the British publishing lord, replying to Sir Charles Forte, British catering magnate. Quoted by George Gamester in the Toronto *Star*, April 15 1975.

Health
See also MEDICINE.

Patients should have rest, food, fresh air, and exercise—the quadrangle of health.

SIR WILLIAM OSLER, world-famous physician and medical teacher, in *Sir William Osler: Aphorisms from His Bedside Teachings and Writings* (1950), edited by W.B. Bean.

Stress is essentially the rate of all the wear and tear caused by life.

*

Stress is the state manifested by a specific syndrome which consists of all the nonspecifically induced changes within a biologic system.

HANS SELYE, Montreal medical researcher, in *The Stress of Life* (1956).

The best insurance against disease is health. Only God can give you insurance against illness.

MAURICE DUPLESSIS, premier of Quebec intermittently between 1936 and 1959, quoted by Pierre Laporte in *The True Face of Duplessis* (1961).

Nowadays I have more trouble with my health than with my virtue.

MAURICE BELLEMARE, ageless, wisecracking leader of Quebec's Union Nationale, when asked at a news conference in Montreal, Nov. 29, 1975, how it was that every year he seemed to look younger.

Heart

And so, not by anything unusual that we did or said, but by the rare and beautiful correspondence that is sometimes to be felt between the sentiment of the hour and the hour itself, this afternoon took its place in the dateless calendar of the heart which is so much more valuable a reference than any other.

SARA JEANNETTE DUNCAN, Ontario novelist, in *The Crow's Nest* (1891).

With glowing hearts we see thee rise,
The True North, strong and free,
And stand on guard, O Canada,
We stand on guard for thee.
R. STANLEY WEIR, jurist, who wrote the lyrics to "O Canada" in 1908.

The world is waiting for the sunrise;
Ev'ry rose is heavy with dew.
The thrush on high his sleepy mate is call-
ing,
And my heart is calling you.
GENE LOCKHART, London-born pianist, from the popular song, "The World Is Waiting for the Sunrise" (1919), by Eugene Lockhart and Ernest J. Seitz.

The earth is such a pale thing in space,
So drab a bleached grey—
There are purer, richer, more translucent
colours
In the heart.
LAWREN HARRIS, painter and poet, from "The Earth Winds," *Contrasts* (1922).

The great sea has set me in motion,
Set me adrift,
Moving me as the weed moves in a river.

The arch of sky and mightiness of storms
Have moved the spirit within me,
Till I am carried away
Trembling with joy.
UVAVNUK, Iglulik Eskimo singer, quoted by Knud Rasmussen in *Across Arctic America* (1927).

It is so with everything in the world: *out of the heart are the issues of life!*
LAURA GOODMAN SALVERSON, writer, conclud-ing words of *Confessions of an Immigrant's Daughter* (1939).

Nobody stuffs the world in at your eyes.
The optic heart must venture: a jail-break
And re-creation.
MARGARET AVISON, poet, from "Snow," in *Winter Sun* (1960).

Ideas often last but a day; feelings, dreams almost forever.
GABRIELLE ROY, Quebec novelist, in a letter of

Aug. 1, 1973, quoted by Joan Hind-Smith in *Three Voices* (1975).

A man's heart melts; a woman's breaks.
RAYMOND CANALE, Italian-born playwright living in Toronto, 1975.

Heaven

We are as near to heaven by sea as by land!
SIR HUMPHREY GILBERT, who claimed New-foundland as England's first colony on Aug. 5, 1583, uttered these last words to his crew on board the *Squirrel* when the ten-ton frigate en-countered rough weather and icebergs near the Azores, on Sept. 9, 1583. The *Squirrel* sank without a trace; the words were overheard by the crew on the companion ship, the *Golden Hind*.

To the man who is not a lover of Nature in all her moods the Barren Ground must al-ways be a howling, desolate wilderness; but for my part, I can understand the feel-ing that prompted Saltatha's answer to the worthy priest, who was explaining to him the beauties of Heaven. "My father, you have spoken well; you have told me that Heaven is very beautiful; tell me now one thing more. Is it more beautiful than the country of the musk-ox in summer, when sometimes the mist blows over the lakes, and sometimes the water is blue, and the loons cry very often? That is beautiful; and if Heaven is still more beautiful, my heart will be glad, and I shall be content to rest there till I am very old."
SALTATHA, a brave of the Yellowknife tribe and a companion of Warburton Pike, who quoted the speech in *The Barren Ground of North-ern Canada* (1892).

The most brilliant description the writer ever heard of the hereafter was from an old Cree squaw, toothless, wrinkled like leath-er, belted at the waist like a sack of wool, with hands of dried parchment, and moc-casins some five months too odiferous. Her version ran *that heaven would be full of the mu-sic of running waters and south winds; that there would always be warm gold sunlight like a mid-summer afternoon, with purple shadows, where tired women could rest; that the trees would be cov-*

ered with blossoms, and all the pebbles on the shore like dewdrops.

> AGNES LAUT, pioneer author, from "Story of the Trapper," quoted by L.J. Burpee and H.J. Morgan in *Canadian Life in Town and Country* (1905).

Two men came to a hole in the sky. One asked the other to lift him up. If only he would do so, then he in turn would lend him a hand.

His comrade lifted him up, but hardly was he up when he shouted aloud for joy, forgot his comrade and ran into heaven.

The other could just manage to peep in over the edge of the hole; it was full of feathers inside. But so beautiful was it in heaven that the man who looked in over the edge forgot everything, forgot his comrade whom he had promised to help and simply ran off into all the splendour of heaven.

> INUGPASUGJUK, Eskimo shaman, recounting a legend, in Knud Rasmussen's *Intellectual Culture of the Iglulik Eskimos* (1929).

Heroes

If I am a great man, then a good many of the great men of history are frauds.

> ANDREW BONAR LAW, Canadian-born prime minister of Great Britain, to Lord Beaverbrook during the Ulster crisis, 1913.

O Commander of the old Fort of Ville-Marie, it is time you were among us! We have such pressing need of a young leader like you, a leader of men. Look, on the frontier where you fell a barbarous throng as menacing as the old threatens our French soul. The work we must now undertake is one of total reconstruction and restoration. Arise, Dollard, and live on your granite pedestal. Summon us, with your virile charm, with a hero's accents. We lift toward you our hands quivering like palm leaves, ardent with ambition to serve. Together we shall work for the reconstruction of our family's house. And should you command it, O Dollard, O powerful leader, we are ready to follow you to the supreme holocaust for the defence of our French tongue and our Catholic faith.

> CANON LIONEL GROULX, influential priest and historian at the University of Montreal, in "Si

Dollard revenait," address at the Monument National, Montreal, Jan. 31, 1919, in *Dix ans d'Action française* (1926). "If Dollard Were Alive Today," *French-Canadian Nationalism* (1969), edited by Ramsay Cook. In 1659, Adam Dollard des Ormeaux made an heroic stand against the Iroguois at Long Sault.

They worship false gods in Europe—that is the trouble—Europe is too full of pictures of Napoleon and statues of the Caesars.

> W.L. MACKENZIE KING, prime minister, to Charles Ritchie, April 21, 1945, quoted by Ritchie in *The Siren Years* (1974).

This is in the true Canadian vein. Heroes impose on others, and Canadians do not like to be imposed on, but they think they are, and hence they are inclined to identify with martyrs, particularly as martyrdom is the kind of fate into which even a moral, rational man can be trapped. What most attracts modern Canadians about Louis Riel is not his micro-patriotism as leader of a few thousand people who called themselves a nation, nor his frenzied chiliasm, but the fact that at his trial he preferred condemnation as a man who acted from reasoned motives to acquittal as an inspired lunatic.

> GEORGE WOODCOCK, author and traveller, in *Canada and the Canadians* (1970).

There's no story so fantastic that I cannot imagine myself the hero. And there's no story so evil that I cannot imagine myself the villain.

> LEONARD COHEN, Montreal poet, quoted by Paul Saltzman in *Maclean's*, June 1972.

I say that we cannot make a hero of Papineau. He died in his bed. All heroes should die young, and not in bed.

> MICHEL BRUNET, Quebec historian, interviewed by Ramsay Cook in *The Craft of History* (1973), edited by Eleanor Cook.

Heroism is not a memory of the past. It is the virtue by which a nation can preserve its identity and fulfill its destiny.

> DONALD CREIGHTON, distinguished historian, in "Heroic Beginnings," CBC-TV, Feb. 21, 1973.

Behind every prime minister stands not

only a beaming mother but a Peter Newman ready to reveal him to posterity and the Book-of-the-Month Club as a maladroit dunderhead.

> JOHNNY WAYNE, comedian, in *Douglas Duncan* (1974).

History
See also HISTORY: CANADIAN.

Often has my declaration of 1829 been repeated, that "MAN IS A RECORDING ANIMAL," but never before, was there such happy opportunity for putting records to profitable use.

> ROBERT GOURLAY, agitator in Upper Canada in the *Banished Briton and Neptunian* (1843-46), April 6, 1843, quoted by Louis D. Milani in *Robert Gourlay, Gadfly* (1971).

In the application of the term *Prehistoric*—introduced, if I mistake not, for the first time in this work,—it was employed originally in reference to races which I then assigned reasons for believing had preceded the oldest historical ones in Britain and Northern Europe. But since then the term has become identified with a comprehensive range of speculative and inductive research, in which the archaeologist labours hand in hand with the geologist and ethnologist, in solving some of the most deeply interesting problems of modern science.

> SIR DANIEL WILSON, Scots-born professor of History and English at University College, University of Toronto, introduced the word "prehistoric" in the first edition of *Prehistoric Annals of Scotland* (1851).

A wise nation preserves its records, gathers up its muniments, decorates the tombs of its illustrious dead, repairs its great public structures, and fosters national pride and love of country, by perpetual references to the sacrifices and glories of the past.

> JOSEPH HOWE, Nova Scotian journalist and statesman, in an address at the Howe Festival, Framingham, Massachusetts, Aug. 31, 1871, *Poems and Essays* (1874).

There is no place, no spot of earth, though e'er so wild and desolate, but has its history . . . there is no place where human beings lived, loved, and wrangled, but has its annals, uttered in some shape.

> ALEXANDER MCLACHLAN, folk poet, in "Sketches from the Wanderer," *The Poetical Works* (1900), edited by E. Margaret Fulton in 1974.

If it's all the same to history, it need not repeat itself any more.

> BOB EDWARDS, writer and publisher, in the Calgary *Eye Opener*, May 31, 1919.

What is not disclosed by contemporary writers will never be disclosed. Hence history can never be a true record, and the exact relation of public men to the causes in which they are concerned never can be determined. If there is reticence in the present and ignorance in the future, at best we can have only light in the darkness.

> SIR JOHN WILLISON, journalist, in *Reminiscences Political and Personal* (1919).

I never realized that there was history too, close at hand, beside my very own home. I did not realize that the old grave that stood among the brambles at the foot of our farm was *history*.

> STEPHEN LEACOCK, renowned Canadian writer and humorist, in "The Place of History in Canadian Education," *Report of the Canadian Historical Association 1925* (1926).

I would rather pass into legend than into history.

> CAMILLIEN HOUDE, the colourful mayor of Montreal from 1928 to 1954, attributed.

The historian is both the guardian and the interpreter of the past. He is a treasure-house of human experience.

> GEORGE M. WRONG, who occupied the chair of Modern History at the University of Toronto from 1895 to 1927, in "The Historian and Society," *Canadian Historical Review*, March 1933.

Without any paradox, I would say boldly that history is the most living of things and that there is nothing so present as the past.

*

We carry in our very bones the mind and marrow of our forbears. No, a nation cannot separate itself from its past any more than a river can separate itself from its source, or sap from the soil whence it arises. No generation is self-sufficient. It can and does happen that a generation forgets its history, or turns its back upon it; such an act is a betrayal of History.

CANON LIONEL GROULX, influential priest and historian at the University of Montreal, address before the Second French Language Congress, Quebec City, June 29, 1937, *Directives* (1959), reproduced by Susan Mann Trofimenkoff in *Abbé Groulx* (1973).

Yesterday's news is tomorrow's history.

BLAIR FRASER, journalist, in *The Search for Identity* (1967).

Ah, but don't get me started on history because then you shall know the meaning of eternity.

JOHN G. DIEFENBAKER, member of Parliament for Prince Albert and former prime minister, quoted by Tom Alderman in the *Canadian*, May 29, 1971.

History is the record of an encounter between character and circumstance . . . the encounter between character and circumstance is essentially a story.

DONALD CREIGHTON, distinguished historian, in *Towards the Discovery of Canada* (1972).

I admit Jogfree is not Histry. Jogfree is what we had to start with, and Histry is the mess we all made of it.

DON HARRON, actor-writer who created Charlie Farquharson, the crotchety farmer from Parry Sound, in *Charlie Farquharson's Jogfree of Canada* (1974).

Historians who tread too closely on the heels of the present are likely to be kicked in the teeth. The dead have few to defend them; the living are easily aroused.

DESMOND MORTON, historian, in *NDP: The Dream of Power* (1974).

History: Canadian
See also HISTORY.

We can enjoy none of these pleasures in *America*. The history of the country can be traced no further, than from the arrival of the Europeans; for every thing that happened before that period, is more like a

fiction or a dream, than any thing that really happened.

PETER KALM, Swedish botanist and traveller, in *Travels into North America* (1770-71), translated from the Swedish by J.R. Forster.

When we contemplate the history of Canada as a whole, from the time of Champlain till our own day, we first remark its two great divisions,—the period of French supremacy, and that of British domination. The annals of the former are replete with the incidents of wars against the savages and the people of the coterminous British colonies, since become the United States; the other portion is signalized by parliamentary antagonism of the colonists to all infractions of their nationality and designs against their religion.

FRANÇOIS-XAVIER GARNEAU, historian, in *History of Canada from the Time of Its Discovery till the Union Year 1840-41* (1862), translated by Andrew Bell.

We live at two opposite poles; you at the pole of naturalism; I at that of supernaturalism; but there is one point on which we meet: that is the love of humanity.

HENRI-RAYMOND CASGRAIN, Quebec abbé and historian, thanking Francis Parkman for a copy of his newly published *The Jesuits in North America in the Seventeenth Century* (1867), quoted by Howard Doughty in *Francis Parkman* (1962).

The historians of Canada (with the conspicuous exception of Garneau) have been literary balloonists. Ascending to a high altitude, they have observed what was on the surface, whilst the character of the Canadian people and its changes in different stages of growth, from the present settlements of the eighteenth century to the confederate nation of today—all this has not yet been written. The people of Canada have been left out of Canadian histories . . . . No work deserving to be called a history of the Canadian people has yet been written.

GEORGE SANDFIELD MACDONALD, historian, *Transactions of the Celtic Society of Montreal* (1884).

Notre maître, le passé.

CANON LIONEL GROULX, influential priest and historian at the University of Montreal, personal maxim: "Our master, the past." It became the slogan of the Association de la Jeunesse, a religious-nationalist group headed by Groulx in the 1910s, and was used as the general title of three volumes of his writings. The motto applies to all of French Canada.

Notre maître, l'avenir,
JOSEPH-ADELARD GODBOUT, twice premier of Quebec during the 1930s and 1940s, played on Lionel Groulx's maxim, "*Notre maître, le passé*," to produce his own: "Our master, the future."

Canada's history is as dull as ditchwater and her politics is full of it.
MAURICE HUTTON, historian, quoted by F.H. Underhill in *Canadian Historical Review*, Sept. 1935.

There are two miracles of Canadian history. The first is the survival of French Canada, and the second is the survival of Canada.
F.R. SCOTT, Montreal man-of-letters, remark made in 1952, quoted by Ramsay Cook in *Canada and the French-Canadian Question* (1966).

You find Canadian history dull and if you were teaching it, what would you teach in the second term?
Better to be a nation without a history than to have too much of it as, say, Bulgaria has. We have just enough. I can remember once at a party somebody sneering at one of the Riel Rebellions: only seven people killed. What on earth would he be satisfied with? Tamburlaine's pyramid of human skulls?
JAMES REANEY, poet and playwright, in "Local Grains of Sand" (1964), *Canada: A Guide to the Peaceable Kingdom* (1970), edited by William Kilbourn.

It is about time that Canada entered history.
CHARLES DE GAULLE, president of the French Republic, observation to a visiting Canadian Cabinet minister who complained of the country's difficulties, quoted by Gerald Clark in *Canada: The Uneasy Neighbour* (1965).

In Europe, you can't move without going down into history.
Here, all is a beginning.
RALPH GUSTAFSON, poet, from "In the Yukon," *Selected Poems* (1972).

Ours is not the only nation which has outtravelled its own soul and now is forced to search frantically for a new identity. No wonder, for so many, the past Canadian experience has become not so much a forgotten thing as an unknown thing.
HUGH MACLENNAN, Montreal novelist, in *Rivers of Canada* (1974).

Canadians are a people who remember their present and think it's their history.
J. MICHAEL BLISS, historian, in "Where Are the Pink Pills?" *Canadian Forum*, June 1975.

Hockey
See also SPORTS.

He shoots! He scores!
FOSTER HEWITT, veteran sports broadcaster, coined this phrase, known to hockey fans around the world, while covering on radio a game between the Toronto Maple Leafs and the Boston Bruins. After five hours of play, at 1:45 a.m., April 4, 1933, Ken Doraty, the smallest player on either team, whipped the puck into the Boston net. Hewitt murmured, exhausted: "He shoots! He scores!"

Les Canadiens sont là!
Rallying cry of the Montreal Canadiens. "It was in the early 1950s that *Les Canadiens* really began to *sont là*," according to Trent Frayne in *The Mad Men of Hockey* (1974). First heard to greet the "Flying Frenchmen" in the 1930s, it translates "the Canadiens are here!"

Imagine being paid to play the game you love!
FRANCIS "KING" CLANCY, former hockey player and referee, probably invented this cliché, according to Trent Frayne and Peter Gzowski in *Great Canadian Sports Stories* (1965).

I don't worry about giving autographs. I'll start to worry when the kids stop asking for them.
GORDIE HOWE, a hockey great, quoted by Foster Hewitt in *Foster Hewitt* (1967).

If you play to win, as I do, the game never ends.
STAN MIKITA, high-scoring Czech-born hockey player, in *I Play To Win* (1969).

This was more emotional than winning the

Stanley Cup. A Stanley Cup's for your team and your city, but beating Russia is for your country.

> PHIL ESPOSITO, high-scoring member of Team Canada in the Canada-Soviet hockey series, in the Toronto *Globe and Mail*, Oct. 2, 1972.

When I scored that final goal, I finally realized what democracy was all about.

> PAUL HENDERSON, hockey player, the left-wing on Team Canada who scored the winning goal in Moscow, Sept. 28, 1972, quoted by Dick Beddoes in *Hockey Night in Minsk* (1972).

Hockey is the Canadian metaphor, the rink a symbol of this country's vast stretches of water and wilderness, its extremes of climate, the player a symbol of our national struggle to civilize such a land.

> *

Hockey captures the essence of the Canadian experience in the New World. In a land so inescapably and inhospitably cold, hockey is the dance of life, an affirmation that despite the deathly chill of winter we are alive.

> BRUCE KIDD, former athlete, in *The Death of Hockey* (1972), by Bruce Kidd and John Macfarlane.

Hockey is the Canadian specific.

> AL PURDY, poet, quoted by Dick Beddoes and John Roberts in *Summit 74* (1974).

Home

For Home and Country.

> ADELAIDE HOODLESS, feminist and founder of the Federated Women's Institutes of Canada, of which this is the motto, in 1897.

O Canada! Our home and native land!

> R. STANLEY WEIR, Montreal lawyer and sometime judge of the Exchequer Court of Canada, first line of "O Canada," written in 1908.

"To make things go well" in a home is an art, and the woman who does this is an artist.

> MARJORY MACMURCHY, writer, in *The Woman—Bless Her* (1916).

War is Hell, but what is homesteading?

> JOHN CHIPMAN KERR, who, with his brother

Roland, set out from their homestead at Spirit River, Alberta, for Edmonton when war was declared, leaving the above note on their cabin door. On Sept. 16, 1916, John won the Victoria Cross while serving with the 49th Battalion during the Battle of the Somme; Roland was killed in France in 1917. From G.C. Machum's *Canada's V.C.'s* (1956).

Honesty

I have felt that when a man and woman live closely together, the only danger to their love lies in the unknown depths of the spirit where strange things are stowed away and hardly ever come to the surface in conversation.

> MARGARET LAWRENCE GREENE, Toronto feminist, in a letter to Benedict Greene in 1942, *Love Letters to Baruch* (1973).

Hope

Hope is a pleasant acquaintance, but an unsafe friend.

> THOMAS CHANDLER HALIBURTON, Nova Scotian editor and writer, in *Sam Slick's Wise Saws* (1853).

Looking forward to things is half the pleasure of them.

> L.M. MONTGOMERY, author, in *Anne of Green Gables* (1908), a sentiment ascribed to Anne.

How dear to us thy broad domain,
From East to Western Sea,
Thou land of hope, for all who toil!
Thou True North, strong and free!

> R. STANLEY WEIR, Montreal lawyer, from "O Canada," written in 1908.

Hope springs eternal—but somehow or other troubles never stay long away.

> ARTHUR MEIGHEN, prime minister, address in 1942, from *Unrevised and Unrepented* (1949).

The one good world that men have always desired will emerge from the consciousness of our common nature, our common destiny and our almost instinctive hope that some day there will be a millennium.

> M.M. COADY, founder of the Antigonish Movement in Nova Scotia, remark made in 1959, from *The Man from Margaree* (1971), edited by Alexander F. Laidlaw.

Horses
See also ANIMALS.

Oh, much I wish that I was able
  To build a house like Cartwright's sta-
  ble,
For it does cause me great remorse
  To be worse lodged than Cartwright's
  horse!

DR. JAMES SAMPSON, then mayor of Kingston, verse about the Regency-style country villa built by J.S. Cartwright in 1842 near Kingston which, with its ornate stable, became an asylum in 1856. Quoted by Agnes Maule Machar in *The Story of Old Kingston* (1909).

Lord Ronald said nothing; he flung himself from the room, flung himself upon his horse and rode madly off in all directions.

STEPHEN LEACOCK, dean of Canadian humorists, from "Gertrude the Governess: or, Simple Seventeen," *Nonsense Novels* (1911). Theodore Roosevelt made use of the sentence in a political address and credited the literary conceit to Leacock; it is one of the few internationally known quotations of Canadian origin.

Remember him.
  Somewhere in God's own space
There must be some sweet-pastured place
Where creeks sing on and tall trees grow;
Some Paradise where horses go,
For by the love which guides my pen
I know great horses live again.

STANLEY HARRISON, prairie versifier, who lost his favourite mare, Delia D, during the First World War, quoted by Grant MacEwan in "Poet of the Qu'Appelle Valley: Stanley Harrison," *Fifty Mighty Men* (1958).

Before I left London, a friend of mine, with a great knowledge of this Dominion, gave me his views on various great cities, and when he came to Toronto he prefaced his remarks, I remember, by saying, "There are two things they understand in Toronto—the British Empire and a good horse."

EARL OF BESSBOROUGH, governor general from 1931 to 1935, in an address to the Canadian Club of Toronto, Nov. 24, 1931.

House of Commons
See also PARLIAMENT.

Hansard.

LUKE HANSARD, printer to the British House of Commons from 1774 to 1828. The official records of speeches and debates in the Canadian Parliament are unofficially known as Hansard. The formal titles are *House of Commons Debates: Official Reports* and *Debates of the Senate: Official Reports.*

Call in de membres.

SIR GEORGE-ETIENNE CARTIER, a Father of Confederation, characteristic reply to Liberal criticism in Parliament in the 1850s and 1860s, quoted by John Boyd in *Sir George Etienne Cartier, Bart.* (1914).

Few of the speeches delivered in the House of Commons can be called inspiring. In fact, when not personal, they are prosaic. This can hardly be helped, for a Canadian parliament, like Congress in the United States, deals, as a rule, with matters from which only genius could draw inspiration.

KARL BAEDEKER, famous German travel-book author, in *Canada: A Guidebook* (1894).

Mr. Speaker, Gentlemen, I might as well give you a blast to wake you up. For one whole year I have thought of nothing but how to exterminate as many of you as possible . . . . The only bills you pass are the ones that line your pockets, while the rest of the country has to eat spaghetti and meat balls.

PAUL JOSEPH CHARTIER, "the Mad Bomber of Parliament Hill," an unemployed truck driver from Alberta who planned to throw a bomb into the Commons chamber from the visitor's gallery, fragments from his "if-I-were-president" speech. He was killed when his homemade bomb exploded in the men's room of the Parliament buildings, May 18, 1966. Quoted by Harry Bruce in "The Mad Bomber of Parliament Hill," the *Canadian*, Sept. 10 and 17, 1966.

Parliament is being turned into a political arena.

ROBERT THOMPSON, former leader of the Social Credit party, quoted by Peter C. Newman in "Robert Thompson" (1967), *Home Country* (1973).

Parliament, basically, is a place of accountability.

GRATTAN O'LEARY, editor and senator, Dec. 11, 1968.

Howe, C.D.

Her Majesty pays me for doing something useful and I don't think I'm doing anything useful when I sit in the House and listen to the kind of blather that's being talked here.

C.D. HOWE, "Minister of Everything," who represented Port Arthur in the House of Commons from 1935 to 1957.

Mr. Green: . . . I am not too sure that this government would not do away with the preferences entirely if they felt they could get away with it as far as the public were concerned.
Mr. Howe: Who would stop us? Don't take yourself too seriously. If we wanted to get away with it who would stop us?
Mr. Green: That is just typical of the minister; if he wanted to get away with anything who would stop him?

C.D. HOWE, minister of Transport, in an exchange with Howard Green in the House of Commons, May 21, 1951. "Who would stop us?" became a household phrase.

What's a million?

C.D. HOWE'S famous quip was never actually uttered by him. What Howe did say in the House of Commons, June 14, 1951, was: "So I hope the hon. member will agree that to operate a department with 1,100 people for a year, $3 million is not exorbitant. Will he go that far with me?"

You keep out of the taxpayer's pocket and I'll stay out of your hair.

C.D. HOWE to Gordon McGregor when the government assumed ownership of TCA (later Air Canada), quoted by Ronald A. Keith in Bush Pilot with a Briefcase (1972).

Today I'm busier'n a whore working two beds.

C.D. HOWE during the 1950s, attributed by Robert Stanfield, quoted by Geoffrey Stevens in Stanfield (1973).

I never give instructions, I just give responsibilities.

C.D. HOWE'S reply when asked, "What are your instructions, C.D.?" Quoted by Peter C. Newman in The Canadian Establishment: Volume One (1975).

Hudson's Bay Company

Pro Pelle Cutem

Motto on the coat of arms of the Hudson's Bay Company, granted to Prince Rupert on May 2, 1670. It means, "Skin for the Sake of the Fleece."

The Governor and Company of Adventurers of England trading into Hudson's Bay.

CHARLES II, king of Great Britain and Ireland, signed the letters patent on May 2, 1670; the above is the official title of the Hudson's Bay Company. The "rights of government" were returned to Queen Victoria when the monopolistic franchise was withdrawn with the Deed of Surrender, Nov. 19, 1869.

The Company have for eighty years slept at the edge of a frozen sea; they have shown no curiosity to penetrate further themselves, and have exerted all their art and power to crush that spirit in others.

JOSEPH ROBSON, HBC supervisor, in An Account of Six Years' Residence in Hudson's-Bay, from 1733 to 1736, and 1744 to 1747 (1752). Critics characterized the Hudson's Bay Company's unwillingness to establish inland posts to compete with the French and English traders as "the sleep by the frozen sea."

After some consideration, and much expectoration, he slowly replied: "Le'ss see, 'B.C.' in ancient history means 'Before Christ,' I b'lieve—'tleast so the school-marm used to tell when I was to school—tharfore, I calc'late 'H.B.C.' to mean 'Here before Christ'; fur this 'tarnal location don't 'pear to've bin much over-run with strangers since that period."

M.E. JOHNSON, writer, in Dayspring in the Far West (1875). The initials appear on the company's flag.

Humour

See also MALAPROPISMS.

The public will pay more for laughing than for any other privilege.

BOB EDWARDS, writer and publisher of the Calgary Eye Opener, May 11, 1918.

An English reviewer writing in a literary journal, the very name of which is enough to put contradiction to sleep, has said of my writing, "What is there, after all, in Professor Leacock's humour but a rather ingenious mixture of hyperbole and myosis?"

The man was right. How he stumbled upon this trade secret, I do not know. But I am willing to admit, since the truth is out, that it has long been my custom in preparing an article of a humorous nature to go down to the cellar and mix up half a gallon of myosis with a pint of hyperbole. If I want to give the article a decidedly literary character, I find it well to put in about half a pint of paresis. The whole thing is amazingly simple.

STEPHEN LEACOCK, dean of Canadian humorists, in *Further Foolishness* (1916).

A man will freely confess that he has no ear for music, or no taste for fiction, or no interest in religion. But I have yet to see the man who announces that he has no sense of humour.

STEPHEN LEACOCK, in "Have the English Any Sense of Humour?" from *My Discovery of England* (1922).

The essence of humour is human kindliness.

*

Humour may be defined as the kindly contemplation of the incongruities of life, and the artistic expression thereof.

STEPHEN LEACOCK, in "On the Nature of Humour," *Humour and Humanity* (1937).

He who laughs, lasts.

PAUL SOLES, television personality, in the 1950s.

Canadians are the only people in the world psychologically capable of distinguishing Wayne from Shuster.

DOUG FETHERLING, Toronto writer, in *Tabloid*, Dec. 1971.

Wit: to indulge in hostilities without having to bear the consequences.

LOUIS DUDEK, Montreal poet, in *Epigrams* (1975).

The laugh is the reverse of a breakdown;
it's a breakup.

BERNARD SLADE, California-based playwright, quoted by Tom Hedley in the *Canadian*, July 26, 1975.

Hydro

We must deliver power to such an extent that the poorest working man will have electric light in his home.

SIR ADAM BECK, founder and chairman of Ontario Hydro from 1906 to 1925, made this pledge in 1908.

Ideals

One of the reasons why the *Eye Opener* has so many high ideals is that Calgary is over 3,000 feet above the level of the sea.

BOB EDWARDS, writer and publisher of the Calgary *Eye Opener*, Aug. 1, 1908.

What great and enduring achievement has the world ever accomplished that was not based on idealism?

SIR WILFRID LAURIER, in an address in New York, 1916, quoted by O.D. Skelton in *The Canadian Dominion* (1919).

Man's spirit will grow in victory as well as in defeat, even in humiliation, as long as he defends noble ideals.

ARVED VIIRLAID, Estonian writer living in Toronto, in *Year of Storms* (1949).

Idealist: a cynic in the making.

IRVING LAYTON, outspoken poet, in *The Whole Bloody Bird* (1969).

Ideas

See also INTELLIGENCE; WISDOM.

New ideas are born in stables and brought up in jails. Whenever a new cause is struggling its way to recognition its adherents frequently have to die for it.

J.B. McLachlan, editor and secretary of the United Mine Workers of America in Cape Breton, in the *Maritime Labour Herald*, Nov. 17, 1923. Quoted by Paul MacEwan in "Labour and Politics in Cape Breton," the *Cape Breton Highlander*, April 17, 1968.

Ideas are born; they develop; they are transformed; but they never die. The history of ideas is the history of the race. They are the real events.
SIR ANDREW MACPHAIL, writer and teacher, in "A History of the Idea of Evolution," *Dalhousie Review*, 1925.

Give the people ideas and they'll put them to work.
FATHER JAMES TOMPKINS, a founder of the Antigonish Movement at St. Francis Xavier University during the 1920s, quoted by E.A. Corbett in "Dr. James Tompkins," *Pioneers in Adult Education in Canada* (1955), edited by Harriet Rouillard.

Ideas have hands and feet. They'll do work for you.
FATHER JAMES TOMPKINS, quoted by John R. Chafe in "God's Greatest Nuisance," from *In Search of Canada* (1971), by the editors of *Reader's Digest*.

No one has ever had an idea in a dress suit.
SIR FREDERICK G. BANTING, Toronto medical researcher who received the Nobel Prize in 1923 for his discovery of insulin, attributed.

I know a lot of my friends who won't drive a car that is of a model more than two years old. A great many of us have machinery in our heads that is of a model a hundred years old.
J.S. WOODSWORTH, leader of the CCF party, quoted by F.H. Underhill in *In Search of Canadian Liberalism* (1960).

This lack of mental aliveness is fundamental. Canada is a non-conductor for any sort of intellectual current.
FREDERICK PHILIP GROVE, novelist, in "The Plight of Canadian Fiction? A Reply," *University of Toronto Quarterly*, July 1938.

Ideology did not end in Canada. It simply did not begin.
JOHN PORTER, social scientist from Carleton

University, in "Canadian Character in the Twentieth Century" (1967), *Canada: A Sociological Profile* (1971), edited by W.E. Mann.

Identity
See NATIONAL IDENTITY.

Immigration
See also EMIGRATION.

In this secluded spot lie the mortal remains of 5,424 persons who, fleeing from pestilence and famine in Ireland in the year 1847, found in America but a grave.
Memorial on Grosse Ile, St. Lawrence River. "Grosse Isle is now an animal quarantine station, and is normally closed to visitors, though there is a suggestive view of it in Montmagny on the southern bank. The fever sheds still stand, and a monument commemorates the Irish who died on the island." James Morris in *Heaven's Command* (1973).

New Canadians.
HOWARD ANGUS KENNEDY, journalist, gave currency to the term in *New Canada and the New Canadians* (1907), a study of Western immigration. The term *New Canadians* for immigrants came into favour around the turn of the century, and was replaced during the centennial year by the word *ethnic*.

I was not long in the country before I ran up against a fact which surprised and startled me: *The English immigrant is not popular in Canada*. This remark applies in a special degree to the Londoner. Professor Mavor has an advertisement cut from a local paper asking for workmen, and which states that no English need apply. Scotsmen, Welshmen and Scandinavians are the favourites, pretty much in the order given. The reason, so far as I could make out, for this strange fact is the Englishman's inveterate habit of grumbling, and his unwillingness to adapt himself to new conditions.
KEIR HARDIE, British socialist and leader of the Independent Labour Party of Great Britain, made these remarks in the *Labour Leader*, Oct. 4, 1907, quoted by Basil Stewart in *The Land of the Maple Leaf* (1908).

When I speak of quality I have in mind, I think, something that is quite different from what is in the mind of the average writer or speaker upon the question of Immigration. I think a stalwart peasant in a sheep-skin coat, born on the soil, whose forefathers have been farmers for ten generations, with a stout wife and a half-dozen children, is good quality.

SIR CLIFFORD SIFTON, minister of the Interior from 1896 to 1905, who encouraged the immigration to western Canada of Ukrainian and Doukhobor farmers and labourers, in "The Immigrants Canada Wants," *Maclean's*, April 1, 1922.

Assimilation is wheat fields and symphonies.

VERA LYSENKO, writer, in *Men in Sheepskin Coats* (1947).

We all want to increase the population of this country and for that purpose if they are equally good people I don't believe that any immigrant, no matter where he comes from or how good he is, is as good as another Canadian baby, because the immigrant has to learn to be a Canadian and the baby is a Canadian to start with.

J.W. PICKERSGILL, minister of Citizenship and Immigration, in a speech made in Victoria, April 15, 1955, repeated in the House of Commons, April 18, 1955.

The refugee is the everyman of our time.

HENRY KREISEL, novelist and academic, in *The Betrayal* (1964).

This place is nice and empty. What you should do is organize reverse immigration, and make it even emptier while you still have a chance.

SLAWOMIR MROZEK, Polish playwright, visiting Toronto in 1969.

Imperialism
See COLONIALISM.

Indians
See also ESKIMOS.

They come like foxes through the woods. They attack like lions. They take flight like birds, disappearing before they have really appeared. [About the Iroquois]

*

We cannot go back very far in our researches in their past history, as they have

no libraries other than the memory of their old men; and perhaps we should find nothing worthy of publication. [About the Algonquins]

JÉRÔME LALEMANT, Jesuit missionary and martyr, in "Relation" (1660), *The Jesuit Relations and Allied Documents* (1954), edited by Edna Kenton.

Ha! Long live the *Hurons*; who without Laws, without Prisons, and without Torture, pass their Life in a State of Sweetness and Tranquility, and enjoy a pitch of Felicity to which the *French* are utter Strangers. We live quietly under the Laws of Instinct and innocent Conduct, which wise Nature has imprinted upon our Minds from our Cradles.

ADARIO, a fictitious Huron based on a chief called "the Rat" who died in 1701, used by the traveller Baron de La Hontan in the third volume of his memoirs (1703) to express his own unorthodox opinions, in *New Voyages to North America* (1905), translated by Reuben Gold Thwaites.

Father, I love your daughter, will you give her to me, that the small roots of her heart may entangle with mine, so that the strongest wind that blows shall never separate them.

Chippewa brave addressing his future father-in-law, quoted by J. Long in *Voyages and Travels of an Indian Interpreter and Trader* (1791).

I do not mean to say that they are without the reasoning faculty, but they certainly appear excessively stupid. I understand that their numbers decrease each year,—if they were wholly extinct, I do not think that human nation would be a great sufferer by it.

HUGH GRAY, traveller, commenting on the Indian population, in *Letters from Canada* (1809).

Should you ask me, whence these stories?
Whence these legends and traditions,
With the odours of the forest,
With the dew and damp of meadows,
With the curling smoke of wigwams,
With the rushing of great rivers,
With their frequent repetitions,
And their wild reverberations,
As of thunder in the mountains?
    I should answer, I should tell you,

"From the forests and the prairies,
From the great lakes of the Northland
. . . ."

HENRY WADSWORTH LONGFELLOW, American
poet, from the opening lines of *The Song of
Hiawatha* (1855), part of which is set in Canada, reprinted from *The Poetical Works of
Longfellow* (1908).

Yes, we must now work for the good of all
the nations. We must establish laws for all
and must work to get them accepted. Are
there not nights when there is danger that
one person may kill another? We must set
this matter right. We must have a league
of nations, so that all may live in peace
and tranquility, undisturbed by the shed-
ding of blood.

HIAWATHA, the semi-legendary Indian chief
who with Dekanahwideh co-founded the Iroquois Confederacy. His traditional words were
recalled by an Onondaga chief at the Six Nations Reserve in 1888. Retold by Ella Elizabeth Clark in *Indian Legends of Canada* (1960).

But the face of the red man is now no
longer seen. All traces of his footsteps are
fast being obliterated from his once favourite haunts, and those who would see the
aborigines of this country in their original
state, or seek to study their native manners
and customs, must travel far through the
pathless forest to find them.

PAUL KANE, painter, in *Wanderings of an Artist
among the Indians of North America* (1859).

Spanish civilization crushed the Indian;
English civilization scorned and neglected
him; French civilization embraced and
cherished him.

FRANCIS PARKMAN, historian who chronicled
the fall of New France, in *Pioneers of France in
the New France* (1865).

Now you see me stand before you all: what
has been done here today has been done
openly before the Great Spirit and before
the nation, and I hope I may never hear
any one say that this treaty has been done
secretly: and now in closing this council, I
take off my glove, and in giving you my
hand I deliver over my birthright and
lands: and in taking your hand I hold fast
all the promises you have made, and I
hope they will last as long as the sun rises

and the water flows, as you have said.

MAWEDOPENAIS, chief spokesman of the Ojib-
way tribes, at Fort Francis when Treaty Number 3 (the North-West Angle Treaty) was
signed, Oct. 1873. Quoted by Alexander Morris in *The Treaties of Canada with the Indians of
Manitoba and the North-West Territories* (1880).

We did not give you our country; you took
it from us. Look how I stand with these
people. Look at me. You think I am a fool,
but you are a greater fool than I am. This
house, the home of the English, is a medicine house and you come here to tell us
lies. We do not want to hear them. Now I
have said enough. You can go back. Say
no more. Take your lies with you. I will
stay with these people. The country we
came from belonged to us; you took it from
us; we will live here.

SITTING BULL, Sioux Indian chief who found
sanctuary in Canada after the battle of Little
Bighorn in 1876, reply to American General
Alfred Terry who urged him to return with his
small band to the United States, quoted by
John Peter Turner in *The North West Mounted
Police: 1873-1893* (1955).

Brothers, we've had a good fight today.
We've worked hard and are hungry.
You've plenty of grub; send us in some.
Tomorrow we'll finish the fight.

ALMIGHTY VOICE, young Cree brave who
evaded capture for three years, at a shoot-out
near Duck Lake, May 30, 1897. Quoted by
Captain Ernest J. Chambers in *The Royal
North-West Mounted Police: A Corps History*
(1906).

One hardly knows whether to take an Indian as a problem, a nuisance, or a possibility. He may be considered from a picturesque, philanthropic, or pestiferous
standpoint, according to your tastes or op-
portunities. You may idealize him, or realize him.

EMILY GOWAN MURPHY, early feminist writer,
Janey Canuck in the West (1910).

Yes, we Indians have lost many things. We
have lost our lands, our forests, our game,
our fish; we have lost our ancient religion,
our ancient dress; some of the younger
people have even lost their fathers' language and the legends and traditions of

their ancestors. We cannot call those old things back to us; they will never come again. We may travel many days up the mountain trails, and look in the silent places for them. They are not there. We may paddle many moons on the sea, but our canoes will never enter the channel that leads to the yesterdays of the Indian people.

JOE CAPILANO, Squamish chief, quoted by Pauline Johnson in *Legends of Vancouver* (1911).

There are those who think they pay me a compliment in saying I am just like a white woman. I am an Indian, and my aim, my joy, my pride, is to sing the glories of my people.

PAULINE JOHNSON, Mohawk poet, in *Legends of Vancouver* (1911).

The Buckskin Curtain

MORRIS C. SHUMIATCHER, Regina lawyer, coined this phrase in "The Buckskin Curtain," *The Beaver*, autumn 1959. "I think the Indian Canadian wishes to enlarge the world in which he lives beyond the buckskin curtain of his reserve."

I think that all of us feel a sense of guilt, not so much toward the Indian as toward the fact that we haven't really addressed our minds to this problem.

PIERRE ELLIOTT TRUDEAU, prime minister, to students at Canada House, London, England, Jan. 13, 1969.

O God! Like the Thunderbird of old I shall rise again out of the sea; I shall grab the instruments of the white man's success—his education, his skills, and with these new tools I shall build my race into the proudest segment of your society. Before I follow the great Chiefs who have gone before us, oh Canada, I shall see these things come to pass.

CHIEF DAN GEORGE, elected chief of the Salish tribe on the West Coast, recited "A Lament for Confederation" at Vancouver's Empire Stadium, July 1, 1967.

When the white man came we had the land and they had the bibles; now they have the land and we have the bibles.

CHIEF DAN GEORGE, actor and spokesman,

quoted by Gerald Walsh in *Indians in Transition* (1971).

My heart soars like a hawk.

CHIEF DAN GEORGE, in the Hollywood film *Little Big Man* (1970). Playing an elderly chief, he addresses these words to his son, played by Dustin Hoffman.

I am a chief, but my power to make war is gone, and the only weapon left to me is speech. It is only with tongue and speech that I can fight my people's war.

CHIEF DAN GEORGE, Indian spokesman, in *My Heart Soars* (1974).

Kemo Sabe. Good friend . . . . Actually, I never did find out what it really means.

JAY SILVERHEELS, Mohawk athlete and actor who from 1949 played the part of Tonto, "the faithful Indian scout and companion" to the Lone Ranger, quoted by Dick Brown in the *Canadian*, Aug. 9, 1975. "Kemo Sabe" was Tonto's characteristic way of addressing the Lone Ranger in countless radio, film and TV adaptations of Fran Striker's character.

Industry
See also LABOUR; MANUFACTURING.

Whenever in social or industrial relations the claims of industry and humanity are opposed, those of industry must make way.

W.L. MACKENZIE KING, future prime minister, in *Industry and Humanity* (1918). The book's motto is "Over all nations is humanity."

Instead of the government taking over industry when the war broke out, industry took over the government.

CLAIRIE GILLIS, socialist M.P., on April 12, 1941, quoted by David A. Frank in *The People's History of Cape Breton* (1971).

If Canada is underdeveloped, so is Brigitte Bardot.

H.R. MACMILLAN, British Columbia lumber magnate, objecting to the inclusion of Canada on a list of underdeveloped countries, at an industrial conference at Versailles, France, in the 1950s.

In 1909, the Canadian Manufacturers' Association launched another crusade for the support of Canadian home industries. One of the first companies proudly advertising its product as "Made in Canada" was Coca-Cola. Things went better . . . .

J. MICHAEL BLISS, historian, "Canadianizing American Business," *Close the 49th Parallel, Etc.* (1970), edited by Ian Lumsden.

Inflation
See also ECONOMICS; MONEY.

Artists stand depressions quite well, depressions look so much like their regular brand of prosperity.

DAVID MILNE, artist, quoted by *Time*, Feb. 10, 1975.

Inflation makes misery unanimous; it is universal poverty.

ARTHUR MEIGHEN, prime minister, from "Socialism," a speech to the Kiwanis Club of Vancouver, Oct. 21, 1943, in *Unrevised and Unrepented* (1949).

A recession is when your neighbour has to tighten his belt. A depression is when you have to tighten your own belt. And a panic is when you have no belt to tighten and your pants fall down.

T.C. DOUGLAS, leader of the New Democratic Party, remark made in 1968, quoted in *T.C. Douglas* (1971).

When you spend money abroad it is not inflationary.

PIERRE ELLIOTT TRUDEAU, prime minister, to Ottawa reporters after returning from a Mediterranean cruise, Sept. 10, 1968.

Having a little inflation is like being a little pregnant—inflation feeds on itself and quickly passes the "little" mark.

DIAN COHEN, Montreal economist, in the Toronto *Star*, Oct. 14, 1972.

We'll wrestle inflation to the ground.

PIERRE ELLIOTT TRUDEAU, prime minister, in a campaign speech on CBC-TV, July 1974.

Insects
See MOSQUITOES.

Intelligence
See also IDEAS; THOUGHT.

You can grow corns or potatoes, but you cannot grow brains. Brains come hard and they come high.

SIR WILLIAM OSLER, physician and medical teacher, from *Sir William Osler: Aphorisms from His Bedside Teachings and Writings* (1950), edited by W.B. Bean.

This is what I call *la nouvelle trahison des clercs*: this self-deluding passion of a large segment of our thinking population for throwing themselves headlong—spiritually and mentally—into purely escapist pursuits.

PIERRE ELLIOTT TRUDEAU, future prime minister, in "New Treason of the Intellectuals" (1962), *Federalism and the French Canadians* (1968).

Intelligence can be used for many things. It seems to me that it should be used especially for living.

JEAN-PAUL DESBIENS, "Brother Anonymous," in *For Pity's Sake* (1965), translated by Frédéric Côté.

A highbrow is a person who can listen to the "William Tell Overture" without thinking of the Lone Ranger.

AL BOLISKA, Toronto radio personality, in *The World's Worst Jokes* (1966).

In the vortex of process there are no fixed points of view. Understanding is never a point of view.

MARSHALL MCLUHAN, media pundit, in a letter to the Toronto *Star*, March 16, 1971.

A lot of people have the wrong idea of me. I'm an omnibrow—not a highbrow, not a lowbrow—an omnibrow.

LISTER SINCLAIR, CBC writer and producer, quoted by Marci McDonald in the Toronto *Star*, July 8, 1972.

Internationalism
See also EXTERNAL AFFAIRS.

Last century made the world a neighbourhood; this century must make it a brotherhood.

J.S. WOODSWORTH, later leader of the Co-operative Commonwealth Federation (CCF), in

Feb. 1917, quoted by Margaret Fairley in *Spirit of Canadian Democracy* (1945).

Nationalism provides the only sure basis for internationalism.

HAROLD ADAMS INNIS, distinguished economic historian, in "Government Ownership and the Canadian Scene" (1933), *Essays in Canadian Economic History* (1956), edited by Mary Quayle Innis.

The real internationalism is the manias we have with each other.

JOHN GRIERSON, founder of the National Film Board in 1939, attributed.

My internationalism, you see, is the internationalism of the English language.

ROBIN SKELTON, writer and editor of the *Malahat Review*, quoted by Linda Sandler in *Books in Canada*, April 1975.

Irish

Ireland is the Israel that failed.

IRVING LAYTON, outspoken poet, in *The Whole Bloody Bird* (1969).

I've been called Black Irish, so it must mean something nice.

MICHAEL HANLON, Toronto journalist, in Dec. 1973.

Isolationism
See also EXTERNAL AFFAIRS.

Splendid isolation.

SIR GEORGE E. FOSTER, prominent Conservative finance minister, in the House of Commons, Jan. 16, 1896: "But he [the patriot] would read the signs of the times not aright in these somewhat troublesome days, when the great mother Empire stands splendidly isolated in Europe, with interest stretching over the wide world . . . ."

It is true, England was—as the Minister of Finance said on a former occasion, and is yet, isolated—whether splendidly isolated or dangerously isolated, I will not now debate; but for my part, I think splendidly isolated, because this isolation of England comes from her superiority, and her superiority today seems to be manifest.

SIR WILFRID LAURIER, prime minister, in the House of Commons, Feb. 5, 1896.

We live in a fire-proof house, far from inflammable materials.

RAOUL DANDURAND, Canadian delegate to the League of Nations Assembly, expressing isolationist sentiment, Oct. 2, 1924, from *Documents on Canadian Foreign Policy: 1917-1939* (1962), edited by Walter A. Riddell.

Jews

We don't attack Jews, we simply defend our country against their conspiracy.

ADRIEN ARCAND, Quebec fascist, quoted by Frederick Edwards in "Fascism in Canada," *Maclean's*, April 15, 1938.

Hampered by racial-religious distinctions to start with, relations between the French, English and Jews of Montreal are still further complicated by the fact that all three groups suffer from an inferiority complex—the French because they are a minority in Canada, the English because they are a minority in Quebec, and the Jews because they are a minority elsewhere.

GWETHALYN GRAHAM, Montreal novelist, in *Earth and High Heaven* (1944).

Well groomed, we stand on broadloomed floors
Inhaling deeply the smell of money,
Well-adjusted children of the new era
Blankly awaiting the next pogrom.

DAVID LEWIS STEIN, Toronto journalist, from "Poem," *First Flowering* (1956), edited by Anthony Frisch.

Jews are not permitted to hand Hitler posthumous victories.

EMIL L. FACKENHEIM, German-born rabbi and philosopher, in *Quest for Past and Future* (1968).

The Jew is neither a race nor a religion but a complaint.

IRVING LAYTON, outspoken poet, in *The Whole Bloody Bird* (1969).

I remember, when I was five or six, falling in love with Edward, Prince of Wales. Of the many arguments with which my Mother might have dampened my ardour, she chose surely the most extraordinary. "You can't marry him. He isn't Jewish."

FREDELLE BRUSER MAYNARD, prairie writer, in *Raisins and Almonds* (1972).

The last thing in the world you did, if you were a teenage Jewish boy in the Sault, was to date a teenage Jewish girl.

MORLEY TORGOV, Sault Ste. Marie-born Toronto lawyer, in *A Good Place To Come From* (1974).

To live in Canada, to write in French, is for me the pursuit of an undertaking that did not end in my ancestors, the Jews of Babylon.

NAÏM KATTAN, Baghdad-born Quebec intellectual, in "Ecrire en français," *Boundary 2*, fall 1974.

Being Jewish cost me the lead in *The Bells of St. Mary's*.

LARRY ZOLF, zany broadcaster, quoted by James Quig in *Weekend*, April 5, 1975.

Coming from Canada, being a writer and Jewish as well, I have impeccable paranoia credentials.

MORDECAI RICHLER, novelist, in "It's a Plot," *Playboy*, May 1975.

Joual
See also LANGUAGE.

Am I cherishing an illusion? It seems to me we used to speak better, not so slurred, not so coarse, not so screechy, not so *joual*. But who will settle that? When the universities get their millions, they will be able to commission linguists to conduct an inquiry into the state of our language. Maybe then we shall learn how many good intentions can bring about such pitiful results.

*

The word *joual* is a summary description of what it is like to talk *joual*, to say *joual* instead of *cheval*, horse.

*

For one is sure not to mangle French when one learns only English. So the language will die, but it will die virgin and martyr.

ANDRÉ LAURENDEAU, Quebec editor, in "The Language We Speak," *Le Devoir*, Oct. 21, 1959.

For primitives, a primitive language is good enough; animals get along with a few grunts. But if you want to attain to human speech, joual is not sufficient. You can make do with a board and some whitewash if you want to paint a barn, but finer tools are necessary for the Mona Lisa.

JEAN-PAUL DESBIENS, who as "Frère Untel" wrote *The Impertinences of Brother Anonymous* (1962), translated by Miriam Chapin.

Journalists
See also NEWS.

A journalist is hardly an authority upon anything—unless perhaps upon the appraisal of the drift of public opinion.

JOHN W. DAFOE, editor of the Winnipeg *Free Press* until his death in 1944, in a convocation address at the University of Manitoba, May 1923, quoted by Murray Donnelly in *Dafoe of the Free Press* (1968).

And I have seen all this company with the goodly fellows of the Press, poets who never wrote a poem, sentimentalists who never shed a tear, cynics who never refused a companion in distress, historians who recorded nothing older than a day.

BEVERLEY BAXTER, Toronto-born journalist and British M.P., contributor of the fortnightly "London Letter" to *Maclean's*, in *Strange Street* (1935).

To become a newspaperman you need the hide of a dinosaur, the stamina of a Chinese coolie, the wakefulness and persistence of a mosquito, the analytic powers of a detective and the digging capacity of a steam shovel.

ROY GREENAWAY, journalist, in *The News Game* (1966).

The only journalism course I feel qualified

to give consists of five words, "Travel, suffer, love, read, write."

RICHARD J. NEEDHAM, Toronto columnist, in *A Friend in Needham, or a Writer's Notebook* (1969).

Over a highball he looks at me and asks, "How do you think you would like it, working for *Time?*"

I tell him I think I might like it a lot. "How do you like it?" I ask.

"Oh, I like it."

"What's it like?" I ask him.

"Well," he says, thoughtfully, "it's like working in the world's finest whorehouse."

DALTON CAMP, influential Conservative, conversing with an anonymous *Time* reporter, in *Gentlemen, Players and Politicians* (1970).

The job of a journalist is to do what he's told by the editors. Period.

JACK CAHILL, bureau chief of the Toronto *Star*, quoted in the *Last Post*, May 1972.

The foreign correspondent is simply a domestic reporter on his way to a distant fire.

MORLEY SAFER, former CBC television reporter and controversial Vietnam war correspondent for CBS, quoted in the Toronto *Globe and Mail*, Aug. 1, 1974.

I think the role of a political journalist is not to have definite partisan loyalties. My interpretation of journalistic objectivity is to be against everybody who's in power.

PETER C. NEWMAN, editor and columnist, quoted by Robert Chodos in *Toronto Life*, Aug. 1974.

Justice

See also CRIME; LAW; PRISON.

It is not a pleasant duty for me to have to sentence you only to prison for life; your crime was unmitigated murder, you deserve to be hanged. Had the jury done their duty I might now have the painful satisfaction of condemning you to death . . . . You, gentlemen of the jury, permit me to say that it would give me great pleasure to see you hanged, each and every one of you, for bringing in a murderer guilty only of manslaughter.

MATTHEW B. BEGBIE, "the hanging judge,"

later chief justice of British Columbia, at the trial of an American gunman named Gilchrist, Jan. 1863, quoted by Edward Nicolls in the *Canadian*, July 1898.

It will take six months or more for the colonial secretary to deal with the matter and months more before we learn of his decision. But you will not be interested in what he decides, for you are to be hanged Monday morning.

MATTHEW B. BEGBIE to an American desperado convicted of murder at the assizes in the Cariboo, who had warned Judge Begbie that he would appeal his sentence, quoted by D.A. McGregor in *Canadian Portraits: CBC Broadcasts* (1940), edited by R.G. Riddell.

The eternal principles of justice are far more important than thousands of millions of acres of land. Let us adhere to those principles of justice, and in so doing we will have the surest foundation for securing justice on every occasion.

SIR WILFRID LAURIER, prime minister, in the House of Commons in 1882, speaking of a boundary dispute between Manitoba and Ontario. Quoted by O.D. Skelton in *Life and Letters of Sir Wilfrid Laurier* (1921).

I maintain that the principle of the demands of the Métis of the North-West Territories, in consideration of extinction of the Indian title, was recognized at that time; justice must be the same on the banks of the Saskatchewan or of the Qu'Appelle, as on those of the Red River or the Assiniboine.

EDWARD BLAKE, leader of the federal Liberal party, in an address on the execution of Louis Riel, in 1885.

If I really thought you were guilty, I would give you ten years.

C.B. ROULEAU, Edmonton judge and member of the Northwest Territories Council, upon dispensing a two-year sentence to a Chinese in 1900.

There have always been those who imagined that "a whiff of grape shot" would stop the cry of the people for justice.

FRED J. DIXON, a leader of the Winnipeg General Strike, in "Kaiserism in Canada," *Western Labour News*, June 23, 1919.

Justice shall be taken to every man's door.

> JACK H. SISSONS, first justice of the Territorial Court of the Northwest Territories from 1955 to 1965, maxim. Judge Sissons, whose bailiwick covered one-third of Canada's land mass, was called *Ekoktoegee* (the One Who Listens to Things) by the Eskimos. From *Judge of the Far North* (1968).

The Just Society.

> PIERRE ELLIOTT TRUDEAU, prime minister, campaign slogan, summer 1968.

King, William Lyon Mackenzie

Hark the herald angels sing
William Lyon Mackenzie King.

> Opening lines of the campaign song popular in the North York constituency in which W.L. Mackenzie King ran as the candidate in the election of 1921, recalled by Alan O. Gibbons in the *Canadian Forum*, April 1974.

KING OR CHAOS.

> Slogan of the Liberal party in the general election of 1935, devised by the editors of *Maclean's* and introduced as a double-page spread in the issue of Oct. 15, 1935. From Floyd S. Chalmers in *A Gentleman of the Press* (1969).

Ultimately, the reason why William Lyon Mackenzie King has been our highly respected prime minister for twenty years is that the anything-but-respectable William Lyon Mackenzie was beaten in 1837. ["Twenty-five Years as Prime Minister" (1946)]

*

He has been the representative Canadian, the typical Canadian, the essential Canadian, the ideal Canadian, the Canadian as he exists in the mind of God. ["The End of the King Era" (1948)]

> FRANK H. UNDERHILL, socialist and later a reluctant Liberal, from *In Search of Canadian Liberalism* (1960).

The mystery of William Lyon Mackenzie King is not the mystery of a man. It is the mystery of a people. We do not understand King because we do not understand ourselves.

> BRUCE HUTCHISON, Vancouver journalist and author, in *The Incredible Canadian* (1952).

How shall we speak of Canada,
Mackenzie King dead?
The Mother's boy in the lonely room
With his dog, his medium and his ruins?

He blunted us.

We had no shape
Because he never took sides,
And no sides
Because he never allowed them to take shape.

He skilfully avoided what was wrong
Without saying what was right,
And never let his on the one hand
Know what his on the other hand was doing.

The height of his ambition
Was to pile a Parliamentary Commission
on a Royal Commission,
To have "conscription if necessary
But not necessarily conscription,"
To let Parliament decide—
Later.

Postpone, postpone, abstain.

Only one thread was certain:
After World War I
Business as usual,
After World War II
Orderly decontrol.
Always he led us back to where we were before.

He seemed to be in the centre
Because we had no centre,
No vision
To pierce the smoke-screen of his politics.

Truly he will be remembered
Wherever men honour ingenuity,
Ambiguity, inactivity, and political longevity.

Let us raise up a temple
To the cult of mediocrity,
Do nothing by halves
Which can be done by quarters.

F.R. Scott, Montreal man-of-letters, in "W.L.M.K." (1957), in *Selected Poems* (1966).

His verbal currency was invariably tendered in the highest denominations; but in practical politics he always dealt in very small change . . . . He made both big words and small deeds serve his turn. There was at once more in him than met the eye, and a great deal less than filled the ear.

> Donald Creighton, distinguished historian, on W.L. Mackenzie King in *Canada's First Century* (1970).

William Lyon Mackenzie King
Sat in the middle & played with string
And he loved his mother like *any*thing—
William Lyon Mackenzie King.

> Dennis Lee, poet, in "William Lyon Mackenzie King," *Alligator Pie* (1974).

Kisses

You may kiss my hand. All emotion begins at the wrist.

> Elinor Glyn, creator of "It" in Hollywood in the 1920s, to Sir Gilbert Parker. Quoted by Lenore Coffee in *Storyline* (1973).

I can't give you too many kisses. The press is watching. Perhaps later.

> Pierre Elliott Trudeau, prime minister, to a pretty campaigner, May 18, 1968.

Klondike

See GOLD RUSH.

Labour

See also CAPITALISM; INDUSTRY; UNIONS.

Your Excellency, I represent the rag, tag and bobtail!

> Daniel J. O'Donoghue, called "the father of the trade union movement in Canada," to Lord Dufferin, governor general of Canada, on being asked for his credentials in the mid-

1870s, quoted by Doris French in *Faith, Sweat and Politics* (1962).

There is something wrong with the government of the people, when it can enact legislation in twenty-five minutes to arrest labour leaders; when we cannot in five years secure legislation in the interests of Canadian working men.

> J.T. Foster, president of the Trades and Labour Council, speaking in Montreal, June 1919, quoted by Charles Lipton in *The Trade Union Movement in Canada* (1967).

We are thankful for these and all the good things of life. We recognize that they are part of our common heritage and come to us through the efforts of our brothers and sisters the world over. What we desire for ourselves we wish for all. To this end may we take our share in the world's work and the world's struggles.

> J.S. Woodsworth, socialist who helped to establish the Labour Church, said this prayer "Grace before Meat" at dinnertime, about 1920. Quoted by Kenneth J. McNaught in *A Prophet in Politics* (1959).

Sorry I can't attend the funeral but I heartily approve of the event.

> J.B. McLachlan, Scottish-born Cape Breton editor of the *Maritime Labour Herald*, sent this telegram declining an invitation to attend the funeral of Samuel Gompers, middle-of-the-road leader of the American Federation of Labor, in 1924. Quoted by Tom McEwan in *He Wrote for Us* (1951).

Mr. Evans: The purpose is to demand from you this programme of work and wages.

Mr. Bennett: And we have made it perfectly clear so far as we are concerned that these camps were not established for that purpose.

Mr. Evans: This is passing the buck. We want work and wages.

Mr. Bennett: Just a moment—

Mr. Evans: You referred to us as not wanting work. Give any of us work and see whether we will work. This is an insidious attempt to propagandize the press on your part, and any body who professes to be premier and uses such despicable tactics is not fit to be premier of a Hottentot village.

Mr. Bennett: I come from Alberta. I remember when you embezzled the funds of your union and were sent to penitentiary.

Mr. Evans: You are a liar . . . .

ARTHUR "SLIM" EVANS, former carpenter and Communist labour organizer, headed the delegation of striking relief-camp workers that met R.B. Bennett and members of his Cabinet in the prime minister's office, East Block, Parliament Buildings, June 22, 1935. Reproduced by Victor Hoar in his edition (1973) of *Recollections of the On to Ottawa Trek* by Ronald Liversedge (1961).

You know my origins; I have always been with, and one of, the workers, and I have neither the desire nor the ability to swing at this late date to the other side. In my official capacity I have travelled the middle of the road, but now that you have put the extreme alternative to me, my place is marching with the workers rather than riding with General Motors. At this late date I cannot oppose unionism and the workers and labour as a whole.

DAVID A. CROLL, Ontario minister of Public Welfare, Labour and Municipal Affairs, in his letter of resignation, addressed to Mitchell Hepburn, premier of Ontario, April 14, 1937, at the height of the Oshawa strike, when 3,700 auto workers were fighting for union recognition and the right to join the CIO. From the Toronto *Star*, April 15, 1937.

Workers have the right to organize and the right *not* to organize. Labour has the right to organize, but not to *dis*organize. [1948 campaign]

MAURICE DUPLESSIS, premier of Quebec intermittently between 1936 and 1959, adapted from Leslie Roberts' *The Chief* (1963).

The working class is the victim of a conspiracy which seeks its destruction and when there is a conspiracy to crush the working class it is the duty of the Church to intervene . . . . We want social peace but we don't want the crushing of the working class. We are attached to man more than to capital. That's why the clergy has decided to intervene. It wants to have justice and charity respected and desires that there shall cease to be a situation where more attention is paid to money interests than to the human element.

MONSEIGNOR JOSEPH CHARBONNEAU, archbishop of Montreal, sermon supporting the strikers at Asbestos, Notre Dame Cathedral, Sunday, May 2, 1949, quoted by Charles Lipton in *The Trade Union Movement in Canada* (1967).

Mangez de la merde!

PIERRE ELLIOTT TRUDEAU, prime minister, yelled this at "the Lapalme guys," striking mail-truck drivers who, on the expiry of their contract on April 1, 1970, were not rehired by the federal government which had taken over the operations of the Lapalme Company.

Labrador
See also NEWFOUNDLAND.

This country shall be named after its natural resources: it shall be called *Markland*.

LEIF THE LUCKY, also known as Leif Ericsson, likely landed at Labrador about 1000 A.D.; "Markland" means "forest-land." From *The Vinland Sagas* (1965), translated from the Old Icelandic by Magnus Magnusson and Hermann Palsson.

Labrador may become another Alaska because it has the largest iron ore deposits in the world waiting to be exploited . . . whoever runs them, Labrador will be an old-age pension for Newfoundland for a very long time. [British House of Commons, March 2, 1949]

*

A Frenchman said that Labrador was the country that God gave to Cain. History may say that it was the country that Britain gave to Canada.

A.P. HERBERT, British humorist and M.P. who visited Newfoundland in 1943, in *Independent Member* (1950).

I go tomorrow, Mr. Speaker, to Labrador to the site of the mighty Churchill Falls. There I will push a switch to create a large new reservoir, a brand new lake, a huge body of water. For some reason—I really don't know why—they've decided to name this magnificent body of water after me. Imagine that, Mr. Speaker! This great new lake, created in the heart of Labrador, Smallwood Lake, *seven times larger than the Sea of Galilee!*

J.R. "JOEY" SMALLWOOD, first premier of

Newfoundland, in the Newfoundland legislature about 1958, attributed by Ray Guy, columnist for the St. John's *Telegram*.

God made the world in six days, and on the seventh, sailed inshore and hurled rocks at Labrador.

Quoted by Richard Gwyn in *Smallwood: The Unlikely Revolutionary* (1968).

Land

I know nothing finer, either from the point of view of the sociologist, the traveller, or the artist, than a month's devotion to even the surface of Canada, over the line of the Great Lakes and the St. Lawrence, the fertile, populous, and happy province of Ontario, the province of Quebec, with another month to the hardy maritime regions of New Brunswick, Nova Scotia, and Newfoundland.

WALT WHITMAN, American poet, in "Notes for a Lecture," Aug. 14, 1880, Hamilton, Ontario, from *Walt Whitman's Diary in Canada* (1904), edited by W.S. Kennedy.

Land ought not to be a commodity, because like air and water it is necessary to human existence; and all men have by birthright equal rights to its use.

PHILLIPS THOMPSON, labour reporter who covered the police court for the Toronto *Telegram* under the name of Jimuel Briggs, in *The Politics of Labour* (1887).

The wholesome Sea is at her gates,
Her gates both East and West,
Then is it strange that we should love
This Land, Our Land, the best?

J.A. RITCHIE, Ottawa barrister and poetaster, from "There Is a Land" (1920). These lines are inscribed in stone over the main entrance to the Parliament Buildings in Ottawa: "THE WHOLESOME SEA IS AT HER GATES . . . HER GATES BOTH EAST AND WEST."

There is no land—I say this is true of any land upon the surface of the earth—there is no land, that will support life, that the race which inhabits it will not in due time come to love.

B.K. SANDWELL, influential editor of *Saturday Night* from 1932 to 1951, in an address to the

Canadian Club, Toronto, March 13, 1920.

This is a beauty
of dissonance,
this resonance
of stony strand. . . .
         *
This is the beauty
of strength
broken by strength
and still strong.

A.J.M. SMITH, poet, from "The Lonely Land" (1929), in *Poems* (1967).

I know a man whose school could never teach him patriotism, but who acquired that virtue when he felt in his bones the vastness of his land, and the greatness of those who founded it.

PIERRE ELLIOTT TRUDEAU, future prime minister, in "Exhaustion and Fulfilment: The Ascetic in a Canoe" (1944), from *Wilderness Canada* (1970), edited by Borden Spears.

"A man without land is nobody. Remember that, Duddel."

MORDECAI RICHLER, Montreal novelist; Grandfather's advice to young Duddy and the motif of *The Apprenticeship of Duddy Kravitz* (1959).

This land is your land, this land is my land,
From Bona Vista to Vancouver Island,
From the Arctic Islands to the Great Lakes waters;
This land was made for you and me.

WOODY GUTHRIE, American folksinger, wrote "This Land Is Your Land" in 1956. The refrain of the Canadian version is an adaptation by Martin Bochner for the Travellers which dates from the late 1950s. The original refrain runs: "From California to the New York Island,/From the redwood forest to the Gulfstream waters."

From the Vancouver Island to the Alberta highland,
Cross the prairie, the Lakes, to Ontario's towers.
From the sound of Mount Royal's chimes, out to the Maritimes,
Something to sing about, this land of ours.

OSCAR BRAND, folksinger and composer of

"Something to Sing About" (sometimes called "This Land of Ours"), written in 1963.

Buy land. They've stopped making it.
> ARTHUR M. PEARSON, chairman of the Special Senate Committee on Land Use, to Senator David Croll, quoted by George Bain in the Toronto *Globe and Mail*, March 17, 1973.

We live in an empty place filled with wonders.
> PETER C. NEWMAN, writer, in *Maclean's*, Oct. 1973.

Language
See also BILINGUALISM; JOUAL; LANGUAGE: ENGLISH; LANGUAGE: FRENCH; SPEECH AND SPEECHES.

I have made all my journeys by means of words. We send our words out to reconnoitre, and they bring back reports on the countries they have seen. We see from these reports whether the countries are real, fairly real, or surreal.
> HECTOR DE SAINT-DENYS-GARNEAU, Quebec poet, on Shrove Tuesday 1936, in *The Journal of Saint-Denys-Garneau* (1962), translated by John Glassco.

No one can ever study language enough, for it is the home of all meanings.
> JEAN-PAUL DESBIENS, writing as "Frère Untel" in *The Impertinences of Brother Anonymous* (1962), translated by Miriam Chapin.

To know the origin of words is to know the cultural history of mankind.
> ERNEST KLEIN, Toronto lexicographer, in *A Comprehensive Etymological Dictionary of the English Language* (1966).

Language: English
See also LANGUAGE.

Speak English, but speak it badly.
> LOUIS-FRANÇOIS-RICHER LAFLÈCHE, bishop of Trois-Rivières from 1870 to 1898, quoted by Télésphore-Damien Bouchard in the House of Commons, June 21, 1944.

He has an accent. So does everyone in Canada.
> DARRYL F. ZANUCK, American film producer,

commenting on the casting of the Danish actor Jean Hersholt as Dr. Dafoe in *The Country Doctor*, a film starring the Dionne Quintuplets released in 1936. Quoted by Mel Gussow in *Don't Say Yes Until I Finish Talking* (1971).

I can write on this controversy with the friendly neutrality of a Canadian. In Canada we have enough to do keeping up with the two spoken languages without trying to invent slang, so we just go right ahead and use English for literature, Scotch for sermons and American for conversation.
> STEPHEN LEACOCK, humorist, in *How to Write* (1943).

When I left Hungary, I lost everything except my accent.
> GEORGE FEYER, Hungarian-born cartoonist, quoted by Beverley Slopen in *Quill and Quire*, July 1972.

Canajan.
> MARK M. ORKIN, lawyer and philologist, in *Canajan, Eh?* (1973). "The nash null language of Anglos." Canajan is to Canadian English what joual is to Canadian French.

Eh?
> MARK M. ORKIN in *Canajan, Eh?* (1973). "Rhymes with hay. The great Canadian monosyllable and shibboleth, 'eh?', is all things to all men."

Language: French
See also LANGUAGE.

In *Canada* nobody ever hears the *French* language spoken by any but *Frenchmen*; for strangers seldom come thither; and the *Indians* are naturally too proud to learn *French*, but obliged the *French* to learn their language.
> PETER KALM, Swedish botanist and traveller, from *Travels into North America* (1770-71), translated from the Swedish by J.R. Forster.

I am an Englishman who speaks French.
> SIR GEORGE-ETIENNE CARTIER, future Father of Confederation, well-known remark in the 1850s, quoted by John Boyd in *Sir George Etienne Cartier, Bart.* (1914).

The more I reflect on the destiny of Canadian literature, the less chance I find for its leaving a mark in history. Canada lacks its own language. If we spoke Iroquois or Huron, our literature would live.

*

Are we not a million Frenchmen forgotten by the mother country on the shores of the St. Lawrence? It is not enough to encourage all those who hold a pen to know that this little people will grow great, and that it will always guard the name and memory of those who aided it to conserve intact the most precious of all treasures, the tongue of its fathers?

> OCTAVE CRÉMAZIE, poet, in a letter to Abbé H.-R. Casgrain, Jan. 29, 1867, from *Les Oeuvres complètes d'Octave Crémazie* (1882), edited by Abbé H.-R. Casgrain.

My native tongue is not French, it is *Franglais*. Learning French was almost like learning a foreign language.

> FERNAND OUELLETTE, Quebec writer, in *Liberté*, March–April 1964. *Franglais* is the term used in France for the anglicized French language.

I haven't practised my French. It's just that you are starting to understand it better.

> JOHN G. DIEFENBAKER, prime minister, at a press conference in St. Hyacinthe, Quebec, Aug. 23, 1965.

Last Words
See also EPITAPHS.

Herewith goodnight to the whole world and my soul into the hand of God.

> JENS MUNK, Danish sea captain searching for the Northwest Passage, concluding words of his will, June 4, 1620. Wintering on the west coast of Hudson Bay near Churchill River, he watched sixty-one of his men die of scurvy, so he drew up the will. Munk and two others survived when they managed to sail the smaller of their two ships back to Europe.

We are made a spectacle to the world, to angels, and to men.

> JÉRÔME LALEMANT, Jesuit missionary, threw himself at the feet of Father Brébeuf, quoting I Corinthians 3:9, before they were both burned to death by the Iroquois in 1649. Quoted by

Francis Parkman in *The Jesuits in North America in the Seventeenth Century* (1867).

I leave the property of Gairbraid, and all other landed property I may die possessed of, to my sisters Helen Boyle Story and Elizabeth Boyle Dunlop; the former because she is married to a minister whom (God help him) she henpecks. The latter because she is married to nobody, nor is she like to be, for she is an old maid, and not market-rife.

*

I leave my silver tankard to the eldest son of old John, as the representative of the family. I would have left it to old John himself, but he would melt it down to make temperance medals, and that would be sacrilege—however, I leave my big horn snuff-box to him: he can only make temperance horn spoons of that.

*

I also leave my late brother's watch to my brother Sandy, exhorting him at the same time to give up Whiggery, Radicalism, and all other sins that do most easily beset him.

*

I leave John Caddle a silver teapot, to the end that he may drink tea therefrom to comfort him under the affliction of a slatternly wife.

> WILLIAM "TIGER" DUNLOP, colonist, prepared his infamous last will and testament three years before his death at Lachine, near Montreal, June 29, 1848. Quoted by Robina Kathleen MacFarlane Lizars in *In the Days of the Canada Company* (1896).

I will love thee in Heaven.

> KATERI TEKAKWITHA, first Indian saint, dying words on April 17, 1860. Other sources claim her last words were: "Jesus, I love thee!" Quoted by Ellen H. Walworth in *The Life and Times of Kateri Tekakwitha* (1891).

J'aime mon Dieu, et j'aime mon Pays.

> SIR LOUIS-HIPPOLYTE LAFONTAINE, French-Canadian reform leader, dying words on Feb. 26, 1864, quoted by G. Mercer Adam in *Canada's Patriot Statesman* (1891).

Get it done more quickly.

> GEORGE MUNRO GRANT, principal of Queen's University, on his deathbed, May 10, 1902,

quoted by P.B. Waite in "Across the Rockies," *Canada: An Historical Magazine*, autumn 1973.

C'est fini.

SIR WILFRID LAURIER, former prime minister, last words, Feb. 17, 1919, quoted by Oscar Douglas Skelton in *Life and Letters of Sir Wilfrid Laurier* (1921).

You are a curious fellow.

ANDREW BONAR LAW, New Brunswick-born prime minister of Great Britain, died on Oct. 30, 1923, murmuring these words to his attendant, Lord Beaverbrook. Law was prime minister for only 209 days. Quoted by Alan Wood in *The True History of Lord Beaverbrook* (1960).

Thank you.

W.L. MACKENZIE KING, former prime minister, dying words, at Kingsmere, Quebec, July 22, 1950.

Laurier, Sir Wilfrid

Had I been born on the banks of the Saskatchewan, I would myself have shouldered a musket to fight against the neglect of governments and the shameless greed of speculators.

SIR WILFRID LAURIER, future prime minister, at a demonstration in the Champ de Mars, Montreal, Nov. 22, 1885, the Sunday following the hanging of Riel. Quoted by O.D. Skelton in *Life and Letters of Sir Wilfrid Laurier* (1921).

I am British to the core.

SIR WILFRID LAURIER, prime minister, address at the Lord Mayor's Banquet, Mansion House, London, England, on July 1, 1897. Quoted by André Siegfried in *The Race Question in Canada* (1907).

Laurier and the Larger Canada.

Banner at an election rally where Laurier was the principal speaker, Massey Hall, Toronto, from the Toronto *Globe*, Oct. 15, 1904.

In 1896 I was excommunicated by the Roman priests and in 1917 by Protestant parsons.

SIR WILFRID LAURIER, prime minister, quoted by F.A. McGregor in *The Fall and Rise of Mac-*

kenzie King (1962). Laurier faced the Manitoba schools question in 1896 and the conscription issue in 1917.

Law

See also CRIME; JUSTICE.

The law! the law! Never mind the law, toorn him oot, toorn him oot!

JOHN STRACHAN, influential Anglican minister and politician in Upper Canada, urged the legal or illegal dismissal of Barnabas Bidwell, the noted reformer, when he was elected to the Legislative Council of Upper Canada in Nov. 1821. On Jan. 22, 1822, Bidwell was declared ineligible to sit in the House, as he had neglected to apply for British citizenship. Quoted by John Charles Dent in *The Story of the Upper Canadian Rebellion* (1885).

The basic principle of the State is compulsion. This is fundamental in its entire organization. It runs through every system of law, both civil and criminal, through practically all the conventions of society; without it law, order, system and organization could not exist.

SIR JAMES LOUGHEED, leader of the Senate in the 1890s and chairman of its Divorce Committee, quoted by Robert M. Hamilton in *Canadian Quotations and Phrases* (1952).

The statute books are exceedingly muddled. I seldom look into them.

MATTHEW B. BEGBIE, "the hanging judge," later chief justice of British Columbia, before an open court, quoted by D.A. McGregor in "Sir Matthew Begbie," *Canadian Portraits: CBC Broadcasts* (1940), edited by R.G. Riddell.

What you say may be in all them books, all right, but it ain't the Law of Killaloe.

The punch line of Ontario Premier Leslie M. Frost's favourite story, about a judge in the small Ontario town of Killaloe Station who objected to the pleas of a big-city lawyer. Quoted by Ron Haggart in *Saturday Night*, Jan. 1972.

What is termed "disrespect for law" in fact may only be the manifestation of a burning desire for justice. Order, like law, to be respected, must deserve respect. Disrespect for an order that does not deserve respect

ought not to be condemned as degeneration, but commended as a healthy regeneration.

> J.C. McRuer, former chief justice of Ontario, in Montreal, Sept. 5, 1966.

There are more Q.C.'s in one office building in Toronto than in all of England.

> Allan Fotheringham, Vancouver columnist, in "Tort, Persiflage, Redundant & Weinstein" (1968), from *Collected and Bound* (1972).

I'm not sure very many of us can understand all this legal jargle.

> John Kushner, former Calgary city councillor and malapropist, in a city council meeting, May 7, 1974.

Leadership
See also PRIME MINISTER.

Du Mont Royal naistra d'une casane,
Qui duc, & compte viendra tyranniser,
Dresser copie de la marche Millane,
Favence, Florence d'or & gens espuiser.

Out of Montreal shall be born in a cottage,
One that shall tyrannize over duke and earl,
He shall raise an army in the land of the rebellion,
He shall empty Favence and Florence of their gold.

> Michel Nostradamus, French prophet, in *Centuries* (1555), Century VII, 32. *The Complete Prophecies of Nostradamus* (1947), translated by Henry C. Roberts, who interprets this to mean: "A Canadian leader, of lowly birth, shall be raised to great power and eventually assume command over men of the nobility."

The Anglo-Saxon leads the van,
  And never lags behind,
For was not he ordained to be
  The leader of mankind?
He carries very little sail,
  Makes very little show,
But gains the havens without fail,
  Whatever winds may blow.

> Alexander McLachlan, folk poet, first stanza of "The Anglo-Saxon," *Poems and Songs* (1888).

I must follow them; I am their leader.

> Andrew Bonar Law, Canadian-born prime

minister of Great Britain who died in 1923, attributed.

Follow my White Plume.

> Sir Wilfrid Laurier, prime minister, on July 11, 1911: "Henry of Navarre at the battle of Ivry said, 'Follow my white plume, and you will find it always in the forefront of honour.' Like Henry IV, I say to you young men, 'Follow my white plume'—the white hairs of sixty-nine years—and you will, I believe I can say it without boasting, find it always in the forefront of honour." Quebec backed Laurier, but his government was defeated.

If the leader strides forward too fast, he may be hidden from his followers by the curvature of the earth.

> George Iles, science writer, in *Canadian Stories* (1918).

Mackenzie King genuinely believed and frequently said that the real secret of political leadership was more in what was prevented than in what was accomplished.

> J.W. Pickersgill, Liberal cabinet minister and Mackenzie King's chief adviser, in *The Mackenzie King Record* (1960), volume I.

Legend
See MYTHOLOGY.

Liberal Party
See also GRITS, THE; LIBERALISM; POLITICS.

I'm neither virtuous nor contemptible, but Liberal.

> Mitchell Hepburn, premier of Ontario from 1934 to 1942, characteristic remark.

The Liberal Party may be defined as a case of the bland leading the bland.

> F.H. Underhill, a founder of the CCF who became a Liberal in later life, attributed.

It is not merely for the well-being of Canadians but for the good of mankind in general that the present Liberal government should remain in office.

> J.W. Pickersgill, Liberal Cabinet minister and Mackenzie King's chief adviser, prior to the 1957 election, quoted by Peter C. Newman in "Jack Pickersgill" (1973), *Home Country* (1973).

I have often thought of my hon. friend the Minister of Citizenship and Immigration [J.W. Pickersgill] as a "Gliberal." He would believe anything twice, as Mencken once said.

> JOHN G. DIEFENBAKER, leader of the Conservative Opposition, in the House of Commons, April 12, 1956.

The Liberals are the flying saucers of politics. No one can make head nor tail of them and they never are seen twice in the same place.

> JOHN G. DIEFENBAKER, prime minister, in an address in London, Ontario, May 5, 1962.

The Liberals give themselves leftist airs but they feed at the table of the rich.

> ROBERT CLICHE, maverick Quebec judge, quoted by Richard Cleroux in the Toronto *Globe and Mail*, May 7, 1975.

Liberalism
See also LIBERAL PARTY.

I have lived too long, I have outlived Liberalism.

> SIR WILFRID LAURIER, leader of the Opposition, to his Liberal caucus, in a despairing mood, from Oscar Douglas Skelton's *Life and Letters of Sir Wilfrid Laurier* (1921).

You ask what Liberalism is? I believe that Liberalism is the leaven which will make prevail, or the means of making prevail, the law of peace, work and health over the law of blood and of death, no matter where this conflict of laws may be found. This is the very work that we, as Liberals, are engaged upon today.

> W.L. MACKENZIE KING, Liberal prime minister, in "The Practice of Liberalism," *The Liberal Way* (1933), opinions expressed at the First Liberal Summer Conference, Port Hope, in Sept. 1933.

A liberal is a man of the centre, moving forward . . . . Liberalism is the middle way between extremes. But while we are in the middle of the road, we don't stand still.

> LESTER B. PEARSON, Liberal prime minister, in a TV interview, Oct. 20, 1966.

Liberty
See also FREEDOM.

Liberty is a gift which can only be realized in a regulated universe and an ordered society.

> SIR ROBERT FALCONER, president of the University of Toronto from 1907 to 1923, in "The Education of National Character," *Idealism in National Character* (1920).

As democracy grows, liberty disappears.

> SIR ANDREW MACPHAIL, physician and author, in "Art in Democracy," *Dalhousie Review* 4, 1924.

The only thing you have to set against the spectacular appeal of the totalitarian State is the spectacle of liberty.

> GEORGE V. FERGUSON, editor of the Montreal *Star*, quoted by John Grierson in "Searchlight on Democracy," *Grierson on Documentary* (1946), edited by Forsyth Hardy.

If you wish to liberate a people, you must use means that put liberty to work.

> FERNAND DUMONT, Laval sociologist, on Radio-Canada, Oct. 20, 1970, quoted by Gérard Pelletier in *The October Crisis* (1971), translated by Joyce Marshall.

Libraries
See also BOOKS.

It is perfectly true that the works of a journalist are ephemeral; they go into the nether world of old files and are forgotten. But does not the same fate befall a good many books? Look at the back stacks of any great library. What a necropolis of the immortals in there.

> GOLDWIN SMITH, British-born journalist, in an address to the Canadian Press Association, June 3, 1881.

The Public and University libraries in Toronto were lacking in modern works on the social, education, and psychologic problems occupying the best minds. "We do not buy books we consider immoral," a local librarian was reported as saying.

> EMMA GOLDMAN, noted anarchist who died in Toronto in 1940, in *Living My Life* (1931).

I am what librarians have made me with a little assistance from a professor of Greek and a few poets.

> B.K. SANDWELL, influential editor of *Saturday*

Night from 1932 to 1951, quoted by J.R. Kidd in *Learning and Society* (1963).

Lies

To the first charge Your Excellency I answer that it is a lie, to the second charge I say that it is a d----d lie, and to the third charge that it is a d----d infernal lie, and Your Excellency I have no more to say.

> THOMAS TREMLETT, chief justice of Newfoundland, made this reply in Oct. 1811 to three charges of partiality and corruption from which he was later exonerated. Quoted by D.W. Prowse in *A History of Newfoundland from English, Colonial, and Foreign Records* (1895).

The only time I tell a lie is when I think I am telling the truth.

> PHILLIP "FLYING PHIL" GAGLARDI, minister of Public Works and Social Improvement in the Social Credit government of W.A.C. Bennett in British Columbia during the 1950s, characteristic remark.

I do not know if the world has lied
I have lied
I do not know if the world has conspired
 against love
I have conspired against love.

> LEONARD COHEN, Montreal poet, from "What I'm Doing Here," *Selected Poems 1956–68* (1968).

Life

Was it a year or lives ago
 We took the grasses in our hands,
And caught the summer flying low
 Over the waving meadow lands,
 And held it there between our hands?

> BLISS CARMAN, New Brunswick poet, from "Low Tide on Grand Pré," *Bliss Carman's Poems* (1929).

Human life is human relatedness. No one lives alone. Robinson Crusoe is a feat of literary imagination.

> GREGORY VLASTOS, teacher, in "The Ethical Foundations," *Towards the Christian Revolution* (1936), edited by R.B.Y. Scott and Gregory Vlastos.

How beautiful the body is; how perfect its parts; with what precision it moves; how

obedient, proud and strong. How terrible when torn. The little flame of life sinks lower and lower, and, with a flicker, goes out. It goes out like a candle goes out. Quietly and gently. It makes its protest at extinction, then submits. It has its say, then is silent.

> NORMAN BETHUNE, Gravenhurst-born medical doctor and hero of Mao's China, in "Wounds," *Canadian Tribune*, June 15, 1940, reprinted in *New Frontiers*, fall 1952.

Let your soul grow a thing apart,
 Untroubled by the restless day,
Sublimed by some unconscious art,
 Controlled by some divine delay.

For life is greater than we think,
 Who fret along its shallow bars:
Swing out the boom to float or sink
 And front the ocean and the stars.

> DUNCAN CAMPBELL SCOTT, Ottawa poet, from "The Ideal," *Selected Poems of Duncan Campbell Scott* (1951), edited by E.K. Brown.

Life, if you have a bent for it, is a beautiful thing. It consists, I do believe, of having a sense of urgency.

> C.L. BURTON, chairman of Simpsons, in *A Sense of Urgency* (1952).

In the early October of that year, in the cathedral hush of a Quebec Indian summer with the lake drawing into its mirror the fire of the maples, it came to me that to be able to love the mystery surrounding us is the final and only sanction of human existence.

> HUGH MACLENNAN, Montreal novelist, in *The Watch That Ends the Night* (1961).

I like a little bit of everything. A little bit of lovin', a little bit of drinkin', and a little bit of workin'. I watch out pretty careful every day for banana peels.

> MARGARET "MA" MURRAY, pioneering newspaper woman, on CBC Radio, Oct. 17, 1967.

Life. Consider the alternative.

> MARSHALL MCLUHAN, media pundit, in *War and Peace in the Global Village* (1968), with Quentin Fiore.

You can sing about life or you can try to understand it. You can't do both.

IRVING LAYTON, outspoken poet, in *The Whole Bloody Bird* (1969).

Reading a dead poet
Who complained in his time
Against bad laws, bad manners,
And bad weather in bad rhyme,

I thought how glad he'd be
To be living in our time
To damn worse laws, worse matters,
And worse weather, in worst rhyme.

LOUIS DUDEK, Montreal poet, in "The Progress of Satire," *Collected Poetry* (1971).

Literature

See also CRITICS; CULTURE; LITERATURE: CANADIAN; PLAYWRIGHTS; POETRY AND POETS; PUBLISHERS AND PUBLISHING; WRITERS AND WRITING.

Literature may be light as a cobweb, but it must be fastened down to life at the four corners.

NELLIE L. MCCLUNG, suffragette leader, in *Clearing in the West* (1936).

The notion that a whole literature can develop out of the happy employment of the odd moments of rather busy men is an unrealistic notion, and one that shows an alarming ignorance of the process by which great works are normally written.

E.K. BROWN, literary critic, quoted by John Gray in "Book Publishing," *Writing in Canada* (1956), edited by George Whalley.

Where are the clerisy? They are people who like to read books . . . the clerisy are those who read for pleasure, but not for idleness; who read for pastime but not to kill time; who love books, but do not live by books.

ROBERTSON DAVIES, Toronto man-of-letters, from *A Voice from the Attic* (1960).

No great literature or art is possible without a great people, a people ripened by experience, stirred by curiosity, and alive to wonder—a people with the daring capacity to expect the wonderful and then attempt to realize it.

LORNE PIERCE, longtime editor of the Ryerson Press, in *An Editor's Creed* (1960).

Literature is a human apocalypse, man's revelation to man, and criticism is not a body of adjudications, but the awareness of that revelation, the last judgement of mankind.

NORTHROP FRYE, literary scholar, in "The Keys to Dreamland," *The Educated Imagination* (1963).

By the way
she moved
away
I could see
her devotion
to literature
was not
perfect.

IRVING LAYTON, outspoken poet, from "Misunderstanding," *The Collected Poems of Irving Layton* (1971).

An article is what *Maclean's* publishes; an essay is what *Maclean's* turns down and you later read in *Saturday Night*.

HUGH GARNER, Toronto author, in *One Damn Thing after Another* (1973).

Great literature is any old stuff you can read without disgust.

LOUIS DUDEK, Montreal poet, in *Epigrams* (1975).

Literature: Canadian

See also LITERATURE.

Has Canada no poet to describe the glories of his parent land—no painter that can delineate her matchless scenery of land and wave? Are her children dumb and blind, that they leave to strangers the task of singing her praise?

The standard literature of Canada must be looked for in her newspapers.

SUSANNA MOODIE, pioneer author, in "Introduction," *Mark Hurdlestone, The Gold Worshipper* (1853).

The cause of this inferiority lies not in the rarity of men of talent, but in the disastrous environment provided for the writer by the indifference of a population which has as yet no taste for letters, at least for works produced by native sons.

OCTAVE CRÉMAZIE, Quebec poet, in a letter to Abbé H.-R. Casgrain on Jan. 29, 1867, in *Les*

Oeuvres complètes d'Octave Crémazie (1882), edited by Abbé H.-R. Casgrain.

If our country becomes an independent, compacted, self-supporting nation, which is, or ought to be, the dream of all of us, its social and climatic conditions will in the course of time evolve a race of people having a peculiar national temperament and bent of mind, and when that is done, we shall have a *Canadian* literature.

*

One May evening somebody lent me *Orion and Other Poems*, then recently published. Like most of the young fellows about me I had been under the depressing conviction that we were situated hopelessly on the outskirts of civilization, where no art and no literature could be, and that it was useless to expect that anything great could be done by any of our companions, still more useless to expect that we could do it ourselves. I sat up all night reading and rereading *Orion* in a state of the wildest excitement and when I went to bed I could not sleep. It seemed to me a wonderful thing that such work could be done by a Canadian, by a young man, one of ourselves. It was like a voice from some new paradise of art, calling to us to be up and doing.

ARCHIBALD LAMPMAN, distinguished poet, "Two Canadian Poets: A Lecture by Archibald Lampman," delivered in Ottawa, Feb. 19, 1891, in *University of Toronto Quarterly*, July 1944. Lampman was a student at Trinity College, Toronto, when he read Sir Charles G.D. Roberts's *Orion* (1880).

Elderly couple apply to orphan asylum for a boy; a girl is sent them.

L.M. MONTGOMERY, author, notebook entry about 1907 that led to the writing of *Anne of Green Gables* (1908), quoted by Hilda M. Ridley in *The Story of L.M. Montgomery* (1956).

The heart is willing, but the head is weak. Modernity and tradition alike demand that the contemporary artist who survives adolescence shall be an intellectual. Sensibility is no longer enough, intelligence is also required. Even in Canada.

A.J.M. SMITH, poet, in "Wanted: Canadian Criticism," *Canadian Forum*, April 1928.

Shall we go round the mulberry bush, or shall
We gather at the river, or shall we
Appoint a Poet Laureate this fall,
Or shall we have another cup of tea?

O Canada, O Canada, Oh can
A day go by without new authors springing
To plant the native maple, and to plan
More ways to set the selfsame welkin ringing?

F.R. SCOTT, Montreal man-of-letters, from "The Canadian Authors Meet" (1945), in *Selected Poems* (1966).

. . . there is no outlet for one's work in Canada, no magazines, and the U.S. is not interested, should the *mise en scène* be Canada and that *mise en scène* not contain a mounted policeman. It is difficult to make a living at 4000 miles distance . . . .

MALCOLM LOWRY, Vancouver-based British novelist, in a letter to Clenens ten Holder, summer 1951, from *Selected Letters of Malcolm Lowry* (1965), edited by Harvey Breit and Margerie Bonner Lowry.

The name Jalna was suggested to me in this way: a member of the Civil Service, in the same department as Caroline, had spent many years in India. When she told him that I was in search of names of military stations there he sent me a list of quite a number. I pored over them and chose Jalna because it was the shortest; it was easy to remember and looked well in print. When I wrote it at the top of my first page of manuscript, it never entered my head that one day it would become well-known to quite a number of people.

MAZO DE LA ROCHE, popular novelist, in *Ringing the Changes* (1957). The country house associated with the fictional Jalna is an attractive residence named "Benares" north of Clarkson, Ontario, still owned and occupied by descendants of the retired British officer who built it in 1837. The Jalna in India is a nondescript, fruit-producing town in Hyderabad State.

We are told that Professor L.E. Horning of the University of Toronto circulated early in 1894 a questionnaire asking anxiously: "What is wrong with Canadian literature?" Goldwin Smith is alleged to have retorted: "*What* Canadian Literature?" In another place his exact answer is reported to have included the sentence: "No such thing as a literature in the local sense exists or is ever likely to exist."

WILFRID EGGLESTON, journalist and author, in *The Frontier and Canadian Letters* (1957).

There is no Canadian writer of whom we can say what we can say of the world's major writers, that their readers can grow up inside their work without ever being aware of a circumference.

*

... everything that is central in Canadian writing seems to be marked by the imminence of the natural world.

*

Literature, we said, is conscious mythology: it creates an autonomous world that gives us an imaginative perspective on the actual one.

NORTHROP FRYE, literary scholar, in *The Bush Garden* (1971).

If I choose to stand in a tradition why not the one to which Tolstoy and Flaubert and Dickens belong, rather than the one that includes Leacock, de la Roche, and Buchan?

JACK LUDWIG, Winnipeg-born novelist, quoted by Mordecai Richler in his introduction to *Canadian Writing Today* (1970).

People put down Canadian literature and ask us why there isn't a *Moby Dick*. The reason there isn't a *Moby Dick* is that if a Canadian did a *Moby Dick*, it would be done from the point of view of the whale. Nobody ever thought of that.

MARGARET ATWOOD, novelist and poet, quoted by John Ayre in *Saturday Night*, Nov. 1972.

Loneliness

One can experience deserts of the soul in Quebec as well as in Arabia Petraea.

PIERRE EMMANUEL, French man-of-letters, in the preface to Anne Hébert's *The Tomb of the Kings* (1967), translated by Peter Miller.

Perhaps the ultimate indignity is loneliness

without privacy.

ALDEN NOWLAN, New Brunswick author, in "Scratchings," *Between Tears and Laughter* (1971).

We are all sick, all lonely, all in need of love.

JEAN VANIER, founder of L'Arche, the home for retarded children, in *Time*, June 18, 1973.

Love

See also MARRIAGE; MEN AND WOMEN.

Come to me, sweet Marie, sweet Marie, come to me;
Not because your face is fair, love, to see,
But your soul, so pure and sweet,
Makes my happiness complete,
Makes me falter at your feet, sweet Marie.

CY WARMAN, American-born resident of London, Ont., wrote the lyrics to "Sweet Marie" in 1893 for his future wife. Set to music by Raymon Moore, the song was a Broadway hit in Moore's musical comedy, *Africa*. Quoted by Ralph L. Woods in *A Second Treasury of the Familiar* (1950).

In the shade of the old apple tree,
Where the love in your eyes I could see,
When the voice that I heard,
Like the song of the bird,
Seem'd to whisper sweet music to me;
I could hear the dull buzz of the bee,
In the blossoms as you said to me,
With a heart that is true,
I'll be waiting for you
In the shade of the old apple tree.

HARRY WILLIAMS, composer, wrote the words to "In the Shade of the Old Apple Tree," a hit song of 1905, said to be inspired by a tree on Glen Edith Drive in Toronto. The melody was composed by an American, Egbert Van Alstyne.

O Canada! Our home and native land!
True patriot-love in all thy sons command.

R. STANLEY WEIR, Montreal lawyer and sometime judge of the Exchequer Court of Canada, wrote the words to "O Canada" in 1908.

The beginning, middle, and end of love is—a sigh.

ARNOLD HAULTAIN, writer and aphorist,

Goldwin Smith's private secretary, in *Hints for Lovers* (1909).

K-K-K-Katy, beautiful Katy,
You're the only g-g-g-girl that I adore,
When the m-m-m-moon shines over the cow-shed,
I'll be waiting at the k-k-k-kitchen door.

GEOFFREY O'HARA, a successful Tin Pan Alley composer born in Chatham, Ont., wrote this "stammering song" in 1882; it was the hit of 1918 and is associated with the ending of World War One. There are many parodies along the lines of:

K-K-K-K-P,
Dirty old K.P.,
That's the only army job that I abhor,
When the m-moon shines over the guard-house,
I'll be mopping up the k-k-k-kitchen floor.

From *"Sound Off!" Soldier Songs from the Revolution to World War II* (1942), edited by Arthur Dolph.

Did you ever get so bored with a woman that you had to make love to her?

NORMAN BETHUNE, Gravenhurst-born medical doctor and later hero of Mao's China, to a startled medical colleague in Montreal, 1933. Quoted by Ted Allan and Sydney Gordon in *The Scalpel, the Sword* (1952).

I'll never smile again
Until I smile at you,
I'll never laugh again,
What good would it do?

RUTH LOWE, song-writer, composed the words and music of "I'll Never Smile Again" in 1939. It was sung in *Las Vegas Nights* (1941) and made the hit parade.

Say: Wisdom is a silver fish
And love a golden hook.

JAY MACPHERSON, poet, from "Go Take the World," *The Boatman* (1957).

One can always love somebody who loves something.

TONY EMERY, director of the Vancouver Art Gallery, in 1968.

I tell you what you do, boy. Or girl.
Go and look at the western sky where

the new moon, the silver shaving of the moon, hangs.

Look at it over your *left* shoulder, and wish.

Wish that your first love shall be your last love.

And if your wish is granted, you will have put on the whole armour of life.

GREGORY CLARK, Toronto writer and author, in *May Your First Love Be Your Last* (1969).

Loving can cost a lot but not loving always costs more, and those who fear to love often find that want of love is an emptiness that robs the joy from life.

MERLE SHAIN, Toronto writer, in *Some Men Are More Perfect Than Others* (1973).

You can command any response—you can even command people to die—but you cannot command love. I think we should replace "Love thy neighbour as thyself" with "Earn thy neighbour's love."

HANS SELYE, theoretician of stress, quoted by Marq de Villiers in *Weekend*, Nov. 23, 1974.

All honest people have difficulty with the word "love."

JOHN HOFSESS, film critic, in *Maclean's*, Dec. 1974.

Love: hours written into life's minutes.

RAYMOND CANALE, Italian-born playwright living in Toronto, in 1975.

Loyalty
See also PATRIOTISM.

U.E., U.E.L.

SIR GUY CARLETON, LORD DORCHESTER, governor-in-chief of British North America, directed in 1789 that as "a Marke of Honour" families of those 50,000 or so immigrants who had left the Thirteen Colonies between 1776 and 1783 might "be distinguished by the letters U.E. affixed to their names." U.E. is an abbreviation of "Unity of the Empire."

They Sacrificed Everything Save Honour.

ROBERT B. BLAUVELDT, Nova Scotian historian of U.E.L. descent, chose the wording on the cairn dedicated to the United Empire Loyalists, Tusket, Nova Scotia, unveiled in 1964.

Canada is not required to be bribed into loyalty.

> SIR CLIFFORD SIFTON, minister of the Interior from 1896 to 1905, paraphrase of a remark made in Ottawa in Dec. 1903.

Loyalty, like affection, is a thing of the heart; it is not of the mouth or the pocket.

> SIR ANDREW MACPHAIL, physician and author, in *Essays in Politics* (1909).

A man can never have too many loyalties.

> JOHN BUCHAN, LORD TWEEDSMUIR, governor general, in an address in Charlottetown in Sept. 1937, from *Canadian Occasions* (1940).

Tell me, are our people in Quebec still loyal?

> PHILIP MOUNTBATTEN, DUKE OF EDINBURGH, to James Eayrs during a visit in 1964, quoted by Eayrs in the Toronto *Star*, Feb. 14, 1972.

Luck

If your luck isn't what it should be, write a "p" in front of it and try again.

> BOB EDWARDS, writer, and publisher of the Calgary *Eye Opener*, Jan. 13, 1912.

Luck nearly always follows after misfortune. If this were not so, people would soon die out.

> QUPAQ, Eskimo shaman, quoted by Knud Rasmussen in *The Netsilik Eskimos* (1931).

I am a great believer in luck, and I find the harder I work the more I have of it.

> STEPHEN LEACOCK, renowned humorist, attributed.

Macdonald, Sir John A.

Well! John A. beats the devil.

> LUTHER H. HOLTON, M.P., expressing surprise that Sir John A. Macdonald had been re-elected following revelations of the Pacific Scandal, September 17, 1878. Quoted by Sir Joseph Pope in *Memoirs of the Right Honourable Sir John Alexander Macdonald* (1894).

Old Tomorrow would be just the name for Sir John.

> COLONEL A.G. IRVINE, commissioner of the North West Mounted Police, made up this nickname for Sir John A. Macdonald after he met the prime minister late in 1881, from E.B. Biggar's *Anecdotal Life of Sir John Macdonald* (1891).

You'll never die, John A.!

> An unidentified person yelled this out at a Toronto gathering to celebrate Sir John's forty years in Parliament, Dec. 17, 1884.

Touché, Taché.

> SIR JOHN A. MACDONALD to Archbishop Alexandre-Antonin Taché in Ottawa, before the hanging of Louis Riel in Nov. 1885. A line of dialogue by John Coulter from his play *Riel* (1962).

John A. Macdonald, cabinet-maker.

> SIR JOHN A. MACDONALD, entering his name in the visitor's book in the Legislative Library, Province House, on his last visit to Prince Edward Island, 1890.

The Old Man, the Old Flag, and the Old Policy.

> LOUIS P. KRIBS, news editor of the Toronto *Empire*, coined the slogan of the Conservative party in the election of 1891. The Conservatives won, returning the "old man," Sir John A. Macdonald, to power. The "old flag" was the Union Jack, and the "old policy," the Na-

tional Policy of protective tariffs vs. Liberal reciprocity.

Dickey: No, I am still a Conservative, and I shall support you whenever I think you are right.

Sir John: That is no satisfaction. Anybody may support me when I am right. What I want is a man that will support me when I am wrong.

SIR JOHN A. MACDONALD in an exchange with Senator A.R. Dickey of Amherst, quoted by E.B. Biggar in *Anecdotal Life of Sir John Macdonald* (1891).

McLuhan, Marshall

Suppose he is what he sounds like, the most important thinker since Newton, Darwin, Freud, Einstein, and Pavlov—what if he is right?

TOM WOLFE, New York journalist, asked this question about Marshall McLuhan and his media theories in "The New Life Out There" (1965), *McLuhan: Hot & Cool* (1967), edited by Gerald Emmanuel Stearn. McLuhan's reply was characteristic: "I'd rather be wrong."

McLuhan put his telescope to his ear;
What a lovely smell, he said, we have here.

A.J.M. SMITH, poet, in "The Taste of Space," *Poems* (1967). McLuhan's response was: "Synaesthesia!"

John Kenneth Galbraith and Marshall McLuhan are the two greatest modern Canadians the United States has produced.

ANTHONY BURGESS, British man-of-letters, quoted by Peter C. Newman in "Home Country" (1971), *Home Country* (1973).

Malapropisms

See also HUMOUR.

Show me the verbal agreement! Show me the verbal agreement!

THOMAS J. IRWIN, mayor of Sault Ste. Marie, to Alderman Harry Lyons, a long-time resident of Steelton, when the two towns amalgamated in 1918. Lyons maintained that there were verbal as well as written agreements. The malapropism is often identified with Sam Goldwyn.

The scaffold at Hamilton is in a state of disrepair. It is a dangerous apparatus and should be demolished.

ARTHUR BARTHOLOMEW ENGLISH, official executioner, in a letter to Sheriff J.W. Lawrason of Wentworth County, Hamilton, 1935, quoted by Frank W. Anderson in *Concise History of Capital Punishment in Canada* (1973).

The patient is still under the doctor's car.

*

Your mother seriously ill, not expected to recover. Don't worry.

*

Had eye operation this morning. Hope to see you soon.

GERALD S. DOYLE would broadcast such items daily on "The Gerald S. Doyle News Bulletin," a radio program popular in Newfoundland in the 1940s and 1950s.

I can walk around this city as if I owned it and say that with pardonable pride.

*

I'm lost, but I'm making record time.

*

If someone's gonna stab me in the back, I wanna be there.

*

In politics you need more of the kind of men who will crawl out from behind the woodwork.

*

It makes good sense to remember the words, "Don't go too close to the edge of the fatal cliff."

*

Let's not just discontinue it, let's stop it.

*

When I'm going over the cliff, I want to be there.

*

Why, I even went so far as to be fair.

*

You can lead a dead horse to water, but you can't make him drink.

ALLAN LAMPORT, mayor of Toronto from 1952 to 1954, and a noted malapropist.

Where is the old mailed fist? Has it gone down the drain?

*

I am in sympathy with the resolution but what I say is this. Why go to work and foul our nest with a mess of pottage? We do not need it. We have got it now. Let us not take a chance.

> A.D. McPHILLIPS, Conservative M.P. from Victoria, speaking against Diefenbaker's proposed Bill of Rights, in the House of Commons, Jan. 6, 1958.

*

The public must learn to obey the laws like everyone else.

> GURZON HARVEY, a Winnipeg alderman, remark made in the early 1960s.

People shouldn't get excited about reports of pollution of the oceans. Everybody knows that oil and water don't mix.

> PHILLIP A. GAGLARDI, lively B.C. Social Credit minister, quoted in *Peter Gzowski's Book About This Country in the Morning* (1974).

Bill Mahoney's a marvellous breast stroker!

> IRENE MACDONALD, former Olympic diver, praising the winner of the men's swimming event on CBC-TV news, 1960s.

What our stories need are more antidotes.

> BELAND HONDERICH, publisher of the Toronto *Star*, 1968.

This agenda shouldn't take long, there's nothing contagious on it.

*

Just give me the headlights. [To a city clerk presenting a report]

*

We're in total darkness but I see the light.

*

Let's get it in black and writing.

*

That's putting the horse before the cart . . . well, isn't that what you normally do, put the horse before the cart?

*

You can't have a gain without a loss. [On a surplus city budget]

> SLAW REBCHUCK, Winnipeg alderman since 1949, councillor since 1962, quoted by Don Atkinson in the Winnipeg *Tribune*, Aug. 2, 1969.

We're not fooling around. We've got the bull by the tail, and we're looking him straight in the eye.

CHIEF DAVE COURCHENE, Indian spokesman, from an interview with Colin Hoath at Island Lake, Manitoba, broadcast on the CBC-TV National News, Feb. 22, 1973.

I'm speaking off the cuff of my head.

*

I don't want any information, I just want the facts.

*

I want to hear from the expertise.

*

Well don't get your dandruff up.

*

Would you please sit down and let me be patient?

> JOHN KUSHNER, Calgary alderman, at city council meetings in the 1970s.

But what of the children of these homosexual unions?

*

There are more important things than survival.

> RÉAL CAOUETTE, Quebec Créditiste leader, remarks attributed.

The onus should be on the other foot.

> DR. EDWIN J. BOUNSALL, member of the Ontario Legislature, to a committee studying labour estimates, October 28, 1974.

The bill is so incredible it is almost unbelievable.

*

W.A.C. Bennett was a man supreme in his ability to walk a straight fence and keep both ears to the ground.

> PATSY JORDAN, Social Credit M.L.A. and former Okanagan beauty queen, quoted by Allan Fotheringham in the Toronto *Star*, Nov. 30, 1974.

We'll be giving them *carte la blanche*.

> EUGENE WHALEN, Liberal minister of Agriculture, attributed, by Richard Gwyn in the Toronto *Star*, Dec. 16, 1974.

If this thing starts to snowball it will catch fire right across the country.

> ROBERT THOMPSON, former chiropractor and leader of the Social Credit party, quoted by Richard Gwyn in the Toronto *Star*, Dec. 26, 1974.

Manitoba

The climate of Manitoba consists of seven months of Arctic weather and five months of cold weather.

From *Settler's Guide to the North-West* (1882), published in New York by the Northern Pacific Railway Company.

Then come sit here awhile e'er you leave us,
Do not hasten to bid us adieu,
Just remember the Red River Valley
And the cowboy who loves you so true.

Chorus of "Red River Valley," American cowboy song popular in Canada, reprinted by Ralph L. Woods in *A Second Treasury of the Familiar* (1950).

Cinderella of Confederation.

JOHN NORQUAY, Manitoba premier, in a budget address of 1884.

Manitoba is a corruption of two Indian words, *Manitou napa*, "the land of the great spirit." The Manitobans translate it more freely as "God's Country."

EMILY GOWAN MURPHY, early feminist writer, in *Janey Canuck in the West* (1910).

A premier of Manitoba should be able to kick manure off tractor wheels!

WALTER WEIR, premier of Manitoba, remark made in 1967.

Mankind

See also MEN; MEN AND WOMEN; PEOPLE; WOMEN.

One topic more and I have done. Society contains not the whole of man. Human societies die; man never dies. Man has a higher destiny than that of states.

EGERTON RYERSON, educator, in "A Lecture on the Social Advancement of Canada," *Journal of Education for Upper Canada*, Dec. 1849.

ABOVE ALL NATIONS IS HUMANITY.

GOLDWIN SMITH, British-born journalist, motto engraved on the stone seat he donated to Cornell University, quoted by Arnold Haultain in *Goldwin Smith* (1913).

We despair of changing the habits of men, still we would alter institutions, the habits of millions of men.

GEORGE ILES, scientific popularizer, in *Canadian Stories* (1918).

The service we render to others is really the rent we pay for our room on this earth.

SIR WILFRED GRENFELL, pioneer Labrador doctor and missionary, in *A Labrador Logbook* (1938).

Only humans are wild.

JACK MINER, pioneer naturalist who banded wildlife at his famous bird sanctuary at Kingsville, Ontario, in *Wild Goose Jack* (1969).

Since I no longer expect anything from mankind except madness, meanness, and mendacity; egotism, cowardice, and self-delusion, I have stopped being a misanthrope.

IRVING LAYTON, outspoken poet, in *The Whole Bloody Bird* (1969).

Ever since man learned to walk upright, he has been looking for a place to sit down.

ARNOLD BRUNER, reporter, in the Toronto *Globe and Mail*, Feb. 21, 1975.

Manufacturing
See also INDUSTRY.

Made in Canada.

Unofficial motto of the Canadian Manufacturers' Association during a "Buy Canadian" campaign in 1903.

We are not manufacturers merely of articles of wood and stone, and iron and cotton and wool, and so on; we manufacture enthusiasms; we manufacture Canadian sentiment; we manufacture a feeling of pride in our country, and we manufacture a spirit of independence, a spirit of national pride.

CYRUS A. BIRGE, president of the Canadian Manufacturers' Association, in *Industrial Canada*, Oct. 1903.

Maple Leaf

The maple is the king of our forest; it is the symbol of the Canadian people.

DENIS-BENJAMIN VIGER, French-Canadian

spokesman, in an address to La Société Saint-Jean-Baptiste, June 24, 1836.

Canada has two emblems which have often appeared to some to point out its position in these respects,—the *Beaver* and the *Maple*. The beaver in his sagacity, his industry, his ingenuity, and his perseverance, is a most respectable animal; a much better emblem for our country than the rapacious eagle or even the lordly lion; but he is also a type of unvarying instincts and old-world traditions. He does not improve, and becomes extinct rather than change his ways. The maple, on the other hand, is the emblem of the vitality and energy of a new country; vigorous and stately in its growth, changing its hues as the seasons change, equally at home in the forest, in the cultivated field, and stretching its green boughs over the dusty streets, it may well be received as a type of the progressive and versatile spirit of a new and growing people.

> Sir John William Dawson, educator and principal of McGill, in *The Duties of Educated Young Men in British America* (1863).

The Maple Leaf, our emblem dear,
    The Maple Leaf forever;
God save our Queen, and Heaven bless
    The Maple Leaf forever.

> Alexander Muir, schoolteacher and later principal, composer of "The Maple Leaf Forever" in 1867.

O Canada! Where pines and maples grow,
Great prairies spread and lordly rivers flow
    . . . .

> R. Stanley Weir, jurist and composer of "O Canada" in 1908.

I love travelling, but I'm always too late or too early. I arrive in Japan when the cherry blossoms have fallen. I get to China too early for the next revolution. I reach Canada when the maple leaves have gone. People are always telling me about something I haven't seen. I find it very pleasant.

> Noël Coward, British playwright, in *The Wit of Noël Coward* (1968), compiled by Dick Richards.

Maritime Provinces

See also: NEW BRUNSWICK; NEWFOUNDLAND; NOVA SCOTIA; PRINCE EDWARD ISLAND.

Let not these Provinces be lost or given away.

> William IV, the "Sailor-King" of England, is credited with this remark, which may date from 1831 when the boundary differences between New Brunswick and Maine were referred to the king of the Netherlands for arbitration. Quoted by James FitzGibbon in *A Few Observations on Canada, and the Other Provinces of British North America* (1849).

We give you ships and tides and men,
Anchors a-weigh and wind-filled sail,
We give you back the sea again
In sailors' songs and rousing tale;
And inland where the dark hills rise
Between you and the salt-thick foam
You hear the surf, the sea gulls' cries
And eastward turn your hearts toward home.

> Eileen Cameron Henry, Maritime versifier, in "Harmony Harbour" (1947), from Will R. Bird's *Atlantic Anthology* (1959).

I had never heard of Ulysses, but before I was ten years old I knew that I was descended from classic heroes.

> Alden Nowlan, New Brunswick author, about his Maritime background, in "Alden Nowlan's Canada," *Maclean's*, June 1971.

Marriage

See also ADULTERY; DIVORCE; LOVE; MEN AND WOMEN.

What a pity it is marryin' spoils courtin'.

> Thomas Chandler Haliburton, Nova Scotian writer and wit, in *Sam Slick's Wise Saws and Modern Instances* (1853).

Many a man in love with a dimple makes the mistake of marrying the whole girl.

> Stephen Leacock, renowned Canadian writer and humorist, attributed.

Marriage: love gone—woman stays.

> Robert Zend, Hungarian-born Toronto writer, in the 1960s.

There is more to marriage than four bare legs under a blanket.

ROBERTSON DAVIES, man-of-letters, from *Love and Libel* (1957), a stage adaptation of the novel *Leaven of Malice* (1954).

A husband suspects one other man; a wife, all other women.

RICHARD J. NEEDHAM, Toronto columnist, in the *Globe and Mail*, April 30, 1971.

Nobody should be married, but everybody should have been.

RICHARD J. NEEDHAM, Toronto columnist, in *Homemaker's Digest*, Jan.–Feb. 1972.

You seem to overlook the fact that happily married men spend their Christmas and New Year's holidays with their families. But married men sometimes take business trips, I am told.

PETER DEMETER, wealthy Toronto business-man found guilty of having arranged the mur-der of his wife, in a letter to his mistress, Ma-rina Hundt, Dec. 7, 1972. Quoted by Farrell Crook in the Toronto *Star*, Nov. 8, 1974.

The world is divided into couples, and so being single can feel like playing musical chairs and every time they stop the music, you're the one who's out.

MERLE SHAIN, Toronto writer, in *Some Men Are More Perfect Than Others* (1973).

Media Theory

See COMMUNICATION.

Medicine

See also DISEASE; DOCTORS; HEALTH; SICKNESS.

Dr. Williams' pink pills for pale people.

GEORGE FULFORD, patent-medicine man and Brockville-born senator, manufacturer of the pills which "purged the blood around the world," in the 1870s.

The practice of medicine is an art, based on science.

*

The desire to take medicine is perhaps the greatest feature which distinguishes man from animals.

SIR WILLIAM OSLER, world-famous physician and medical teacher, in *Sir William Osler: Apho-risms from His Bedside Teachings and Writings* (1950), edited by W.B. Bean.

Tie off pancreas ducts of dogs. Wait six or eight weeks. Remove and extract.

SIR FREDERICK G. BANTING, medical re-searcher and discoverer of insulin, scribbled these words in his medical notebook at 2:00 a.m., Oct. 30, 1920. The procedure led to the isolation of insulin in May 1921, to the control of diabetes, and to the Nobel Prize for Medi-cine in 1923 (shared with J.J.R. Macleod). Quoted by Lloyd Stevenson in *Sir Frederick Banting* (1946).

The problem of medical economics is a part of the problem of world economics and is inseparable and indivisible from it. Medicine, as we are practising it, is a lux-ury trade. *We are selling bread at the price of jewels.*

NORMAN BETHUNE, Gravenhurst-born medical doctor and hero of Mao's China, to the Mont-real Medico-Chirurgical Society, April 17, 1936. Quoted by Ted Allan and Sydney Gor-don in *The Scalpel, The Sword* (1952).

You can only cure retail but you can pre-vent wholesale.

BROCK CHISHOLM, psychiatrist who from 1948 to 1953 was the first director-general of the World Health Organization, Geneva, remark made in 1936.

A great many people know a great deal about mental illness and mental health. Unfortunately, a great deal of what they know is not true.

J.D. GRIFFIN, psychiatrist and general director of the Canadian Mental Health Association from 1951 to 1971, in 1953, from *Let Just Praise Be Given* (1971).

Memory

Memory is cultivated and praised, but who will teach us to forget?

GEORGE ILES, scientific popularizer, in *Canadian Stories* (1918).

Memory, after all, is the sweetest story ever told.

GREGORY CLARK, journalist and story writer, attributed.

Men

See also MANKIND.

The natural man has only two primal passions, to get and to beget.

SIR WILLIAM OSLER, world-famous physician and medical teacher, in *Sir William Osler: Aphorisms from His Bedside Teachings and Writings* (1950), edited by W.B. Bean.

A good man who goes wrong is just a bad man who has been found out.

BOB EDWARDS, writer and publisher of the Calgary *Eye Opener*, Sept. 22, 1917.

When a man gets up on his hind legs, no one can walk on him.

FATHER JAMES TOMPKINS, educator who helped found the co-operative Antigonish Movement at St. Francis Xavier University during the 1920s, quoted by John R. Chafe in "God's Greatest Nuisance" in *In Search of Canada* (1971), by the editors of *Reader's Digest*.

Men are all alike. They say yours. But they mean mine.

MAZO DE LA ROCHE, popular novelist, in *Delight* (1926).

We have forgotten the truth that there is no sense in pasting wings on a man unless you can give him a winged nature.

GRATTAN O'LEARY, Conservative spokesman and senator, in an address to the Empire Club of Canada in 1950.

Man cannot add an inch to his stature, but by taking thought he can stand erect.

LORD BEAVERBROOK, Canadian-born British press lord, in *The Three Keys to Success* (1956).

The opposite of a male is a husband.

ROBERT ZEND, Hungarian-born Toronto writer, in the 1960s.

. . . the contradiction that is man; the mind that wrestles with black despair, the spirit that soars.

ROBERT KROETSCH, Alberta-born novelist, in *The Words of My Roaring* (1966).

There are no perfect men of course, but some are more perfect than others, and we can use all of those we can get.

MERLE SHAIN, Toronto writer, in *Some Men Are More Perfect Than Others* (1973).

Men are very fragile creatures. Their psyches are so closely tied to their epididymis.

BETTE STEPHENSON, past-president of the Canadian Medical Association, went on to explain: "The epididymis is the little tube that carries the sperm from the testicle to the *vas deferens*." Quoted by Christina Newman in the Toronto *Globe and Mail*, July 12, 1975.

Men and Women

See also LOVE; MANKIND; MARRIAGE; SEX.

A woman's tears are a man's terrors.

*

A woman can say more in a sigh than a man can say in a sermon.

*

A man imagines he wins by strenuous assault. The woman knows the victory was due to surrender.

ARNOLD HAULTAIN, writer and aphorist who was Goldwin Smith's private secretary, in *Hints for Lovers* (1909).

The trouble with wives is they expect too much. Because their husbands kiss them on Monday they look for the same on Tuesday, Wednesday and every day, whereas the husbands, in their ignorance of women's ways, consider the pleasant duty performed for the whole week.

JEAN BLEWETT, writer, quoted in *Canadian Days* (1911).

. . . women know men better than they know themselves and better than men ever suspect . . . .

SIR JOHN WILLISON, journalist, in *Reminiscences ‑ Political and Personal* (1919).

To define a man: he must be a creature who makes me feel that I am a woman.

ELINOR GLYN, British-born Hollywood writer raised in Ontario, creator of "It" in the 1920s.

Women become dangerous when they have no husbands to lie with them.

NAUKATJIK, Eskimo shaman, in Knud Rasmussen's *Intellectual Culture of the Iglulik Eskimos* (1929).

. . . the sexes are only tolerable when mingled.

ROBERTSON DAVIES, man-of-letters, in *The Table Talk of Samuel Marchbanks* (1949).

So it is probably appropriate that I should quote an unknown source which said: "The battle of the sexes will never be won by either side. There is too much fraternizing with the enemy."

ELLEN L. FAIRCLOUGH, M.P. and first woman to become a Canadian Cabinet minister, in "Canadian Women as Citizens," an address to the Empire Club of Canada in 1957.

Every woman needs one man in her life who is strong and responsible. Given this security, she can proceed to do what she really wants to do—fall in love with men who are weak and irresponsible.

RICHARD J. NEEDHAM, Toronto columnist, in A Friend in Needham, or a Writer's Notebook (1969).

Society has given women the role of being decorative; it has given men the role of being competent.

DR. JOHN RICH, Toronto marriage counsellor, in Chatelaine, April 1971.

The true liberation of women cannot take place without the liberation of men.

MADAME THÉRÈSE-FORGET CASGRAIN, Quebec M.L.A., in A Woman in a Man's World (1972).

To me, the apex of life is to have dinner with a beautiful woman—my wife, preferably.

ARTHUR HAILEY, best-selling novelist, quoted by George Gamester in the Toronto Star, March 1975.

Mining

And in some places we have found stones like Diamants, the most faire, pollished and excellently cut that it is possible for a man to see. When the Sunne shineth upon them, they glister as it were sparkles of fire.

JACQUES CARTIER, French explorer, in "The Third Voyage of Discovery" (1541), The Voyages of Jacques Cartier (1924), edited by H.P. Biggar. Cartier's quarry is known to this day as Cape Diamond.

Along the shores of the said Quebec are diamonds in the slate rocks which are better than those of Alençon.

SAMUEL DE CHAMPLAIN, the "Father of New France," in "Of Savages, or Voyages of Sam-

uel Champlain of Brouage" (1603), in The Works of Samuel de Champlain (1922-36), translated by H.P. Biggar. The "diamonds" encountered near present-day Quebec City, June 22, 1603, were quartz.

For we'll sing a little song of Cobalt,
If you don't live there it's your fault.
Oh you Cobalt, where the wintry breezes blow,
Where all the silver comes from
And you live a life and then some,
Oh you Cobalt, you're the best old town I know.

L.F. STEENMAN wrote the words and R.L. MacAdam the music, about 1910, to "The Cobalt Song"; from Canada's Story in Song (1965), edited by Edith Fowke and Alan Mills.

Rings on my fingers, corns on my toes,
Gold up in Porcupine, everybody knows.
Put on your snowshoes, and hit the trail with me,
For P-o-r-c-u-p-i-n-e—that's me!

From "The Porcupine Song," in Canada's Story in Song (1965), edited by Edith Fowke and Alan Mills.

It's an elephant!

GILBERT A. LABINE, uranium prospector, when his geiger counter made extra-loud crackling noises, indicating the presence of uranium near Beaverlodge Lake, Northwest Territories, 1925; quoted by D.M. LeBourdais in Metals and Men (1957).

My object in purchasing the Globe was not to make money out of it—at least that was not my main object. I thought I could do something for the country by making our mining industries better known. Anything that is of advantage to mining is of advantage to the country as a whole.

WILLIAM H. WRIGHT, mining magnate and newspaper publisher, in Mining World, Oct. 24, 1936. Quoted by Brian J. Young in "C. George McCullagh and the Leadership League," Canadian Historical Review, Sept. 1966.

What's Algoma? A new vegetable?

SALVADOR DALI, the surrealist painter, asked this of Sir James Dunn, head of Algoma Steel Corporation. Quoted by Lord Beaverbrook in Courage: The Story of Sir James Dunn (1961).

I would say that ninety per cent of our natural wealth still awaits discovery.

*

We always hear of the fortunes gained in mining. What about those that are lost?

STEPHEN B. ROMAN, mining executive, quoted by George Lonn in *Historical Highlights of Canadian Mining* (1973).

Monarchy

See also GOVERNOR GENERAL; ROYAL VISITS.

God save our gracious Queen,
Long live our noble Queen,
God save the Queen!

The opening lines of "God Save the Queen," the national anthem of the United Kingdom and the royal anthem of Canada. The words are traditional and go back to the sixteenth century.

Hail our great Queen in her regalia;
One foot in Canada, the other in Australia.

JAMES GAY, eccentric Canadian bard and "Royal Poet," attributed.

The time has gone by when Europe could give Monarchies to America; on the contrary, a new epoch is now approaching when America will give Republics to Europe.

LOUIS-JOSEPH PAPINEAU, French-Canadian patriot and later leader of the Rebellion of 1837 in Lower Canada, in an address to the House in 1835, quoted by John Mercier McMullen in *The History of Canada from Its First Discovery to the Present Time* (1892).

NOW KNOW YE that by and with the advice of Our Privy Council for Canada We do by this Our Royal Proclamation establish for Canada Our Royal Style and Titles as follows, namely, in the English language:

Elizabeth the Second, by the Grace of God of the United Kingdom, Canada and Her other Realms and Territories Queen, Head of the Commonwealth, Defender of the Faith.

And in the French language:

Elisabeth Deux, par la grâce de Dieu, Reine du Royaume-Uni, du Canada et de ses autres royaumes et territoires, Chef du Commonwealth, Défenseur de la Foi.

ELIZABETH II, Queen of Canada, in "Proclamation of the Queen's Title," May 28, 1953, reproduced by R.A. Mackay in *Canadian Foreign Policy 1945-1954* (1971).

It is as Queen of Canada that I am here, Queen of Canada and of all Canadians, not just of one or two ancestral strains. I would like the Crown to be seen as a symbol of national sovereignty belonging to all. It is not only a link between Commonwealth nations, but between Canadian citizens of every national origin and ancestry.

ELIZABETH II, on a Royal Visit, in an address at the Royal York Hotel in Toronto, June 26, 1973.

Like most Canadians I'm indifferent to the visit of the Queen . . . . We're a little annoyed at still being dependent.

JOYCE DAVIDSON, TV personality, observations on Dave Garroway's "Today Show," June 18, 1959. Mayor Nathan Phillips of Toronto said that the remarks "are not the feelings of the people of Canada" and demanded an apology; Miss Davidson refused to recant.

I think it is a complete misconception to imagine that the monarchy exists in the interest of the monarchy. It does not. It exists in the interest of the people in the sense that we do not come here for our health . . . we can think of other ways of enjoying ourselves.

*

If at any stage people feel that it has no further part to play then for goodness sake let's end the thing on amicable terms without having a row about it.

PHILIP MOUNTBATTEN, DUKE OF EDINBURGH, at a press conference in Ottawa, Oct. 1969.

A republic can swallow a top hat but not a crown.

MCKENZIE PORTER, columnist, in the Toronto *Telegram*, May 3, 1971.

Why should Canada not pay? They want to have the circus but not to feed the bloody horses.

WILLIE HAMILTON, British M.P., on Canada's lack of financial support for the monarchy, quoted by Ross Henderson in the Toronto *Globe and Mail*, Feb. 12, 1975.

Money

See also FINANCE; INFLATION.

A dollar looks larger going out than it does coming in.

    *

We sometimes lost dollars by being too careful with our cents.

> R.D. CUMMING, writer, in *Skookum Chuck Fables* (1915).

It is much easier to make money than it is to use it wisely.

> J.S. MCLEAN, founder of Canada Packers, quoted by Douglas Dacre in "The Butcher with a Poet's Soul," *Maclean's*, Oct. 1, 1951.

If you loan money to a friend, you will loose either the money or the friend.

> ROBERT ZEND, Hungarian-born Toronto writer, in 1974.

Money: The Poor Man's Credit Card.

> MARSHALL MCLUHAN, media pundit, in *Understanding Media* (1964).

Where your treasury is, there your heart is also.

> W.A.C. BENNETT, premier of British Columbia, quoted by Paddy Sherman in *Bennett* (1966).

Money in itself doesn't bring happiness. But often the *pursuit* of money does.

> JACK CLYNE, former chairman of MacMillan Bloedel Ltd., quoted by Peter C. Newman in *The Canadian Establishment: Volume One* (1975).

Montcalm, Marquis de

See also CONQUEST OF 1759.

"It's nothing, it's nothing," replied the death-stricken man; "don't be troubled for me, my good friends."

    *

"I am happy that I shall not live to see the surrender of Quebec."

> FRANCIS PARKMAN, historian who chronicled the fall of New France, recounted the Marquis de Montcalm's dying words in *Montcalm and Wolfe* (1884). Louis-Joseph de Montcalm-Gazon, Marquis de Montcalm de Saint-Servan, and leader of the French forces at the Battle of the Plains of Abraham on Sept. 13, 1759, died

the following day and was buried in the Ursuline Chapel in Quebec City.

>   Honneur à Montcalm
>   Le Destin
> En lui dérobant la Victorie
>   L'a récompensé
> Par une Mort glorieuse

> LORD AYLMER, governor of Lower Canada, composed the inscription for Montcalm's monument on the Plains of Abraham in 1831. "Honour to Montcalm/ Destiny/ in robbing him of victory/ compensated him/ with a glorious death." S. Macnaughtan in *My Canadian Memories* (1920) and Agnes Repplier in *Mère Marie of the Ursulines* (1931).

Montreal

And amidst these fields is situated the town of Hochelaga, near to and touching a mountain, which is around it, very fertile and cultivated, from the summit of which one can see far off. We called this mountain "le Mont Royal."

> JACQUES CARTIER, French navigator, exploring the site of present-day Montreal in 1535, in *Jacques Cartier and His Four Voyages to Canada* (1890), edited by Hiram B. Stephens.

The whole of this day was passed in devotions, thanksgivings, and hymns of praise to the Creator. There were no lighted lamps before the Holy Sacrament, but there were some fire-flies which shone there very pleasantly day and night, hung by threads in a beautiful and marvellous manner altogether fitting for the honour of the most revered of our mysteries, considering the rudeness of this savage country.

> FRANÇOIS DOLLIER DE CASSON, a French officer who gave an account of the founding of Montreal, May 18, 1642, in *A History of Montreal: 1640-1672* (1928), translated by Ralph Flenley.

I have not come here to deliberate, but to act. It is my duty and my honour to found a colony at Montreal; and I would go, if every tree were an Iroquois!

> SIEUR DE MAISONNEUVE, who founded the colony of Ville-Marie (later Montreal) on May 18, 1642, quoted by Francis Parkman in *The Jesuits of North America in the Seventeenth Century* (1867).

Stowed away in a Montreal lumber room
The Discobolus standeth and turneth his
    face to the wall;
Dusty, cobweb-covered, maimed, and set
    at naught,
Beauty crieth in an attic and no man re-
    gardeth:
               O God! O Montreal!

Beautiful by night and day, beautiful in
    summer and winter,
Whole or maimed, always and alike
    beautiful—
He preached gospel of grace to the skins of
    owls
And to one who seasoneth the skins of
    Canadian owls:
               O God! O Montreal!

SAMUEL BUTLER, British writer, in "A Psalm of
Montreal" (1875), which first appeared in the
Spectator, May 18, 1878.

The English people of Montreal would be
much gayer & happier & cultured if they
allowed a little French sunlight to warm
and illuminate their lives.

EARL GREY, governor general, to Edward VII,
on Feb. 3, 1905, quoted by R.H. Hubbard in
Rideau Hall (1967).

As I approached this great city [of
Montreal] I recollected the time when only
a line of frail palisades lay between its population and utter barbarism, and when a
sudden rush of savages might have driven
Europe entirely from these parts. I assure
you that I felt as much veneration as I
know you feel when you approach the historical centres of Europe.

SIR ARTHUR CONAN DOYLE, creator of Sher-
lock Holmes, in "The Future of Canadian
Literature," an address to the Canadian Club
of Montreal on June 4, 1914.

The outcome of it all was a vague general
impression that Montreal consists of banks
and churches. The people in this city
spend much of their time laying up their
riches in this world or the next.

RUPERT BROOKE, English poet, who visited
North America in 1913, in *Letters from America*
(1916).

Well, never mind, what you lack in
weather you make up in the means of

grace. This is the first time I was ever in a
city where you couldn't throw a brick
without breaking a church window. Yet I
was told that you were going to build one
more. I said, the scheme is good, but where
are you going to find the room? They said,
we will build it on top of another church
and use an elevator. This shows that the
gift of lying is not yet dead in the land.

MARK TWAIN, American humorist, quoted by
Stephen Leacock in "Mark Twain and
Canada," *Queen's Quarterly*, summer 1935.

In the Montreal telephone directory, the
Macs fill six pages. Tear them out, and
Montreal is no longer a financial capital,
but simply an immense French village
with a little English garrison!

ANDRÉ SIEGFRIED, French author, in *Canada:
An International Power* (1937), translated by
H.H. and Doris Hemming.

Montreal is wide-open—but honest.

CAMILLIEN HOUDE, the colourful mayor of
Montreal from 1928 to 1954, attributed.

Montreal has something of American lux-
ury, the sagacity of London, the briskness
of New York, the gaiety of Europe.

V.S. PRITCHETT, British essayist, in "Across
the Vast Land," *Holiday*, April 1964.

Montreal is the only place where a good
French accent isn't a social asset.

BRENDAN BEHAN, Irish playwright, in *The Wit
of Brendan Behan* (1968), compiled by Sean
McCann.

The Channukah lights are going out.

IRVING LAYTON, poet, giving this as his reason
for leaving Montreal, the city he was identified
with, for Toronto, in 1968.

Westmount Rhodesians.

KEITH SPICER, the commissioner of official languages, at a luncheon meeting of the Canadian Studies Institute, Johns Hopkins University, Washington campus, April 1973. Spicer
compared the Anglo-Saxons in the wealthy
Montreal district of Westmount with the
"outlaw regime" of Ian Smith's Rhodesia.

There was a young girl from Montreal
Who wore a newspaper dress to a ball.
    But her dress caught on fire

And burnt her entire
Front page—sporting section and all.
Anonymous limerick, dating from the 1950s.

Mosaic
See also SOCIETY.

It is indeed a mosaic of vast dimensions
and great breadth, essayed of the Prairie.
VICTORIA HAYWARD, American travel-writer,
describing the contributions of New Canadians to the architecture of the prairies, in
Romantic Canada (1922).

. . . the word "mosaic" . . . was used for the
first time, so far as I know, by an American
writer, Victoria Hayward, who used to
come every summer to Canada with her
friend, Edith Watson, to write about and
photograph the country folk, both in the
East and in the West. These two collabo-
rated on a book, published in 1922 . . . .
JOHN MURRAY GIBBON, writer who popularized the concept, in *Canadian Mosaic* (1938).

The Vertical Mosaic.
JOHN PORTER, social scientist from Carleton
University who examined the structure of
Canadian society horizontally to study ethnici-
ty, and vertically to study class, in *The Vertical
Mosaic* (1965). "One of the most persistent im-
ages that Canadians have of their society is
that it has no classes."

Mosquitoes

Hudson's Bay is certainly a country that
Sinbad the Sailor never saw, as he makes
no mention of mosquitoes.
DAVID THOMPSON, geographer, at Prince of
Wales's Fort, now Churchill, Manitoba, in
1784-85, from *Travels in Western North America,
1784-1812* (1971), edited by Victor G. Hop-
wood.

A certain northern chronicler relates that
Kitch Manitou became angry when, one
day, all the men married all the women
and a universal honeymoon began so that
no one would harvest the rice or the corn.
At this juncture Kitch created *saw-gi-may*,
the mosquito, and sent him forth to work
his will and, as the chronicler puts it, "this
took the romance out of the situation" so
that the honeymoon suddenly waned.

EMILY GOWAN MURPHY, early feminist writer,
in *Janey Canuck in the West* (1910).

An old woman was once found among
corpses. All her neighbours were dead.
And she was the only one alive among the
dead.
Have you eaten of human flesh?
"No."
"Then what have you lived on?"
"Lice."
No one believed her. So they killed her
and opened her stomach. It was full of lice.
But when her stomach was opened all the
lice became alive, put on wings, and flew
out over the country and turned into mos-
quitoes. In that way the old woman took
vengeance on the people who would not
believe her word. And she gave them the
worst plague of hot summers.
MANÉLAQ, Eskimo shaman, recounting the
Eskimo legend, "How the First Mosquitoes
Came," quoted by Knud Rasmussen in *The
Netsilik Eskimos* (1931).

And the black flies, the little black flies,
Always the black fly no matter where you
go.
I'll die with the black fly a-pickin' my
bones
In North Ontario, io, in North Ontario.
WADE HEMSWORTH, engineer, refrain from
"The Black Fly Song" (1949), in *Canada's Story
in Song* (1964), edited by Edith Fowke and
Alan Mills.

Mothers
See also CHILDREN.

Mothers can get weaned as well as babies.
THOMAS CHANDLER HALIBURTON, Nova Sco-
tian writer and wit, in *The Attaché; or, Sam Slick
in England* (1843-44).

Maternal dislike is more crippling than
clubs.
JUNE CALLWOOD, woman-of-all-causes, in
"The Needs of the Young," *Probings* (1968), es-
says contributed to the Canadian Mental
Health Association for its golden jubilee.

There was this old lady in Calgary, they
called her Mother Melville, and she used
to go down to the jungle on the Bow River
and she'd have a purse full of envelopes.

Envelopes with stamps on them and a sheet of paper inside each one and she'd go among the boys, all these guys riding the rods and she'd hand out these envelopes and say, "Write your mother, son, please write her just a line or two. She's worried, I know." After Mother Melville had gone through, you'd see fifteen or twenty guys sitting around, passing a pencil around, writing notes home.

Unidentified survivor of the Great Depression, quoted by Barry Broadfoot in *Ten Lost Years* (1973).

Mottos

Country, Province or Territory: Date of Confederation; Floral Emblem; Motto. Capital; motto.

Canada: July 1, 1867; Maple Leaf; "A Mari Usque ad Mare" (From Sea to Sea; D'un océan à l'autre). Ottawa; "Advance—Ottawa—*En Avant*."

Alberta: September 1, 1905; Wild Rose; no official motto (unofficially "Next Year Country"). Edmonton; "Industry, Integrity, Progress."

British Columbia: July 20, 1871; Dogwood; "*Splendor Sine Occasu*" (Splendour Undiminished; Splendour Without Diminishment). Victoria; "*Semper Liber*" (Always Free [an allusion to its free-port facilities]).

Manitoba: July 15, 1870; Prairie Crocus; no official motto (unofficially "Home of the [Hudson's] Bay," "The Prairie Province"). Winnipeg; "*Unum cum Virtute Multorum*" (One with the Strength of Many).

New Brunswick: July 1, 1867; Purple Violet; "*Spem Reduxit*" (She [England] Restored Hope). Fredericton; "*Fredericopolis Silvae Filia Nobilis*" (Fredericton, Noble Daughter of the Forest).

Newfoundland: March 31, 1949; Pitcher Plant; "*Quaerite Prime Regnum Dei*" (Seek Ye First the Kingdom of God), unofficially "The Great Island." St. John's; no official motto (unofficially "The Most Easterly City of America").

Nova Scotia: July 1, 1867; Trailing Arbutus, "*Munit Haec et Altera Vincit*" (One Defends and the Other Conquers). Halifax; "*E Mari Merces*" (Wealth from the Sea), unofficially "Warden of the North."

Ontario: July 1, 1867; White Trillium;

"*Ut Incepit Fidelis Sic Permanet*" (Loyal She Began, Loyal She Remains [an allusion to the Loyalist settlers]). Toronto; "Industry, Intelligence, Integrity."

Prince Edward Island: July 1, 1873; Lady's Slipper; "*Parva sub Ingenti*" (The Small under the Protection of the Great), unofficially "The Garden of the Gulf. Charlottetown; no official motto (unofficially "Cradle of Confederation").

Quebec: July 1, 1867; White Garden Lily; "*Je me Souviens*" (I Remember), unofficially "*La Belle Province*" (The Beautiful Province). Quebec City; "*Don de Dieu Feray Valoir*" (God's Gift to Make the Most).

Saskatchewan: September 1, 1905; Prairie Lily; no official motto (unofficially "Wheat Province," "Home of the RCMP"). Regina; "*Floreat Regina*" (Let Regina Flourish).

Northwest Territories: July 15, 1870 (the three administrative districts of Mackenzie, Keewatin and Franklin were created July 1, 1920); Mountain Avens; no official motto (unofficially "The New North"). Yellowknife; "*Multum in Parvo*" (Much from Little).

Yukon Territory: June 13, 1898; Purple Fireweed; no official motto (unofficially "Home of the Klondike"). Whitehorse; no official motto (unofficially "Trail of '98" and "Sourdough City").

Mountains

But the greater part of the mainland is "a sea of mountains"; and the Province will have to depend mainly on its rich grazing resources, its valuable timber, its fisheries, and minerals, for any large increase of population.

GEORGE MUNRO GRANT, principal of Queen's University, in *Ocean to Ocean: Sandford Fleming's Expedition through Canada in 1872* (1873).

Until these surveys are thoroughly completed, and until we have found the least impracticable route through that inhospitable country, that "sea of mountains," it is folly to talk of commencing the work of construction.

EDWARD BLAKE, brilliant Liberal leader, at Aurora, Ontario, Oct. 3, 1873. W. Stewart

Wallace, "Aurora Speech," *Canadian Historical Review*, Sept. 1921.

The Rockies have no majesty; they do not elevate the mind to contemplation of Almighty God any more than they warm the heart by seeming sentinels to watch over the habitations of one's fellow men.
ALEISTER CROWLEY, the self-styled poet and black magician who travelled from British Columbia to Niagara Falls in 1906, in *The Confessions of Aleister Crowley* (1970).

I said that he fell straight to the ice where they found him.
And none but the sun and incurious clouds have lingered
Around the marks of that day on the ledge of the Finger,
That day, the last of my youth, on the last of our mountains.
EARLE BIRNEY, distinguished poet, in the concluding stanza of "David" (1940), from *Selected Poems* (1966).

When they said Canada, I thought it would be up in the mountains somewhere.
MARILYN MONROE, movie star, interviewed on the set of *Niagara* by Jock Carroll in 1952, in *The Death of the Toronto Telegram and Other Newspaper Stories* (1971).

The mountains are all right, I guess, but they sure do block the view.
PETER BERGLUND, retired Saskatchewan farmer living in Kelowna, B.C., as told to Ed Ogle, *Time* bureau chief, in 1958.

Multiculturalism
See also CULTURE.

I want the marble to remain the marble; I want the granite to remain the granite; I want the oak to remain the oak.
SIR WILFRID LAURIER, prime minister, on the need for diversity, quoted by Richard M. Nixon before a joint sitting of the Canadian Senate and the House of Commons, April 14, 1972.

You will be better Canadians for being Ukrainians.
JOHN BUCHAN, LORD TWEEDSMUIR, governor general, to a Ukrainian group in 1936, quoted by Elizabeth Wangenheim in "The Ukraini-

ans: A Case Study of the 'Third Force,'" *Nationalism in Canada* (1966), edited by Peter Russell.

Leave them alone and pretty soon the Ukrainians will think they won the battle of Trafalgar , , , ,
STEPHEN LEACOCK, renowned Canadian writer and humorist, in "Monarchy in the West," *My Discovery of the West* (1937).

An apocryphal yarn has it that when a Canadian newsman covering President Nixon's visit to Moscow asked Leonid Brezhnev how many Soviet missiles were aimed at Toronto, the Soviet Communist party chief replied: "None. I've got nothing against the Italians."
A reference to Leonid Brezhnev, the Soviet leader, in *Time*, July 10, 1972.

ENGLISH SPOKEN HERE
Sign seen in a shopwindow in the Italian section of Toronto, reported by Max Braithwaite in *Braithwaite's Ontario* (1974).

Beauty is the business of Italians.
ROLOFF BENY, talking about his book of Italian photographs to Helen Hutchison on "Canada A.M.," CTV, Dec. 9, 1974.

Multinational Corporation
See also BUSINESS; ECONOMIC NATIONALISM.

The multinational firm.
HOWE MARTYN, Canadian citizen teaching in the United States, coined this widely used term in 1958. "Origins of the Multinational Firm," *The Multinational Corporation in World Politics* (1973), edited by Abdul Said.

The multinational corporation is like the man who came to dinner. You welcome him as a guest and then find that he's making the rules and giving the orders for the household.
MELVILLE H. WATKINS, nationalist and author of the Watkins Report, in *Gordon To Watkins To You* (1970), edited by Dave Godfrey and Mel Watkins.

The so-called multi-national enterprises are really national enterprises with multinational operations.
HERB GRAY, Liberal cabinet minister, in

Foreign Direct Investment in Canada, popularly known as the Gray Report (1972).

Munsinger, Gerda

STAR MAN FINDS GERDA MUNSINGER

Munich—The girl Canada calls Olga Munsinger is alive and well.

Her real name is Gerda Munsinger. She is tall, blonde and shapely.

I found her in a chintzy flat in an affluent district of Munich, wearing a gold September birthstone ring that was the gift of a former Canadian cabinet minister . . . .

ROBERT REGULY, Toronto *Star* reporter, made "the scoop of the sixties" when he found Mrs. Gerda Munsinger (the former Miss Garmisch-Partenkirchen, who was intimate with at least one Canadian cabinet minister) alive and well and living in Munich, West Germany, in the Toronto *Star*, March 11, 1966.

I want my bedtime Tory.

GERDA MUNSINGER, attributed by James Johnston in *The Party's Over* (1971).

There was a young lady from Munich
Whose bosom distended her tunic.
Her main undertaking
Was cabinet making
In fashions *bilingue et unique*.

GILLIS PURCELL, general manager of Canadian Press, in a limerick celebrating the achievements of Gerda Munsinger; it won first prize in a contest sponsored by *Maclean's* in 1967.

Murder

See CRIME.

Music

See also CANADIAN BOAT SONG; COMPOSERS; CULTURE; NATIONAL ANTHEMS; NATIONAL SONGS.

The Sweetest Music This Side of Heaven.

Motto of GUY LOMBARDO and His Royal Canadians, dating from 1931. *Auld Acquaintance* (1975), by the popular bandleader who was born in London, Ont., and Jack Altshul.

Music is no more the exclusive property of musicians than law is the property of lawyers. Music belongs to the masses.

It would be wonderful if I could live to see Canada made a singing nation.

EDWARD JOHNSON, Guelph-born singer and general manager of the Metropolitan Opera in New York from 1935 to 1950.

And I will sing to the barren rock
Your difficult, lonely music, heart,
Like an old proud king in a parable.

A.J.M. SMITH, poet, from "Like an Old Proud King in a Parable" (1943), in *Poems* (1967).

When people ask me what I think of opera in Maple Leaf Gardens I reply we only hope ice hockey will look as well in the Metropolitan Opera House.

RUDOLF BING, manager of the Metropolitan Opera, in "This Business of Opera" (1957), an address to the Empire Club of Canada in 1957.

Don't call me Callas.

TERESA STRATAS, Toronto-born opera singer, quoted by George Kidd in the Toronto *Telegram*, Jan. 10, 1958.

Look for the word *music* in the index of almost any book of Canadian history and you will find that the M's stop at "Murray, James, governor of Quebec!"

HELMUT KALLMANN, musicologist, in *A History of Music in Canada* (1960).

Canada is a great school—I should know, all my training was in Canada—but it is in danger of remaining a school.

JON VICKERS, opera singer, quoted in the Toronto *Globe and Mail*, Feb. 2, 1968.

The habit of concert-going and concert-giving, both as a social institution and as chief symbol of musical mercantilism, will be . . . dormant in the twenty-first century.

GLENN GOULD, pianist, quoted by Richard Kostelanetz in "The Glenn Gould Variations," *Master Minds* (1969), reprinted by William Kilbourn in *Canada: A Guide to the Peaceable Kingdom* (1970).

Dear God, you gave me a voice, I didn't ask for it. So help me.

LOUIS QUILICO, baritone, mock prayer quoted by Blaik Kirby in the Toronto *Globe and Mail*, Feb. 12, 1972.

If you close your eyes and think of a naked Anne Murray, parts of her always come up airbrushed.

LARRY LeBLANC, freelance writer, in "The Flip Side of Anne Murray," *Maclean's*, Nov. 1974.

I can't stand to see moonlight go to waste . . . perhaps it's the merchant in me.

LEONARD COHEN, poet and singer, at a concert at the Théâtre du Nouveau Monde, Montreal, Feb. 10, 1975.

I've been in show business for thirty years. At last I've arrived—I've been goosed in Toronto.

LIBERACE, pianist, when presented with a carved Canada goose at the O'Keefe Centre in Toronto where he was performing, April 7, 1975.

Mythology

As to ghosts or spirits they appear totally banished from Canada. This is too matter-of-fact country for such supernaturals to visit. Here there are no historical associations, no legendary tales of those that came before us. Fancy would starve for lack of marvellous food to keep her alive in the backwoods. We have neither fay nor fairy, ghost nor bogle, satyr nor wood-nymph; our very forests disdain to shelter dryad or hamadryad. No naiad haunts the rushy margin of our lakes, or hallows with her presence our forest-rills. No Druid claims our oaks; and instead of pouring with mysterious awe among our curious limestone rocks, that are often singularly grouped together, we refer them to the geologist to exercise his skill in accounting for their appearance: instead of investing them with the solemn characters of ancient temples or heaven altars, we look upon them with the curious eye of natural philosophy alone.

CATHARINE PARR TRAILL, pioneer writer, on May 9, 1833, from *The Backwoods of Canada* (1836).

Reader, did you ever see a ghost? A tall spectral-looking figure, with large saucer eyes, glides before you; and ere you summon courage to address it, vanishes from your astonished sight? Well, Canada is no place for ghosts. The country is too new for such gentry. We have no fine, old, ruined castles, crumbling monastic walls, or ivy-clad churches—no shelter here but the wild, wild wood.

MAJOR SAMUEL STRICKLAND, brother of Catharine Parr Traill, in *Twenty-Seven Years in Canada West* (1853), edited by Agnes Strickland.

No monuments or landmarks guide the stranger
Going among this savage people, masks
Taciturn or babbling out an alien jargon
And moody as barbaric skies are moody.

DOUGLAS LePAN, poet and essayist, in "A Country Without a Mythology," *The Wounded Prince and Other Poems* (1948).

No ghosts in Canada? The country which too vigorously asserts its normality and rationality is like a man who declares that he is without imagination; suddenly the ghosts he has denied may overcome him, and then his imaginative flights make poets stare . . . .

However, nations have a way of whispering the inner truth about themselves, sufficiently disguised to deceive those who would keep the truth hidden . . . this self-appraisal now begins to reveal, among much else, that the Canadian writers of the past must have been much more perceptive, more prophetic and disenchanted, than their readers have guessed. In the land which pretends to have no ghosts, they have seen ghosts; in the country without a mythology, they have heard the ground bass of myth; in a country born not of love and struggle but of politics, they have fought battles; and, with reserve and irony, they have offered their country love.

ROBERTSON DAVIES, man-of-letters, in "The Northern Muse," *Holiday*, April 1964.

National Anthems
See also MUSIC.

God save our gracious Queen,
Long live our noble Queen,
God save the Queen!
Send her victorious,
Happy and glorious,
Long to reign over us,
God save the Queen!

Dieu sauve notre Reine,
Notre gracieuse Reine,
Vive la Reine!
Qu'elle soit victorieuse,
Heureuse et glorieuse,
Que Dieu protège notre Reine,
Vive la Reine!

First verse of "God Save the King," in English and French. The words and music for the "best-known tune in the world" were first printed in their present form in 1744. Since 1967, "God Save the King" has been Canada's royal anthem, and the music (but not the words) of "O Canada" the national anthem.

O Canada! terre de nos aïeux,
Ton front est ceint de fleurons glorieux.
    Car ton bras sait porter l'épée,
        Il sait porter la croix;
    Ton histoire est une épopée
        Des plus brillants exploits;
    Et ta valeur, de foi trempée,
Protégera nos foyers et nos droits.

SIR ADOLPHE-BASILE ROUTHIER, prominent Quebec City lawyer and versifier, wrote "Chant national," better known as "O Canada," and Calixa Lavallée set it to music for the Fête Nationale des Canadiens-français in Quebec City on St. Jean-Baptiste Day, June 24, 1880. The lyrics were published in *Les Echos* (1882). In 1967, Parliament recognized the melody and the French lyrics of "O Canada" and proclaimed them the national anthem.

Here is a translation by William McLennan from *Songs of Old Canada* (1886): "O Canada! land of our sires, / Whose brow is bound with glorious bays, / The sword thy valorous hand can wield / And bear the Cross that faith inspires, / What mighty deeds hast thou beheld, / An epopee of glorious sights! / The faith, thy shield through all thy days, / Shall still protect our homes and rights, / Shall still protect our homes and rights." (The final line is usually repeated.)

O Canada! Our home and native land!
True patriot-love in all thy sons command.
With glowing hearts we see thee rise,
The True North, strong and free,
And stand on guard, O Canada,
We stand on guard for thee.

O Canada, glorious and free!
We stand on guard, we stand on guard for thee.
O Canada, we stand on guard for thee!

O Canada! Where pines and maples grow,
Great prairies spread and lordly rivers flow,
How dear to us thy broad domain,
From East to Western Sea,
Thou land of hope, for all who toil!
Thou True North, strong and free!

O Canada, glorious and free!
We stand on guard, we stand on guard for thee.
O Canada, we stand on guard for thee!

O Canada! Beneath thy shining skies
May stalwart sons and gentle maidens rise,
To keep thee steadfast through the years
From East to Western Sea,
Our own beloved native land!
Our True North, strong and free!

O Canada, glorious and free!
We stand on guard, we stand on guard for thee.
O Canada, we stand on guard for thee!

R. STANLEY WEIR, Montreal lawyer and sometime judge of the Exchequer Court of Canada, prepared the generally accepted English version of the lyrics of "O Canada" for Quebec's tercentenary celebration in 1908. In 1967, Parliament accepted the song as the national anthem, but did not accept the English words. In 1972 Parliament made minor revisions to the English version.

While other states take up a war-like stance,

"No price too high to live secure," the
  plea;
My native land, with gay insouciance,
Slashes her "Stand on Guards" from five to
  three.

> CLAUDE T. BISSELL, former president of the
> University of Toronto and poetaster, from
> "Lines written on hearing about Changes in
> the Words of the Canadian National
> Anthem," from an address on "Continentalism
> and Nationalism," June 23, 1971.

With glowing hearts we see thee rise,
The true North, strong and free,
And stand on guard, O Canada,
While Exxon's doing it to thee.

> DAVE BROADFOOT, as "The Honourable Mem-
> ber for Kicking Horse Pass," in *Sex and Security*
> (1974).

National Emblems
See BEAVER; MAPLE LEAF; MOTTOS.

National Identity
See also NATIONAL INFERIORITY COMPLEX;
NATIONALISM.

Is the northern land which we have chosen, a congenial home for the growth of a
free and a dominant race? What is the
stock from which we are sprung? Who are
the men of the north and what is their
place in history? Can the generous flame of
national spirit be kindled and blaze in the
icy bosom of the frozen north?

> ROBERT GRANT HALIBURTON, son of Thomas
> Chandler Haliburton and a founder of the
> Canada First movement, in *The Men of the
> North and Their Place in History*, a lecture to the
> Montreal Literary Club on March 31, 1869.

The old Norse mythology, with its Thor
hammers and Thor hammerings, appeals
to us,—for we are a Northern people,—as
the true out-crop of human nature, more
manly, more real, than the weak marrow-
bones superstition of an effeminate South.

> WILLIAM A. FOSTER, a founder of the Canada
> First movement, in *Canada First* (1871), the key
> text of the movement which, between 1868
> and 1874, encouraged pan-Canadianism.

But how long is this talk in the newspaper
and elsewhere, this talk which I find in
very high places, of the desirability, aye, of
the necessity of fostering a national spirit
among the people of Canada, to be mere
talk? It is impossible to foster a national
spirit unless you have national interests to
attend to, or among people who do not
choose to understand the responsibilities
and to devote themselves to the duties to
which national attributes belong.

> EDWARD BLAKE, brilliant Liberal leader, in his
> speech at Aurora, Ontario, Oct. 3, 1873. Re-
> printed by W. Stewart Wallace as "Aurora
> Speech," *Canadian Historical Review*, Sept. 1921.

For forty years we have been teaching in
Canada everything but Canada and Canadianism and if generations are now
growing up who are not particularly concerned about Canada, her future, her ideals, her national life and her destiny who is
to be blamed?

*

We have decided that our own Supreme
Court was not good enough for the people
of Canada, we have never had enough national spirit to provide ourselves with a distinctive flag; we have people in Canada
objecting to standing up when "O
Canada" is sung, we have trifled with the
question of citizenship and nationality until the young Canadian is never quite sure
whether he is a Canadian or a Hottentot
because he had a Hottentot grandmother.

> JOHN W. DAFOE, Winnipeg editor, Convention
> of Canadian Clubs in 1921, from *Dafoe of the
> Free Press* (1968), by Murray Donnelly.

Canada isn't exactly underdeveloped, but
living here is like living in a civilized Con-
go: there's just as much search for identity.

> NICHOLAS MONSARRAT, best-selling novelist
> resident in Ottawa in the 1950s, quoted by
> Gerald Clark in *Canada: The Uneasy Neighbour*[9]
> (1965).

We moved from British influence to American influence without much feeling of
purely national identity in between.

> LESTER B. PEARSON, prime minister, in an in-
> terview upon his retirement in 1968.

If the national mental illness of the United
States is megalomania, that of Canada is
paranoid schizophrenia . . . . We are all
immigrants to this place even if we were
born here: the country is too big for any-

one to inhabit completely, and in the parts unknown to us we move in fear, exiles and invaders. This country is something that must be chosen—it is so easy to leave—and if we do choose it we are still choosing a violent duality.

MARGARET ATWOOD, poet and novelist, in an afterword to *The Journals of Susanna Moodie* (1970).

Canada demands a great deal from people and is not, as some countries are, quick to offer in return a pleasant atmosphere or easy kind of life .... Canada is not really a place where you are encouraged to have large spiritual adventures.

ROBERTSON DAVIES, man-of-letters, in "The Master's Voice: The Table Talk of Robertson Davies," quoted by Peter C. Newman in *Maclean's*, Sept. 1972.

Team Canada probably did more to create a Canadian identity by defeating Russia by four games to three than did ten years of Canada Council fellowships.

JAMES GIBSON, president of Brock University, to the Ontario Committee on Economic and Cultural Nationalism, Feb. 20, 1973.

National Inferiority Complex
See also NATIONAL IDENTITY.

Fortunately, I am not only an authority on the [national] inferiority complex but possibly one of the greatest living authorities. I don't claim to be the inventor of the famous cliché—some of the credit must be shared with Sigmund Freud—but I was probably the first to diagnose the symptoms and immortalize them on the printed page .... I never expected that it would become part of the national folklore and live to become a tedious and shop-worn cliché. For my sins, I have been doing my best to combat it ever since.

MERRILL DENISON, Montreal company historian, in "That Inferiority Complex," an address to the Empire Club of Canada in 1949.

National Policy of 1878
See also TRADE.

I say what Canada wants is a national policy—a policy that shall be in the interest of Canada, apart from the principles of free-trade, apart from the principles of protection.

SIR CHARLES TUPPER, Nova Scotian leader, in the House of Commons, Feb. 25, 1876. Tupper's speech included the phrase "national policy," which two years later Sir John A. Macdonald appropriated.

I move: That the Speaker do not now leave the Chair, but that this House is of the opinion that the welfare of Canada requires the adoption of a National Policy, which, by a judicious readjustment of the Tariff, will benefit and foster the agricultural, the mining, the manufacturing and other interests of the Dominion; that such a policy will retain in Canada thousands of our fellow countrymen now obliged to expatriate themselves in search of the employment denied them at home, will restore prosperity to our struggling industries, now so sadly depressed, will prevent Canada from being made a sacrifice market, will encourage and develop an active inter-provincial trade, and moving (as it ought to do) in the direction of a reciprocity of tariffs with our neighbours, so far as the varied interests of Canada may demand, will greatly tend to procure for this country, eventually, a reciprocity of trade.

SIR JOHN A. MACDONALD, leader of the Opposition, in the House of Commons, March 7, 1878, moved an amendment to the budget speech and declared the principles of his protectionist National Policy.

National Songs
See also MUSIC.

O Alouette, gentille Alouette,
Alouette, je t'y plumerai.

Je t'y plumerai la têt',
Je t'y plumerai la têt',

Et la têt', et la têt',
Alouett', Alouett'.

O Alouette, gentille Alouette,
Alouette, je t'y plumerai.

The lyrics of the famous French-Canadian song "Alouette." To sing it, repeat the above, replacing la têt' (head) in the second verse with: le bec (beak), le nez (nose), les yeux (eyes), le cou (neck), les ail's (wings), le dos (back), les patt's (feet), la queue (tail). In the third verse, repeat the new word and then work backwards through the series to la têt', so that the song grows by one line with each repetition. Loosely translated:

O Alouette, gentle Alouette,
Alouette, I'll pluck your feathers yet.

Pluck your plumage from your head,
Pluck your plumage from your head,

And your head, and your head,
Alouett', Alouett'.

O Alouette, gentle Alouette,
Alouette, I'll pluck your feathers yet.

Comme le dit un vieil adage
Rien n'est si beau que son pays;
Et de le chanter, c'est l'usage;
Le mien je chante à mes amis
L'étranger voit avec un oeil d'envie
Du Saint-Laurent le majestueux cours;
A son aspect le Canadien s'écrie:
O Canada! mon pays! mes amours!

SIR GEORGE-ETIENNE CARTIER, future Father of Confederation, composed "O Canada, mon pays, mes amours" (which almost became a national anthem) in 1834, while still a student. *Sir George Etienne Cartier, Bart.* (1914), by John Boyd, who included the following verse translation:

"One's own land is best of all,"
  So an ancient adage says;
To sing it is the poet's call,
  Mine be to sing my fair land's praise.
Strangers behold the envious eyes
  St. Lawrence's tide so swift and grand,
But the Canadian proudly cries,
  O Canada, my own beloved land!

Souvent de la Grande Bretagne,
On vante de les moeurs et les lois;
Par leur vins, la France et l'Espagne
A nos éloges ont des droits.
Admirez le ciel d'Italie
Louez l'Europe, c'est fort bien;
Moi, je préfère ma patrie:
Avant tout je suis Canadien.

SIR GEORGE-ETIENNE CARTIER, future Father of Confederation, composed "Avant tout je suis Canadien" ("Before all I am a Canadian"), which was the marching song of the Sons of Liberty during the Rebellion of 1837 in Lower Canada, quoted by John Boyd

in *Sir George Etienne Cartier, Bart.* (1914). The title is sometimes given as "Avant tout soyons Canadiens" ("Before all let us be Canadians"). Boyd included the following prose translation: "Often they boast of the customs and laws of Great Britain; France and Spain, on account of their wines, have a right to our praises; to admire the skies of Italy and to laud Europe is all very well, but for me I prefer my own country. Before all I am a Canadian."

Un Canadien errant,
Banni de ses foyers,
Parcourait en pleurant
Des pays étrangers.

Un jour, triste et pensif,
Assis au bord des flots,
Au courant fugitif
Il adressa ces mots:

"Si tu vois mon pays,
Mon pays malheureux,
Va, dis à mes amis
Que je me souviens d'eux.

"O jours si pleins d'appas,
Vous êtes disparus,
Et ma patrie, hélas!
Je ne la verrai plus.

"Non, mais en expirant,
O mon cher Canada,
Mon regard languissant
Vers toi se portera."

ANTOINE GÉRIN-LAJOIE, French-Canadian nationalist, in "Un Canadien errant: 1838," a lament for those who fled or were exiled for taking part in the Rebellion of 1837, written a few years later. From A.J.M. Smith's *The Oxford Book of Canadian Verse in English and French* (1960). John Boyd, journalist and versifier, prepared a translation, which he called "The Canadian Exile," in *Canadian Poetry in English* (rev., 1954), edited by Bliss Carman, Lorne Pierce, and V.B. Rhodenizer:

Weeping sorely as he journeyed / Over many a foreign strand, / A Canadian exile wandered, / Banished from his native land.
Sad and pensive, sitting lonely, / By a rushing river's shore, / To the flowing waters spake he / Words that fondest memories bore:
"If you see my own dear country— / Most unhappy is its lot— / Say to all my friends, O river, / That they never are forgot.

"Oh! those days so full of gladness, / Now forever are they o'er, / And alas! my own dear country, / I shall never see it more.

"No, dear Canada, O my homeland! / But upon my dying day, / Fondly shall my last look wander / To thee, beloved, far away."

In days ot yóre, from Britain's shore,
   Wolfe, the dauntless hero, came,
And planted firm Britannia's flag
   On Canada's fair domain.

Here may it wave, our boast and pride,
   And, joined in love together,
The Thistle, Shamrock, Rose entwine
   The Maple Leaf forever!

The Maple Leaf, our emblem dear,
   The Maple Leaf forever;
God save our Queen, and Heaven bless
   The Maple Leaf forever.
   ALEXANDER MUIR, a Toronto school teacher and later principal, wrote "The Maple Leaf Forever" in 1867, from *Selections from Scottish Canadian Poets* (1900), edited by Dr. Daniel Clark. The pro-British words have never been acceptable to French Canadians.

CA-NA-DA—We love Thee—
(One little two little three little Canadians)
CA-NA-DA—Proud and Free—
(Now we are Twenty Million)
North, South, East, West,
(Four little five little six little Provinces)
There'll be Happy Times,
(Now we are ten and the Territories Sea to Sea)
   *
Le Centenaire! That's the order of the day.
Frère Jacques, Frère Jacques,
Merrily we roll along
Together, all the way.
   BOBBY GIMBY, west-coast composer and bandleader, wrote the catchy words and tune of "Canada: A Centennial Song," nicknamed "CA-NA-DA," for *Preview '67*, a feature film produced by the Centennial Commission early in 1966. It was the song hit of the centennial.

Nationalism

See also CANADA FIRST MOVEMENT; ECONOMIC NATIONALISM; INTERNATIONALISM; NATIONAL IDENTITY; NATIONALISM: CANADIAN; PATRIOTISM.

To make a nation there must be a common life, common sentiments, common aims, and common hopes. Of these, in the case of Quebec and Ontario, there are none.
   GOLDWIN SMITH, British-born journalist, in the *Bystander*, Dec. 1889.

Nationalism is simply a stop on the way to internationalism.
   JOHN W. DAFOE, Winnipeg editor, a remark characteristic of his later years, from *Dafoe of the Free Press* (1968), by Murray Donnelly.

Most nations have been formed, not by people who desired intensely to live together, but rather by people who could not live apart.
   JEAN-CHARLES BONENFANT, Quebec sociologist, in "L'Esprit de 1867," *Revue d'histoire de l'Amérique française*, June 1963, quoted by Ramsay Cook in *Canada and the French-Canadian Question* (1966).

Nationalism may be a bad thing, but nihilism is worse.
   W.L. MORTON, historian, attributed in the 1960s.

A nation is a body of people who have done great things together in the past and who hope to do great things together in the future.
   FRANK H. UNDERHILL, historian, in *The Image of Confederation* (1964).

In other words, the nation first decides what the state should be; but then the state has to decide what the nation should remain.
   PIERRE ELLIOTT TRUDEAU, future prime minister, in "Federalism, Nationalism and Reason" (1964), *Federalism and the French Canadians* (1968).

The glue of nationalism must become as obsolete as the theory of the divine right of kings.
   PIERRE ELLIOTT TRUDEAU in an interview, June 11, 1964.

What is nationalism? It is simply the manifestation of the natural and spontaneous solidarity that exists among members of a human group sharing a historical and cultural tradition from which the group derives its distinctive identity. This manifestation of solidarity is more or less conscious and more or less complete, according to the peculiar circumstances which have influenced and continue to condition the development of each collectivity.

MICHEL BRUNET, Quebec historian, in "The French Canadians' Search for a Fatherland," *Nationalism in Canada* (1966), edited by Peter Russell.

For my part I believe in the quality of small nations: here is where common values have a chance to sink deep roots.

FERNAND DUMONT, Laval sociologist, quoted by René Lévesque in *An Option for Quebec* (1968).

Nationalism: a snarl wrapped up in a flag.

IRVING LAYTON, outspoken poet, in *The Whole Bloody Bird* (1969).

The conquest of any nation takes place not on battlefields, not in business boardrooms, but with the soul of its people and the minds of its leaders.

PETER C. NEWMAN, journalist and editor, receiving an honorary degree at York University, quoted in the Toronto *Star*, June 7, 1975.

Nationalism: Canadian
See also NATIONALISM.

The Dutch may have their Holland, the
    Spaniard have his Spain,
The Yankee to the south of us must south
    of us remain;
For not a man dare lift a hand against the
    men who brag
That they were born in Canada beneath
    the British flag.

PAULINE JOHNSON, Mohawk poet, in the final stanza of "Canadian Born," *Canadian Born* (1903); text taken from *Flint and Feather* (1912).

Canadian nationalism! How old-fashioned can you get?

E.P. TAYLOR, long-time chairman of Argus Corporation, remark made in the winter of 1963, quoted by George L. Grant in *Lament for a Nation* (1965).

What confronts us is either the breaking-up of our country or its continuance as a fragmented, decentralized nation, firmly

152

integrated in the American economic and military empire, with all its assets, down to the last treasures of its birthright, freely expendable in the service of the government and people of the United States. Our only hope of deliverance from this fate lies in the reassertion of Canadian nationalism in its first and integral form. The vain and perilous pursuit of dualism, which was not an original object of Confederation and has nearly brought about its undoing, must be abandoned. One nation, not two nations in one, can alone maintain an effective defence of Canada.

DONALD CREIGHTON, distinguished historian, in "The Coming Defeat of Canadian Nationalism," an address to the Empire Club of Canada on Nov. 16, 1970.

The Canadian breed sometimes has missed its way. It has never failed a single decisive test when the alternatives were clear. If you can clarify the present alternatives, the right choice will be made again. *Whatever else it may lack, the nation is rich in sanity.*

BRUCE HUTCHISON, popular author, in "An Open Letter to Pierre Trudeau," *Maclean's*, July 1971.

Radicalism in Canada has to mean nationalism.

ABRAHAM ROTSTEIN, influential political economist, aphorism dating from 1972.

The thing is that you must not have a kind of nationalism which is an insistence on the protection of the third-rate, do you see? All you should say is, I know it's excellent, and the world will discover it *is* excellent. They'll discover it's Canadian, because they'll ask where it came from.

MORLEY CALLAGHAN, Toronto novelist, interviewed by Donald Cameron in *Conversations with Canadian Novelists* (1973).

For God's sake. Either we have a country or we don't. Let's decide!

PIERRE JUNEAU, characteristic remark while chairman of the CRTC; testifying before the Senate Committee on Transportation and Communications about the cost of operating the CBC, Oct. 1974.

Native People
See ESKIMOS; INDIANS.

Nature

See also CONSERVATION; TREES.

Canada is essentially a country of the larger air, where men can still face the old primeval forces of Nature and be braced into vigour, and withal so beautiful that it can readily inspire that romantic patriotism which is one of the most priceless assets of a people.

> JOHN BUCHAN, LORD TWEEDSMUIR, governor general and author, in 1901, quoted by Janet Adam Smith in *John Buchan* (1965).

The greatest joy in nature is the absence of man.

> BLISS CARMAN, poet, in *The Kinship of Nature* (1904).

Nature is great; but man is greater still.

> ANARULUNGUAQ, Caribou Eskimo, quoted by Knud Rasmussen in *Across Arctic America* (1927).

Give me a good canoe, a pair of Jibway snowshoes, my beaver, my family and ten thousand square miles of wilderness and I am happy.

> GREY OWL, Indian spokesman, quoted by Hugh Eayrs in his foreword to *Pilgrims of the Wild* (1935).

PLEASE WALK ON THE GRASS.

> TOMMY THOMPSON, parks commissioner for Metropolitan Toronto, devised this friendly invitation. The first sign was erected in Edwards Gardens in 1960; the words have become the motto of the Parks Department.

NDP

See NEW DEMOCRATIC PARTY.

New Brunswick

See also MARITIME PROVINCES.

"Father, what country do we live in?"
"My dear son, you have no country, for Mr. Tilley has sold us all to the Canadians for eighty cents a head."

> ANDREW R. WETMORE, New Brunswicker, in an imaginary dialogue used in an anti-Confederation address in the province, March 1865, quoted by Laurier LaPierre in *Genesis of a Nation* (1967). The "eighty cents" referred to

the per capita grant the province would receive upon entering Confederation.

Sweet maiden of Passamaquoddy
Shall we seek for communion of souls
Where the deep Mississippi meanders,
Or the distant Saskatchewan rolls?

Ah no,—for in Maine I will find thee,
A sweetly sequestrated nook,
Where the winding Skoodoowabskooksis
Conjoins with the Skoodoowabskook.
 *
Let others sing loudly of Saco,
Of Quoddy, and Tattamagouche,
Of Kenneneccasis, and Quaco,
Of Merigonishe, and Buctouche.

Of Nashwaak, and Magaguadavique,
Or Memmerimammericook,—
There's none like the Skoodoowabskooksis
Excepting the Skoodoowabskook!

> JAMES DE MILLE, New Brunswick author and teacher, stanzas of "Lines to Florence Huntingdon, Passamaquoddy, Maine," from the *New Dominion and True Humorist*, April 16, 1870.

Each and every year, health permitting, I will visit the university and take part in the Encaenia exercises. At the same time I will take advantage of the opportunity to fish in New Brunswick streams and will go back and tell the world what a grand and glorious land this is.

> LOUIS B. MAYER, founder of MGM who was raised in Saint John, N.B., in a convocation address at the University of New Brunswick, accepting an honorary LL.D., May 18, 1939.

I appear respectable again, riding the waves of sloth towards some climax as dramatic as the twenty-foot tidal drop at Saint John, in the Bay of Fundy. For forty-five minutes, in that New Brunswick harbour, between the ebb and flow of the tide, a ship can traverse the gorge between river and harbour. Forty-five minutes and no more. Just about the time taken by a bout of activity between spells of *accidie*.

> ALAN PRYCE-JONES, British critic, in "Viewpoint," *Times Literary Supplement*, Oct. 27, 1972.

New Democratic Party

See also POLITICS; SOCIALISM.

The League for Social Reconstruction is an association of men and women who are working for the establishment in Canada of a social order in which the basic principle regulating production, distribution and service will be the common good rather than private profit.

FRANK H. UNDERHILL, a founder of the CCF, in the manifesto of the League for Social Reconstruction (LSR), founded in Toronto in Jan. 1932 by F.R. Scott and F.H. Underhill, with J.S. Woodsworth as honorary president. From *The Anatomy of a Party* (1969) by Walter D. Young.

Beatty: What would be your first act if you became prime minister of Canada?
Lewis: Nationalize the CPR, sir.

DAVID LEWIS, future leader of the New Democratic Party, in an exchange with Sir Edward Beatty, president of the CPR and chairman of the selection committee for the Rhodes scholarships, Dec. 1931 or Jan. 1932, in the CPR boardroom, Montreal. Lewis was awarded the scholarship and studied at Oxford.

The stars in their courses are fighting for the cause of socialism.

J.S. WOODSWORTH, socialist leader, devised the CCF slogan, in *New Commonwealth*, April 18, 1936.

You cannot build an island of socialism in a sea of capitalism.

T.C. "TOMMY" DOUGLAS, socialist and premier of Saskatchewan, in the Throne Speech, June 1944.

I've realized that it's possible to plan an economy without owning it.

T.C. DOUGLAS, future leader of the New Democratic Party, remark made at the formation of the new party in 1960.

You won't find me very interesting. I never do anything but work.

T.C. DOUGLAS, former NDP leader, to his biographer Doris Shackleton in *Tommy Douglas* (1975).

Well, I'd rather waffle to the left than waffle to the right.

ED BROADBENT, NDP member of Parliament, when accused at a public meeting in 1969 of waffling on an issue. The word *waffle* stuck as

the name of the unofficial ginger group within the NDP which sought to unite socialism and economic nationalism.

Our aim as democratic socialists is to build an independent socialist Canada. Our aim as supporters of the New Democratic Party is to make it truly a socialist party.

MELVILLE H. WATKINS, economist and nationalist, in *The Waffle Manifesto* (1969), from *Gordon To Watkins To You* (1970), edited by Dave Godfrey and Mel Watkins.

The left in Canada is more *gauche* than *sinister*.

JOHN PAUL HARNEY, NDP thinker and former M.P., in 1970.

These fearful little socialists have a majority in only one place in B.C.—in the legislature.

W.A.C. BENNETT, former premier of British Columbia, to a group of Social Crediters, on March 26, 1973.

As socialists, we will be hard-nosed capitalists in business ventures.

DAVID "DAVE" BARRETT, NDP premier of British Columbia, in the *Financial Post*, March 17, 1973.

We have lost nothing tonight in terms of getting people to understand that there is a more loving way of building a community.

DAVE BARRETT, NDP leader in British Columbia, the evening of his defeat as premier, Dec. 11, 1975.

Voting NDP for the first time is like committing adultery for the first time: the chances are you'll do it a second and maybe even a third time.

LARRY ZOLF, zany broadcaster, *Saturday Night*, Dec. 1975.

New France

See also COUREUR DE BOIS; FRENCH CANADA; QUEBEC.

Now, as New France is so immense, so many inhabitants can be sent here that those who remain in the Mother Country will have enough honest work left them to do, without launching into those vices which ruin Republics; this does not mean that ruined people, or those of evil lives, should be sent here, for that would be to build Babylons.

> PAUL LE JEUNE, Jesuit missionary in 1635, from *The Jesuit Relations and Allied Documents* (1954), edited by Edna Kenton.

You ask me for seeds and bulbs of the flowers of this country. We have those for our garden brought from France, there being none here that are very rare or very beautiful. Everything is savage here, the flowers as well as the men.

> MARIE DE L'INCARNATION, Ursuline nun, in a letter to a French sister, Quebec, Aug. 12, 1653, from *Word from New France* (1967), translated by Joyce Marshall.

The girls destined for this country, besides being strong and healthy, ought to be entirely free from any natural blemish or anything personally repulsive.

> JEAN TALON, intendant of New France, in a letter to Jean-Baptiste Colbert, Nov. 10, 1670, quoted by Francis Parkman in *The Old Régime in Canada* (1874).

Let us fight to the death. We are fighting for our country and our religion. Remember that our father has taught you that gentlemen are born to shed their blood for the service of God and the King.

> MADELEINE DE VERCHÈRES, in her fourteenth year, rallied the spirits of her two younger brothers and three others when their seigniory on the St. Lawrence River was attacked by Indians, Oct. 22, 1692. Quoted by Francis Parkman in *Count Frontenac and New France Under Louis XIV* (1877).

The Colony of Canada is good only inasmuch as it can be useful to the Kingdom.

> LOUIS XIV, the Sun King of France, on New France in 1702, quoted by Mason Wade in *The French Canadians: 1760-1967* (1968).

It seems to me that in the choice of girls, good looks should be more considered than virtue.

> DUCLOS, intendant of Louisiana, in a letter to the French colonial minister in 1717 concerning the "king's girls," quoted by Francis Parkman in *A Half-Century of Conflict* (1892).

New Nationalism

See CONFEDERATION.

New Year's

When I go I'm going to take New Year's with me.

> GUY LOMBARDO, popular band-leader who, with his Royal Canadians, has greeted the New Year from the main ballrooms of leading New York hotels on radio and television since 1930.

Newfoundland

See also LABRADOR; MARITIME PROVINCES.

Now we have two tasks on our hands. On alternate days we must gather grapes and cut vines, and then fell trees, to make a cargo for my ship.

> LEIF THE LUCKY, also known as Leif Ericsson, landed at Newfoundland about 1000 A.D. He called the country "Vinland" or "Wine-land." *The Vinland Sagas* (1965), translated from the Old Icelandic by Magnus Magnusson and Herman Palsson.

A piece of rock entirely surrounded by fog.
*
A home entirely surrounded by hospitality.

> Anonymous descriptions of Newfoundland, "the Great Island."

Terra Primum Vista.

> JOHN CABOT, Genoese navigator and explorer for England, made his historic landfall at Cape Bonavista, Newfoundland, June 24, 1497. When he returned with the news of his discovery, Henry VII made payment of £10 "to hym that founde the new Isle," Aug. 10-11, 1497. The phrase means "first-seen land."

The Aire in Newfound-land is wholesome, good;
The Fire, as sweet as any made of wood;
The waters, very rich, both salt and fresh;
The Earth more rich, you know it is no lesse.
Where all are good, *Fire, Water, Earth,* and *Aire,*
What man made of these foure would not live there?

> ROBERT HAYMAN, governor of the colony at Harbour Grace, Conception Bay, Newfoundland, in *Quodlibets, Lately Come Over from New Britaniola, Old Newfound-land* (1628). This publi-

cation has been called the first book of original verse written on the North American continent.

Licence my roaving hands, and let them
go,
Before, behind, between, above, below
O my America! my new-found-land,
My kingdome, safeliest when with one
man man'd,
My Myne of precious stones, My Emperie,
How blest am I in this discovering thee!
To enter in these bonds, is to be free;
Then where my hand is set, my seal shall
be.

JOHN DONNE, English poet, comparing his mistress' body with "My America! my new-found-land," in "Elegie XIX," first published in 1633. The poem might have been written as early as 1590, some seven years after Sir Humphrey Gilbert claimed Newfoundland as an English colony. From *Complete Poetry and Selected Prose* (1932), edited by John Hayward.

Then hurrah for our own native isle, Newfoundland!
Not a stranger shall hold one inch of its
strand!
Her face turns to Britain, her back to the
Gulf.
Come near at your peril, Canadian Wolf!

Last verse of "An Anti-Confederation Song" (1869), *Old-Time Poetry and Songs of Newfoundland* (1940), edited by Gerald S. Doyle.

Cinderella of the Empire.

LORD ROSEBERY, prime minister of Great Britain (1894-95), epithetical description of Newfoundland, quoted by J.R. Smallwood in *I Chose Canada* (1973).

I find that Newfoundland is said to be celebrated for its codfish, its dogs, its hogs, its fogs and bogs. That is a very erroneous opinion, I assure you.

SIR WILLIAM WHITEWAY, prime minister of Newfoundland, in an address in London, England, on his retirement, July 5, 1897.

Sport of historic misfortune.

LORD BIRKENHEAD, British statesman, epithet for Newfoundland, widely used at the turn of the century, quoted by Joey Smallwood in *I Chose Canada* (1973).

When sun rays crown thy pine-clad hills,
And Summer spreads her hand,
When silvern voices tune thy rills,
We love thee, smiling land.

We love thee, we love thee,
We love thee, smiling land.

SIR CAVENDISH BOYLE, governor of Newfoundland from 1901 to 1904, first verse of "Ode to Newfoundland," *The Book of Newfoundland* (1937), edited by J.R. Smallwood.

We'll rant and we'll roar like true Newfoundlanders,
We'll rant and we'll roar on deck and below;
Until we see bottom inside the two sunkers,
When straight through the Channel to
Toslow we'll go.
*
Farewell and adieu to ye, fair ones of Valen,
Farewell and adieu to ye, girls in the cove;
I'm bound to the westward, to the wall
with the hole in,
I'll take her from Toslow the wild world to
rove.

H.W. LE MESSURIER, song-writer, verses from "The Girls from Toslow," a popular Newfoundland song, reproduced from *The Book of Newfoundland* (1937), edited by J.R. Smallwood, where the contemporary folksong is titled "The Ryans and the Pittmans."

Take me back to my Western boat,
Let me fish off Cape St. Mary's,
Where the hog-downs sail and the
foghorns wail
With my friends the Browns and the
Clearys.
Let me fish off Cape St. Mary's.

OTTO P. KELLAND, song-writer, last verse of the popular Newfoundland song, "Let Me Fish off Cape St. Mary's."

Every man can build his own house, his own boat: but he won't build a parish council. They have all the crafts except the political.

A.P. HERBERT, British humorist and M.P., who visited the "great island" in 1943, quoted in *Independent Member* (1950).

Oh! this is the place where the fishermen
gather,

In oil skins and boots and Cape Anns battened down;

All sizes of figures with squid lines and jiggers,

They congregate here on the squid-jiggin' ground.

A R. SCAMMELL, song-writer, first verse of the famous Newfoundland air "The Squid-Jiggin' Ground," written in 1944 and published in *My Newfoundland* (1966).

The only thing wrong with Confederation is that we didn't join in 1867.

*

This poor bald rock . . . .

J.R. "JOEY" SMALLWOOD, "the only living Father of Confederation" and first premier of Newfoundland when the island joined the mainland in 1949, quoted by Richard Gwyn in *Smallwood: The Unlikely Revolutionary* (1968).

The world will end at midnight tonight; 12:30 in Newfoundland.

PETER GZOWSKI, writer and host of the CBC Radio show, "This Country in the Morning," in *Peter Gzowski's Book About This Country in the Morning* (1974).

News

See also BROADCASTING; CENSORSHIP; JOURNALISTS; NEWSPAPERS.

But words are things, and a small drop of ink,

Falling like dew, upon a thought, produces

That which makes thousands, perhaps millions think . . . .

LORD BYRON, English poet, from the Third Canto of *Don Juan* (1818-24), *Byron's Poems* (1963), edited by V. de Sola Pinto. Charles A. Bowman, an Ottawa editor, selected the last three lines to adorn the fireplace of the Press Gallery Lounge, Parliament Buildings, Ottawa, in 1920.

What I want to see in the *Montreal Star* is the sort of news, or item, or story or article which you would be tempted to read aloud to the person next to you if you saw it in a newspaper or book.

SIR HUGH GRAHAM, founder of the Montreal *Star*, advice to John W. Dafoe, then a cub reporter, in June 1883, quoted by Murray Donnelly in *Dafoe of the Free Press* (1968).

World news is Canadian news.

*

Put a punch in every paragraph.

HARRY COMFORT HINDMARSH, editor of the Toronto *Star* in the 1920s, characteristic remarks, quoted by Ross Harkness in *J.E. Atkinson of the Star* (1963).

What is editorial content? The stuff you separate the ads with.

ROY THOMSON, Canadian-born British press lord, 1950s, attributed.

Here are the news.

*

Everything good now.

*

This is end the news.

EDITH JOSIE, Indian correspondent for the Whitehorse *Star* in Old Crow, six hundred miles north of Whitehorse, and author of a collection of spontaneous and unedited reports, *Here Are the News* (1966).

To borrow a line from Mark Twain, "First get your facts, and then you can distort them as much as you please." As for headlines, which, after all, are the only journalistic things that matter, they are, of course, outside your control—or, so far as I can gather, anybody else's.

LESTER B. PEARSON, prime minister, to newspapermen, quoted by I. Norman Smith in *The Journal Men* (1974).

Max Aitken Lord Beaverbrook was quite a Somebody. Those who loved him have one dream in life: that the telephone will ring again and the familiar voice ask, "What's the news?"

A.J.P. TAYLOR, British historian, in *Beaverbrook* (1972).

The four elements of news are: love, money, conquest, disaster.

GORDON SINCLAIR, radio and TV personality, in a news broadcast on CFRB, Toronto, 1972.

Newspapers

See also NEWS.

It is too late in the day to stop men thinking. If allowed to think they will speak. If they speak they will write, and what they write will be printed and published. A newspaper is only a thought-throwing machine, a reflex of the popular mind. If it is not, it cannot live. We are not disposed to send our proof-sheets to anyone to correct.

AMOR DE COSMOS, journalist, in the editorial of the *British Colonist* in 1859, when the governor of British Columbia, Sir James Douglas, failed in his attempt to suppress the newspaper, quoted by Roland Wilde in *Amor de Cosmos* (1958).

Printed in the sage brush country of the Lillooet every Thursday, God Willing. Guarantees a chuckle every week and a belly laugh once a month, or your money back. Subscription: $5 in Canada. Furriners: $6. This week's circulation 1769, and every bloody one of them paid for.

MARGARET "MA" MURRAY, peppery veteran journalist, on the editorial page of the Bridge River-Lillooet *News*, which she published in the 1950s, quoted by Georgina Keddell in *The Newspapering Murrays* (1967).

"When Paul Martin, the cabinet minister, formally opened the Guelph *Mercury's* new building, he said in his speech that whenever he entered a strange town he always bought a paper. At this Thomson grinned broadly, and interjected: 'Me too—and its plant!' "

ROY THOMSON, LORD THOMSON OF FLEET, newspaper baron, quoted by Russell Braddon in *Roy Thomson of Fleet Street* (1965).

I want *The Journal* to enter homes with grace, as a guest.

E. NORMAN SMITH, publisher of the Ottawa *Journal*, quoted by his son, I. Norman Smith, in *The Journal Men* (1974).

My own observation is that there is no Canadian community which is as dull as the newspaper it reads.

ROBERT FULFORD, Toronto cultural journalist, in "The Press in the Community" (1962), *Crisis at the Victory Burlesk* (1968).

What this country now needs, to achieve the sort of editorial competition that is our best guarantee of a good society, is a journalistic equivalent of the Volkswagen.

KEITH DAVEY, senator, in the *Report of the Special Senate Committee on Mass Media, Volume I: The Uncertain Mirror* (1971).

Nobody is bigger than the *Star*.

BELAND HONDERICH, publisher of the Toronto *Star*, the newspaper with the largest circulation in Canada, attributed in 1972 when its rival, the Toronto *Telegram*, folded.

Newspapers are born free, and everywhere they are in chains.

F.R. SCOTT, Montreal man-of-letters, aphorism from his commonplace book, 1973.

It's not a question of how bad the *Star* is, but of how good it could be.

WILLIAM MCILWAIN, American journalist briefly employed by the Toronto *Star*, on CBC-TV, Feb. 4, 1975.

I used to say "the universe is unfolding as it should," but here there is one *Star*, one *Sun* and one *Globe* badly out of order.

PIERRE ELLIOTT TRUDEAU, prime minister, at a Liberal fund-raising dinner in Toronto, referring to the three daily newspapers, reported the following day by John Marshall in the *Globe and Mail*, April 19, 1975.

Niagara Falls

Four leagues from Lake Frontenac there is an incredible Cataract or Waterfall, which has no equal. The Niagara river near this place is only the eighth of a league wide, but it is very deep in places, and so rapid above the great fall, that it hurries down all the animals which try to cross it, without a single one being able to withstand its current. They plunge down a height of more than five hundred feet, and its fall is composed of two sheets of water and a cascade, with an island sloping down. In the middle these waters foam and boil in a fearful manner.

LOUIS HENNEPIN, Recollet missionary, first eyewitness description of the falls of Niagara on Dec. 6, 1678, in *Description de la Louisiane* (1683); *Description of Louisiana* (1880), translated by John Gilmary Shea.

Beheld the duteous son, the sire decay'd,
The modest matron, and the blushing maid,
Forc'd from their homes, a melancholy train,
To traverse climes beyond the western main;

Where wild Oswego spreads her swamps around,

And Niagara stuns with thund'ring sound?

OLIVER GOLDSMITH, Irish poet and novelist, in *The Traveller* (1764), from *The Complete Poetical Works of Oliver Goldsmith* (1906), edited by Austin Dobson.

The grand leap of the whale up the Falls of Niagara is esteemed, by all who have seen it, as one of the finest spectacles in nature.

BENJAMIN FRANKLIN, American statesman, in "To the Editor of a London Newspaper, Intending to Chaff the English for Their Ignorance of America," 1765.

What has come over my soul and senses?—I am no longer Anna—I am metamorphosed—I am translated—I am an ass's head, a clod, a wooden spoon, a fat weed growing on Lethe's bank, a stock, a stone, a petrifaction,—for have I not seen Niagara, the wonder of wonders; and felt—no words can tell *what* disappointment!

ANNA JAMESON, British writer resident in Upper Canada, in *Winter Studies and Summer Rambles in Canada* (1838).

Shooting Niagara

THOMAS CARLYLE, British man-of-letters, title of an article (and the origin of the phrase) that appeared in *Macmillan's* magazine in 1867.

Niagara Falls is simply a vast unnecessary amount of water going the wrong way and then falling over unnecessary rocks. The wonder would be if the water did not fall.

*

Niagara Falls must be the second major disappointment of American married life.

OSCAR WILDE, Anglo-Irish playwright, at a news conference in New York in 1882, attributed.

You purchase release at last by the fury of your indifference, and stand there gazing your fill at the most beautiful object in the world.

HENRY JAMES, Anglo-American novelist, in "Niagara," *Portraits of Places* (1883).

North, The

See also ARCTIC; NORTH, THE TRUE; NORTHWEST TERRITORIES.

Who can doubt of the future of these British Provinces, or of the entire and palpable reality of that vision which rises so grandly before us of the Great British Empire of the North—of that new English-speaking nation which will at one and no distant day people all this Northern continent—a Russia, as has been well said, it may be, but yet an English Russia, with free institutions, with high civilization, and entire freedom of speech and thought—with its face to the south and its back to the pole, with its right and left resting on the Atlantic and the Pacific, and with the telegraph and the iron road connecting the two oceans!

ALEXANDER MORRIS, lieutenant-governor of Manitoba, in a Montreal address, winter 1858.

Canada was bound to the North-West by the ties of discovery, possession, and interest.

ALEXANDER MORRIS, lieutenant-governor of Manitoba, in the House of Commons, Dec. 5, 1867.

Why did I desire so ardently to reach the Pole? The attainment of the Pole meant at the time simply the accomplishing of a splendid, unprecedented feat—a feat of brain and muscle in which I should, if successful, signally surpass other men. This imaginary spot held for me the revealing of no great scientific secrets. I never regarded the feat as of any scientific value. The real victory would lie, not in reaching the goal itself, but in overcoming the obstacles which exist in the way of it.

DR. FREDERICK COOK, the first person to reach the North Pole on April 21, 1908, in *My Attainment of the Pole* (1911). The counterclaim of Robert Peary is dismissed by Farley Mowat in *The Polar Passion* (1967).

I have the Pole, April 6, 1909.

ROBERT PEARY, American naval officer, sent this telegram from Smokey Tickle, Labrador, on Sept. 6, 1909, claiming to be the first person to reach the North Pole. Farley Mowat, in *The Polar Passion* (1967), credits Dr. Frederick Cook with the achievement.

The North has got him.

ROBERT W. SERVICE, "the poet of the Yukon," who refers to this as a "Yukonism" in "The

Ballad of Pious Pete," *Ballads of a Cheechako* (1909).

The northward course of empire.

VILHJALMUR STEFANSSON, outspoken Arctic explorer, took the familiar phrase, "Westward the course of empire takes its way," and adapted it as the title and theme of his book, *The Northward Course of Empire* (1922), which emphasizes the importance of the Arctic explorations of the fur traders. The phrase is associated with Bishop Berkeley who coined it in 1752 in a verse titled "On the Prospect of Planting Arts and Learning in America." It was also used by John Quincy Adams in 1802.

We should not regard the Eskimos as foreigners but as friends. They are your fellow citizens. Their future is bound up in our future. If Canada is but a thin southern strip across which plies a shuttle railway we shall have no remarkable future.

VILHJALMUR STEFANSSON, Manitoba-born Arctic explorer, quoted by Margaret Fairley in *Spirit of Canadian Democracy* (1945).

The Russians live North and look North, but the Canadians live North and look South.

VILHJALMUR STEFANSSON, Arctic explorer and author, attributed.

The artistic cult of the North is, as a matter of fact, pure romanticism at its worst, and bears little relation to the real life of Canada. Far from seeking inspiration among the rocks and winds, the normal Canadian dreams of living in a big city where he can make his pile quickly and enjoy such urban luxuries as are familiar to him in the advertising columns of our national magazines.

FRANK H. UNDERHILL, historian and writer, in "False Hair on the Chest," *Saturday Night*, Oct. 3, 1936.

Many countries—and they are to be envied—possess in one direction or another a window which opens out on to the infinite—on to the potential future . . . . The North is always there like a presence; it is the background of the picture without which Canada would not be Canadian.

ANDRÉ SIEGFRIED, French author, in *Canada:*

An International Power (1937), translated by H.H. and Doris Hemming.

"It's only the North can mend what the North breaks."

JOHN BUCHAN, LORD TWEEDSMUIR, governor general, line of dialogue from his novel *Sick Heart River* (1941).

It has been said that Great Britain acquired her Empire in a state of absence of mind. Apparently we have administered these vast territories of the North in an almost continuing absence of mind.

LOUIS ST LAURENT, prime minister, in the House of Commons, Dec. 8, 1953, on second reading of the bill to establish the Department of Northern Affairs and National Resources.

One Canada, one Canada where Canadians will have preserved to them the control of their own economic and political destiny. Sir John A. Macdonald gave his life to this party. He opened the west. He saw Canada from east to west. I see a new Canada—a Canada of the North!

JOHN G. DIEFENBAKER, prime minister, in a Winnipeg address, Feb. 12, 1958.

To me, as to most northerners, the country is still an unknown quantity, as elusive as the wolf, howling just beyond the rim of the hills. Perhaps that is why it holds its fascination.

PIERRE BERTON, author and TV personality, in *The Mysterious North* (1959).

We sing about the North but live as far south as possible.

J.B. "HAMISH" MCGEACHY, Toronto columnist and broadcaster, attributed.

Today only a few people are caught by the magnetism of the North.

R.A.J. PHILLIPS, northern-affairs expert, in *Canada's North* (1967).

The presence of a North in man is even more critical than the presence of men in the North.

JACK WARWICK, professor, in *The Long Journey* (1968).

I have my own vision of the high North. I

envision it being transformed—restored—into a symbol of sanity in a world where madness is becoming the accepted mode of action.

FARLEY MOWAT, popular writer, from *Tundra* (1973).

North, The True

See also NORTH, THE.

Witness, too, the silent cry,
The prayer of many a race and creed, and clime—
Thunderless lightnings striking under sea
From sunset and sunrise of all thy realm,
And that true North, whereof we lately heard
A strain to shame us, "Keep you to yourselves;
So loyal is too costly! friends—your love
Is but a burthen: loose the bond, and go."
Is this the tone of empire? here the faith
That made us rulers? this, indeed, her voice
And meaning, whom the roar of Hougoumont
Left mightiest of all people under heaven?
What shock has fool'd her since, that she should speak
So feebly? wealthier—wealthier—hour by hour!
The voice of Britain, or a sinking land,
Some third-rate isle half-lost among her seas?

ALFRED LORD TENNYSON, poet laureate of Great Britain, in "To the Queen," epilogue to "O Loyal to the Royal in Thyself," *Idylls of the King* (1873). "That true North" is a direct reference to Canada, composed immediately after reading an editorial in the *Times*, Oct. 30, 1872, in which Canada was advised to seek its independence. From *Tennyson's Poetical Works* (1897), edited by Eugene Parsons.

With glowing hearts we see thee rise,
The True North, strong and free,
And stand on guard, O Canada,
We stand on guard for thee.

R. STANLEY WEIR, Montreal lawyer and sometime judge of the Exchequer Court of Canada, from "O Canada," written in 1908.

Northwest Passage

For there is no doubt but that there is a straight and short way open into the West, even unto Cathay.

RICHARD HAKLUYT, British historian, in *Divers Voyages Touching the Discovery of America* (1582).

And now it may be that som expect I should give my opynion conserning the passadge. To those my answere must be, that doubtles theare is a passadge.

WILLIAM BAFFIN, English navigator who discovered Baffin Island in 1616 and predicted that the Northwest Passage would be found through Davis Strait, in "Fourth Recorded Voyage," *The Voyages of William Baffin, 1612-1622* (1881), edited by Clements R. Markham.

The weather was bad, with even poorer visibility all the way down the coast of Baffin Island and Labrador. The first vessel we sighted was a Newfoundland fishing schooner, off Bateau Harbour in Labrador where she was heading for the harbour itself. I followed her in to the small fishing village and there we had a few days' well-earned rest. Because of the gale the fishermen were in port and they were surprised to learn who we were and the length of time we had been away from home, although I somehow had a feeling that they didn't completely grasp the fact that we had come all the way around the Arctic.

HENRY A. LARSEN, RCMP sergeant, completed his first voyage through the Northwest Passage in his motor schooner, *St. Roch*, with little fanfare, Sept. 1942.

On September 27 we passed through the Bering Strait and docked in Vancouver on October 16, at 6:00 P.M. Behind us were 7,-295 nautical miles, which we had covered in eighty-six days!

There was nobody to meet us at the wharf. Canada was still at war and had no time for frivolous things.

HENRY A. LARSEN, RCMP sergeant, completed his return voyage on the *St. Roch* in Oct. 1944, again without fanfare. From *The Big Ship* (1967), by Henry A. Larsen with Frank R. Sheer and Edvard Omholt-Jensen.

Had I done it alone by canoe, I might have boasted a little.

F.S. FARRAR, RCMP sergeant, third mate and

photographer aboard the *St. Roch*, the first vessel to circumnavigate the North American continent on May 29, 1950. On one trip Farrar sailed the Northwest Passage, on another the Panama Canal. Quoted by Nora and William Kelly in *The Royal Canadian Mounted Police* (1973).

Northwest Rebellion
See also RIEL, LOUIS.

Eagle Hills, May 19th, 1885. Sir.—I am camped with my people at the east-end of the Eagle Hills, where I am met by the news of the surrender of Riel. No letter came with the news, so that I cannot tell how far it may be true. I send some of my men to you to learn the truth and the terms of peace, and hope you will deal kindly with them. I and my people wish you to send us the terms of peace in writing, so that we may be under no misunderstanding, from which so much trouble arises. We have twenty-one prisoners, whom we have tried to treat well in every respect. With greetings,

His
(Signed) POUNDMAKER X
Mark

POUNDMAKER, chief of the Crees, letter to Sir Fred Middleton at Duck Lake, Sask., reproduced by Middleton in *Suppression of the Rebellion in the North West Territories of Canada* (1948), edited by G.H. Needler.

POUNDMAKER.—I have utterly defeated the half-breeds and Indians at Batoche, and have made prisoners of Riel and most of his council. I have made no terms with them, neither will I make terms with you. I have men enough to destroy you and your people, or, at least to drive you away to starve, and will do so unless you bring in the teams you took and yourself and councillors, with your arms, to meet me at Battleford on Monday, the 26th. I am glad to hear you have treated the prisoners well and have released them.

(Signed) FRED MIDDLETON,
Major-General

GENERAL SIR FRED MIDDLETON, reply to Poundmaker's request for peace terms, May 23, 1885, reproduced by Middleton in *Suppression of the Rebellion in the North West Territories of Canada* (1948), edited by G.H. Needler.

Northwest Territories
See also NORTH, THE.

It is impossible to describe the country, for it is built on a scale outside that of humanity.

JOHN BUCHAN, LORD TWEEDSMUIR, governor general, reaction to the north country around Great Slave Lake, at Fort Providence, N.W.T., Sept. 1937, quoted by Janet Adam Smith in *John Buchan* (1965).

The land of feast and famine.

JOHN HORNBY, bizarre English explorer of the Barrens in the 1920s, called that stark country "the land of feast and famine." Quoted by Pierre Berton in *The Mysterious North* (1959).

Tomorrow's Country.

Slogan associated with the Centennial of the Northwest Territories, celebrated in 1970.

Yer North Waste Terrortory: Our Froze Asset.

DON HARRON, actor-writer who created the crotchety farmer from Parry Sound, in *Charlie Farquharson's Jogfree of Canada* (1974).

Nova Scotia
See also BLUENOSE; MARITIME PROVINCES.

Nova Scotia is a peninsula entirely surrounded by fish.

From an early travel book.

Farewell to Nova Scotia, the sea-bound coast!
Let your mountains dark and dreary be,
For when I am far away on the briny ocean tossed
Will you ever heave a sigh and a wish for me?

Refrain from "Nova Scotia," *Folk Songs of Canada* (1954), edited by Edith Fowke and Richard Johnston.

Are the streets being paved with gold over there? I fully expect to awake one morning in Versailles to see the walls of the fortress rising above the horizon.

LOUIS XV, French monarch, reply to Sebastien de Vauban, when the military architect pressed for further funds to complete the Fortress of Louisbourg, Cape Breton Island. By the 1740s, Louisbourg was the most expensive fortress in all North America.

The province of Nova Scotia was the youngest and the favourite child of the board. Good God! What sums the nursing of that ill-thriven, hard-visaged, and ill-favoured brat, has cost to this wittol nation! Sir, this colony has stood us in a sum of not less than seven hundred thousand pounds. To this day it has made no repayment. It does not even support those offices of expenses, which are miscalled its government; the whole of that job still lies upon the patient, callous shoulders of the people of England.

> EDMUND BURKE, British statesman, in "Speech on Economic Reform," delivered in the British House of Commons, Feb. 11, 1780, from *The Speeches of the Right Hon. Edmund Burke* (1853), edited by James Burke. A "wittol" is a contented cuckold.

Breathes there the man, with soul so dead,
Who never to himself hath said,
    This is my own, my native land.

> The last line was the motto of a series of articles on Nova Scotia published in the *Acadian Register* in 1826. The passage comes from Sir Walter Scott's *The Lay of the Last Minstrel* (1805).

Nova Scotia is an excellent poor man's country, because almost any man, in any walk of industry, by perseverance and economy, can secure the comforts of life.

> JOSEPH HOWE, editor and future statesman, in the *Novascotian*, July 31, 1834.

. . . and my pride and hope is, that we shall make Nova Scotia, by her loyalty, intelligence, and spirit, as it were, a Normal school for British North America, to show how far British liberty may be assumed in a Colony, and at what point it should stop, and the people be content.

> JOSEPH HOWE, "The Tribune of Nova Scotia," speech at a Reform dinner, Nov. 23, 1840. From *Joseph Howe: Voice of Nova Scotia* (1964), edited by J. Murray Beck.

We are sold for the price of a sheepskin.

> JOSEPH HOWE, anti-Confederation spokesman, bitter remark made when it became apparent that Nova Scotia would enter Confederation

the following year, in the *Novascotian*, Aug. 13, 1866.

Boys, brag of your country. When I'm abroad, I brag of everything that Nova Scotia is, has, or can produce; and when they beat me at everything else, I turn round on them and say, "How high does your tide rise?"

> JOSEPH HOWE, quoted by George Munro Grant in *Joseph Howe* (1904).

Millions for Corruption, but not a Cent for Nova Scotia.

> WILLIAM STEVENS FIELDING, leader of the Liberal party of Nova Scotia which was returned to office on a platform of secession in the election of 1886, the only election ever conducted on an anti-Confederation platform. The resolution favouring independence was never implemented. Fielding became Laurier's finance minister.

In the town of Springhill, Nova Scotia,
Down in the dark of the Cumberland Mine,
There's blood on the coal and the miners lie,
In roads that never saw sun nor sky,
Roads that never saw sun nor sky.

> EWAN MACCOLL, British-born folk-singer, with his American-born wife, Peggy Seeger, wrote the ballad, "The Springhill Mining Disaster," about the Nova Scotia catastrophe of 1958.

Nova Scotia is a part of the world which is particularly proud of its ability to select from among the cultural influences that might impinge on it.

> EDGAR Z. FRIEDENBERG, Louisiana-born educator who teaches at Dalhousie University, quoted by Harry Bruce in *Saturday Night*, Feb. 1973.

North America is a large island to the west of the continent of Cape Breton. (Pronounced: Caybrittn)

> RAY SMITH, novelist, in *Cape Breton Is the Thought Control Center of Canada* (1969).

October Crisis
See also SEPARATISM.

The provisions of sections 6, 10, 11 and 13 of this Act shall be in force during war, invasion, or insurrection, real or apprehended.

The War Measures Act, 1914, section 3, assented to Aug. 22, 1914, reproduced in *Historical Documents of Canada: Volume V* (1972), edited by C.P. Stacey, who notes: "This drastic measure, which gives the Governor in Council virtually unlimited powers in a time of emergency, is (with adjustments) still on the statute books."

We have a gift for Mr. Cross. You'll have to sign for it.

JACQUES LANCTÔT, separatist kidnapper, began the October Crisis by taking as hostage the British trade official James Cross on Oct. 5, 1970. Ron Haggart and Aubrey E. Golden, in *Rumours of War* (1971), report Lanctôt's first words as: "Birthday present for Mr. Cross."

This is a wind of madness blowing across the province. I hope it won't last long.

PIERRE LAPORTE, Quebec minister of Labour and Immigration, on learning of the kidnapping of the British trade commissioner, James Cross, by the FLQ on Oct. 5, 1970.

My dear Robert . . . . You have the power to dispose of my life . . . . I am convinced that I am writing the most important letter of my life . . . .

PIERRE LAPORTE, Quebec Cabinet minister, lines from a note written on Oct. 12, 1970, while in the hands of FLQ kidnappers, addressed to Quebec Premier Robert Bourassa. Quoted by Ron Haggart and Aubrey E. Golden in *Rumours of War* (1971).

Trudeau: Yes, well there are a lot of bleeding hearts around who just don't like to see people with helmets and guns. All I can say is, go on and bleed, but it is more important to keep law and order in the so-

ciety than to be worried about weak-kneed people who don't like the looks of . . . .

Ralfe: At any cost? How far would you go with that? How far would you extend that?

Trudeau: Well, just watch me . . . . Yes, I think the society must take every means at its disposal to defend itself against the emergence of a parallel power which defies the elected power in this country and I think that goes at any distance. So long as there is a power in here which is challenging the elected representatives of the people, I think that power must be stopped and I think it's only, I repeat, weak-kneed bleeding hearts who are afraid to take these measures.

PIERRE ELLIOTT TRUDEAU, prime minister, in a interview with CBC-TV reporter Tim Ralfe on Oct. 13, 1970, during the FLQ crisis. The transcript was published the following day in the Toronto *Star*.

There is no more freedom.

JEAN MARCHAND, Cabinet minister, attributed, when the Trudeau administration imposed the War Measures Act on Oct. 16, 1970.

It was a case of six kids trying to make a revolution.

JAMES R. CROSS, remark made after his release 3 Dec. 1970, quoted by Ron Haggart and Aubrey E. Golden in *Rumours of War* (1971).

I do not recognize the foreign law under which I am charged. However my lawyers advise me that this law applies in this case. I acknowledge the facts mentioned in the indictment. It is true that I committed these acts but I surely committed them because I believe that this is the only attitude that can free the people of Quebec from the colonial domination and yoke which burden them.

ROBERT LEMIEUX, separatist lawyer, English translation of the statement prepared by the legal counsel for the FLQ terrorists who pleaded guilty to acts of terrorism.

Oil
See also ENERGY CRISIS.

1. No well shall be drilled before 6:00 A.M. or after 3:00 P.M. Operations at that

time are liable to disturb the paying guests while in the midst of beautiful dreams of vast wealth and permanent gushers.

2. No more than one well shall be drilled in each leather chair, or sofa, during one time interval. It is exhausting to the furniture.

3. No well shall be drilled in a tone of voice which is audible within the three-mile zone, and causes the skylight to flutter.

4. No well shall be drilled within one foot from any door, window, or passageway, and no disputes shall be indulged in, or any lease located in such areas.

5. No dry holes will be tolerated in the lobby. All wells brought in must be in the thousand barrel class, or larger.

> Drilling regulations at the Palliser Hotel in Calgary, reproduced by John Patrick Gillese in *Chinook Arch* (1967).

All the wheels of industry turn on oil.

> NATHAN E. TANNER, Alberta Social Credit mines minister and Trans-Canada Pipe Line president, in "Petroleum Development," *Canada: Nation on the March* (1953).

I've been working on the pipe line all the
  day through,
I've been working on the pipe line just to
  make the Tories blue.
Can't you hear the Tories moaning, getting up so early in the morn';
Hear the C.C.F.'ers groaning, for the pipe
  line's getting warm.

> New words for "I've Been Working on the Railroad," sung by Liberal members in the House of Commons on June 1, 1956, during the pipeline debate.

This is black Friday, boy.

> THOMAS M. BELL, Conservative member, describing the undemocratic procedures that marked the pipeline debate in the House of Commons on Friday, June 1, 1956.

What shall it profit Canada if we gain a pipeline, and lose a nation's soul? What shall it profit the people of Canada, if we gain a thousand pipelines, and lose Parliament!

> STANLEY KNOWLES, CCF spokesman during the 1956 pipeline debate, quoted by Christina and Peter Newman in "The Great Pipeline

Debate," *Historic Headlines* (1967), edited by Pierre Berton.

Olympics

The Montreal Olympics can no more have a deficit than a man can have a baby.

> JEAN DRAPEAU, mayor of Montreal, announcing a "self-financing" Olympic budget of $310 million at a press conference, Jan. 29, 1973.

'Ello, Morgentaler?

> TERRY MOSHER, under the pen-name Aislin, attributed this line to Mayor Drapeau in an editorial cartoon in the Montreal *Gazette* that depicted the mayor, pregnant, phoning Dr. Henry Morgentaler for an abortion. Reproduced in *Time*, Jan. 20, 1975.

I can't say that my opinion is definitely accepted by the government, but I remain firm on my stand. The tap has to flow until the tub is full.

> JEAN DRAPEAU, Montreal mayor and promoter of the 1976 Montreal Olympics, stand taken in Feb. 1974, on federal funding for the games. Quoted by Mary Kate Rowan in the *Canadian*, June 7, 1975.

The Olympics present a vision of humanity, an enduring insight into physical beauty, the possibility of perfection, the drive to excellence and the indomitable human spirit.

> ABBY HOFFMAN, athlete and teacher, in *Weekend*, July 19, 1975.

Ontario

On the Old Ontario Strand, my boys,
Where Queen's forever shall stand!
  For has she not stood
  Since the time of the flood
On the Old Ontario Strand!

> Chorus of "On the Old Ontario Strand," the college song of Queen's University, first sung at convocation ceremonies on April 26, 1886. The song is sometimes identified with Victoria University, which moved in 1892 from Cobourg to Toronto.

One by one they all clear out,
Thinking to better themselves, no doubt,
Caring little how far they go
From the poor little girls of Ontario.

Refrain of "The Poor Little Girls of Ontario," in *Canada's Story in Song* (1965), edited by Edith Fowke and Alan Mills.

Ontario is a state of mind, bounded on the east by a foreign language, on the north by wilderness, on the west by the hungry prairies, and on the south by another country.

DOROTHY DUNCAN, Montreal writer, in *Here's to Canada* (1941).

Old Man Ontario.

LESLIE FROST, premier of Ontario in the 1950s, accepted this sobriquet, created for him by Allister Grosart (who himself went on to become "architect" of Diefenbaker's successful campaign of 1957).

Give us a place to stand
And a place to grow
And call this land
Ontario.

RICHARD MORRIS, song-writer, wrote the lyrics to "Ontar-i-ar-i-ar-io," the rousing theme song from *A Place to Stand*, a documentary film directed by Christopher Chapman for the Ontario pavilion at Expo 67. The music was composed by Dolores Claman.

I am as willing to talk about our disappointments as about your achievements. The people of Ontario have never been spoiled by perfection in government.

WILLIAM DAVIS, premier of Ontario, in the Ontario Legislature on Aug. 11, 1975.

Opinions

A man's reputation is the opinion people have of him; his character is what he really is.

JACK MINER, pioneer naturalist who banded wildlife at his famous bird sanctuary at Kingsville, Ontario, in *Wild Goose Jack* (1969).

Do you wish to know what public opinion is? It is the opinion of those who are against us.

MAURICE DUPLESSIS, premier of Quebec intermittently between 1936 and 1959, quoted by Pierre Laporte in *The True Face of Duplessis* (1961).

We all have opinions, but some of us happen to be right.

LOUIS DUDEK, Montreal poet, in *Epigrams* (1975).

Opposition
See GOVERNMENT.

Ottawa

On the whole, therefore, I believe that the least objectionable place is the city of Ottawa. Every city is jealous of every other city except Ottawa.

SIR EDMUND HEAD, governor general from 1854 to 1861, in "Confidential Memorandum by Sir E. Head, Containing Reasons for Fixing the Seat of Government for Canada at Ottawa," Oct. 1857. Reprinted by James A. Gibbon in *Canadian Historical Review*, Dec. 1935.

The subject is a delicate one. I would not wish to say anything disparaging of the capital, but it is hard to say anything good of it. Ottawa is not a handsome city and does not appear destined to become one either.

SIR WILFRID LAURIER, future prime minister, in a Montreal address on May 14, 1884, from *Wilfrid Laurier on the Platform* (1890).

Ottawa is a sub-arctic lumber-village converted by royal mandate into a political cockpit.

GOLDWIN SMITH, British-born journalist, quoted by Edwin C. Guillet in *Pioneer Inns and Taverns* (1956).

But what Ottawa leaves in the mind is a certain graciousness—dim, for it expresses a barely materialized national spirit—and the sight of kindly English-looking faces, and the rather lovely sound of the soft Canadian accent in the streets.

RUPERT BROOKE, English poet who visited North America in 1913, in *Letters from America* (1916).

The atmosphere of Ottawa after Washington is like Belfast after Dublin.

LORD MORAN, British statesman who visited Ottawa during the Second World War, in *Churchill: Taken from the Diaries of Lord Moran* (1966).

Moscow wonderful, concerts wonderful,

ballet wonderful, opera wonderful, Moscow big city—Ottawa nothing (*nichevo*)—cinema, cinema, cinema.

MADAME ZARUBIN, wife of the Soviet ambassador to Ottawa, at a dinner in Ottawa on March 3, 1945, reported by Charles Ritchie in *The Siren Years* (1974).

The best thing about Ottawa is the train to Montreal.

JEAN MARCHAND, former minister of Transport, in 1972, attributed.

Pacific Scandal
See also CANADIAN PACIFIC RAILWAY.

These hands are clean!

J.W. BENGOUGH, political cartoonist, in the most famous of all Canadian political cartoons, "Whither Are We Drifting?" from the Toronto comic weekly *Grip*, Aug. 6, 1873. The cartoon depicts Prime Minister Sir John A. Macdonald absolving himself of all charges of corruption in connection with the Pacific Scandal. Yet in his left hand he holds a sign that says, "Send me another $10,000," and in his right a charter for the "Prorogation and Suppression of the Investigation."

I admit I took the money and bribed the electors with it. Is there anything wrong about *that*?

J.W. BENGOUGH, cartoonist, in *Grip*, Sept. 27, 1873. These words issue from the lips of Sir John A. Macdonald. Bengough also quotes the prime minister's actual words: "We in Canada seem to have lost all idea of justice, honour and integrity" (reported in the *Mail*, Sept. 26, 1873).

I throw myself upon this house; I throw myself upon this country; I throw myself upon posterity; and I believe that I know, that, notwithstanding the many failings in my life, I shall have the voice of this country, and this house, rallying around me. [Cheers] And, sir, if I am mistaken in that,

I shall confidently appeal to a higher court—to the court of my own conscience, and to the court of posterity.

SIR JOHN A. MACDONALD, first prime minister, in a reply to allegations concerning the Canadian Pacific Railway charter, in the House of Commons, Nov. 3, 1873. From "The Pacific Scandal," reprinted by G. Mercer Adam in *Canada's Patriot Statesman* (1891).

Painting
See also ART; GROUP OF SEVEN.

In summer it was green, raw greens all in a tangle; in autumn it flamed with red and gold; in winter it was wrapped in a blanket of dazzling snow, and in the springtime it roared with running waters and surged with new life, and our artists were advised to go to Europe and paint *smelly canals*.

A.Y. JACKSON, member of the Group of Seven, in "Canadian Art," an address to the Empire Club of Canada in 1925.

For many years we had a country with little or no art, now it seems we are to have art without a country.

A.Y. JACKSON, famous artist, in *A Painter's Country* (1958).

My name is written all over it.

JAMES WILSON MORRICE, Franco-Canadian artist, refusing to sign a painting. Quoted by Donald W. Buchanan in *James Wilson Morrice* (1936).

To return to the term "Creative Art." This is the definition a child once gave it: "I think and then I draw a line round my think." Children grasp these things more quickly than we do. They are more creative than grown-ups. It has not been knocked out of them.

EMILY CARR, west-coast painter and writer, from "Fresh Seeing" (1930) in *Fresh Seeing* (1972), two addresses with a preface by Doris Shadbolt.

I suppose each painter has his own way of launching into the adventures in shape, colour, texture and space that we call painting. I mostly fall into them.

DAVID MILNE, Ontario artist, from "Notes for an Exhibition of Little Pictures," Oct. 24, 1936.

The thing that "makes" a picture is the thing that "makes" dynamite—compression. It isn't a fire in the grass; it is an explosion. Everything must hit at once.

DAVID MILNE, Ontario artist, in *David Milne 1882-1953* (1967), edited by Ralph Allen.

Every damn pine tree in the country has been painted.

GRAHAM COUGHTRY, Toronto artist whose specialty is abstract figures, remark made in 1955. Quoted by Barrie Hale in *Toronto Painting* (1972).

A picture can become for us a highway between a particular thing and a universal feeling.

LAWREN HARRIS, member of the Group of Seven, in *Lawren Harris* (1969), edited by Bess Harris and R.C.P. Colgrove.

Art is simply to transfer one's visions from the real to the unreal.

KENOJUAK, Cape Dorset printmaker, quoted by James Houston in the preface to *Arts of the Eskimo* (1974), edited by Ernest Roch.

Salvador Dali? I think I know that guy's name. What reservation is he on?

JAMES SIMON, a young Indian artist, to art collector Robert McMichael at the Wikwemikong Reservation, Manitoulin Island, Ontario, in summer 1975, after McMichael had noted the Dali-esque quality of Simon's painting "Autumn Spirit."

Parliament

See also GOVERNMENT; GOVERNOR GENERAL; HOUSE OF COMMONS; POLITICS; PRIME MINISTER; SENATE.

My only guiding star in the conduct and maintenance of my official relations with your public men is the Parliament of Canada, in fact, I suppose I am the only person in the Dominion whose faith in the wisdom and in the infallibility of Parliament is never shaken. Each of you, gentlemen, only believe in Parliament so long as Parliament votes according to your wishes and convictions. I, gentlemen, believe in Parliament, no matter which way it votes, and to those men alone whom the absolute will of the Confederated Parliament of the Dominion may assign me as my responsible advisers, can I give my confidence.

LORD DUFFERIN, governor general from 1872 to 1878, in a Halifax address, Aug. 8, 1873, in response to urgings by the Liberals to dismiss the government during the Pacific Scandal. Quoted by George Stewart in *Canada Under the Administration of the Earl of Dufferin* (1878).

The privileges of Parliament are the privileges of the People, and the rights of Parliament are the rights of the People.

EDWARD BLAKE, brilliant Liberal leader, in *Three Speeches by the Hon. Edward Blake, Q.C., M.P., on the Pacific Scandal* (1873), in London, Aug. 28, 1873.

It is for parliament to decide whether or not we should participate in wars in different parts of the world, and it is neither right nor proper for any individual or for any groups of individuals to take any step in which in any way might limit the rights of parliament in a manner which is of such great concern to all the people of our country.

W.L. MACKENZIE KING, prime minister, in the House of Commons, on Feb. 1, 1923. "It is for Parliament to decide" or "Parliament will decide" or "Let Parliament decide" was King's way of dealing with difficult situations. The formula was first used during the Chanak crisis of 1922, according to James Eayrs in *The Art of the Possible* (1961).

Guy Fawkes was the only person to approach Parliament in the proper manner.

GERRY McGEER, former mayor of Vancouver, allegedly spoken in the Senate, to which he was summoned in 1945.

Past

See also PRESENT.

We can only pay our debt to the past by putting the future in debt to ourselves.

JOHN BUCHAN, LORD TWEEDSMUIR, governor general, in an address to the people of Canada on the coronation of George VI, May 12, 1937.

Our Master, the Past, that is to say, the past, master of the future.

CANON LIONEL GROULX, influential priest and historian at the University of Montreal, in

"L'originalité de nôtre histoire," *Centenaire de l'histoire du Canada de François-Xavier Garneau* (1945).

The past must no longer be used as an anvil for beating out the present and the future.

PAUL-ÉMILE BORDUAS, famous Quebec artist, excerpts from *Refus global*, the manifesto issued in Montreal by Borduas and other Quebec artists in 1948. "Global Refusal," *French-Canadian Nationalism* (1969), edited by Ramsay Cook.

To remember the old is to add strength and background to the new.

LESLIE M. FROST, former premier of Ontario, in *Fighting Men* (1967).

Patriotism

See also LOYALTY; NATIONALISM.

So let it be with British America—let every national distinction cease from among us—let not the native Canadian look upon his Irish or Scottish neighbour as an in- truder, nor the native of the British Isles taunt the other about stupidity and inca- pacity. Rather let them become as one race, and may the only strife among us be a praiseworthy emulation as to who shall attain the honour of conferring the greatest benefits on the country of our birth—or the land of our choice.

WILLIAM LYON MACKENZIE, newspaperman and reformer in Upper Canada, in the *Colonial Advocate*, March 30, 1826, reproduced by Margaret Fairley in her edition of *The Se- lected Writings of William Lyon Mackenzie* (1960).

We can hardly join the Americans on our own terms, and we never ought to join them on theirs. A Canadian nationality, not French-Canadian, nor British-Canadi- an, nor Irish-Canadian—patriotism rejects the prefix—is, in my opinion, what we should look forward to,—that is what we ought to labour for, that is what we ought to be prepared to defend to the death . . . .

THOMAS D'ARCY MCGEE, future Father of Confederation, in "American Relations and Canadian Duties," an address before the Irish Protestant Benevolent Society of Quebec, May 10, 1862, from *Speeches and Addresses Chiefly on the Subject of British-American Union* (1865).

Some men, and all cattle, lack patriotism.

GEORGE MUNRO GRANT, principal of Queen's University, quoted by William Lawson Grant and Frederick Hamilton in *Principal Grant* (1904).

There is Ontario patriotism, Quebec patri- otism, or Western patriotism, each based on the hope that it may swallow up the others, but there is no Canadian patriot- ism, and we can have no Canadian nation when we have no Canadian patriotism.

HENRI BOURASSA, French-Canadian national- ist, in "The Nationalist Movement in Quebec," an address to the Canadian Club of Canada on Jan. 22, 1907.

O Canada! Our home and native land! True patriot-love in all thy sons command.

R. STANLEY WEIR, Montreal lawyer and some- time judge of the Exchequer Court of Canada, from "O Canada," written in 1908.

He stole, and boasted of his swag.
  And, when his victims would rebel,
He wrapped himself in England's flag
  And sang, "God Save the King," like Hell.

WILSON MACDONALD, Toronto poet, final stanza of "The Member of Parliament," *Comber Cove* (1937).

Patronage

See also CORRUPTION.

As usual it was a Psalm-singing Protestant dissenter who, holding seven or eight votes in the palm of his hand, volunteered to do the greasing process for a consideration. Upon my word I do not think there was much to be said in favour of the Canadians over the Turks when contracts, places, free tickets on railways, or even cash was in question.

SIR EDMUND HORNBY, a leading British barris- ter who visited Turkey and Quebec in 1858 on business, from *An Autobiography* (1928).

We must support our supporters.

*

What the hell has Strathroy done for me?

JOHN SANDFIELD MACDONALD, Ontario premi- er, to a delegation from a Liberal stronghold that wanted a registry office, in the *Globe*, Aug.

24, 1871. Quoted by Bruce W. Hodgins in *John Sandfield Macdonald* (1971).

A former master dispenser of patronage, Sir Charles Tupper, had devised an ingenious plan. Sir William Van Horne complained to Sir Charles that he was sending a preposterous number of recommendations for passes on the Canadian Pacific. "True," Sir Charles replied, "but it is difficult to decline what people consider costs me nothing. Hereafter, when I send you a letter recommending a pass, and sign it 'Yours truly,' throw it into the waste-basket; when I sign it 'Yours sincerely,' please give it consideration; but when I sign it 'Yours very sincerely,' you simply must not refuse it." "And," added Sir William, "after that, every blessed letter from Tupper asking for a pass was signed, 'Yours very sincerely.' "

O.D. SKELTON, economist and civil servant, in *Life and Letters of Sir Wilfrid Laurier* (1921).

"Patronage!" The udder of democracy!

ROBERT RUMILLY, Quebec historian, in *History of Saint-Laurent* (1970), translated by Cameron Nish.

There is a clear distinction between being a Liberal contractor and being dishonest.

ROBERT BOURASSA, premier of Quebec, remark made in March 1973.

In any case, it's only puritans from outside Quebec who worry about little things like that.

ROBERT BOURASSA, Quebec premier, on a possible conflict of interest between party workers and those who benefit from government contracts, reported the following day in the Toronto *Globe and Mail*, May 10, 1975.

Peace

I, Dekanahwideh, and the Confederated Chiefs, now uproot the tallest pine tree, and into the cavity thereby made we cast all weapons of war. Into the depth of the earth, deep down into the underwater currents of water flowing to unknown regions, we cast all weapons of strife. We bury them from sight and we plant again the tree. Thus shall the Great Peace be established.

DEKANAHWIDEH, semi-legendary Iroquois statesman, giving the Pledge of the Confederacy, which founded the Great League of the Iroquois (or the Five Nations Confederacy) in the 1450s. Quoted by Stanley B. Ryerson in *The Founding of Canada* (rev. ed., 1963).

I do not believe that universal peace is either possible or desirable. If it were possible and could be brought about, I feel sure that it would result in universal rottenness. All the manliness of the civilized world is due to wars or the need of being prepared for wars. All the highest qualities of mankind have been developed by wars or the dangers of wars. Our whole civilization is the outgrowth of wars. Without wars, religion would disappear. All the enterprise of the world has grown out of the aggressive, adventurous, and warlike spirit engendered by centuries of wars.

SIR W.C. VAN HORNE, railroad builder, in a letter to S.S. McClure in 1910, quoted by Walter Vaughan in *The Life and Work of Sir William Van Horne* (1920).

To God in His glory. We two nations dedicate this garden and pledge ourselves that as long as men shall live, we will not take up arms against one another.

Inscription on the cairn of the International Peace Garden, composed of lands donated by Manitoba and North Dakota, opened July 14, 1932.

Make peace as exciting as war.

JOHN GRIERSON, founder of the National Film Board in 1939, characteristic saying.

The grim fact is that we prepare for war like precocious giants and for peace like retarded pygmies.

LESTER B. PEARSON, diplomat and future prime minister, accepting the Nobel Prize for Peace in Oslo, Dec. 10, 1957.

There's panic in the papers
Stocks and bonds are cutting capers
Rich men jumping from skyscrapers.

What's the rumpus all about?
Peace broke out.

JOE WALLACE, Communist poet, in "Panic," *A Radiant Sphere* (1964).

Man has reached out and touched the

tranquil moon. Puisse ce haut fait permettre à l'homme de redécouvrir la terre et d'y trouver la paix.

> PIERRE ELLIOTT TRUDEAU, prime minister, a message on the moon. This was one of seventy-three from world leaders miniaturized and reproduced on a disc the size of a fifty-cent piece, taken to the moon on the Apollo flight and deposited there by Neil Armstrong on July 20, 1969. The translation reads: "May that high accomplishment allow man to rediscover the earth, and there find peace."

I sometimes wonder if there is any other sphere of human activity in which so many fine words have been uttered, and so little achieved as in the pursuit of disarmament and a stable peace.

> E.L.M. BURNS, lieutenant-general of the Canadian Armed Forces, from *A Seat at the Table* (1972).

Any peace is honourable.

> MORLEY SAFER, Toronto-born television reporter who covered the Vietnam War for CBS and incurred Richard Nixon's wrath when he criticized the American president's "peace with honour" policy, from the Toronto *Star*, Jan. 27, 1973.

People
See also MANKIND.

The only way a man achieves greatness is by getting it from the people—the people make giants.

> FATHER JAMES TOMPKINS, who helped found the co-operative Antigonish Movement at St. Francis Xavier University during the 1920s, quoted by E.A. Corbett in "Dr. James Tompkins," *Pioneers in Adult Education in Canada* (c. 1955), edited by Harriet Rouillard.

The little people together is a giant. You've got to give them ideas. Then they'll blow the roof off.

> FATHER JAMES TOMPKINS, Nova Scotian educator, quoted by John R. Chafe in "God's Greatest Nuisance," *In Search of Canada* (1971), by the editors of *Reader's Digest.*

Everyone is against me but the people.

*

There are great interests against us—national and international—but the people of Canada have an appointment with destiny.

> JOHN G. DIEFENBAKER, prime minister, at Port Hope, Ontario, March 8, 1963. This is an echo of Franklin Delano Roosevelt's stirring statement in 1936, "This generation of Americans has a rendezvous with destiny."

Philosophy

It takes as long to become a man as it does to become a philosopher.

> R.D. CUMMING, writer and aphorist, in *Skookum Chuck Fables* (1915).

The philosophers of the Middle Ages demonstrated both that the earth did not exist and also that it was flat. Today they are still arguing about whether the world exists, but they no longer dispute about whether it is flat.

> VILHJALMUR STEFANSSON, outspoken Arctic explorer, in *The Standardization of Error* (1927).

Philosophy, informed by the psychological and social sciences, offers a wisdom that will enable a man to integrate the whole of his being, a wisdom not subject, like all other personal goods, to the mutations of time.

> JOHN A. IRVING, philosopher and professor, in *Science and Values* (1952).

Being a philosopher, I have a problem for every solution.

> ROBERT ZEND, Hungarian-born Toronto writer, in the 1960s.

One has apparently to choose between a competent discussion of trivialities and a series of emotional outbursts about what matters.

> FRANCIS SPARSHOTT, philosopher and poet, in *Looking for Philosophy* (1972).

Pioneers
See also NEW FRANCE.

Reader! it is not my intention to trouble you with the sequel of our history. I have given you a faithful picture of a life in the backwoods of Canada, and I leave you to draw from it your own conclusions. To the poor, industrious working man it presents many advantages; to the poor gentleman, *none!*

> SUSANNA MOODIE, pioneer author, in *Roughing It in the Bush* (1852).

Life is a great adventure and every one of you can be a pioneer, blazing by thought and service a trail to better things.

> GEORGE VI, king of Great Britain, in an address at Government House, Winnipeg, May 24, 1939.

The pioneer's present is always so rough that he quickly learns to live for tomorrow.

> GEORGE V. FERGUSON, editor of the Montreal *Star*, from *John W. Dafoe* (1948).

All around me, when I was a child, men broke the land under the fierce promise of the Homestead Act—a quarter section free if within three years you could plough the prairie, raise house and barn, and survive. It can never come again, that free wild perilous world. No one who has known it would willingly return. No one who has left it can forget.

> FREDELLE BRUSER MAYNARD, Prairie author, in *Raisins and Almonds* (1972).

Planning

The first question in political economy should be, can the mass of the people live comfortably under this or that arrangement? But this most necessary question was forgotten, and many of the people have perished.

> ROBERT GOURLAY, social agitator, in *Statistical Account of Upper Canada, Compiled with a View to a Grand System of Emigration* (1822).

"Rich by nature, poor by policy," might be written over Canada's door. Rich she would be if she were allowed to embrace her destiny and be part of her own continent; poor, comparatively at least, she is in striving to remain a part of Europe.

> GOLDWIN SMITH, British-born journalist, in *Canada and the Canadian Question* (1891). The phrase within quotation marks appeared earlier in Smith's introduction to *Handbook of Commercial Union* (1888).

It is not enough to have good principles;
we must have organization also. Principles without organization may lose, but organization without principles may often win.

> SIR WILFRID LAURIER, prime minister, in an address to the Reform Club, Ottawa, June 19, 1893.

When schemes are laid in advance, it is surprising how often the circumstances fit in with them.

> SIR WILLIAM OSLER, world-famous physician and medical teacher, in *Sir William Osler: Aphorisms from His Bedside Teachings and Writings* (1950), edited by W.B. Bean.

In Canada, for example, there are 2.6 persons per square mile; in other countries perhaps 16, 18, 20, or 26 persons. Well, no matter how stupidly one managed one's affairs in such a country, a decent living would still be possible.

> ADOLF HITLER, Nazi leader, in a Berlin address, Dec. 10, 1940, from *Hitler's Words* (1944), edited by Gordon W. Prange.

Playwrights

See also LITERATURE; WRITERS AND WRITING.

I find writing about the Canadian theatre or drama depressingly like discussing the art of dinghy sailing among the Bedouins. There is so little to be said on the subject save to point out why there is none. Depending on one's expository habits this can be done tersely, as in the case of the Bedouins, by saying "there are no dinghys because there is no water," or at appalling and splendid length by re-examining the geology of the Mediterranean basin and recalling all the flood-mythology one can remember.

> MERRILL DENISON, Montreal playwright and author, in "Nationalism and Drama," *Yearbook of the Arts in Canada: 1928-29* (1929), edited by Bertram Brooker.

The two great Canadian dramatists are Chekhov and Ibsen. The Ibsen and Chekhov situations can be paralleled in Canada twenty times over.

> ROBERTSON DAVIES, man-of-letters, interviewed by Donald Cameron in *Conversations with Canadian Novelists* (1973).

"Canadian playwright." The words seem a little incongruous together, like "Panamanian hockey-player," or "Lebanese fur-trapper."

JULIAN NOVICK, American drama critic, in his review of George Ryga's *The Ecstasy of Rita Joe* at the Washington Theatre Club, in the New York *Times*, May 13, 1973.

A beginning Canadian playwright is a depressing sight—like watching a caterpillar set off across the freeway.

ERIC NICOL, Vancouver humorist and playwright, in *Letters to My Son* (1974).

Poetry and Poets

See also LITERATURE; POETRY AND POETS: CANADIAN.

I am not a great poet and I never was. Greatness in poetry must proceed from greatness of character, from force, fearlessness, brightness. I have none of these qualities. I am, if anything, the very opposite. I am weak; I am a coward. I am a hypochondriac. I am a minor poet of a superior order and that is all.

ARCHIBALD LAMPMAN, Ottawa poet, in a letter of Aug. 29, 1895, from *Archibald Lampman's Letters to E.W. Thomson* (1956), edited by Arthur S. Bourinot.

The poet's daily chore
Is my long duty;
To keep and cherish my good lens
For love and war
And wasps about the lilies
And mutiny within.

ANNE WILKINSON, Toronto poet, from "Lens" (1955), *Selected Poems* (1968), edited by A.J.M. Smith.

Poetry is a verdict.

LEONARD COHEN, Montreal poet and singer, attributed remark, in the 1960s.

A poem is an Alka-Seltzer tablet: orthodoxies begin to fizz when one is dropped into their midst. Distrustful of abstractions, poetry is in love with the concrete and the particular.

IRVING LAYTON, outspoken poet, from "Poets: The Conscience of Mankind" (1963), in *Engagements* (1972), edited by Seymour Mayne.

And me happiest when I compose poems.
Love, power, the huzza of battle
are something, are much;
yet a poem includes them like a pool
water and reflection.
*
I am their mouth; as a mouth I serve.

IRVING LAYTON, poet, from "The Birth of Tragedy," *The Collected Poems of Irving Layton* (1971).

I write poems like spiders spin webs, and perhaps for much the same reason: to support my existence.

ALFRED PURDY, poet and writer, interviewed by Gary Geddes in *Canadian Literature*, summer 1969.

As a poet I need to experience ecstasy.
(English poetry never went crazy, a Frenchman said.
It was not a compliment.)

ELDON GRIER, poet and artist, from "An Ecstasy," *Selected Poems 1955-1970* (1971).

"Poetry is when words sing"—six-year-old boy.

R. MURRAY SCHAFER, west-coast composer and teacher, in *When Words Sing* (1970).

Poetry is studying
how the spirit soars
on learned as on simple
ignorant things.

ROBIN SKELTON, British-born, Victoria-based poet, in "Robert Graves in Deya, Mallorca," *Timelight* (1974).

A good poet is someone who manages, in a lifetime of standing out in thunderstorms, to be struck by lightning five or six times; a dozen or two dozen times and he is great.

ROBIN SKELTON, poet and editor, from *The Poet's Calling* (1975).

Prose is the kind of writing everybody understands, poetry is the other kind.

LOUIS DUDEK, Montreal poet and critic, in *Epigrams* (1975).

Poetry and Poets: Canadian

See also POETRY AND POETS.

To Dr. C.L. Alfred Tennyson,
Poet Laureate of England, Baron, &c.

Dear Sir,

Now Longfellow is gone there are only two of us left. There ought to be no rivalry between us.

"A poet's mind is clear and bright,
No room for hatred, malice or spite."

. . . I do not know whether a Baron or a Poet Laureate gets any wages in England. In Canada there is no pay . . . . It is a solemn thing to reflect that I am the link connecting two great countries. I hope when I am gone another may raise up . . . .
Yours alway,
    James Gay,
        (this day).

Poet Laureate of Canada and Master of All Poets.
Royal City of Guelph, Ontario.

> JAMES GAY, an eccentric Ontario bard and self-styled "Royal Poet," a letter sent to Alfred Lord Tennyson in 1882. From *Canada's Poet* (1884).

No country on the face of the globe has produced, proportionately, so many volumes of verse as Canada.

> JOHN A. COOPER, literary-magazine editor who became a motion-picture distributor, in *Canada Under Victoria* (1901). A highly dubious statement.

Speaking of personal matters, the first time I ever felt the necessity or inevitableness of verse, was in the desire to reproduce the peculiar quality of feeling which is induced by the flat spaces and wide horizons of the virgin prairie of western Canada.

> T.E. HULME, British philosopher and founder of Imagism, who worked as a labourer in western Canada in 1906, in "Lectures on Modern Poetry" (written about 1914), quoted by Michael Roberts in *T.E. Hulme* (1938).

In Eskimo the word to make poetry is the word to breathe; both are derivatives of *anerca*, the soul, that which is eternal: the breath of life.

> EDMUND CARPENTER, anthropologist and editor of *Anerca* (1959).

And like dear bad poets
    Who wrote
    Early in Canada

And never were of note.

> JAMES REANEY, poet and playwright, from "To the Avon River above Stratford, Canada," *Twelve Letters to a Little Town* (1962).

I say the best Canadian poet is Phil Esposito, and that is not a joke.

> YEVGENY YEVTUSHENKO, Russian poet touring Canada, quoted by John Fraser in the Toronto *Globe and Mail*, Dec. 6, 1973.

Whatever happened to Bliss Carman?

> JOHN BETJEMAN, poet laureate of the United Kingdom, in a letter written in the spring of 1975 concerning a visit to McMaster University in Hamilton, Ontario.

Political Parties

See also POLITICS.

My opinions are mine, but my vote belongs to my party.

> ALONZO WRIGHT, Ottawa County M.P. from 1867 to 1891, known as "King of the Gatineau," attributed.

Canadian Liberals believe in the autonomy of the Dominion and the maintenance of the unity of the Empire, whereas Canadian Conservatives believe in the unity of the Empire and the preservation of the autonomy of the Dominions.

> HENRI BOURASSA, French-Canadian nationalist, quoted by R. MacGregor Dawson in *The Government of Canada* (1952).

I'm not a leftist; I'm where the righteous ought to be.

> M.M. COADY, who helped found the self-help Antigonish Movement in Nova Scotia in the 1920s, quoted by J.R. Kidd in 1973 as a characteristic remark.

Perhaps my political views can best be described by saying that I am the hyphen in the phrase Liberal-Conservative.

> FLOYD S. CHALMERS, Toronto publisher, in "The World Economic Crisis and the Canadian Monetary Situation," *The Liberal Way* (1933), opinions expressed at the first Liberal summer conference in Port Hope, Sept. 1933.

Intellectuals in large numbers will sink the

raft of any party, and if allowed to write a program will kill it.

> HAROLD ADAMS INNIS, economist and historian, in "Discussion in the Social Sciences," *Dalhousie Review*, autumn 1935.

No one can kick over the party traces in Canada and politically ever again be heard from.

> C.L. BURTON, chairman of Simpsons, on H.H. Stevens who broke with the Conservatives and formed his own party in 1935, in *A Sense of Urgency* (1952).

An exciting party should have both blondes and brunettes.

> PIERRE ELLIOTT TRUDEAU, prime minister, on March 10, 1968.

Socialists belong to movements, capitalists support parties.

> WALTER D. YOUNG, historian, in *The Anatomy of a Party* (1969).

I don't mind someone stealing my pyjamas, but he should wear all of them if he doesn't want to appear indecent.

> T.C. DOUGLAS, former leader of the New Democratic Party, on the appropriation of CCF-NDP programs by the Liberals and Conservatives, in *Time*, May 3, 1971.

Politicians
See also POLITICS.

A politician is anyone who manages to get elected: more to the point, he is someone who is elected again.

> CHARLES G. "CHUBBY" POWER, prominent politician, in *A Party Politician* (1966), edited by Norman Ward.

Whenever I see a hand sticking out of a sleeve, I shake it.

> GEORGE HEES, as minister of Trade and Commerce in the late 1950s, political credo, quoted by Peter C. Newman in *Renegade in Power* (1963).

A politician these days has to sit on a fence and still keep both ears to the ground.

> ALLAN LAMPORT, mayor of Toronto in the 1950s and malapropist, attributed.

He must be a politician's brother:

He talks one way
And he walks another.

> JOE WALLACE, Communist versifier, from "Verse," *A Radiant Sphere* (1964).

A candidate is a person who stands for what he thinks the public will fall for.

> AL BOLISKA, broadcaster, in *The Mahareeshi Says* (1968).

Ultimately there is one thing that destroys a politician, and that is lack of judgement in public.

> JONATHAN MANTHORPE, journalist, in *The Power and the Tories* (1974).

A statesman has been defined as "a politician held upright by equal pressures from all sides."

> ED FINN, public-relations director for a labour union, in the Toronto *Star*, Sept. 1, 1975.

Politics
See also ELECTIONS; PARLIAMENT; POLITICAL PARTIES; POLITICIANS; POLITICS: CANADIAN; STATESMEN.

Representation by Population.

> GEORGE BROWN, future Father of Confederation, platform in the election of 1851. The demand for "Rep by Pop" came ten years earlier when Upper and Lower Canada were united to form the Province of Canada. Eastern Canada demanded more seats because it had a larger population; ten years later western Canada made the same demand. "Rep by Pop" was achieved with Confederation in 1867.

Poetry was my first love, but politics was the harridan I married.

> JOSEPH HOWE, Nova Scotian editor and statesman, remark made in his later years (frequently reproduced as "Poetry was the maiden I loved, but politics was the harridan I married"). Quoted by George Munro Grant in *Joseph Howe* (1904).

A nest of traitors.

> SIR MACKENZIE BOWELL, prime minister, remark made when half the ministers in his Cabinet, including Sir George Foster and Sir Charles Tupper, resigned on Jan. 4, 1896, over their leader's handling of the Manitoba

schools issue. Bowell himself resigned on April 27, 1896.

The member for Winnipeg North Centre is the leader of the party and I am the party.

WILLIAM IRVINE on his fellow M.P., J.S. Woodsworth, both of whom were identified as belonging to "the labour party" because they had participated in the Winnipeg General Strike of 1919. Quoted by F.H. Underhill in *In Search of Canadian Liberalism* (1960).

I have no politics, I am a Canadian.

GEORGE McCULLAGH, publisher of the Toronto *Globe and Mail* and founder of the Leadership League for unemployed youth in the 1930s; in an address, June 1938, quoted by Brian J. Young in "C. George McCullagh and the Leadership League," *Canadian Historical Review*, Sept. 1966.

Canadian politics in British Columbia is an adventure, on the prairies a cause, in Ontario a business, in Quebec a religion, in the Maritimes a disease.

PAUL ST. PIERRE, writer and M.P. for Coast Chilcotin from 1968 to 1972.

Nothing I ever do is political.

JOHN G. DIEFENBAKER, former prime minister, in Ottawa, Jan. 16, 1968.

Following Canadian politics closely is a little like being a devoted reader of *Peanuts* or even *Pogo*; it's the characters that hold your interest, not the story line.

EDGAR Z. FRIEDENBERG, Louisiana-born educator who teaches at Dalhousie University, in "Good Manners," the *New York Review of Books*, May 17, 1973.

Loose fish.

SIR JOHN A. MACDONALD, prime minister, used this term in the 1880s for members of Parliament not subject to party discipline. This is the opposite of George Drew's "trained seals."

Trained seals.

GEORGE DREW, premier of Ontario from 1943 to 1948, first used this phrase to describe the behaviour of Liberal backbenchers, House of Commons, May 15, 1956.

Red Tory.

GAD HOROWITZ, Winnipeg political scientist, popularized this term to define "a conscious ideological Conservative with some 'odd' socialist notions (W.L. Morton) or a conscious ideological socialist with some 'odd' tory notions (Eugene Forsey)." From the *Canadian Journal of Economics and Political Science*, May 1966.

Politics: Canadian

See also POLITICS.

This then is politics. That part of our duty which teaches us to study the welfare of our whole country, and not to rest satisfied altho' our own household is well off when our neighbours are in difficulty and danger. The honest politician is he who gives all he can of his time and means to promote the public good, whose charity begins at home *but does not end there*. The man who says he is no politician, is either ignorant of what he is saying, or a contemptible selfish creature, unworthy of the country or community of which he is a part.

WILLIAM LYON MACKENZIE, Upper Canadian reformer, in the *Colonial Advocate*, June 27, 1833. Reproduced by Margaret Fairley in her edition of *The Selected Writings of William Lyon Mackenzie* (1960).

Politics makes a man as crooked as a pack does a pedlar, not that they are so awful heavy, neither, but it teaches a man to stoop in the long run.

THOMAS CHANDLER HALIBURTON, Nova Scotian writer and wit, in *The Clockmaker* (1836).

Politics, the noblest of all callings, but the meanest of all trades . . . .

GOLDWIN SMITH, British-born journalist, in *Essays on Questions of the Day, Political and Social* (1893).

Ah! Politics, politics, always politics.

GOLDWIN SMITH, writer and political commentator, quoted by Hector Charlesworth in *Candid Chronicles* (1925).

There is much gold amid the mud of politics.

SIR RICHARD CARTWRIGHT, Liberal spokesman and senator who died in 1912, attributed.

No man should enter politics unless he is either independently rich or independently poor.

ROBERT JAMES MANION, politician who died in 1943, quoted by Dalton Camp in *Gentlemen, Players and Politicians* (1970).

Politics is largely made up of irrelevancies.

DALTON CAMP, Toronto advertising man and Conservative, quoted by Rae Murphy in the *Last Post*, April-May 1971.

Politics is the skilled use of blunt objects.

LESTER B. PEARSON, former prime minister, on "The Tenth Decade," CBC-TV, 1972.

Politics is man's best game, next to war.

JOHN PHILIP MACLEAN, novelist, in *Backroom Boys and Girls* (1973).

In politics there are no thank you's.

MORTON SHULMAN, controversial member of the Ontario legislature, announcing his intention to retire from public life, quoted by Norman Webster in the Toronto *Globe and Mail*, Sept. 19, 1974.

For me, politics is a vehicle to achieve things—not a power trip, not a game of charades that you play with the vested interests, but a natural extension of social work, a way to alleviate misery.

DAVE BARRETT, former premier of British Columbia, quoted by Christina Newman in the Toronto *Globe and Mail*, March 1, 1975.

In politics, you can't beat a somethin' with a nothin'.

GEORGE HEES, old-guard Conservative M.P., quoted by Norman Webster in the Toronto *Globe and Mail*, Sept. 5, 1975.

Poverty

Visitor: Why don't you give these things you wear to the poor?

La Peltrie: I prefer to see the poor in new clothes.

MARIE-MADELEINE DE LA PELTRIE, founder of the Ursuline Convent in Quebec, who died Nov. 19, 1671, always wore tattered garments. Adapted from Thomas B. Costain's *The White and the Gold* (1954).

We live in a rickety house,
  In a dirty dismal street,
Where the naked hide from day,
  And the thieves and drunkards meet.

ALEXANDER MCLACHLAN, folk poet, from "We Live in a Rickety House," *The Emigrant and Other Poems* (1861).

I love my own country and race,
  Nor lightly I fled them both,
Yet who would remain in a place
  Where there's too many spoons for the broth?

ALEXANDER MCLACHLAN, folk poet, from "Song," *The Emigrant and Other Poems* (1861).

One of the greatest assets any man or woman can have on entering life's struggle is poverty.

R.B. BENNETT, prime minister who died in England as Viscount Bennett of Mickleham, Calgary and Hopewell, attributed.

We can't go on living on a planet that's two-thirds slum—not with safety.

ARNOLD SMITH, secretary-general of the Commonwealth of Nations, 1968.

Social Credit once had a war on poverty. Phil Gaglardi started to throw rocks at beggars.

GRAHAM LEAD, B.C. NDP minister of Highways, referring to the minister of Highways in the previous administration, quoted by Allan Fotheringham in the Toronto *Star*, May 23, 1975.

Power

. . . and beside, power has a nateral [*sic*] tendency to corpulency.

THOMAS CHANDLER HALIBURTON, Nova Scotian writer and wit, in *The Clockmaker* (1836).

We have less control over others and more power over ourselves than we like to think.

STEPHEN VIZINCZEY, Budapest-born Canadian author, in *The Rules of Chaos* (1969).

Authoritarianism is the temptation of power; alarmism that of opposition.

GÉRARD PELLETIER, secretary of State during the October Crisis, in *The October Crisis* (1971), translated by Joyce Marshall.

Power without love is tyranny. Power with love is charity in action.

> JEAN VANIER, founder of L'Arche, the community in France for the mentally retarded, sign at the centre, quoted by James H. Clarke in *L'Arche Journal* (1973).

Prairies

See also WEST, THE.

The Prairie Province.

> JAMES CLELLAND HAMILTON, Toronto lawyer and author, used this term in his study of Manitoba, *The Prairie Province: Sketches of Travel from Lake Ontario to Lake Winnipeg* (1876). When Saskatchewan and Alberta were formed in 1905, the term *prairie provinces* was used to refer to all three.

O Canada! Where pines and maples grow,
Great prairies spread and lordly rivers flow
. . . .

> R. STANLEY WEIR, Montreal lawyer and sometime judge of the Exchequer Court of Canada, from "O Canada," written in 1908.

Once, while we halted a woman drove straight down at us from the sky-line, along a golden path between black ploughed lands. When the horse, who managed affairs, stopped at the cars, she nodded mysteriously, and showed us a very small baby in the hollow of her arm. Doubtless she was some exiled Queen flying North to found a dynasty and establish a country. The Prairie makes everything wonderful.

> RUDYARD KIPLING, British man-of-letters, in *Letters to the Family: Notes on a Recent Trip to Canada* (1908), reprinted in *Letters of Travel 1892-1913* (1920).

The Landless Man and the Manless Land.

> A.C. FLUMERFELT, speaker, title of an address on the under-populated west, to the Canadian Club of Montreal on Jan. 22, 1917. Robert Forke, minister of Immigration and Colonization from 1926 to 1929, adopted this expression as a slogan to encourage immigration to the west.

It is a country to breed mystical people, egocentric people, perhaps poetic people. But not humble ones. At noon the total sun pours on your single head; at sunrise or sunset you throw a shadow a hundred yards long. It was not prairie dwellers who invented the indifferent universe or impotent man. Puny you may feel there, and vulnerable, but not unnoticed. This is a land to mark the sparrow's fall.

> WALLACE STEGNER, American author, whose family homesteaded from 1911 to 1920 in the region of the Cypress Hills, Sask. From *Wolf Willow* (1962).

A writer of our acquaintance, sitting on the train going west across the repetitive prairies, finally burst out savagely, "This country could do with a great deal of editing!"

> DEREK PATMORE, traveller and writer, in *Canada* (1967), by Derek Patmore and Marjory Whitelaw.

Prayer

What a Friend we have in Jesus,
All our sins and griefs to bear!
What a privilege to carry
Everything to God in prayer!
Oh, what peace we often forfeit,
Oh, what needless pain we bear—
All because we do not carry
Ev'rything to God in prayer!

> JOSEPH MEDLICOTT SCRIVEN, resident of the Port Hope area, Ontario, wrote "What a Friend We Have in Jesus" about 1857. Quoted by Rev. Jas. Cleland in *What a Friend We Have in Jesus and Other Hymns by Joseph Scriven with a Sketch of the Author* (1895).

"Why must people kneel down to pray? If I really wanted to pray I'll tell you what I'd do. I'd go out into a great big field all alone or into the deep, deep woods, and I'd look up into the sky—up—up—up—into that lovely blue sky that looks as if there was no end to its blueness. And then I'd just *feel* a prayer."

> L.M. MONTGOMERY, novelist, expresses these sentiments through the young Anne in *Anne of Green Gables* (1908).

Pre-Cambrian Shield
See CANADIAN SHIELD.

Prejudice

It has been spread abroad that " 'Uncle Tom' is coming," and that is what has brought you here. Now allow me to say that my name is not Tom, and never was Tom, and that I do not want to have any other name inserted in the newspapers for me than my own. My name is Josiah Henson, always was, and always will be. I never change my colours.

JOSIAH HENSON, Kentucky slave who escaped and settled near Dresden, Ontario, in 1830, quoted by Robin W. Winks in *The Blacks in Canada* (1971). Henson was repeatedly introduced as Uncle Tom at public lectures, long after the American Civil War.

"Person" means a male person, including an Indian, and excluding a person of Mongolian or Chinese race.

From the Electoral Franchise Act, assented to July 20, 1885, from *Acts of the Parliament of the United Kingdom and Great Britain and Ireland* (1885). It was frequently cited by Nellie McClung, suffragette leader, as a racist clause.

No Aliens Need Apply.

SIR RICHARD MCBRIDE, British Columbia politician and later the province's first native-born premier, was defeated in the federal election of 1896 on this anti-Oriental platform.

No Englishmen Need Apply.

From an advertisement for a "position vacant" in a Winnipeg newspaper, Aug. 1909, which coincided with a meeting of the British Association in that city.

We will not march on Ottawa. When we go we will go as M.P.s in Pullman cars.

ADRIEN ARCAND, Quebec fascist leader, in Feb. 1938, quoted by Lita-Rose Betcherman in *The Swastika and the Maple Leaf* (1975).

I am a man of sound prejudice.

ALLAN LAMPORT, Toronto mayor in the 1950s and malapropist, attributed.

There is absolutely no bias in Vancouver. I know because I just had dinner with your Negro.

DICK GREGORY, black American comedian, quoted by Jay and Audrey Walz in *Portrait of Canada* (1970).

I resent that they think that because the chairman is an immigrant boy from Slovakia and the president is a Polack, we are third-class citizens.

STEPHEN B. ROMAN, mining magnate, statement to the press on learning in 1970 that the Trudeau administration would block the sale of Denison Mines, the world's largest supplier of uranium, to U.S. interests.

Toleration of differences is the measure of civilization.

VINCENT MASSEY, first native-born governor general, quoted by Richard M. Nixon before a joint sitting of the Canadian Senate and the House of Commons, April 14, 1972.

To be black and female, in a society which is both racist and sexist, is to be in a unique position of having nowhere to go but up.

ROSEMARY BROWN, member of the B.C. legislature and black feminist, quoted by Allan Fotheringham in *Saturday Night*, July-Aug. 1975.

Present
See also FUTURE; PAST.

The present seems to be a thing of the past.

R.D. CUMMING, writer and aphorist, in *Skookum Chuck Fables* (1915).

Today is the tomorrow you worried about yesterday.

JACK MINER, pioneer naturalist who banded wildlife at his famous bird sanctuary at Kingsville, Ontario, a "Minerism."

All men are powerless against chance, but the defeated know the secret. They live for the present—the future has already betrayed them. They are the children of reality.

STEPHEN VIZINCZEY, Budapest-born Canadian author, in *The Rules of Chaos* (1969).

Prime Minister
See also LEADERSHIP; PARLIAMENT.

Do I want to be Prime Minister of Great Britain? Yes, but only if I can be Leader of the Opposition at the same time!

LORD BEAVERBROOK, Canadian-born British press lord, attributed by A. Beverley Baxter in *Strange Street* (1935).

Alexander wept; there were no more

worlds to conquer. What would make a Canadian Prime Minister weep?

PATRICK WATSON, author and TV personality, in *Conspirators in Silence* (1969).

I've never been a president and wonder what it would be like.

PIERRE ELLIOTT TRUDEAU, prime minister, at a Toronto dinner, April 15, 1971.

The Canadian kid who wants to grow up to be Prime Minister isn't thinking big, he is setting a limit to his ambitions rather early.

MORDECAI RICHLER, Montreal novelist, quoted in *Time*, May 31, 1971.

I've achieved my objective. I'm a has-been.

JOHN P. ROBARTS, premier of Ontario, resigning as premier and Conservative leader on Feb. 13, 1970, quoted by Jonathan Manthorpe in *The Power and the Tories* (1974).

When the goals are known and the means are known, people want a bureaucrat. (Louis St. Laurent?)
When the goals are known but the means are unknown, people want an entrepreneur. (Sir John A. Macdonald?)
When the goals are unknown but the means are known, people want a scholar. (Pearson? Trudeau?)
When the goals and the means are unknown, people want a Machiavelli. (Mackenzie King?)

MARY McIVER STEWARD, writer, in *Leadership* (1975), a publication based on the "Human Journey" TV series.

"Every man must be his own Prime Minister, serving under the Queen."

ROBERTSON DAVIES, man-of-letters, in a line of dialogue from *Question Period*, premiered at the St. Lawrence Centre in Toronto, Feb. 24, 1975.

Prince Edward Island
See also MARITIME PROVINCES.

It needs only the nightingale.

JACQUES CARTIER, French explorer, on Prince Edward Island in 1530-40, quoted by Stephen Leacock in "The Island of the Blest" in *My Discovery of the West* (1937).

Prince Edward Island will have to come in, for if she does not we will have to tow her into the St. Lawrence.

THOMAS D'ARCY McGEE, politician and future Father of Confederation, attributed, in 1865, when P.E.I. was against Confederation.

I found the Island in a high state of jubilation and quite under the impression that it is the Dominion that has been annexed to Prince Edward; and in alluding to the subject I had adopted the same tone.

LORD DUFFERIN, governor general from 1872 to 1878, who visited Prince Edward Island three weeks after the colony joined Confederation, on July 1, 1873, in a letter to Sir John A. Macdonald later that year. Quoted by D.C. Harvey in "Confederation and Prince Edward Island," *Canadian Historical Review*, June 1933.

Prison
See also JUSTICE.

And I seriously declare, I had rather die by the most severe tortures ever inflicted on this continent, than languish in one of your prisons for a single year. Great Spirit of the Universe!—and do you call yourselves Christians?

JOSEPH BRANT, Mohawk leader, in a letter of 1803. Quoted by William L. Stone in *Life of Joseph Brant* (1838).

And there, in the office, we were put through an examination the like of which I had never before experienced, even in the Peter-Paul fortress. For in the Czar's fortress the police stripped me and searched me in privacy, whereas here our democratic allies subjected us to this shameful humiliation before a dozen men.

LEON TROTSKY, Russian revolutionary, about his incarceration in Canada on April 3, 1917, when he and his family were forcibly removed from a Norwegian vessel at Halifax. His wife and children were kept under close surveillance in Halifax while Trotsky was kept in a prisoner-of-war camp at Amherst; released on April 29, he and his family returned to Russia. From *My Life* (1931).

If we are to have human dignity, then we have to break the law. Jails are made for men. We might as well explore them.

MICHEL CHARTRAND, leader of the left wing of the Quebec labour movement and president of the Montreal Central Council of the CNTU, in a Toronto address, June 15, 1973.

Privacy

I shun publicity wherever I can find it.
ALLAN LAMPORT, Toronto mayor in the 1950s and malapropist, attributed.

There's no place for the state in the bedrooms of the nation.
PIERRE ELLIOTT TRUDEAU, then minister of Justice and future prime minister, tossed off this now-celebrated *bon mot* in an Ottawa interview, Dec. 22, 1967. What he actually said, in reference to changes in the Criminal Code, was, "The state has no place in the nation's bedrooms." The aphorism is an adaptation of lines from an editorial in the Toronto *Globe and Mail*: "Obviously, the state's responsibility should be to legislate rules for a well-ordered society. It has no right or duty to creep into the bedrooms of the nation." The unsigned editorial, written by Martin O'Malley, appeared on Dec. 12, 1967.

I knew he would never marry Barbra Streisand or any American girl. I can recall him saying the States has no place in the bedrooms of the nation.
ROBERT L. STANFIELD, leader of the Opposition, in a luncheon speech at the Variety Club, Toronto, on May 27, 1971, shortly after Prime Minister Trudeau's marriage to Margaret Sinclair of Vancouver.

Progress

True progress can come only as the result of thoughtful, continuous, co-operative effort. This progress will necessarily be slow, but it must be continuous. Nothing can hinder it more than the mistakes of thoughtless impatience.
HENRY WISE WOOD, president of the United Farmers of Alberta, in the *Grain Growers' Guide*, Jan. 29, 1919.

All this progress is marvellous . . . now if only it would stop!
ALLAN LAMPORT, Toronto mayor in the 1950s and malapropist, attributed.

The march of social progress is like a long and straggling parade, with the seers and prophets at its head and a smug minority bringing up the rear.
PIERRE BERTON, author and TV personality, in *The Smug Minority* (1968).

The worst superstition of the nineteenth and twentieth centuries is called progress. It is certain there will be no progress until there is an end to this kind of progress.
GEORGE FALUDY, Hungarian-born poet and humanist living in Toronto, characteristic remark.

Prohibition
See also DRINKING.

I am a Prohibitionist. What I propose to prohibit is the reckless use of water.
BOB EDWARDS, writer and publisher of the Calgary *Eye Opener*, March 17, 1904.

I wish somehow that we could prohibit the use of alcohol and merely drink beer and whisky and gin as we used to.
STEPHEN LEACOCK, renowned humorist, from "This Strenuous Age," *Frenzied Fiction* (1917).

I was not aware that Canada was under Prohibition until two gentlemen offered me bottles of whiskey within fifteen minutes of my arrival here.
ISRAEL ZANGWILL, well-known Anglo-Jewish novelist, in a Toronto address, quoted by Hector Charlesworth in *More Candid Chronicles* (1928).

I am against prohibition on both grounds. I think it would be inexpedient if it were possible, and it is impossible if it were expedient.
MATTHEW B. BEGBIE, "the hanging judge," later chief justice of British Columbia, quoted by Roy St. George Stubbs in "Matthew Baillie Begbie," *Papers read before the Historical and Scientific Society of Manitoba* (1968-69).

Prostitution
See also SEX.

To hell with Pearl Harbor
Remember Pearl Miller!
PEARL MILLER was a popular Calgary madam

in the 1930s. The Calgary Highlanders tell the story that the Princess Pats erected this sign in their sergeant's mess shortly before D–Day, after seeing the American slogan "Remember Pearl Harbor."

The prostitute is never an enemy of the man's wife.
MARTHA ADAMS, most famous of Montreal madams, who ran against Claude Wagner in the federal election of 1972, in *Martha Adams* (1972).

I now make more money vertically than I ever did horizontally.
XAVIERA HOLLANDER, Toronto-based author of *The Happy Hooker* (1972).

You know what I think Oshawa needs? A good brothel.
XAVIERA HOLLANDER, author and former madam, quoted by David Cobb in *Toronto Life*, July 1973.

Publishers and Publishing
See also LITERATURE.

The market for Canadian literary wares of all sorts is self-evidently New York, where the intellectual life of the continent is rapidly centralizing. It is true that it will never become a great or profitable market until some original process of development is applied to the transplanted romance of our North-west, to the somewhat squat and uninteresting life of Ontario, to our treasure trove, Quebec; but when this is done, we may be sure that it will be with an eye upon immediate American appreciation, and in the spirit and methods of American literary production.
SARA JEANNETTE DUNCAN, novelist, in *The Week*, July 1887.

Publishers are procurers.
HUGH KANE, publishing executive, at the Canadian Authors' Association convention in Winnipeg in 1957, quoted by Stan Obodiac in *My Experiences at a Canadian Authors' Convention* (1957).

A writer's best friend is his publisher.
LORNE PIERCE, editor of the Ryerson Press, at the Canadian Authors' Association convention

in Winnipeg in 1957, quoted by Stan Obodiac in *My Experiences at a Canadian Authors' Convention* (1957).

I once defined a publisher as: Somebody looking for someone who has something to say.
LORNE PIERCE, long-time editor, in *An Editor's Creed* (1960).

Most of the men who call themselves publishers in Toronto might as well be selling soap.
ROBERT WEAVER, CBC executive, in "Books," *Mass Media in Canada* (1962), edited by John A. Irving.

Then, to repeat a favourite story of mine, there is the editor of a major New York publishing house who told me that one afternoon he and his associates compiled a list of twelve deserving but ineffably dull books with which to start a publishing firm that was bound to fail. Leading the list of unreadables was *Canada: Our Good Neighbour to the North*.
MORDECAI RICHLER, Montreal novelist, in the introduction to *Canadian Writing Today* (1970).

If [Frederick Philip] Grove were any good, he would have been published in New York and London.
MORDECAI RICHLER, Montreal novelist, quoted by Henry Makov in *Weekend*, April 26, 1975.

If Canadians spoke Swahili and dealt in razbuckniks, Canada would have a healthy and vigorous Canadian-owned book publishing industry. But, because we have the misfortune of speaking English and dealing in dollars, our publishing industry is fighting for its survival.
PETER MARTIN, Toronto publisher, in a brief to the Ontario Royal Commission on Book Publishing, March 1971, reprinted in *Independence* (1972), edited by Abraham Rotstein and Gary Lax.

Publishers have half a brain among them, and they pass it around.
JOHN PETER, Victoria novelist, at the annual meeting of the Writers' Union in Ottawa, quoted by William French in the Toronto *Globe and Mail*, Oct. 28, 1974.

Xerox gives power to the people. It makes everyone a publisher.

> MARSHALL MCLUHAN, media pundit, at the Montreal International Book Fair, quoted by Christie McCormick in the Montreal *Gazette*, May 16, 1975.

Quebec

See also CONQUEST OF 1759; FRENCH CANADA; FRENCH CANADIANS; NEW FRANCE; QUEBEC CITY; QUIET REVOLUTION; SEPARATISM.

Your answer positive in an hour returned by your own trumpet, with the return of mine, is required upon the peril that will ensue.

> SIR WILLIAM PHIPS, leader of the British forces at Quebec, sent this order for immediate surrender to le Comte de Frontenac on Oct. 15, 1690. Quoted by Francis Parkman in *Count Frontenac and New France under Louis XIV* (1877).

I have no reply to make to your general other than from the mouths of my cannon and muskets. He must learn that it is not in this fashion that one summons a man such as I. Let him do the best he can on his side as I will do on mine.

> COMTE DE FRONTENAC, governor of New France, to Major Thomas Savage, envoy of Admiral Phips who demanded the surrender of Quebec, Oct. 15, 1690. Quoted by W.J. Eccles in *Canada under Louis XIV: 1663-1701* (1964).

Oh, we're marching down to Old Quebec
And the fifes and the drums are abeating,
For the British boys have gained the day,
And the Yankees are retreating,
So we'll turn back and we'll come again
To the place where we first started,
And we'll open the ring and we'll take a
    couple in,
Since they proved that they are true-hearted.

> From "Marching Down to Old Quebec"

(1775), *Canada's Story in Song* (1965), edited by Edith Fowke and Alan Mills.

Je me souviens.

> EUGÈNE TACHÉ, architect, chose the motto of the province of Quebec, first inscribed beneath its coat of arms on Feb. 9, 1883. The phrase translates, "I remember," and is an allusion to the glory of the *ancien régime*.

Certainly it cannot be too often repeated, that the most solid basis for a nation is the possession of the land; that the question of "repatriation," that is of the return to the agricultural districts of the province of Quebec, remains the order of the day. Lay hold of the land, as far as circumstances will permit.

> EDMOND DE NEVERS, French-Canadian author, in *L'avenir du peuple canadien-français* (1896). Quoted by Ramsay Cook in "Quebec: The Ideology of Survival," *The Prospect of Change* (1965), edited by Abraham Rotstein.

Strangers have surrounded us whom it is our pleasure to call foreigners; they have taken into their hands most of the rule, they have gathered to themselves much of the wealth; but in this land of Quebec nothing has changed. Nor shall anything change, for we are the pledge of it. Concerning ourselves and our destiny but one duty have we clearly understood: that we should hold fast—should endure. And we have held fast, so that, it may be, many centuries hence the world will look upon us and say:—These people are a race which knows not how to perish . . . . In this land of Quebec naught shall die and naught change . . . .

> LOUIS HÉMON, French author of *Maria Chapdelaine* (1921), translated by W.H. Blake.

The daughter of Maria Chapdelaine who was an ammunition-factory worker at Valcartier during the war now lives with her own family of five children in the Rosemount ward of Montreal. Maria's married brothers are employees of the Aluminum Company at Arvida and Shipshaw after having been workers at the Jonquière pulp plant.

> JEAN-CHARLES FALARDEAU, Quebec sociologist, from "The Changing Social Structures," *Essais sur le Québec Contemporain* (1953). Quoted by

Ramsay Cook in "Quebec: The Ideology of Survival," *The Prospect of Change* (1965), edited by Abraham Rotstein.

The English papers in Quebec act like British administrators in an African colony. Wise in the arts of political science, the British rarely destroy the political institutions of a conquered country. They keep a close check on the nigger-king but they wink at his whims. On occasion they permit him to chop off a few heads; it's just part of the local folklore. But one thing would never occur to them: to expect the nigger-king to conform to the high moral and political standards of the British.

The main thing is to get the nigger-king to support and protect British interests. Once this collaboration is assured, the rest is less important. Does the princeling violate democratic principles? What else can you expect of the natives? . . .

ANDRÉ LAURENDEAU, Quebec editor, in "The Nigger-King Hypothesis," *Le Devoir*, July 4, 1958, from *André Laurendeau* (1973), translated by Philip Stratford. This celebrated *roi nègre* editorial appeared following the failure of a single English-language paper in Quebec to report Maurice Duplessis's expulsion of a *Le Devoir* reporter from one of his press conferences.

Quebec is not a province like the others. She is a little more stupid.

GÉRARD FILION, editor of *Le Devoir*, quoted by Brian Moore in *Canada* (1963).

You are not aware of the meaning you have for France. There is nowhere in the world where the spirit of France works so movingly as it does in the Province of Quebec.

ANDRÉ MALRAUX, novelist and French minister of Culture, in an Montreal address, Oct. 15, 1963.

This province is a country within a country. Québec the original heart. The hardest and deepest kernel. The core of first time. All around, nine other provinces form the flesh of this still-bitter fruit called Canada.

ANNE HÉBERT, poet and novelist, in "Quebec: The Proud Province," *Century 1867-1967* (1967).

As for me, a Québécois, proletarian, white nigger of America, one of the "wretched of the earth," to take responsibility for our history was, inevitably, to begin by denouncing and exposing the inhuman conditions of our existence, to build up a body of concrete knowledge and orient it entirely in the direction of "the practical results of action," of revolutionary action, of total liberation.

PIERRE VALLIÈRES, FLQ sympathizer, in *White Niggers of America* (1971), translated by Joan Pinkham. The book was written in the Manhattan House of Detention for Men in 1966 and 1967.

Quebec City
See also QUEBEC.

I never saw anything more superb than the position of this town. It could not be better situated as the future capital of a great empire.

LE COMTE DE FRONTENAC, "Father of New France," on first seeing Quebec in Sept. 1672, quoted by Francis Parkman in *Count Frontenac and New France under Louis XIV* (1877).

Push on, brave boys, Quebec is ours!

RICHARD MONTGOMERY, American brigadier-general, gave this last command to his invading army outside the ramparts of Quebec, New Year's Eve, 1775. Quoted by John Codman II in *Arnold's Expedition to Quebec* (1901).

Something assures one that Quebec must be a city of gossip; for evidently it is not a city of culture. A glance at the few booksellers' windows gives evidence of this. A few Catholic statuettes and prints, two or three Catholic publications, a festoon or so of rosaries, a volume of Lamartine, a supply of ink and matches, form the principal stock.

HENRY JAMES, American novelist, in "Quebec," *Portraits of Places* (1883).

Quebec is the most interesting thing by much that I have seen on this Continent, and I think I would sooner be a poor priest in Quebec than a rich hog-merchant in Chicago.

MATTHEW ARNOLD, British writer, in a letter to Walter Arnold, New York, Feb. 28, 1884.

From *Letters of Matthew Arnold* (1895), edited by George W.E. Russell.

There was a young man of Quebec
Who was frozen in snow to his neck,
    When asked, "Are you Friz?"
    He replied, "Yes I is,
But we don't call this cold in Quebec.

RUDYARD KIPLING, British man-of-letters, quoted by Stephen Leacock in "Comic Verse: The Lighter Notes," *Humour and Humanity* (1937). Kipling never claimed authorship of this widely quoted limerick.

A tailor, who sailed from Quebec,
In a storm ventured once upon deck;
    But the waves of the sea
    Were as strong as could be,
And he tumbled in up to his neck.

Anonymous limerick, first published in England in 1822, according to Iona and Peter Opie in *The Oxford Dictionary of Nursery Rhymes* (1951).

Quiet Revolution

See also QUEBEC.

Maîtres chez nous. C'est l'temps qu'ça change!

JEAN LESAGE, premier of Quebec from 1960 to 1966, used these political slogans ("Masters in our own house," "It's time for a change!"), which are associated with the Quiet Revolution.

Jean Lesage is the only person I know who can strut sitting down.

JOHN G. DIEFENBAKER, former prime minister, adapted from Thomas Van Dussen in *The Chief* (1968).

We, the Liberal government, had just called an election on the nationalization of private power companies. A couple of nights later, a small group of us came up with a campaign slogan: "*Maîtres chez nous*" (Masters in our own home). The moment those three words rang out, the search was over. Even though instinct and common sense cried out that here, potentially, was much more than a call for the takeover of a handful of private utilities.

RENÉ LÉVESQUE, in 1962 a Quebec Liberal Cabinet minister, in "To Be Masters in Our

Own House" (1968), from *Canada: A Guide to the Peaceable Kingdom* (1970), edited by William Kilbourn. The election on Nov. 14, 1962, confirmed the Liberal mandate.

J'ai le goût du Québec.

RENÉ LÉVESQUE, founder of the separatist Parti québécois, adopted this low key slogan ("I have a taste for Quebec") for the provincial election in Oct. 1973.

Quotation

Perhaps the reader may ask, of what consequence is it whether the author's exact language is preserved or not, provided we have his thought? The answer is, that inaccurate quotation is a sin against truth. It may appear in any particular instance to be a trifle, but perfection consists in small things, and perfection is no trifle.

ROBERT W. SHANNON, writer, in the *Canadian*, Oct. 1898.

Nothing can stand against a really resolute quoter.

GOLDWIN SMITH, British-born journalist and man-of-letters, attributed.

To be apt in quotation is a splendid and dangerous gift. Splendid, because it ornaments a man's speech with other men's jewels; dangerous, for the same reason.

ROBERTSON DAVIES, man-of-letters, in the Toronto *Star*, Oct. 1, 1960.

An aphorism should be like a burr: sting, stick, and leave a little soreness afterwards.

IRVING LAYTON, outspoken poet, in *The Whole Bloody Bird* (1969).

Radio

See also BROADCASTING.

Canadian radio listeners want Canadian broadcasting.

SIR JOHN AIRD, chairman of the Royal Commission on Broadcasting, from the Aird Report which was tabled in the House of Commons in Sept. 1929.

The question before this committee is whether Canada is to establish a chain that is owned and operated and controlled by Canadians, or whether it is to be owned and operated by commercial organizations associated or controlled by American interest. The question is, the State or the United States?

GRAHAM SPRY, early enthusiast for national broadcasting, in an address to the Parliamentary Committee on Broadcasting, April 18, 1932, quoted by E. Austin Weir in *The Struggle for National Broadcasting in Canada* (1965).

Knock-knock.
Who's there?
It's the Happy Gang!
Well, c'mon in!

BERT PEARL, Winnipeg-born radio personality, introduction to CBC Radio's long-running (1937–59) daily comedy program, "The Happy Gang," which employed the talents of Cliff McKay, Bobby Gimby, Lloyd Edwards, Joe and Bert Niosi, Jimmy Namaro, Lou Snider and many others.

Good evening. This is James Bannerman.

JAMES BANNERMAN, Toronto broadcaster, characteristic salutation before introducing the cultural programs to be heard on "CBC Wednesday Night," during the 1950s and 1960s.

Privately owned radio has often been successful in its own terms: profitability, stability, unflagging mediocrity.

KEITH DAVEY, Liberal senator, in *The Report of the Special Senate Committee on Mass Media, Volume I: The Uncertain Mirror* (1971), commonly called the Davey Report.

Railroads

See also CANADIAN PACIFIC RAILWAY.

I am neither a prophet, nor a son of a prophet, yet I will venture to predict that in five years we shall make the journey hence to Quebec and Montreal, and home through Portland and St. John, by rail; and I believe that many in this room will live to hear the whistle of the steam engine in the passes of the Rocky Mountains, and to make the journey from Halifax to the Pacific in five or six days.

JOSEPH HOWE, Nova Scotian editor and future statesman, in an address at Mason's Hall, Halifax, May 15, 1851, from *The Speeches and Public Letters of The Hon. Joseph Howe* (1858), edited by William Annand.

Railroads are my politics.

SIR ALLAN MACNAB, president of the Great Western Railway, and leader of the Tory Opposition in the Legislative Assembly of Upper Canada, maxim dating from 1853.

The base banner under which they fight, bears the motto, "Expediency is our God! RAILROADS are our politics!"

ROBERT JACKSON MACGEORGE, editor of the Streetsville *Weekly Review*, Nov. 25, 1854, referring to the interests of Canadian newspaper publishers.

Canada Linked.

Terse two-word cable sent to Queen Victoria as Engine 374 steamed into Vancouver on May 23, 1887, with the first Montreal-to-Vancouver passengers.

I often say to my directors that I am almost ashamed to take the salary that they pay me because it is the easiest thing in the world to be a railway president. All you have to do is to satisfy the public.

SIR EDWARD W. BEATTY, president of the CPR, quoting an unnamed American railway president of many years standing with whom he agreed, in "Confederation," an address to the Canadian Club of Toronto, March 28, 1927.

The provinces were literally railroaded into Confederation.

ERIC NICOL, Vancouver humorist, in *100 Years of What?* (1966); illustrated by Peter Whalley.

"Ready, Aye, Ready"

See WAR, CANADIANS AT.

Rebellion of 1837

In the name of every regiment of militia in Upper Canada, I publicly promulgate, *let them come if they dare.*

FRANCIS BOND HEAD, ebullient lieutenant-governor of Upper Canada during the Rebellion of 1837, in an address in the House of Assembly prior to the election of June 20, 1837, from *A Narrative* (1839).

As for me, I am of a different opinion from that of M. Papineau. I claim the time has come to melt down our pewter plates and spoons into bullets.

WOLFRED NELSON, leader of the rebellion in Lower Canada, at a political meeting in St. Charles, Oct. 23, 1837. Quoted by Alfred D. DeCelles in *The "Patriotes" of '37* (1920).

"Remember the *Caroline.*"

This phrase became a slogan of the patriots in the Rebellion of 1837. Captain Andrew Drew claimed he had cut adrift and set afire the American steamer, *Caroline*, and sent it flaming over Niagara Falls, Dec. 29, 1837.

I have not had a fair trial. There are witnesses here who have sworn my life away. The perjured evidence of William Gymer, William Crew, and David Bridgeford will haunt them in after years. These perjurers will never die a natural death; and when you, sir, and the jury shall have died and perished in hell's flames, John Montgomery will yet be living on Yonge Street.

JOHN MONTGOMERY, popular proprietor of Montgomery's Tavern, which acted as a meeting place for the rebels of 1837, prophecy allegedly made in the dock of the Toronto court house in the presence of Chief Justice John Beverley Robinson, April 2, 1838. Montgomery, convicted of high treason, was sentenced to death, but the sentence was commuted to imprisonment. He escaped to the United States, was eventually pardoned, and died in Toronto in 1879. According to Edwin C. Guil-

let in *The Lives and Times of the Patriots* (1938, 1969): "The prophecy was partially fulfilled, for one man shot himself and another cut his throat, and Montgomery outlived judge, jurors, witnesses, and prosecutors."

Be of good cheer, boys. I am not ashamed of anything I've done. I trust in God, and I'm going to die like a man.

SAMUEL LOUNT, patriot who forged spearheads for the Rebellion, was hanged in Toronto, April 12, 1838. Quoted by John Ross Robertson about 1900 in *Old Toronto* (1954), edited by E.C. Kyte.

He lived a Patriot, and died for popular rights.

Inscription on the monument erected to honour the memory of Samuel Lount and Peter Mathews, both hanged for treason, April 12, 1838. The monument was erected in 1893 in St. James Cemetery, Toronto.

And now that the rebellion's o'er
  Let each true Briton sing,
Long live the Queen in health and peace,
  And may each rebel swing.

From "New Words to an Old Song; or, John Gilpin Travestied" (1938), reproduced by John S. Moir in *Rhymes of Rebellion* (1965).

I carried my musket in '37.

SIR JOHN A. MACDONALD, prime minister of Canada, remark characteristic of his later years.

Mackenzie was a crazy man,
He wore his wig askew.
He donned three bulky overcoats
In case the bullets flew.
Mackenzie talked of fighting
While the fight went down the drain.
But who will speak for Canada?
Mackenzie, come again!

DENNIS LEE, poet and editor, final verse of "1838," *Nicholas Knock and Other People* (1974).

Reciprocity

See also TRADE.

It is in vain to suppose that a free trade system will be beneficial to a new and struggling colony, which has nothing to export but raw materials; it is rather calculated to enrich an old commonwealth, whose people by their skill and labour make such raw materials valuable, and then return them for consumption. The result of the system alluded to has been that the suppliers of the raw material at last become hewers of wood and drawers of water to the manufacturers.

ABRAHAM GESNER, the scientist who devised a method of producing kerosene in Halifax in 1846, and a critic of reciprocity, from *The Industrial Resources of Nova Scotia* (1849).

Now is the accepted time. Canada is at the parting of the ways. Shall she be an isolated country, as much separated from us as if she were across the ocean, or shall her people and our people profit by the proximity that our geography furnishes and stimulate trade across the border that nothing but a useless, illogical and unnecessary tariff wall created?

WILLIAM HOWARD TAFT, United States president, in an address in the Illinois legislature, Springfield, Feb. 11, 1911.

No Truck Nor Trade with the Yankees!

SIR GEORGE E. FOSTER, M.P. who became Robert Borden's minister of Trade and Commerce when the Conservatives defeated the Liberals under Laurier in the anti-reciprocity election of 1911, was the author of the Conservative election slogan.

No Navy made in London; no reciprocity made in Washington.

CHARLES H. CAHAN, M.P. and later secretary of State in R.B. Bennett's government, coined this slogan for Robert Borden's Conservatives in the election of Sept. 21, 1911. Borden defeated Laurier's Liberals who favoured establishing a navy and reciprocity with the United States. Quoted by Mason Wade in *The French Canadians: 1760–1967* (1968).

It is her own soul that Canada risks today.

RUDYARD KIPLING, British man-of-letters, in a message cabled on the eve of the general election, Sept. 21, 1911. The country saved "her own soul," when the electorate rejected the reciprocity agreement reached by Prime Minister Sir Wilfrid Laurier and American President William Howard Taft. Laurier was replaced by Sir Robert Borden, who favoured imperial preference in matters of trade.

Red River
See MANITOBA.

Red River Rebellion
See also RIEL, LOUIS.

You go no farther!

LOUIS RIEL, leader of the Métis in the Red River and Northwest Rebellions, to the British surveyors stopped on Oct. 11, 1869. "The métis simply stood on the chain while Riel declared that the territory south of the Assiniboine belonged to the people of Red River and not to Canada, and that the métis would not allow the survey to proceed any further." George F.G. Stanley in *Louis Riel* (1963).

REMEMBER BUTLER, 69TH REGIMENT.

SIR WILLIAM FRANCIS BUTLER, British officer, cable sent to Colonel Garnet Wolseley, who was organizing the Red River Expedition in 1870, reproduced in Field-Marshal Viscount Wolseley's *The Story of a Soldier's Life* (1903). Butler immediately left England for Montreal, where Wolseley agreed to take him on as an intelligence officer.

Reform

You can't reform 'em, the only way is to chloroform them.

THOMAS CHANDLER HALIBURTON, Nova Scotian satirist and judge, in *Sam Slick's Wise Saws* (1853).

But in this country what is there for Conservatives to conserve or for Reformers to reform?

GOLDWIN SMITH, British-born journalist, in *Canadian Monthly and National Review*, April 1872.

Disaster precedes reform.

PETER MCARTHUR, rural Ontario writer and columnist who died in 1924, attributed.

And, to my mind, reform means Government intervention. It means Government control and regulation. It means the end of *laissez faire*. Reform heralds certain recovery. There can be no permanent recovery without reform! Reform or no reform! I raise that issue squarely. I nail the flag of progress to the masthead. I summon the power of the State to its support.

R.B. BENNETT, prime minister, in his first radio address, Jan. 2, 1935, quoted by J.R.H. Wilbur in *The Bennett New Deal* (1968).

Religion
See also CHRISTIANITY.

About the only people who don't quarrel over religion are the people who haven't any.
BOB EDWARDS, writer and publisher of the Calgary *Eye Opener*, Oct. 15, 1910.

To be Catholic or Jewish isn't chic. Chic is Episcopalian.
ELIZABETH ARDEN, Ontario-born American cosmetic queen, quoted by Alfred Allan Lewis and Constance Woodworth in *Miss Elizabeth Arden* (1972).

When someone asked me what it felt like to be outside the Roman Catholic Church, I found myself spontaneously answering: it is as if I had rejoined the human race.
CHARLES DAVIS, former British Jesuit theologian teaching in Montreal, in *A Question of Conscience* (1967).

Had every Christian in Hitler's Europe followed the example of the king of Denmark and decided to put on the yellow star, there would be today neither despair in the church nor talk of the death of God.
EMIL L. FACKENHEIM, German-born rabbi and philosopher, in *Quest for Past and Future* (1968).

Responsibility

When everyone is responsible then nobody is, and that is comfortable, finally.
MAVIS GALLANT, Paris-based Montreal short-story writer, in the introduction to *The Affair of Gabrielle Russier* (1971).

It's not true that men in my position have power. We only have responsibility.
W. EARLE MCLAUGHLIN, president of the Royal Bank of Canada, interviewed by Dean Walker in an advertisement published in the Toronto *Globe and Mail*, Aug. 5, 1975.

Any society that denies the concept of individual responsibility must either perish in a chaos of criminal and vigilante lawlessness or end up denying all of its citizens

any individual freedom.
BARBARA AMIEL, Toronto journalist, in "In Defence of Vengeance," *Saturday Night*, Sept. 1975.

Responsible Government

Why do they talk of responsible government when we have responsible government? As Governor of this country I am responsible to the King.
SIR PEREGRINE MAITLAND, autocratic lieutenant-governor of Upper Canada (1818-28), attributed remark, quoted by E.J. Hathaway in *Jesse Ketchum and His Times* (1929).

Responsible Government.
ROBERT BALDWIN, moderate reformer in Upper Canada, in a memorandum to the colonial secretary in 1836 recommended responsible government (elected rather than appointed Cabinet members) in local affairs. His father, William Warren Baldwin, Upper Canadian doctor, lawyer and reform leader, had been the first colonist to suggest the application of the principle of responsible government to the colonies, in a letter to the Duke of Wellington in 1828. The idea was adopted by Lord Durham in his famous report.

Retirement

But as to this retirement business, let me give a word of advice to all of you young fellows around fifty. Some of you have been talking of it and even looking forward to it. Have nothing to do with it. Listen; it's like this. Have you ever been out for a late autumn walk in the closing part of the afternoon, and suddenly looked up to realize that the leaves have practically all gone? You hadn't realized it. And you notice that the sun has set already, the day gone before you knew it—and with that a cold wind blows across the landscape. That's retirement.
STEPHEN LEACOCK, humorist who died in Toronto in 1944, in "When Men Retire," *Too Much College* (1939).

Don't resign. Wait until you're sacked.
Don't retire. Wait until you're dead.
SIR JAMES DUNN, president of Algoma Steel Corporation, quoted by Lord Beaverbrook in *Courage: The Story of Sir James Dunn* (1961).

Dunn took his own advice, resisted C.D. Howe's pressure to resign, and died in his eighty-second year planning a twenty-year program.

Retiring is for automobiles.

LORNE GREENE, the Ottawa-born actor who went from being CBC's "Voice of Doom" to Canada's only multi-millionaire star, quoted by Frank Rasky in the Toronto *Star*, Nov. 12, 1974.

Revolution

The great lesson to draw from revolutions is not that they devour humanity but rather that tyranny never fails to generate them.

PIERRE ELLIOTT TRUDEAU, prime minister, in "When the People Are in Power" (1958), *Approaches to Politics* (1970), translated by I.M. Owen.

I don't understand the revolutionary who does not take the trouble to make love well.

PAUL CHAMBERLAND, Quebec separatist poet, explaining the significance of the title of his book, *L'afficheur hurle* (1964), which translates "The poster-hanger screams." Quoted by Malcolm Reid in *The Shouting Signpainters* (1972).

When one is a victim of aggression one does not waste time preparing the menu for the victory banquet.

LOUIS LABERGE, militant president of the Quebec Federation of Labour, replying to charges that the FLQ lacked specific long-term goals, in the Toronto *Star*, Feb. 7, 1972.

A revolution is a good thing as long as it doesn't succeed.

LOUIS DUDEK, Montreal poet, in *Epigrams* (1975).

Riel, Louis

See also NORTHWEST REBELLION; RED RIVER REBELLION.

I am the half-breed question.

LOUIS RIEL, leader of the Métis in the Red River and Northwest Rebellions, remark made about 1884, quoted by O.D. Skelton in *Life and Letters of Sir Wilfrid Laurier* (1921).

The day of my birth I was helpless and my mother took care of me although she was not able to do it alone, there was some one to help her to take care of me and I lived. Today, although a man, I am as helpless before this Court, in the Dominion of Canada and in this world as I was helpless on the knees of my mother the day of my birth. The North West is also my mother, it is my mother country, and although my mother country is sick and confined in a certain way, there are some from Lower Canada who came to help her to take care of me during her sickness, and I am sure that my mother country will not kill me more than my mother did . . . .

*

If it is any satisfaction to the doctor to know what kind of insanity I have, if they are going to call my pretentions insanity, I say humbly, through the grace of God I believe I am the prophet of the New World.

*

I know that through the grace of God I am the founder of Manitoba.

LOUIS RIEL, messianic Métis leader, in his eloquent defence speech, Regina, July 31, 1885. From "The Prisoner's Address," *The Queen vs. Louis Riel, Accused and Convicted of the Crime of High Treason* (1886).

He shall hang though every dog in Quebec bark in his favour.

SIR JOHN A. MACDONALD, prime minister, comment prior to Louis Riel's execution on Nov. 16, 1885. Quoted by Sir George R. Parkin in *Sir John A. Macdonald* (1908).

Gave up his right to pardon. Was ordered hanged as a traitor.
But they say his body made a great wound in the air,
and God Damn the English judge that put him there.

PATRICK ANDERSON, British-born poet in Montreal, from "The Country Still Unpossessed," *The White Centre* (1946).

How many other Riels exist in Canada, beyond the fringe of accepted conduct, driven to believe that this country offers no answer to their needs and no solutions to their problems?

It is all too easy, should disturbances erupt, to crush them in the name of law and order. We must never forget that, in the long run, a democracy is judged by the way the majority treats the minority. Louis Riel's battle is not yet won.

PIERRE ELLIOTT TRUDEAU, prime minister, in an address at the unveiling of the Louis Riel Monument, Regina, Oct. 2, 1969.

Rights
See CIVIL RIGHTS.

Rivers

. . . that great river [St. Lawrence], associated with memories of Cartier, Champlain, LaSalle, Frontenac, Wolfe and Montcalm,—that river already immortalized in history by the pen of Parkman—will be as noted in song and story as the Rhine, and will have its Irving to make it as famous as the lovely Hudson.

SIR J.G. BOURINOT, clerk of the House of Commons from 1880 to 1902, in *Our Intellectual Strength and Weakness* (1893).

O Canada! Where pines and maples grow,
Great prairies spread and lordly rivers flow
. . . .

R. STANLEY WEIR, Montreal lawyer and sometime judge of the Exchequer Court of Canada, from "O Canada," written in 1908.

A river is never quite silent; it can never, of its very nature, be quite still; it is never quite the same from one day to the next. It has its own life and its own beauty and the creatures it nourishes are alive and beautiful also. Perhaps fishing is for me only an excuse to be near rivers. If so, I'm glad I thought of it.

RODERICK HAIG-BROWN, naturalist and magistrate in British Columbia, in *A River Never Sleeps* (1950).

A dull people,
but the rivers of this country
are wide and beautiful.

IRVING LAYTON, outspoken poet, from "From Colony to Nation," *The Collected Poems of Irving Layton* (1971).

The Thousand Island region is a place of storms—of equinoctial storms that come sliding over the surface of the earth when the world tilts, of summer thunderstorms and winter gales.

JOHN KEATS, the American social critic, described his way of life on a two-acre island in the Thousand Islands region of the St. Lawrence in *Of Time and an Island* (1974).

I wanted to return to the rivers, and please don't laugh at this: I wanted to try to *think* like a river even though a river doesn't think. Because every river on this earth, some of them against incredible obstacles, ultimately finds its way through the labyrinth to the universal sea.

HUGH MACLENNAN, Montreal novelist, in *Rivers of Canada* (1974).

Royal Canadian Mounted Police

They are to be purely a civil, not a military body, with as little gold lace, fuss, and fine feathers as possible: not a crack cavalry regiment, but an efficient police force for the rough and ready—particularly ready—enforcement of law and justice.

SIR JOHN A. MACDONALD, prime minister, introducing the bill to establish the North West Mounted Police, in the House of Commons, May 3, 1873.

Maintiens le droit.

Official motto of the Mounties: the North West Mounted Police (1873-1904), Royal North West Mounted Police (1904-1920), Royal Canadian Mounted Police (from 1920). The French phrase is officially translated "Uphold the Right." Its use was advocated in 1873 and adopted two years later.

Without fear, favour or affection.

From the oath of office, assented to May 23, 1874.

The advice given me and my people has proved to be very good. If the police had not come to this country, where would we all be now? Bad men and whiskey were killing us so fast that very few of us would have been alive today. The Mounted Police have protected us as the feathers of the bird protect it from the frosts of winter. I wish them all good, and I trust that all our hearts will increase in goodness from this time forward. I am satisfied! I will sign the treaty.

> CROWFOOT, great Blackfoot chief, at the signing of Blackfoot Treaty Number Seven, Sept. 22, 1877, at Blackfoot Crossing. Quoted by Alexander Morris in *The Treaties of Canada with the Indians* (1880).

They always get their man.

> Expression associated with the RCMP but not its motto. After the Mounted Police closed down Fort Whoop-Up, a whiskey fort that was operated in the Cypress Hills by John J. Healy, the enterprising American turned to publishing the *Fort Benton Record*. On April 13, 1877, he referred to the Mounties' action in suppressing the liquor traffic: ". . . but the M.P.'s are worse than bloodhounds when they scent the track of a smuggler, and they fetch their men every time."

And though we win no praise or fame
  In the struggle here alone—
To carry out good British law
  And plant old England's throne;
Yet when our task has been performed,
  And law with order reigns,
The peaceful settler long will bless
  The Riders of the Plains.

> "The Riders of the Plains" (1878), a ballad attributed to numerous authors and constables. The entire work was published in Charles Pelham Mulvaney's *The History of the North-West Rebellion of 1885* (1885).

On the 17th inst., I, Corporal Hogg, was called to the hotel to quiet a disturbance. I found the room full of cowboys, and one Monaghan, or "Cowboy Jack," was carrying a gun and pointed it at me, against sections 105 and 109 of the Criminal Code. We struggled. Finally I got him handcuffed behind and put him inside. His head being in bad shape I had to engage the services of a doctor, who dressed his wound and pronounced it as nothing serious. To the doctor Monaghan said that if I hadn't grabbed his gun there'd be another death in Canadian history. All of which I have the honour to report.

> CORPORAL C. HOGG, of the Wood Mountain detachment, filed this report of his actions in quelling a disturbance instigated by an armed badman in a North Portal hotel, quoted by A.L. Haydon in *The Riders of the Plains* (1910).

Oh, Rose-Marie. I love you!
I'm always dreaming of you.
No matter what I do,
I can't forget you.
Sometimes I wish that I had never met you!
And yet if I should lose you,
'Twould mean my very life to me;
Of all the queens that ever lived I'd choose you
To rule me, my Rose-Marie.

> RUDOLF FRIML, Vienna-born American composer who wrote the music to *Rose-Marie*, the operetta that was the hit of the 1924 Broadway season. The lyrics were written by Otto Harbach and Oscar Hammerstein II. In 1936, Jeanette MacDonald and Nelson Eddy starred in the Hollywood movie, *Rose-Marie*. Within the ranks of the RCMP, a soft assignment is known to this day as "a Rose-Marie posting."

The Silent Force.

> Epithet from *The Silent Force* (1927), by the Philadelphia writer, T.M. Longstreth.

I never did like that emblim they have up on the wall, "We always gits our man." Fur a change, they deserves to git the gurl. It's helthier.

> DON HARRON, actor-writer who created Charlie Farquharson, the crotchety farmer from Parry Sound, in *Charlie Farquharson's Jogfree of Canada* (1974).

I must say, Mr. Speaker, that when the RCMP tell me something I listen.

> PIERRE ELLIOTT TRUDEAU, prime minister, explaining why he acquired an $85,000 Cadillac with bullet-proof wheels, in the House of Commons, Dec. 11, 1974.

Royal Commissions

Paris, history reminds us, was worth a mass. Perhaps Canada is worth a royal commission.

> ANDRÉ LAURENDEAU, editor of *Le Devoir*, in "A Proposal for an Inquiry into Bilingualism," *Le Devoir*, Jan. 20, 1962. The following year the Royal Commission on Bilingualism and Biculturalism was established, with Laurendeau and Davidson Dunton as co-chairmen. *André Laurendeau: Witness for Quebec* (1973), translated by Philip Stratford.

A chance remark by somebody coming out of a bank or a supermarket might tell the man of the future a lot more about the 1970's than a whole shelf of Royal Commission reports.

ANDREW ALLAN, well-known radio director, in *Andrew Allan* (1974)

Royal Visits
See also MONARCHY.

It is only repetition when I say that I hope to be often in Canada again and in Toronto, where I have had such a wonderful time, and I will try never to forget the great kindness which you have shown me this year. As you know, my right hand has been out of action for nearly two months. When asked why I shake hands with my left hand, I always reply that my right hand was "done in" in Toronto. Though painful at the time, I shall always look back on that as a great compliment.

EDWARD VIII, as the Duke of Windsor, visited Canada in 1919, 1923, 1924, and 1927, before renouncing the British throne in 1936; an address at Massey Hall to the joint meeting of the Canadian Club and the Empire Club of Canada, Nov. 4, 1919.

And of all the information that I brought back I think what delighted him [King George V] most was the following doggerel picked up in a Canadian border town:
Four and twenty Yankees, feeling very dry,
Went across the border to get a drink of rye.
When the rye was opened, the Yanks began to sing,
"God bless America, but God save the King!"

EDWARD VIII, as the Duke of Windsor, on his first Canadian tour in 1919, when he was twenty-five, from *A King's Story* (1951).

You know, Your Majesty, some of this is for you.

CAMILLIEN HOUDE, long-time mayor of Montreal, remark to King George VI and Queen Elizabeth when they heard the cheers of the crowds while driving through Montreal, May 18, 1939.

The more balconies, the better.

GEORGE VI, king of Canada, quoted by Gustave Lanctot in *The Royal Tour of King George VI*

and Queen Elizabeth in Canada and the United States of America 1939. (1964).

Thank you for being just the way you are.

ELIZABETH II, queen of Canada, to Eskimos at Resolute Bay, July 6, 1970, too shy to approach the first reigning monarch to visit the Northwest Territories, quoted by Pat Carney in *Tiara and Atigi* (1971).

Thank you for bringing Her Majesty, your charming wife, to Thunder Bay.

W.M. ASSEF, lively mayor of Thunder Bay, to Prince Philip at a civic reception to honour Queen Elizabeth and the Duke of Edinburgh, at City Hall, Thunder Bay, July 3, 1971.

The Son of the Big Boss.

Eskimo name given to Prince Charles, Prince of Wales, when he visited the eastern Arctic in April 1974. The phrase in Eskimo is *Attaniout Ikeneega.*

So where, may I ask,
Is the monarchy going
When princes and pressmen
Are on the same Boeing?

PRINCE CHARLES, PRINCE OF WALES, composed and recited this verse before Eskimos and reporters (who travelled on his jet), Resolute Bay, April 27, 1975.

Virtually any female I meet is liable to be sized up as a future spouse. So I shall be very careful as to whose nose I rub.

PRINCE CHARLES, PRINCE OF WALES, quoted by *Time*, May 5, 1975, was denounced for making this remark on his Arctic travels as it showed "no respect for Inuit integrity."

Rules and Regulations

CODE OF RULES

1. Guests will be provided with breakfast and supper but must rustle their own dinner.

2. Boots and spurs must be removed at night before retiring.

3. Dogs are not allowed in the bunks, but may sleep underneath.

4. Candles, hot water and other luxuries charged extra, also soap.

5. Two or more persons must sleep in one bed when so requested by the proprietor.

6. Baths furnished free down at the river, but bathers must furnish their own soap and water.

7. Jewelry or other valuables will not be locked in the safe. The hotel has no such ornament as a safe.

8. The proprietor will not be responsible for anything. In case of fire, guests are requested to escape without unnecessary delay.

9. Guests without baggage may sleep in the vacant lot.

10. Meals served in bedrooms will not be guaranteed in any way. Our waiters are hungry and not above temptation.

11. All guests are requested to rise at 6 A.M. This is imperative as sheets may be needed for tablecloths.

12. No tips to be given to any waiters or servants. Leave them with the proprietor and he will distribute them if considered necessary.

13. The following tariff subject to change: Board $25 a month. Board and lodging with wooden bench to sleep on, $50 a month. Board and lodging with bed, $60 a month.

14. When guests find themselves or their baggage thrown over the fence, they may consider that they have received notice to quit.

> HARRY "KAMOOSE" TAYLOR, innkeeper at Hotel Fort Macleod, his "Code of Rules," Sept. 1, 1882, reproduced by Grant MacEwan in "The Keeper of Hotel Fort Macleod: Harry Taylor," *Fifty Mighty Men* (1958). Taylor's nickname, Kamoose, is said to be Indian for "wife-stealer."

Russia

See UNION OF SOVIET SOCIALIST REPUBLICS.

Saskatchewan

A paradise of fertility.

> HENRY YOULE HIND, geologist, used this phrase to describe the Red River Valley in his *Narrative of the Canadian Red River Exploring Expedition of 1857* (1860).

The Lord said "let there be wheat" and Saskatchewan was born.

> STEPHEN LEACOCK, dean of Canadian humorists, in "Saskatchewan and Wheat," *My Discovery of the West* (1937).

Silence and solitude—the finest gifts Saskatchewan has to offer bedevilled modern man.

> EDWARD MCCOURT, writer and academic, in *Saskatchewan* (1968).

Science and Scientists
See also EDUCATION; TECHNOLOGY.

A romantic age stands in need of science, a scientific and utilitarian age stands in need of the humanities.

> GOLDWIN SMITH, British-born journalist, in *The Week*, April 28, 1893.

There is a saying that "it is the first step that counts," and it is clear that to McGill belongs whatever credit is due for the early ideas and experiments which opened up the way into the unknown.

> ERNEST RUTHERFORD, professor of Physics at McGill University from 1898 to 1907, where he did work in radioactivity that led to his receiving the Nobel Prize for Chemistry in 1908. Quoted by Rollo O. Earl in "Science," *The Culture of Contemporary Canada* (1957), edited by Julian Park.

We talk about the American way, the British way. If we had any sense, we would know that there is no American way, no British way. There is only one way—the scientific way that cuts across racial lines with international boundaries.

M.M. COADY, educator who helped found the Antigonish Movement in Nova Scotia in the 1920s, in *The Man from Margaree* (1971), edited by Alexander F. Laidlaw.

, , , the academic atmosphere, produced mainly by the humanities, is the only atmosphere in which pure science can flourish.

E.W. STEACIE, former director of the National Research Council, in an address in 1956. From *Science in Canada* (1965), edited by J.D. Babbitt.

A scientist is one who can look at a platinum blonde and tell whether she is a Virgin Metal or a Common Ore.

AL BOLISKA, Toronto joke-collector, in *The World's Worst Jokes* (1966).

The history of technology shows that many of the major developments of the last hundred years are based on discoveries made by scientists motivated by the quest for knowledge. If we want to ensure further beneficial development of technology in Canada, we shall have a much better chance of success if we support basic research with all possible freedom for the individual scientist than if we support only those missions in which we can foresee immediate advantages.

GERHARD HERZBERG, winner of the Nobel Prize for Physics, in a convocation address at York University, Nov. 7, 1969. Quoted by F. Ronald Hayes in *The Chaining of Prometheus* (1973).

A scientist has as much luck in communicating with the federal bureaucracy as you would have reciting Gaelic poetry to a deaf seagull.

DR. PETER LARKIN of the University of British Columbia at a meeting of the Pacific Science Congress in Vancouver, Aug. 26, 1975.

Scots

The chieftain of the Clan MacNab emigrated to Canada with a hundred followers; and, on reaching Toronto, called on his namesake Sir Allan MacNab. He left his card, which bore the words: "The MacNab." Sir Allan next day returned the visit, and left *his* card. It said, simply: "The Other MacNab."

SIR ALLAN MACNAB, president of the Great Western Railway, and later Tory premier of the Province of Canada, in *The Wit of the Scots* (1968), by Gordon Irving.

The Scots are the backbone of Canada. They are all right in their three vital parts—heads, heart and haggis.

SIR WILLIAM OSLER, famous physician and medical teacher, from *Sir William Osler: Aphorisms from His Bedside Teachings and Writings* (1950), edited by W.B. Bean.

One may be a little homesick for Oxfordshire here, but not for Scotland, for Canada is simply Scotland on an extended scale.

JOHN BUCHAN, LORD TWEEDSMUIR, governor general, in a letter to Stanley Baldwin, about 1938, quoted by Janet Adam Smith in *John Buchan* (1965).

Seasons

Along the line of smoky hills
  The crimson forest stands,
And all the day the blue-jay calls
  Throughout the autumn lands.

WILLIAM WILFRED CAMPBELL, poet who aspired to become the first poet laureate of the British Empire, first verse of "Indian Summer," *Lake Lyrics and Other Poems* (1889).

And yet to me not this or that
  Is always sharp or always sweet;
In the sloped shadow of my hat
  I lean at rest, and drain the heat;
Nay more, I think some blessèd power
  Hath brought me wandering idly here:
In the full furnace of this hour
  My thoughts grow keen and clear.

ARCHIBALD LAMPMAN, Ottawa poet, from "Heat," *The Poems of Archibald Lampman* (1900), edited by Duncan Campbell Scott.

There is an honesty about the very seasons in Canada. In the winter it is cold. In the summer it is hot.

BEVERLEY BAXTER, Toronto-born journalist and British M.P. who contributed a fortnightly "London Letter" to *Maclean's*, in "From the Heart of Things" (1937), an address to the Empire Club of Canada.

September has a touch of the year's death

in it—one notices that a little more sadly and fearfully as one grows older.

RODERICK HAIG-BROWN, British Columbia magistrate and author, from *A River Never Sleeps* (1946).

I know of only one other season in one other country which compares in beauty with the Canadian fall. It is the English spring. The two seasons evoke different thoughts and emotions. The one cries "Hail!" and the other says "Farewell!" The one is concerned with birth and the other with death. One expresses joy and the other sorrow. Their moods contrast widely. But for sheer, aesthetic beauty they are peers in perfection.

*

October is the loveliest Canadian month. For some time frosts have been stealing down at night from the north and forcing that sad crisis in the woods—the death of the leaves. Nothing in Nature is more memorable than the transformation which then takes place. The funeral rites of the Canadian trees are celebrated with pageantry of startling gorgeousness. Gradually the dark, sultry green of the summer foliage is changed into many lighter, gayer, more vivid hues. Each day the wonder grows until in the first half of October it reaches its climax.

MALCOLM MACDONALD, British high commissioner in Ottawa from 1941 to 1945, in *The Birds of Brewery Creek* (1947).

The rain of the monsoon falls, an inescapable treasure,
Hundreds of millions live
Only because of the certainty of this season,
The turn of the wind.

F.R. SCOTT, Montreal man-of-letters, from *Selected Poems* (1966).

Mon pays ce n'est pas un pays c'est l'hiver
Mon jardin ce n'est pas un jardin c'est la plaine
Mon chemin ce n'est pas un chemin c'est la neige
Mon pays ce n'est pas un pays c'est l'hiver

*

My country is not a country it's the winter
My garden is not a garden it's the plain
My road is not a road it's the snow

My country is not a country it's the winter

GILLES VIGNEAULT, well-known *chansonnier*, from "Mon Pays," *Avec les vieux mots* (1965), with English translation.

Secord, Laura
See also WAR OF 1812.

By this time daylight had left me. Here I found all the Indians encamped; by moonlight the scene was terrifying, and to those accustomed to such scenes, might be considered grand. Upon advancing to the Indians they all rose, and, with some yells, said "Woman," which made me tremble. I cannot express the awful feeling it gave me; but I did not lose my presence of mind. I was determined to persevere. I went up to one of the chiefs, made him understand that I had great news for Capt. Fitzgibbon, and that he must let me pass to his camp, or that he and his party would be all taken. The chief at first objected to let me pass, but finally consented, after some hesitation, to go with me and accompany me to Fitzgibbon's station, which was at the Beaver Dam, where I had an interview with him. I then told him what I had come for, and what I had heard—that the Americans intended to make an attack upon the troops under his command, and would, from their superior numbers, capture them all. Benefitting by this information, Capt. Fitzgibbon formed his plans accordingly, and captured about five hundred American infantry, about fifty mounted dragoons, and a field-piece or two was taken from the enemy. I returned home next day, exhausted and fatigued.

LAURA SECORD, the thirty-seven-year-old Loyalist lady who trekked through the woods for nineteen miles in June 1813 to warn Captain James FitzGibbon of the intended American attack, quoted by Gilbert Auchinleck in *A History of the War Between Great Britain and the United States of America during the Years 1812, 1813 & 1814* (1855).

One, two, three, alora,
Four, five, six, alora,
Seven, eight, nine, alora,
Ten, A-Laura Secord!

Ball-bouncing rhyme, traditional.

She is not without honour in Canada.

Across the country there are Laura Secord candy stores. At one time the face on the candy boxes was Laura's own determined middle-aged visage framed by a stiff bonnet, but American influence has subversively transformed Canada's heroine. Currently a misty-eyed maiden, a gentle immigrant from the Old South, purports to be Laura on the candy boxes.

JAY WALZ, Ottawa correspondent for the New York *Times*, in *Portrait of Canada* (1970), by Jay and Audrey Walz.

Senate
See also PARLIAMENT.

In the Upper House, the controlling and regulating, but not initiating, branch, we have the sober second thought in legislation.

*

A large qualification should be necessary for membership in the Upper House, in order to represent the principle of property. The rights of the minority must be protected, and the rich are always fewer in number than the poor.

SIR JOHN A. MACDONALD, future prime minister, discussing the proposed Senate, on April 6, 1865, quoted by Sir Joseph Pope in *Confederation* (1895).

The Senate is the saucer into which we pour legislation to cool.

SIR JOHN A. MACDONALD, prime minister, quoted by Sir Joseph Pope in *Memoirs of The Right Honourable Sir John Alexander Macdonald* (1894).

The Senate is a bulwark against the clamour and caprice of the mob.

SIR JAMES LOUGHEED, summoned to the Senate in 1889, attributed.

A Senate seat is a legitimate aspiration of any Canadian.

ARTHUR MEIGHEN, prime minister, replying to an ambitious mother who wrote him, "My daughters are both married. May I dream of reaching to the Upper House, Ottawa?" Quoted by F.A. Kunz in *The Modern Senate of Canada, 1925-1963* (1965).

I have never thought of the state looking after me, never. I never thought of it, I ex-

pect, until I guiltily entered this Chamber in this Senate.

GRATTAN O'LEARY, Conservative spokesman, in his maiden speech in the Senate, quoted by I. Norman Smith in *The Journal Men* (1974).

I don't think I'd do too well in the Senate. I speak too fast for them.

ROBERT L. STANFIELD, leader of the Opposition, in a luncheon speech to the Variety Club, Toronto, May 27, 1971.

Here I am going to point out that I find it easier to say Senate than to keep repeating the euphemism "the other place." I have listened enough to that in all my thirteen years here. I think the Senate is the Senate, and the House of Commons is the House of Commons. I propose to call the Senate the Senate, unless I am taken away in chains!

R. GORDON L. FAIRWEATHER, Conservative M.P., alluding to the Commons practice of referring to the Senate indirectly as "the other place," in the House of Commons, Dec. 12, 1974.

I have passed around a copy of the amendments to the shareholders, the directors, er, I mean the Senators.

SALTER HAYDEN, a Toronto senator who holds twenty-three directorships, is alleged to have made this slip of the tongue. Mentioned in the House of Commons, March 22, 1975.

Separatism
See also OCTOBER CRISIS; QUEBEC.

Laurentia

CANON LIONEL GROULX, influential priest and historian at the University of Montreal, "believed in 'Laurentia,' a separate French and Catholic state, rather than in Canada," and once almost expressed his view openly at the Second Congress of the French Language at Quebec in 1937, according to Mason Wade in *The French-Canadian Outlook* (1946).

Too little, too late.

RENÉ LÉVESQUE, separatist leader, reiterated this phrase throughout the late 1950s and early 1960s to dramatize English-Canadian concessions to Quebec demands. The phrase goes back to the 1930s, for Allan Nevins used it in *Current History* (1935).

Famine and wars, these are the things that change the world, not the separation of Quebec.

> MONIQUE LEYRAC, Quebec *chanteuse*, quoted by David Cobb in the Toronto *Telegram*, Feb. 18, 1967.

Vive le Quebec! Vive le Québec libre!
Vive le Canada français! Vive la France!

> CHARLES DE GAULLE, French president, voicing the separatist slogan to a crowd of ten thousand from the balcony of the Montreal City Hall, July 24, 1967. Quoted by Mason Wade in *The French Canadians* (1968).

We are an uncultured stammering people
yet we are not deaf to the uniqueness of a tongue
speak with the accent of Milton and Byron and Shelley and Keats
speak white
and forgive us if we reply
only in the harsh songs of our ancestors
and the deep pain of Nelligan.

> MICHÈLE LALONDE, Quebec poet, author of "Speak White," a long poem that expresses French dissatisfactions with life on a continent with the English that was distributed by students demonstrating for French instruction at McGill University, Feb. 1969. Reproduced in French and English in *How Do I Love Thee* (1970), edited by John Robert Colombo.

There's no question of your obtaining socialist independence gradually in Quebec. So it must of course be through violence. I do not say this light-heartedly, it is the same everywhere.

> JEAN-PAUL SARTRE, French intellectual, in a videotape interview shown in Montreal, Jan. 16, 1971. Quoted by Gérard Pelletier in *The October Crisis* (1971).

If Quebec decided to separate from Canada, *and if the rest of the country let it go peacefully*, it would be the greatest moment in the history of Canadian civilization. It would be. And, of course, also the most tragic.

> HERSCHEL HARDIN, Vancouver playwright and nationalist, in *A Nation Unaware* (1974).

Vive le Québec libre et socialiste.

> VICTOR-LÉVY BEAULIEU, Quebec novelist, to Governor General Jules Léger who had just

198

presented him with the Governor General's Award for Literature, Government House, Ottawa, May 22, 1975. "Long live a free, socialist Quebec."

Sex

See also ADULTERY; MEN AND WOMEN; PROSTITUTION.

Would you care to sin
Like Elinor Glyn
On a tiger skin
Or would you prefer
To err
On some other fur?

> ELINOR GLYN, Ontario-raised scriptwriter in Hollywood in the 1920s, the subject of this popular ditty, quoted by Lenore Coffee in *Storyline* (1973).

I cannot find that reproduction of the human race is contrary to morals.

> MR. JUSTICE MIDDLETON, Toronto judge, came to this conclusion in court concerning the "Stork Derby" will of the eccentric lawyer, Charles Millar, in 1926.

Among the porcupines, rape is unknown.

> GREGORY CLARK, Toronto journalist and short-story writer, to the late Jimmy Frise at Lake Scugog in 1933, who passed the observation on to Gillis Purcell.

In some of the poorer areas of the world it is sadly true that sex is the only luxury available to the ordinary man. Whether the ordinary woman also considers it a luxury is perhaps open to question.

> HUGH L. KEENLEYSIDE, External Affairs officer, in an address to the Third World Conference on Medical Education, New Delhi, Nov. 21, 1966.

I pick up a recent copy of *Maclean's* magazine and what do I read? That modesty has more sex appeal than nudity.

> GRATTAN O'LEARY, Conservative spokesman and senator, before the Davey Commission, quoted in the *Last Post*, June 1970.

Orgasms really have very little to do with making love, and men who require their woman to respond with *petit mal* seizures that can be picked up on the Richter scale are not making love but asking for reassurance.

> MERLE SHAIN, Toronto writer, in *Some Men Are More Perfect Than Others* (1973).

So far, I've lost every appeal except my sex appeal.

> XAVIERA HOLLANDER, former New York madam living in Toronto since 1972 as a landed immigrant, fighting a deportation order before the Supreme Court. Quoted by Frank Rasky in the Toronto *Star*, Dec. 17, 1974.

I never wanted to be a hooker, I just wanted to please people.

> XAVIERA HOLLANDER, author of *The Happy Hooker*, quoted by Dennis Braithwaite in the Toronto *Star*, Jan. 29, 1975.

I doubt if any man ever ceases to be amazed at the capacity of a woman's complete sexual abandonment.

> RAYMOND CANALE, Italian-born playwright living in Toronto, in 1975.

Shaw Festival
See THEATRE: CANADIAN.

Ships and Sailing

I sprang from the oars to my feet, and lifted the anchor above my head, threw it clear just as she was turning over. I grasped her gunwale and held on as she turned bottom up, for I suddenly remembered that I could not swim.

> JOSHUA SLOCUM, the first man to sail solo around the world, between April 1895 and July 1898, in *Sailing Alone Around the World* (1900). The Nova Scotian never learned to swim.

Wooden Ships and Iron Men.

> FREDERICK WILLIAM WALLACE, author and historian, title of his book published in 1924 with the subtitle: "The story of the Square-rigged Merchant Marine of British North America, the Ships, their Builders and the Men who Sailed Them."

The fog still hangs on the long tide-rips,
The gulls go wavering to and fro,
But where are all the beautiful ships
I knew so long ago?

> BLISS CARMAN, New Brunswick-born poet,

"The Ships of Saint John," *Bliss Carman's Poems* (1929).

The wood of the vessel that will beat the *Bluenose* is still growing!

> ANGUS J. WALTERS, captain of the *Bluenose*, the most famous sailing ship of the century and the last of the great Nova Scotian clippers. Launched at Lunenburg in 1921, it sank off Haiti in 1946. Oland's Brewery built a replica, *Bluenose II*, in 1963. Quoted by Brian and Phil Backman in *Bluenose* (1965).

Sickness
See also MEDICINE.

A patient with a written list of symptoms—neurasthenia.

*

To talk of diseases is a sort of Arabian Nights' entertainment.

> SIR WILLIAM OSLER, world-famous physician and medical teacher, from *Sir William Osler: Aphorisms from His Bedside Teachings and Writings* (1950), edited by W.B. Bean.

Doctor Body is the best—
Sends no bills and takes no rest.
Brings to pain and broken bone
Pharmacopia all his own.

His assistant, Dr. Bed,
Likes to coddle me instead.
Soothes me in my private room,
Recreates the healthy womb.

Meet the jolliest of the three,
My psychiatrist, Dr. B.
Dear old Bottle! Slaps my back
When I'm just about to crack.

> F.R. SCOTT, Montreal poet and wit, in "My Three Doctors" (1975), an unpublished poem.

Silence

There is no silence upon the earth or under
   the earth like the silence under the sea;
No cries announcing birth,
No sounds declaring death.

> E.J. PRATT, epic poet, opening lines of "Silences" (1937), in *The Collected Poems of E.J. Pratt* (second ed., 1958), edited by Northrop Frye.

The silence of our Western forests was so profound that our ears could scarcely comprehend it. If you spoke your voice came back to you as your face is thrown back to you in a mirror. It seemed as if the forest were so full of silence that there was no room for sounds.

EMILY CARR, west-coast artist, in "Silence and Pioneers," *The Book of Small* (1942).

Silence is a pocket of possibility. Anything can happen to break it.

R. MURRAY SCHAFER, west-coast composer and teacher, in *Ear Cleaning* (1967).

The arctic expresses the sum total of all wisdom:

Silence. Nothing but silence.
The end of time.

WALTER BAUER, German-born Toronto poet, in "Canada," *The Price of Morning* (1968), translated from the German by Henry Beissel.

Sleep

And after all, why should I go to bed every night? Sleep is only a habit.

SIR W.C. VAN HORNE, railroad builder, quoted by C. Lintern Sibley in the *Canadian*, Sept. 1913.

If ye break faith with us who die
We shall not sleep, though poppies grow
In Flanders fields.

JOHN MCCRAE, soldier poet, from "In Flanders Fields," *In Flanders Fields and Other Poems* (1919), edited by Sir Andrew Macphail.

In sleep too deep for dreams I'll lie,—
Till One shall knock, and bid me rise
To quest new ventures, fare new roads,
Essay new suns and vaster skies.

SIR CHARLES G.D. ROBERTS, poet and writer, in "The Vagrant of Time" (1927), *Selected Poetry and Critical Prose* (1974), edited by W.J. Keith.

Snow

You know that these two nations have been at war over a few acres of snow near Canada, and that they are spending on this fine struggle more than Canada itself is worth.

VOLTAIRE, French satirist, celebrated observation in chapter 23 of *Candide, ou l'optimisme* (1759), which was published the year Quebec

fell to the British. *Candide, or Optimism* (1966), translated by Robert A. Adams.

If two Canadians understand snow
they are then both Canadians.
If one Canadian understands snow
and another doesn't understand
snow at all, then one is a Canadian
and the other is no Canadian at all.

CARL SANDBURG, Chicago poet, from "Canadians and Pottawatomies" (1928), *Complete Poems* (1950).

The brown Brazilians asked me: "What is snow?"
"Snow has no taste, no colour and no smell,
nor joy of touch, and speaks no syllable;
snow is the flower and quintessence of no;
snow is our rule of churches, work and laws,
our reticence, our loneliness, our pause,
the emptiness we live in. This is snow . . . ."

E.A. LACEY, Ontario-born poet who resides in Brazil, in "Canadian Sonnets," *Path of Snow* (1974).

Social Credit Party
See also POLITICS.

The Eyes of the World are on Alberta.

WILLIAM ABERHART, leader of Alberta's Social Credit party, slogan in the election of Aug. 22, 1935, which brought Aberhart's reform party to power. Quoted by John A. Irving in *The Social Credit Movement in Alberta* (1959).

Congratulations. There will be others but only one first.

MAJOR C.H. DOUGLAS, British theorist of Social Credit, cable of congratulations to William Aberhart when the party came to power in Alberta, Aug. 22, 1935. Quoted by L.P.V. Johnson and Ola J. MacNutt in *Aberhart of Alberta* (1970).

I trust the Alberta Elections have renewed your faith in humanity.

EZRA POUND, Anglo-American poet, referring to the Social Credit victory, in a letter dated Sept. 1, 1935, to John Buchan before his appointment as governor general. Quoted by Janet Adam Smith in *John Buchan* (1965).

If we cannot feed, clothe and shelter the people of Alberta, tell me who else is going to do it?

> WILLIAM ABERHART, Social Credit premier of Alberta, in "Social Credit," an address to the Canadian Club of Toronto, Sept. 13, 1935.

Whatever you wear, Mr. Aberhart, will be a social credit to Alberta.

> JOHN BUCHAN, LORD TWEEDSMUIR, governor general, reply when William Aberhart inquired what he should wear to the Coronation in 1937. Quoted by Janet Adam Smith in *John Buchan* (1965).

Social Credit is above politics.

> ROBERT THOMPSON, former leader of the Social Credit party, quoted by Peter C. Newman in "Robert Thompson" (1967), *Home Country* (1973).

What have you got to lose?

> RÉAL CAOUETTE, Quebec Créditiste leader. "Il n'y a rien à perdre?" was the Créditiste slogan in the 1962 federal election when the provincial party under Caouette took one-third of the Quebec seats.

You don't have to understand Social Credit in order to vote for it.

> RÉAL CAOUETTE, fiery and folksy Créditiste leader, in the federal election of 1962.

I'd hire a Socred if I could find one with any brains.

> DAVE BARRETT, former premier of British Columbia, quoted by Christina Newman in the Toronto *Globe and Mail*, March 1, 1975.

Social Sciences

The Social Sciences are good at accounting for disasters once they have taken place.

> CLAUDE T. BISSELL, former president of the University of Toronto, in an address, "The Future of Liberal Education in Canada," Oct. 28, 1971.

I am a sociologist, God help me.

> JOHN O'NEILL, York University social scientist, in *Sociology as a Skin Trade* (1972).

Socialism

See also NEW DEMOCRATIC PARTY.

The cause of socialism is the cause of love and hope and humanity: the cause of competition is the cause of anarchy, pessimism, and a disbelief in a possible Manhood for human nature just emerging from its barbarous infancy.

> ARCHIBALD LAMPMAN, distinguished poet, in "Untitled Essay on Socialism" (1886), *Archibald Lampman* (1975), edited by Barrie Davies.

What we desire for ourselves, we wish for all.

> J.S. WOODSWORTH, leader of the CCF from 1932 to 1942, characteristic remark recalled by his daughter, Grace MacInnes.

Emergency measures, however, are of only temporary value, for the present depression is a sign of the mortal sickness of the whole capitalist system, and this sickness cannot be cured by the application of salves. These leave untouched the cancer which is eating at the heart of our society, namely, the economic system in which our natural resources and our principal means of production and distribution are owned, controlled and operated for the private profit of a small proportion of our population.

No C.C.F. Government will rest content until it has eradicated capitalism and put into operation the full programme of socialized planning which will lead to the establishment in Canada of the Co-operative Commonwealth.

> FRANK H. UNDERHILL, a founder of the CCF, final paragraphs of the "Regina Manifesto" read before the founding convention of the CCF, July 1933. Reproduced in *The Anatomy of a Party* (1969), by Walter D. Young.

There is more in common between two managers, one of whom is a socialist, than there is between two socialists, one of whom is a manager.

> FRANK H. UNDERHILL, socialist and historian, in *The Image of Confederation* (1964).

The essential basis of socialism is ethical, not economic.

> FRANK H. UNDERHILL, socialist (whom F.R. Scott called "the most Shavian of the Fabians"), attributed sentiments.

Socialism is only a bright soap bubble, light as ignorance and floating with its own gas. It would only work in a community of impossible people, guided by impossible leaders, and inspired by an inconceivable good-will. The angels, no doubt, are Socialists.

STEPHEN LEACOCK, political economist and renowned humorist, in *Stephen Leacock's Plan to Relieve the Depression in Six Days, to Remove It in Six Months, to Eradicate It in Six Years* (1933).

Never mind the difference between the two; it's only that a socialist shares the workroom and a communist shares the bathroom.

STEPHEN LEACOCK, professor of economics at McGill, in *Model Memoirs and Other Sketches from Simple to Serious* (1938).

Socialism won't work except in Heaven where they don't need it and in Hell where they already have it.

STEPHEN LEACOCK, humorist and economist, quoted by Ralph L. Curry in *Stephen Leacock* (1959).

Also it [dining in a smart restaurant in wartime London] restored my lust for the things that money can buy—smart women, fashionable glitter, all the frivolities that charm the eye. What I really dread from the sober reasonable socialism of the future is the eclipse of style, the disappearance of distinction—for mixed and intermingled with the vulgarity of our age is the survival of pleasant, ornamental, amusing people and things—and one's soul shrinks from the austere prospect of cotton stockings. The intellectuals do not mind, because they despise the glitter and speciousness of rich life. But the aesthetes—like myself—have their misgivings.

CHARLES RITCHIE, a member of the high commissioner's staff in London, England, on June 16, 1941, in *The Siren Years* (1974).

Till power is brought to pooling
And outcasts share in ruling
There will not be an ending
Nor any peace for spending.

F.R. SCOTT, Montreal man-of-letters, from "Dedication" (1945), in *Selected Poems* (1966). When the poem was first published in 1941,

the second word in the second line was originally "masses," not "outcasts."

Socialists are Liberals in a hurry.

LOUIS ST. LAURENT, prime minister, in a speech reported in the Montreal *Gazette*, April 25, 1949, quoted by Dale C. Thomson in *Louis St. Laurent* (1967). The phrase "Liberals in a hurry" was applied to those Progressives and Liberal-Progressives in the House of Commons who joined the Liberal party in 1926.

For consolation, the socialist need only look southward.

GAD HOROWITZ, social scientist, concluding sentence of *Canadian Labour in Politics* (1968).

A Canadian and Socialist? Philistinism raised to the second power.

IRVING LAYTON, outspoken poet, in *The Whole Bloody Bird* (1969).

Socialism is people working together to bring out the best qualities in each individual.

GRACE MacINNIS, daughter of J.S. Woodsworth and member of Parliament, interviewed by Bill Zimmerman in *Speaking of Winnipeg* (1974), edited by John Parr.

There's no percentage in being socialistic.

JOHN ANGUS "BUD" McDOUGALD, head of the Argus Corporation, quoted by Peter C. Newman in *Maclean's*, Sept. 1975.

For socialists, going to bed with the Liberals is like getting oral sex from a shark.

LARRY ZOLF, zany broadcaster, *Saturday Night*, Dec. 1975.

Society
See also CLASSES, SOCIAL; MOSAIC.

Excesses correct themselves, and I have no doubt that the violence of the disaffected will elicit a great counter-demonstration.—At the same time I confess I did not before know how thin is the crust of order which covers the anarchical elements that boil and toss beneath our feet.

LORD ELGIN, governor general of the Province of Canada, in a letter to Earl Grey, April 30, 1847, when opponents of the Rebellion Losses Act had set fire to the Parliament Buildings at

Montreal. Quoted by J.M.S. Careless in *The Union of the Canadas* (1967).

Society, my dear, is like salt water, good to swim in but hard to swallow.
> ARTHUR STRINGER, Chatham-born American novelist, in *The Silver Poppy* (1903).

The discovery of society is, indeed, the anchor of freedom.
> KARL POLANYI, distinguished political economist who spent the last years of his life in Canada, in *The Great Transformation* (1944).

Real society, the total body of what humanity has done and can do, is revealed to us only by the arts and sciences; nothing but the imagination can apprehend what reality as a whole, and nothing but literature, in a culture as verbal as ours, can train the imagination to fight for the sanity and the dignity of man.
> NORTHROP FRYE, literary scholar, in "Elementary Teaching and Elementary Scholarship" (1964), *The Stubborn Structure* (1970).

Songs
See MUSIC.

Speech and Speeches
See also LANGUAGE.

Have something to say. Say it. Shut up. Sit down.
> A.L. HORTON, editor of the Vegreville *Observer* from 1906 to 1958, giving advice on public speaking. Quoted by Tony Cashman in *Chinook Arch* (1967), edited by John Patrick Gillese.

A good speech should contain a lot of shortening.
> KATE AITKEN, popular broadcaster in the 1940s and 1950s, attributed.

It has a rather sad tone, as if someone once dear and now lost and forgotten is still being endlessly regretted. Many of the men hardly move their lips, conversing in a melancholy mumble. Even the gay and pretty girls, for all their sparkling glances, sound as if they were inwardly fixed in some sad enchantment. You look up in the

aeroplane to see the handsome stewardess smiling at you, like a favourite niece; and then she murmurs, "Would you care for some carfee?"
> J.B. PRIESTLEY, British playwright, discussing Canadian speech patterns in 1953, quoted by Joseph Barber in *Good Fences Make Good Neighbours* (1958).

I can only testify that the ugliest, most raucous and unattractive speaking I have heard in Canada has come from the lips, not of roughnecked, horny-handed sons of toil, but from nicely-come-home, expensively educated, sophisticated ladies in Westmount and Rosedale. It was speech, which, as an expert, I would declare to be thoroughly bad in every important respect. Nevertheless it was perfectly acceptable in a Society which was evidently exclusive.
> TYRONE GUTHRIE, Irish-born director, in "A Long View of the Stratford Festival," *Twice Have the Trumpets Sounded* (1954), by Tyrone Guthrie, Robertson Davies, and Grant Macdonald.

I published a collection of my speeches—ignoring the warning made in an observation by someone that "speeches don't keep any better than fish."
> VINCENT MASSEY, first native-born governor general, in *What's Past Is Prologue* (1963).

"Splendid Isolation"
See ISOLATIONISM.

Sports
See also FOOTBALL; HOCKEY; SWIMMING; VIOLENCE.

Norse am I when the first snow falls;
Norse am I till the ice departs.
The fare for which my spirit calls
Is blood from a hundred viking-hearts.
> WILSON MACDONALD, Toronto versifier, opening lines of "The Song of the Ski," *Out of the Wilderness* (1926).

Championship is a state of mind.
> ANDY O'BRIEN, Montreal sports writer, in "Ring Champ's Fight with Fear," *My Friend the Hangman* (1970).

I shudder to think what would have happened to the Canadian World War II effort if we had depended on track and swimming participants instead of mannish hockey players.

> STAN OBODIAC, publicity director of Maple Leaf Gardens, quoted in the Toronto *Telegram*, June 7, 1970.

The sportswriting confraternity is burdened with hacks who make tin-can gods out of cast-iron jerks.

> DICK BEDDOES, popular Toronto sportswriter, before the Special Senate Committee on Mass Media (the Davey Commission) in 1971.

Have you ever noticed what golf spells backwards?

> AL BOLISKA, broadcaster and joke-collector, in *Fore-Play: Every Golf Joke Ever Told* (1971).

The average Canadian male is weakest in his arms. He just doesn't use 'em enough. We may soon reach the stage where the Canadian bride carries the Canadian groom over the threshold.

> LLOYD PERCIVAL, former athlete and founder of the Fitness Institute, quoted by Bob Pennington in the Toronto *Star*, April 15, 1972.

Athletics is poetry in motion.

> GUS MACFARLANE, M.P., in a debate on the creation of a department of sports, in the House of Commons, March 21, 1975.

Spring

See SEASONS.

Statesmen

See also POLITICS.

Now I know what a statesman is; he's a dead politician. We need more statesmen.

> BOB EDWARDS, writer and publisher of the Calgary *Eye Opener* from 1902 to 1922, attributed.

This thing they call irresolution is often the very pith and marrow of statesmanship.

> SIR JOHN WILLISON, political journalist, in *Sir Wilfrid Laurier and the Liberal Party* (1926).

Over and over again, I have thought . . . that some day the world will know some of the things that I have prevented . . . I must make increasingly clear to the world that

prevention of wrong courses of evil and the like means more than all else that man can accomplish.

> W.L. MACKENZIE KING, prime minister, on Dec. 8, 1944, in *The Mackenzie King Record: Volume 2: 1944-45* (1968), edited by J.W. Pickersgill and D.F. Forster.

If politics is the art of the possible, it should be recognized that statesmanship is the art of making things possible . . . .

> KENNETH MCNAUGHT, political commentator, in *A Prophet in Politics* (1959).

You know, the trouble with the Department of Finance is we have no civil servants here—they're all statesmen.

> J.L. ILSLEY, wartime Finance minister, to Mitchell Sharp, interviewed by Bill Zimmerman in *Speaking of Winnipeg* (1974), edited by John Parr.

Stratford Festival

See also THEATRE: CANADIAN.

This is Tom Patterson. Will you come to Canada and give advice? We want to start a Shakespeare festival in Stratford, Ontario. We will pay your expenses and a small fee.

> TOM PATTERSON, Stratford-born journalist, on a long-distance telephone call to Tyrone Guthrie in Northern Ireland during the summer of 1952, which resulted in the founding of the Stratford Festival. Quoted by Tyrone Guthrie in *A Life in the Theatre* (1959).

Now is the winter of our discontent
Made glorious summer by this sun of York.

> WILLIAM SHAKESPEARE, playwright, opening lines of *The Tragedy of King Richard III*, written about 1593. These were the first words heard from the open stage of the Stratford Festival, on July 13, 1953, recited by Alec Guinness.

But there is one person to whom we must pay special tribute. A man of so great genius and such profound humility that we are apt to overlook him. I ask you to rise with me and pay tribute to the man who more than any other has been responsible for the success of the Festival and who belongs to us all—Will Shakespeare.

> ALEC GUINNESS, British actor, at the end of the last performance of *Richard III*, stepped out on

the makeshift stage of the Stratford Festival, still in costume, and paid tributes to Tom Patterson, Tyrone Guthrie, and the other prime movers. He concluded with the above tribute, Sept. 1953.

July 13, 1953, was the most exciting night in the history of Canadian theatre. I doubt if there will ever be another night to match it, for me and for a great many others who were at that opening of the first Stratford Festival.

HERBERT WHITTAKER, drama critic for the Toronto *Globe and Mail*, in the introduction to *The Stratford Festival 1953-1957* (1958).

To go to Stratford today is more than a duty—it is a pleasure.

NICHOLAS MONSARRAT, bestselling British author resident in Ottawa, remark made in 1953, from *To Stratford with Love* (1963).

Lister Sinclair: What do you think of our wonderful Stratford Festival?

Gilbert Harding: I rather thought we'd started it!

GILBERT HARDING, British radio and television personality, interviewed by Lister Sinclair, quoted in *CBC Times*, Oct. 13, 1957.

We have never considered playing at Stratford-on-Avon any more than we would think of bringing vodka to Poland.

WILLIAM HUTT, actor and associate director of the Stratford Festival, touring eastern Europe, speaking at a press conference in Warsaw, Poland, Feb. 6, 1973.

Success

See also ACHIEVEMENT; FAILURE; WINNERS.

Success invariably makes a man philosophical.

PETER MCARTHUR, columnist who wrote about farm life in western Ontario, in *The Best of Peter McArthur* (1967), edited by Alec Lucas.

There is an old motto that runs, *"If at first you don't succeed, try, try again."* This is nonsense. It ought to read—"If at first you don't succeed, quit, quit, at once."

STEPHEN LEACOCK, humorist, in "Simple Stories of Success, or How to Succeed in Life," *Frenzied Fiction* (1917).

There is always room at the top and plenty of room at the bottom. But it gets mighty crowded in the middle.

ALAN YOUNG, Hollywood comedian who left the CBC for radio and films in the United States, in the *Christian Science Monitor*, Oct. 25, 1965.

Treat those twin imposters, triumph and disaster, just the same.

LESTER B. PEARSON, leader of the Liberal party, quoted these words, which appear above a doorway at Oxford University where he studied as a youth, the night his party lost in the Conservative landslide, March 31, 1960. Quoted by Peter Dempson in *Assignment Ottawa* (1968).

Not to seek success but to deserve it.

LESTER B. PEARSON, recipient of the Nobel Prize for Peace, personal motto, from *Words and Occasions* (1970).

I married him for better or for worse, not just for lunch.

*

Behind every successful man there is a surprised woman.

MARYON PEARSON, wife of the prime minister, quoted by Lester B. Pearson in *Mike: The Memoirs of the Right Honourable Lester B. Pearson: Volume I* (1972).

My theory is that if you can make it in Canada, you can make it anywhere.

BERNARD SLADE, St. Catharines-born TV scriptwriter—*The Flying Nun, The Partridge Family, Brigit Loves Bernie*—and Broadway playwright, quoted by David Cobb in the *Canadian*, June 17, 1972.

Even when you hit the jackpot, it turns out there's no jackpot.

MORDECAI RICHLER, Montreal novelist, on the apparent commercial success of the film *The Apprenticeship of Duddy Kravitz* (1974), quoted by Martin Knelman in the Toronto *Globe and Mail*, March 8, 1975.

Suffering

All true wisdom is only to be found far from the dwellings of men, in the great solitudes; and it can only be attained through suffering. Suffering and privation are the

205

only things that can open the mind of man to that which is hidden from his fellows.

IGJUGARJUK, Caribou Eskimo, quoted by Knud Rasmussen in *Across Arctic America* (1927).

If the people have not suffered enough, it is their God-given right to suffer some more.

WILLIAM ABERHART, premier of Alberta, quoted by Jon Whyte in "The Ballad of Twain and Abel" in *The Unfinished Revolt* (1971), edited by John Barr and Owen Anderson.

Is our capacity for suffering commensurate with our capacity for happiness: *infinite?*

HECTOR DE SAINT-DENYS-GARNEAU, French-Canadian poet, *The Journal of Saint-Denys-Garneau* (1962), translated by John Glassco, June 1936.

Suffragettes
See WOMEN AND THE LAW.

Suicide

I certainly did try my very best to kill myself and from what they have told me I nearly succeeded. They gave me up for hopeless three or four times.

A. ROY BROWN, fighter pilot who downed the "Red Baron," in a letter to his father, Aug. 1, 1918.

When a man truly despairs, he does not write; he commits suicide.

GEORGE P. GRANT, professor of Religion at McMaster University, in *Lament for a Nation* (1965).

To contemplate suicide is surely the best exercise of the imagination.

PHYLLIS WEBB, west-coast poet, quoted by Merle Shain in *Chatelaine*, Oct. 1972.

Summer
See SEASONS.

Swimming
See also SPORTS.

I did it for Canada!

MARILYN BELL, first woman to swim Lake Ontario, Sept. 9, 1954, quoted by Ron McAllister in *Swim to Glory* (1954).

It's your lake now.

MARILYN BELL, marathon swimmer, to Cindy Nicholas, when the sixteen-year-old girl conquered the lake on Aug. 16, 1974, reported the following day in the Toronto *Star*.

I really did it for Canada.

CINDY NICHOLAS, marathon swimmer, to the reception committee in Toronto after successfully swimming the English Channel, Aug. 6, 1975.

Marathon swimming isn't a bed of roses.

ANGELA KONDRAK, the fourteen-year-old swimmer who failed to cross Lake Ontario on Aug. 19, 1974. The Toronto *Star*, Aug. 24, 1974.

Taste

I have not the slightest desire to improve the taste of the Canadian public.

JAMES WILSON MORRICE, Franco-Canadian painter, in a letter to Edmund Morris, Feb. 12, 1911. Quoted by J. Russell Harper in *Painting in Canada* (1966).

"There is no disputing about tastes," says the old saw. In my experience there is little else.

ROBERTSON DAVIES, man-of-letters, in *Marchbanks' Almanack* (1967).

Good taste is the first refuge of the non-creative. It is the last-ditch stand of the artist.

MARSHALL MCLUHAN, media pundit, in *Through the Vanishing Point* (1968), with Harley Parker.

Good taste can be defined as making war while refusing to say shit.

*

Good taste is the enemy of art. Good taste is the last refuge of the middlebrow. Good taste is Stanley Kramer, CBC television, Neil Simon, C.P. Snow, and the Toronto *Globe and Mail*.

ROBERT FULFORD, Toronto editor and film reviewer, in 1970, from *Marshall Delaney at the Movies* (1974).

Taxes

See also FINANCE.

Tears and taxes are the price of liberty. The pockets that pay are more blessed than the eyes that weep.

> JOHN "BLACK JACK" ROBINSON, Toronto newspaper editor, in an editorial urging the conscription of wealth in 1928, quoted by Ron Poulton in *The Paper Tyrant* (1971).

The promises of yesterday are the taxes of today.

> W.L. MACKENZIE KING, leader of the Opposition, replying to the Conservative budget in the House of Commons, June 16, 1931.

Remember, there's only one taxpayer—you and me.

> JOHN KUSHNER, Calgary alderman, about 1960.

You can't drink yourself sober, you can't spend yourself rich, and the power to tax is the power to destroy.

> COLONEL ERIC PHILLIPS, corporation executive, in his last address to the Argus Corporation in 1964.

I'm a Bahamian.

> E.P. TAYLOR, capitalist, quoted by the *Sunday Times*, Dec. 22, 1968.

Teachers

See also EDUCATION.

I can always tell a good teacher. All I have to do is to speak to him of some transforming idea and then watch him light up just as an electric bulb does when the current is connected.

> M.M. COADY, educator who helped found the Antigonish Movement in Nova Scotia in the 1920s, quoted by J.R. Kidd in *How Adults Learn* (1959).

To go into teaching was a matter of sheer necessity. My education had fitted me for nothing except to pass it on to the other people.

> STEPHEN LEACOCK, professor of economics at McGill and humorist, in "Teaching School," *The Boy I Left Behind Me* (1946).

The people who have the most to say about what goes on in schools never see a pupil.

> EMMETT HALL, Ontario chief justice and co-author of the Hall-Dennis Report, quoted by Walter Stewart in *Maclean's*, July 1975.

Technology

See also SCIENCE AND SCIENTISTS.

Our technology is more lovable than the Russian technology, and in the end it is bound to prevail. We are only beginning. We have just reached the outer fringes of the Solar System. Can any sane man possibly argue that we should stop there?

> HUGH MACLENNAN, Montreal novelist, from "Remembrance Day, 2010 A.D.," *Scotchman's Return and Other Essays* (1960).

The two big tricks of the twentieth century are: technology instead of grace, and information instead of virtue.

> ULYSSE COMTOIS, Quebec painter, quoted by Beverly Carter in "Conversations with Four Montreal Artists," *Artscanada*, Feb.-March 1971.

Engineers should be on tap, not on top.

> A.B. MACCALLUM, biologist and first head of the National Research Council, quoted by R. Ronald Hayes in *The Chaining of Prometheus* (1973).

The most recent development at the Centre for Culture and Technology is the completion of a study on "The Laws of the Media," which has led to the discovery that the most human thing about people is technology.

> MARSHALL MCLUHAN, media theorist and director of the Centre for Culture and Technology at the University of Toronto. Private communication, April 30, 1976.

Telephone

Yes, Alec, it is I, your father, speaking.

> MELVILLE BELL, father of Alexander Graham Bell, who invented the telephone, in the first message ever carried over a long-distance telephone line on Aug. 10, 1876. Melville Bell spoke into a primitive transmitter in Brantford to his son in a shoe store in Paris, Ont., eight miles away. The first long-distance conversation lasted three hours.

The telephone, devised in Brantford, was not made until 1875, when it appeared in Boston; so that the telephone was conceived in Brantford in 1874, and born in Boston in 1875.

*

But Canada was also associated with a very important development of the practical telephone in the early days. It was in Brantford that the first transmission of speech to a distance occurred. . . . That was in August, 1876.

ALEXANDER GRAHAM BELL, inventor of the telephone, in "The Substance of My Latest Research," an address to the Empire Club of Canada in 1917.

Television
See also BROADCASTING.

You know, it's just like having a licence to print your own money.

ROY THOMSON, LORD THOMSON OF FLEET, to colleagues after being awarded a licence to operate a TV station in Scotland, in the fall of 1957. The observation is usually quoted as, "A TV franchise is a licence to print money."

I told him—Julie, don't go.

JOHNNY WAYNE and FRANK SHUSTER, the comedy team, made this line famous in their fondly remembered Julius Caesar skit for "The Ed Sullivan Show," May 4, 1958. Sylvia Lennick, playing Calpurnia, recited the line.

It's hard to remember what we used to do before television.

BERNIE BRADEN, Vancouver-born British TV personality, quoted by John Gray in *Maclean's*, Nov. 7, 1959.

Hi, Mom! Good-night, Mom!

JULIETTE, popular singer Juliette Sysak, familiar opening and closing remarks from her CBC-TV show in the 1960s.

This season we are matching *our* strong U.S. imports against *their* strong U.S. imports.

MICHAEL HIND-SMITH, CTV director, commenting on the commercial rivalry between the privately owned CTV network and the publicly owned CBC-TV network, in 1961.

I am Laurier LaPierre and you are you.

LAURIER LaPIERRE, Montreal historian and broadcaster, characteristic sign-off on CBC-TV and CBC Radio programs in the 1960s and 1970s.

It should be possible to turn on one's television set and know what country one is in. One would almost never be in doubt in the United States; one is frequently in doubt in Canada.

MORRIS WOLFE, television critic for *Saturday Night* and principal author of the brief *Saving the CBC*, "an intervention before the Canadian Radio-Television Commission concerning the CBC's application for renewal of its English-language television licence," Feb. 1974.

Television brought the brutality of war into the comfort of the living room. Vietnam was lost in the living rooms of America—not on the battlefields of Vietnam.

MARSHALL McLUHAN, media pundit, at the Montreal International Book Fair, quoted by Christie McCormick in the Montreal *Gazette*, May 16, 1975.

All TV networks should end with the letters BS.

LOUIS DUDEK, Montreal poet, in *Epigrams* (1975).

Theatre
See also ACTORS AND ACTRESSES; AWARDS; CRITICS; CULTURE;·PLAYWRIGHTS; STRATFORD FESTIVAL; THEATRE: CANADIAN.

There are no comedies of manners, because there are no more manners.

RAYMOND MASSEY, Toronto-born American actor, characteristic remark.

I've been in the business long enough to determine to entertain.

ROBERT WHITEHEAD, Montreal-born Broadway producer, married to Zoe Caldwell, quoted in the Toronto *Globe and Mail*, May 17, 1958.

I love show business and the theatre. I just wish I could afford it.

SAMMY SALES, performer, quoted by Morris Duff in the Toronto *Star*, Oct. 31, 1959.

Three-quarters of acting is listening.

KATE REID, leading lady, quoted by Herbert Whittaker in the Toronto *Globe and Mail*, Nov. 25, 1967.

Acting is not being emotional, but being able to express emotions.

KATE REID, stage and film star, quoted by Joanne Strong in the Toronto *Globe and Mail*, June 4, 1973.

The theatre is like fireworks. Look at it, look at it, it may not come again.

GRATIEN GÉLINAS, Montreal man-of-the-theatre, quoted by Joanne Strong in the Toronto *Globe and Mail*, June 11, 1973.

I've learned that a serious actor must sometimes show his soul to an audience and unashamedly take from every remembered passion of the past.

*

I truly believed in our artistic credo, "There are no small stages—only large actors."

PAUL KLIGMAN, Toronto actor, quoted by Frank Rasky in the Toronto *Star*, Sept. 7, 1974.

Theatre: Canadian
See also THEATRE.

It may be easily conceived how despicably low the Canadian theatricals must be, when boys are obliged to perform the female characters: the only actresses being an old superannuated demirep, whose drunken Belvideras, Desdemonas, and Isabellas, have often *enraptured* a Canadian audience.

JOHN LAMBERT, writer, in *Travels through Lower Canada and the United States of North America* (1810).

If this organization becomes a success, it will have been founded on love and whisky.

COLONEL HENRY E. OSBORNE, honorary director of the Dominion Drama Festival from 1933 to 1939, quoted by Betty Lee in *Love and Whisky* (1973). This was a self-fulfilling prophecy, for during the 1950s the festival came to be sponsored by Calvert Distillers.

The spectre of bankruptcy rather than the *spectre de la rose* is what haunts some of our stages.

PETER M. DWYER, late director of the Canada Council, in the *Seventh Annual Report of the Canada Council* (1964).

For Canada itself, the Charlottetown Festival is already of greater value than the one in Stratford.

NATHAN COHEN, Toronto drama critic, quoted by Mavor Moore in *Maclean's*, June 4, 1966. The summer festival opened in the new Confederation Centre in 1965.

Alas, once they have made their names abroad they are generally lost to us, priced out of our modest market. We get them on the way up and on the way down, and sometimes in between.

THOMAS HENDRY, arts administrator, referring to expatriates like Lorne Greene and Zara Nelsova, in "The Performing Arts," *The Canadians 1867-1967* (1967), edited by J.M.S. Careless and R. Craig Brown.

To come across a really elegant production of *Heartbreak House* in this setting is a little like finding a Watteau at a country auction. Or would be, if you hadn't heard so many good things in advance about Niagara's Shaw Festival.

DAN SULLIVAN, drama critic, in a review of the Shaw Festival in the New York *Times*, July 6, 1968. The Watteau reference was used in promotional literature for the next five years.

There are no laughs or applause soaked into the walls yet. We've got to put those in.

STANLEY HOLLOWAY, British actor appearing in *You Never Can Tell*, which opened the new Shaw Festival Theatre, June 12, 1973, quoted by Brian Doherty in *Not Bloody Likely* (1974).

Thought
See also INTELLIGENCE.

How utterly destitute of all light and charm are the intellectual conditions of our people and the institutions of our public life! How barren! How barbarous! It is true that this is a new and struggling country, but one would think that the simplest impulse of patriotism, if it existed at all in our governing bodies, would suffice to provoke some attempt at remedy.

ARCHIBALD LAMPMAN, Ottawa poet, in the *Globe* of Toronto, Feb. 27, 1892, from *At the Mermaid Inn* (1958), edited by Arthur S. Bourinot.

Descriptions of our meadows, prairies and forests, with their wealth of herbage and foliage, or artistic sketches of pretty bits of lake scenery have their limitations as respects their influence on a people. Great thoughts or deeds are not bred by scenery.

SIR J.G. BOURINOT, clerk of the House of Commons from 1880 to 1902, in *Our Intellectual Strength and Weakness* (1893).

One of Canada's greatest tragedies is that sober second thoughts so often prevail.

RICHARD J. NEEDHAM, Toronto columnist, in *A Friend in Needham, or a Writer's Notebook* (1969).

Think until it hurts.

ROY THOMSON, LORD THOMSON OF FLEET, delivered this maxim in a television interview, Sept. 15, 1975.

Transcendental meditation, the prolonged effort to think of nothing, is a technique perfectly suitable for Canadians. They've been doing it now for almost a century.

LOUIS DUDEK, Montreal poet, in *Epigrams* (1975).

Time

It would farther be expedient to distinguish the proposed new system from sidereal, astronomical, civil or local time. For this purpose either of the designations, "common," "universal," "non-local," "uniform," "absolute," "all world," "terrestrial," or "cosmopolitan," might be employed. For the present it may be convenient to use the latter term.

SIR SANDFORD FLEMING, "the Father of Standard Time," in "Time-Reckoning" (1879), *Proceedings of the Canadian Institute, Toronto* (1884). At the Washington Meridian Conference, Oct. 1884, Fleming's resolutions for fixing a prime meridian (Greenwich) were passed and widely endorsed by national governments.

Deeds are not accomplished in a few days, or in a few hours. A century is only a spoke in the wheel of everlasting time.

LOUIS RIEL, leader of the Métis in the Red River and Northwest Rebellions, on Aug. 27, 1885, quoted by Nick and Helma Mika in *The Riel Rebellion 1885* (1972).

Time is the small change of eternity.

IRVING LAYTON, outspoken poet, in *The Whole Bloody Bird* (1969).

Time solves every problem and in the process adds a couple of new ones.

RICHARD J. NEEDHAM, Toronto columnist, in the Toronto *Globe and Mail*, April 28, 1975.

Titles
See also AWARDS.

How could I accept a knighthood? Good heavens! I shovel off my own sidewalk and stoke my own furnace.

JOHN W. DAFOE, editor of the Winnipeg *Free Press*, declining a knighthood in 1919. From *Dafoe of the Free Press* (1968), by Murray Donnelly.

Away with tunics, cocked hats, swords
In proof of stern endeavour
We'll wear (where Adam wore the fig)
The Maple Leaf for Ever.

LORD GARNER, British high commissioner in Ottawa from 1956 to 1961, submitted this verse to Lester B. Pearson, who had requested all External Affairs officers to refuse foreign honours. "Mike: An Englishman's View," *International Journal*, winter 1973-74. Lord Garner attributed the piece of doggerel to (now Sir) Raymond Bell, a member of his staff.

John Diefenbaker: Why burden your sons and successors with the incubus of this thing [a hereditary title]?

Lord Thomson of Fleet: It's the best way I can prove to Canadians that I'm a success.
*

Canada intimated that they wouldn't mind Lord Thomson of Mississauga, but that's all—and that's a hell of a name anyway. I can't even spell it myself. [The Thomson estate is in Mississauga, near Toronto]

Roy Thomson, British press baron, quoted by Russell Braddon in *Roy Thomson of Fleet Street* (1965).

Toronto

The inhabitants do not possess the fairest character.

Duc de La Rochefoucauld-Liancourt, French nobleman, assessment of the inhabitants of York (later Toronto) in 1795, in *Voyages dans les Etats-Unis d'Amérique, fait en 1795, 1796, et 1797* (1799).

Where the blue hills of old Toronto shed
Their evening shadows o'er Ontario's bed;
Should trace the grand Cataraqui, and glide
Down the white rapids of his lordly tide
. . . .

Thomas Moore, Irish poet, from "To the Lady Charlotte Rawdon, from the Banks of the St. Lawrence" (1804), in *The Poetical Works of Thomas Moore* (1910).

The streets of York are regularly laid out, intersecting each other at right angles. Only one of them, however, is yet completely built; and in wet weather the unfinished streets are, if possible, muddier and dirtier than those of Kingston. The situation of the town is very unhealthy, for it stands on a piece of low marshy land, which is better calculated for a frog-pond or beaver-meadow than for the residence of human beings.

Edward Allen Talbot, colonist, in *Five Years' Residence in the Canadas* (1824).

Every body who has ever been at Dover knows that it is one of the vilest blue-devil haunts on the face of the earth except Little York in U. Canada, when he has been there one day.

John Galt, colonist and novelist, in *An Autobiography of John Galt* (1838).

"There is no *society* in Toronto," is what I hear repeated all around me—even by those who compose the only society we have. "But," you will say, "what could be expected in a remote town, which forty years ago was an uninhabited swamp, and twenty years ago only began to exist?"

Toronto is, as a residence, worse and better than other small communities—*worse* in so much as it is remote from all the best advantages of a high state of civilisation, while it is infested by all its evils, all its follies; and *better*, because, beside being a small place, it is a *young* place; and in spite of this affectation of looking back, instead of looking up, it must advance—it may become the thinking head and beating heart of a nation, great, and wise, and happy;—who knows?

Anna Jameson, British writer, in *Winter Studies and Summer Rambles in Canada* (1838).

The country round this town [Toronto], being very flat, is bare of scenic interest; but the town itself is full of life and motion, bustle, business, and improvement. The streets are well paved, and lighted with gas; the houses are large and good; the shops excellent. Many of them have a display of goods in their windows, such as may be seen in thriving county towns in England; and there are some which would do no discredit to the metropolis itself.

Charles Dickens, British novelist, who first visited eastern Canada in 1842, in *American Notes for General Circulation and Pictures from Italy* (1905).

We are off, off into Toronto Bay (soon the wide expanse and cool breezes of Lake Ontario). As we steam out a mile or so we get a pretty view of Toronto from the blue foreground of the waters,—the whole rising spread of the city, groupings of roofs, spires, trees, hills in the background. Good-bye, Toronto, with your memories of a very lively and agreeable visit.

Walt Whitman, American poet, who visited Toronto on July 26-27, 1880, in *Walt Whitman's Diary of Canada* (1904), edited by William Sloane Kennedy.

Toronto the Good.

Sobriquet associated with the city, especially during the reform administration of Mayor William Howland (1886-88), quoted by Desmond Morton in *Mayor Howland* (1973).

Houses of ill-fame in Toronto? Certainly not. The whole city is an immense house of ill-fame . . . .

C.S. CLARK, writer, in *Of Toronto the Good* (1898).

Toronto as a city carries out the idea of Canada as a country. It is a calculated crime both against the aspirations of the soul and the affection of the heart.

ALEISTER CROWLEY, self-styled black magician who travelled from British Columbia to Niagara Falls in 1906, in *The Confessions of Aleister Crowley* (1970).

Toronto (pronounce *T'ranto*, please) is difficult to describe. It has an individuality, but an elusive one; yet not through any queerness or difficult shade of eccentricity; a subtly normal, and indefinably obvious personality. It is a healthy, cheerful city (by modern standard); a clean-shaven, pink-faced, respectably dressed, fairly energetic, unintellectual, passably sociable, well-to-do, public-school-and-varsity sort of city.

*

But Toronto—Toronto is the subject. One must say something—*what* must one say about Toronto? What can one? What has anybody ever said? It is impossible to give it anything but commendation. It is not squalid like Birmingham, or cramped like Canton, or scattered like Edmonton, or sham like Berlin, or hellish like New York, or tiresome like Nice. It is all right. The only depressing thing is that it will always be what it is, only larger, and that no Canadian city can ever be anything better or different. If they are good they become Toronto.

RUPERT BROOKE, English poet who visited North America in 1913, in *Letters from America* (1916).

First prize, one week in Toronto. Second prize, two weeks in Toronto. Third prize, three weeks in Toronto.

Quebec joke, probably 1920s.

Lastly, Toronto is known as Toronto the Good, because of its alleged piety. My guess is that there's more polygamy in Toronto than Baghdad, only it's not called that in Toronto.

AUSTIN F. CROSS, Montreal journalist, in *Cross Roads* (1936).

Indeed I have always found that the only thing in regard to Toronto which faraway people know for certain is that McGill University is in it.

STEPHEN LEACOCK, humorist who lived in both Toronto and Montreal, in "So This Is Winnipeg," *My Discovery of the West* (1937).

At this juncture it may be as well to tell you that I did not exactly hit it off with the intellectuals of Toronto. Toronto is probably not a good place to be an intellectual in, and I suppose that it is too much to expect that intellectuals from more clement regions (more clement towards the Intelligence) should be welcomed . . . .

WYNDHAM LEWIS, British writer and painter, in a letter to Lorne Pierce, June 17, 1941, from *The Letters of Wyndham Lewis* (1963), edited by W.K. Rose.

Short of a job I shall simply die in a flophouse if I stop here. There is not a minute to be lost if I am to save myself from this last degradation.

WYNDHAM LEWIS, British literary figure, in a draft of a letter to Frank Morley, Oct. 17, 1941, quoted by Walter Michel in *Wyndham Lewis* (1971).

I'll be happy to come back to Toronto to kick your balls off any time you want.

CAMILLIEN HOUDE, long-time mayor of Montreal, attending a Grey Cup game in Toronto about 1946.

"But we all hate Toronto."
"That's just it. We *all* hate Toronto! It's the only thing everybody's got in common."

LISTER SINCLAIR, radio and television writer, in "We All Hate Toronto," *A Play on Words and Other Radio Plays* (1948).

Witness the French-Canadian politician, who, in the course of a Parliamentary debate, remarked that he had "spent a week in Toronto, one Sunday."

P.T. O'GORMAN, travel writer, in *Magnificent Ontario* (1950).

Toronto is an excellent town to mind one's business in.

NORTHROP FRYE, literary scholar, quoted by

Pelham Edgar in *Across My Path* (1952).

No one should ever visit Toronto for the first time.

*

Toronto is the city of the future—and always will be.

ALLAN LAMPORT, mayor of Toronto (1952-54) and malapropist, attributed.

There were four buildings on this corner [at the intersection of King and Simcoe Streets, Toronto]—Government House itself, Upper Canada College, a church, and a saloon (to use the venerable term); a pale little joke of the time was that the four buildings represented legislation, education, salvation, and damnation.

VINCENT MASSEY, first native-born governor general, in *What's Past Is Prologue* (1963).

No one ever tried harder than I to live up to the name, and I believe that I *was* Mayor of All the People, regardless of race, colour, creed, national origin or political affiliation.

NATHAN PHILLIPS, mayor of Toronto in the 1950s and 60s, in *Mayor of All the People* (1967).

Last night I had a dream about Toronto. I was on my bicycle, cruising about in front of the old house. And, as usual in my dreams, I was a little girl again. A little girl in Toronto, with long golden curls.

MARY PICKFORD, Toronto-born Hollywood star and "America's Sweetheart," in a telephone interview with Clyde Gilmour in the Toronto *Telegram*, June 22, 1968.

You're going to have a great town here if you ever get it finished.

BOB HOPE, American comedian, commenting on the growth of Toronto, to Elwood Glover, Aug. 21, 1969.

This is the *only* North American city where people skate and dance at the seat of power.

DAVID CROMBIE, mayor of Toronto, alluding to the skating rink in Nathan Phillips Square, surrounding the new City Hall, in his address to the City Council, Jan. 3, 1973.

He is tiny. He is perfect. He is ours.

He is our tiny perfect mayor.

GARY DUNFORD, columnist, was the first person to describe David Crombie, mayor of Toronto, as the "tiny perfect mayor," in his column in the Toronto *Sun*, Oct. 14, 1973. The phrase recalls the description of Maharishi Mahesh Yogi as "the tiny perfect master."

But what moved Bech, with their intimations of lost time and present innocence, were the great Victorian piles, within the university and along Bloor Street, that Canadians, building across the lake from grimy grubbing America, had lovingly erected—brick valentines posted to a distant dowager queen.

*

Clean straight streets. Cities whose cores are not blighted but innocently bustling. Anglo-Saxon faces, British once removed, striding long-legged and unterrorized out of a dim thin past into a future as likely as any. Empty territories rich in minerals. Stately imperial government buildings. Parks where one need not fear being mugged.

JOHN UPDIKE, New England author, in "Australia and Canada," *Playboy*, May 1975.

Trade

See also ECONOMIC NATIONALISM; NATIONAL POLICY OF 1878; RECIPROCITY.

Fifty bullocks from Illinois would frighten every butcher out of Montreal!

PORTUS BAXTER, representative from Vermont, in the House of Representatives, Washington, from the *Congressional Globe*, May 26, 1864, discussing the termination of the Reciprocity Treaty signed in 1854.

I will blast a way into the markets of the world.

R.B. BENNETT, leader of the Conservative party, in a Winnipeg address, June 9, 1930. What Bennett actually said was: "You say our tariffs are only for the manufacturers. I will make them fight for you as well. I will use them to blast a way into the markets that have been closed to you." These phrases were inserted into the address by Bennett's brother-in-law, W.H. Herridge, ambassador to the United States, and hence do not appear in the *Globe*'s full report the following day.

Canada is the largest trading partner of the United States.

Hon. Members: Hear, Hear!

Mr. Nixon: It is very important that that be noted in Japan, too.

Hon. Members: Hear, hear!

RICHARD M. NIXON, American president, in an address before a joint sitting of the Canadian Senate and the House of Commons, April 14, 1972. At a press conference in the White House, Washington, Sept. 16, 1971, Nixon had said that Japan was the biggest customer of the United States. Peter C. Newman, in "I Love Canada," the New York *Times*, Jan. 28, 1972, noted: "The fact is that in 1970 United States–Canadian trade exceeded the value of United States–Japanese trade by some $10 billion."

Tradition

We have here no traditions and ancient venerable institutions; here, there are no aristocratic elements hallowed by time or bright deeds; here, every man is the first settler of the land, or removed from the first settler one or two generations at the furthest; here, we have no architectural monuments calling up old associations; here, we have none of those old popular legends and stories which in other countries have exercised a powerful share in the government; here, every man is the son of his own works.

THOMAS D'ARCY McGEE, future Father of Confederation, in the Legislative Assembly in Quebec, Feb. 9, 1865, from *Parliamentary Debates on the Subject of the Confederation of the British North American Provinces* (1865).

Canada only needs to be known in order to be great.

J. CASTELL HOPKINS, Toronto editor, in the preface to *The Story of the Dominion* (1901).

Tradition is the father of persecutions, the uncle of falsehoods, the brother of ignorance, and the grandsire of a thousand hideous sins against sweetness and light.

BLISS CARMAN, New Brunswick-born poet, in *The Friendship of Art* (1904).

It is that feeling of fresh loneliness that impresses itself before any detail of the wild. The soul—or the personality—seems to have indefinite room to expand. There is no one else within reach, there never has been anyone, no one else is *thinking* of the lake and hills you see before you. They have no tradition, no names even; they are only pools of water and lumps of earth, some day, perhaps to be clothed with loves and memories and the comings and going of men, but now dumbly waiting their Wordsworth or their Acropolis to give them individuality, and a soul.

RUPERT BROOKE, English poet who visited North America in 1913, in *Letters from America* (1916).

Travel

May you get to the place you are aiming for.

The Netsilik farewell, quoted by Knud Rasmussen in *The Netsilik Eskimos* (1931).

There was a young lady named Bright
Whose speed was far faster than light;
　She set out one day
　In a relative way
And returned on the previous night.

＊

To her friends said the Bright one in chatter,
"I have learned something new about matter:
　My speed was so great,
　Much increased was my weight,
Yet I failed to become any fatter!"

A.H. REGINALD BULLER, one-time professor of botany at the University of Manitoba and a world-wide authority on fungi, wrote the limerick "Relativity," published in *Punch*, Dec. 19, 1923. Its sequel appeared in *The Lure of the Limerick* (1968), by William S. Baring-Gould.

Travels are dreams translated into action.

DOROTHY DUNCAN, Montreal writer, in *Here's to Canada* (1941).

Somnolent through landscapes and by trees
nondescript, almost anonymous,
they alter as they enter foreign cities—
the terrible tourists with their empty eyes
longing to be filled with monuments.

P.K. PAGE, poet, in "The Permanent Tourists," *The Metal and the Flower* (1954).

Airline travel is hours of boredom interrupted by moments of stark terror.

AL BOLISKA, Toronto joke-collector, in *The Mahareeshi Says* (1968).

Live, and let Nelson Eddy live. And if the tourists turn up on Dominion Day with skis, just switch on the artificial snow machines.

From *To Know and Be Known* (1969), report of the task force on government information, D'Iberville Fortier, chairman.

If we go far enough down this road we'll find Nineveh.

A.Y. JACKSON, member of the Group of Seven, about a country road near Kleinburg, Ontario, quoted by Neil Loutit in the Toronto *Globe and Mail*, July 17, 1971.

If you are moving at the speed of light, you are already there.

MARSHALL MCLUHAN, media pundit, at the Montreal International Book Fair, quoted by Christie McCormick in the Montreal *Gazette*, May 16, 1975.

Trees

See also NATURE.

The pity I have for the trees in Canada, shows how far I am from being a true Canadian. How do we know that trees do not feel their downfall? We know nothing about it.

*

A Canadian settler *hates* a tree, regards it as his natural enemy, as something to be destroyed, eradicated, annihilated by all and any means. The idea of useful or ornamental is seldom associated here even with the most magnificent timber trees, such as among the Druids had been consecrated, and among the Greeks would have sheltered oracles and votive temples. The beautiful faith which assigned to every tree of the forest its guardian nymph, to every leafy grove its tutelary divinity, would find no votaries here. Alas! for the Dryads and Hamadryads of Canada!

ANNA JAMESON, British writer, in *Winter Studies and Summer Rambles in Canada* (1838).

Life to a man in Fredericton without the elms above him is unthinkable.

BRUCE HUTCHISON, west-coast editor and author, in *The Unknown Country* (1942).

Those trees weren't put on that mountain by God to be praised, they were put there to be chopped down.

PHILLIP A. GAGLARDI, minister of Public Works and Social Improvement in the B.C. Social Credit government of W.A.C. Bennett, characteristic remark, quoted by Paddy Sherman in *Bennett* (1966).

" . . . But only God can make a tree." (He'll never try it in Sudbury.)

RAYMOND SOUSTER, Toronto poet, from "Very Short Poem," *Selected Poems* (1972).

Troubles

Have you ever noticed how much larger your troubles appear at night?

BOB EDWARDS, writer and publisher of the Calgary *Eye Opener*, Sept. 24, 1921.

Trouble is good for mankind. When you are in trouble you get an understanding of life and you find the answers to many questions.

F.H. VARLEY, member of the Group of Seven, quoted by McKenzie Porter in *Maclean's*, Nov. 7, 1959.

A St. Valentine's Day Massacre is just a word until you have one.

MAX FERGUSON, broadcaster and humorist, in *And Now . . . Here's Max* (1967).

It is a long lane that has no ash-cans.

JOHN G. DIEFENBAKER, former prime minister, over a government motion defeated during Prime Minister Lester B. Pearson's absence from the House of Commons, Feb. 19, 1967.

There are two kinds of problems, those that get better . . . and those that get worse.

JOHN TURNER, minister of Finance, quoted by Barbara Frum in *Maclean's*, Aug. 1973.

After the pendulum there is always the pit.

LARRY ZOLF, zany broadcaster, on "As It Happens," March 6, 1975.

Trudeau, Pierre Elliott

La raison avant la passion.

PIERRE ELLIOTT TRUDEAU's personal maxim, which translates "Reason over passion."

Have you ever seen him kiss a farmer?

JOHN G. DIEFENBAKER, former prime minister, alluding to Prime Minister Pierre Elliott Trudeau's "kissing campaign" of 1968.

The only constant factor to be found in my thinking over the years has been opposition to accepted opinions. Had I applied this principle to the stock market, I might have made a fortune. I chose to apply it to politics, and it led me to power—a result I had not really desired, or even expected.

*

My political action, or my theory—insomuch as I can be said to have one—can be expressed very simply: create counterweights.

PIERRE ELLIOTT TRUDEAU, future prime minister, in *Federalism and the French Canadians* (1968).

Biafra? Where's Biafra?

To Ron Collister on CBC-TV, outside the East Block on Parliament Hill in 1968, when asked what the government was "going to do" about Biafra. The flip reply was frequently quoted when Nigeria forcibly re-established its control over secessionist Biafra in April 1970. Trudeau was familiar with the region and the issues, having canoed down its principal river in the summer of 1957.

In Pierre Elliott Trudeau, Canada has at last produced a political leader worthy of assassination.

IRVING LAYTON, outspoken poet, in *The Whole Bloody Bird* (1969).

I'll tell you one thing that's certain. From now on, no more philosopher-king.

PIERRE ELLIOTT TRUDEAU, to a cabinet minister on election night, Oct. 30, 1972, when it became apparent there would be a minority government.

I'm glad I won a majority. Now I can go back to being arrogant and telling everyone to fuddle-duddle off.

PIERRE ELLIOTT TRUDEAU, at a celebration at 24 Sussex Drive, following the federal election of 1974, attributed by Richard Gwyn in the Toronto *Star*, Oct. 3, 1974.

Well, I would have to concede that I have been called worse things by worse men.

PIERRE ELLIOTT TRUDEAU, response on learning that in a taped conversation, Richard M. Nixon, the American president who had recently resigned, had referred to him as "that asshole Trudeau," reported Oct. 21, 1974.

Truth

Flattery is an agreeable untruth.

SIR JOHN A. MACDONALD, prime minister, attributed by John G. Diefenbaker in the House of Commons, Feb. 5, 1971.

Error held in truth has much the effect of truth.

GEORGE ILES, science writer, in *Canadian Stories* (1918).

It is a hard thing to speak the truth. It is difficult to make hidden forces appear.

HORQARNAQ, Eskimo shaman, observation quoted by Knud Rasmussen in *Intellectual Culture of the Copper Eskimos* (1932).

And of course it may be that all I have been telling you is wrong. For you cannot be certain about a thing you cannot see. And people say so much!

NULIAJUK, Eskimo remark made ironically, quoted by Knud Rasmussen in *The Netsilik Eskimos* (1931).

There is nothing too amazing to be true.

ALLAN SPRAGGETT, "Canada's foremost authority on ESP," last sentence of *The Unexplained* (1967).

Truth: lie's lie.

NICHOLAS CATANOY, Romanian-born literary figure, from "The Second Truth," *Hic et Nunc* (1968).

When truth in science seems to teach us that we are accidental inhabitants of a negligible planet in the endless spaces, men are forced to seek meaning in other ways than through the intellect. If truth leads to meaninglessness, then men in their thirst for meaning turn to art. To hope to find in the products of the imagination that meaning which has been cast out of the intellect may, in the light of Socrates, be known to be a fruitless quest. Nevertheless, it is a thirst which is the enemy of tyranny.

> GEORGE P. GRANT, a leading spokesman for conservatism, in "The University Curriculum," *Technology and Empire* (1969).

I'm constantly reminded of what my grandfather told me: the moon shines just as much on a handful of water as on a lake. We may find truth under a pebble. Truth is probably very small.

> RAYMOND MORIYAMA, Vancouver-born Toronto architect, quoted by Marjorie Harris in *Maclean's*, March 1970.

Every dogma has its day.

> ABRAHAM ROTSTEIN, influential political economist, in Dec. 1974.

It's all right to tell the truth and shame the devil.

> MARGARET "MA" MURRAY, pioneer newspaperwoman, on CBC-TV, June 3, 1975.

Truth I have no trouble with, it's the facts I get all screwed up.

> FARLEY MOWAT, author and environmentalist, on CFRB radio, Toronto, Dec. 14, 1975.

Twentieth Century

Let me utter one concluding word. Canada is here to stay. The beginning of this century marks an epoch of phenomenal progress in British North America. The nineteenth century was the century of the United States. The twentieth century is Canada's century.

> JAMES W. LONGLEY, attorney-general of Nova Scotia, in an address to the Canadian Club of Boston, April 8, 1902; from the Toronto *Globe*, April 12, 1902.

The twentieth century belongs to Canada.

> SIR WILFRID LAURIER, prime minister, in 1904. This is the most celebrated of all Canadian aphorisms, a touchstone of national aspiration measured against national achievement. In an address to the Canadian Club of Ottawa on Jan. 18, 1904, Laurier actually said: "The nineteenth century was the century of the United States. I think we can claim that it is Canada that shall fill the twentieth century."

I remember a Toronto in which the admirably true phrase—the twentieth century was to be Canada's—was accepted as the general watchword; only nobody had begun to realize what a rotten century the twentieth was going to be.

> B.K. SANDWELL, influential editor of *Saturday Night* from 1932 to 1951, in "On Being Sorry for Ourselves," an address to the Empire Club of Canada in 1924.

Today we think in more modest terms.

> EUGENE FORSEY, unionist and senator, in "The Nature of the Canadian Economy," *Social Planning for Canada* (1935), by the Research Committee of the League for Social Reconstruction.

The twentieth century was once supposed to belong to Canada, but it seems more and more likely that only the first quarter of the century was really ours.

> F.W. BURTON of St. John's College, Winnipeg, in the *Canadian Journal of Economics and Political Science*, Nov. 1936.

The twentieth century *did* belong to Canada.

> BRIAN MOORE, well-known novelist, in *Canada* (1963, 1968).

The future really belongs to those who will build it. The future can be promised to no one.

> PIERRE ELLIOTT TRUDEAU, prime minister, at Yarmouth, Nova Scotia, May 30, 1968.

The twenty-first century belongs to Japan.

> HERMAN KAHN, American research scientist, about 1970.

The 20th Century belongs to the Moon.

> EARLE BIRNEY, distinguished poet, in *What's So Big About Green* (1973).

Twenty-Fourth of May
See VICTORIA DAY.

"Two Solitudes"
See also CANADA: FRENCH AND ENGLISH.

And this more human love (that will fulfill itself, infinitely considerate and gentle, and good and clear in binding and releasing) will resemble that which we are with struggle and endeavour preparing, the love that consists in this, that two solitudes protect and touch and greet each other.

RAINER MARIA RILKE, great German poet, in letter seven, Rome, May 14, 1904, from *Letters to a Young Poet* (1934), translated from the German by M.D. Herter Norton. Hugh MacLennan adapted the last fifteen words and cited them in his well-known novel, *Two Solitudes* (1945), to represent the isolation of the French and English in Quebec and Canada.

I did not, of course, "invent" the phrase "two solitudes." It comes from a sentence of Rainer Maria Rilke and I still think it is one of the supreme poetic utterances of our century, though actually it was a line of prose in a letter to a friend . . . . "Love consists in this, that two solitudes protect and touch and greet each other." Surely the best practical definition of love ever uttered, whether applied to individuals or to two nations sharing a single state.

HUGH MACLENNAN, Montreal novelist, in "Two Solitudes that Meet and Greet in Hope and Hate," *Maclean's*, Aug. 1971.

Unemployment

I will end unemployment or perish in the attempt.

R.B. BENNETT, leader of the Conservative party, in a Winnipeg address, June 9, 1930. What Bennett actually said was: "I propose that any government of which I am the head will at the first session of Parliament initiate whatever action is necessary to that end, or perish in the attempt." W.H. Herridge, brother-in-law of the Conservative leader, inserted these words into the address. Quoted by J.R.H. Wilbur in *The Bennett New Deal* (1968).

A very regrettable side effect.

PIERRE ELLIOTT TRUDEAU, prime minister, gave a new definition of unemployment as "a very regrettable side effect of inflation," in the House of Commons, April 16, 1970.

Unemployment, I guess. The switch is because we have won last year's victory, the one against inflation.

PIERRE ELLIOTT TRUDEAU, prime minister, reply when asked to identify the main problem facing Canadians, and why the nation faces a new one, on Dec. 23, 1970. Quoted by Walter Stewart in *Divide and Con* (1973).

The government is doing something about unemployment—it's creating it.

DON HARRON, actor-writer who created Charlie Farquharson, the crotchety farmer from Parry Sound, in a skit in Toronto in 1973.

Union of Soviet Socialist Republics

Canada and Russia are the largest countries of the world. They lie within the same latitudes. They share a climate of extremes. They share a sense of wind and plain, of airy desolation; and they enclose huddles of people within the harsh rhythms of the north. I've always felt that Canada has this kind of elemental kinship with Russia, a kinship more mysterious and so tougher than that with the sultry United States . . . it was time we shared not only snow but visions.

MICHAEL BAWTREE, dramaturge, in "The Government Inspector," *The Stratford Scene: 1958-1968* (1968), edited by Peter Raby.

[I can foresee the day when Canada and Russia might] reach agreement on a program of trans-Arctic co-operation of a yet unforeseen nature. That may be a dream, but surely there is an element of reality in it—the reality of two peoples overcoming the rigors of the same climate, subduing the same untamed reaches, taking up the challenge of our common Everest, the Far North.

PIERRE ELLIOTT TRUDEAU, prime minister, in a speech in Leningrad, May 27, 1971.

For Canada to be great, Canada must realize it is a great country and most of it is North. The difference between Canada and Russia is that the Russians look north and Canadians look south.

DOUG WILKINSON, author, quoted by Nancy Naglin in the Toronto *Star*, Jan. 29, 1972.

Unions

See also LABOUR.

United to Support, Not Combined to Injure.

Motto of the International Typographical Society, No. 91, since 1844, the oldest of Canada's printing associations. Noted by H.A. Logan in *Trade Unions in Canada* (1948).

Where the Fraser River flows, each fellow worker knows,
They have bullied and oppressed us, but still our Union grows.
And we're going to find a way, boys, for shorter hours and better pay, boys!
And we're going to win the day, boys; where the River Fraser flows.

JOE HILL, martyred labour hero and singer-composer, wrote "Where the Fraser River Flows" (to the tune of "Where the River Shannon Flows") to support the striking construction workers laying track for the Canadian Northern Railroad in British Columbia. The strike broke out on March 27, 1912. Hill wrote the song at Yale, B.C., shortly thereafter. The strikers, supported by the Wobblies, won. Quoted by Gibbs M. Smith in *Labour Martyr* (1969).

From a thousand hills, a thousand rills father into a mighty river which sweeps on to the ocean. An attempt to damn the Niagara, in the hope that it would never reach the sea, would be no more foolish than the attempt to damn labour from its resistless onward sweep towards its natural outlet—co-operative industry.

*

One might as well tell the full-grown man to resolve himself into a boy again and "be seen and not heard" as tell labour it cannot have a voice in the management of industry through collective bargaining. Grass will grow, the river will reach the sea, the boy will come a man, and labour will come into its own.

FRED J. DIXON, a leader of the Winnipeg General Strike, which paralyzed the city from May 15 to June 25, 1919, in *Strike Bulletin* no. 27.

Co-operation, Yes. Domination, No!

PERCY BENGOUGH, president of the Trades and Labour Congress, is identified with this celebrated statement of Canadian labour sovereignty, when an attempt was made by the American Federation of Labor to disenfranchise Canadian members. *Trades and Labour Congress Journal*, March 1949, quoted by Charles Lipton in *The Trade Union Movement in Canada* (1967).

We are only loggers.

H. LANDON LADD, president of the International Wood Workers of America, coined the slogan of District 2 (Newfoundland local) after a retired logger heard him speak and commented: "What you say is right, and what you are trying to do is right. But you'll never get it. We are only loggers." From Richard Gwyn's *Smallwood: The Unlikely Revolutionary* (1968).

We can count only on ourselves.

MICHEL CHARTRAND, leader of the left wing of the Quebec labour movement and president of the Montreal Central Council of the CNTU, title of the manifesto, *Ne comptons que sur nos propres moyens*, issued in Sept. 1971 by the CNTU and advocating the overthrow of capitalism in Quebec.

The state is our exploiter.

LOUIS LABERGE, militant president of the Quebec Federation of Labour, title of working papers distributed by the Quebec Federation of Labour at its convention in Nov. 1971.

The first thing I'd do is nationalize all the American trade unions. Canadian unions must be independent. Let them cry how much they want.

GUNNAR MYRDAL, Swedish social scientist, quoted by Peter C. Newman in "Sweden" (1971), *Home Country* (1973).

United Empire Loyalists
See LOYALTY.

United States of America
See also CANADA: ANGLO-AMERICAN RELATIONS; CANADA: UNITED STATES RELATIONS.

For my part—I never made any secret of it—I have the greatest possible admiration for the American people. I have always admired their many strong qualities. But I have found in the short experience during which it has been my privilege and my fortune to be placed at the head of affairs, by the will of the Canadian people, that the best and most effective way to maintain friendship with our American neighbours is to be absolutely independent of them.

> SIR WILFRID LAURIER, prime minister of Canada, in the House of Commons, July 30, 1903.

The American way of life:
You can get away with murder
If you use a golden knife.

> JOE WALLACE, Communist versifier, in "Verse," *A Radiant Sphere* (1964).

The Americans are our best friends, whether we like it or not.

> ROBERT THOMPSON, former leader of the Social Credit party, quoted by Peter C. Newman in "Robert Thompson" (1967), *Home Country: People, Places, and Power Politics* (1973).

The old platitude must be repeated once again: the United States is the society with the least history prior to the age of progress.

> GEORGE P. GRANT, philosopher and prominent conservative, in "From Roosevelt to L.B.J.," *The New Romans* (1968), edited by Al Purdy.

A country which elected, but survived, McKinley, Harding, Coolidge, Hoover, and Nixon as vice-president can't be all bad.

> JACK LUDWIG, Winnipeg-born, New York-based novelist, in "Balancing the Books," *The New Romans* (1968), edited by Al Purdy.

My generation of Canadians grew up believing that, if we were very good or very smart, or both, we would someday *graduate* from Canada.

> ROBERT FULFORD, Toronto journalist and editor, in "Notebook," *Saturday Night*, Oct. 1970.

Unity, National
See also FEDERAL-PROVINCIAL RELATIONS.

So long as the majority of Canadians have two countries, one here and one in Europe, national unity will remain a myth and a constant source of internecine quarrels.

> HENRI BOURASSA, French-Canadian nationalist, in a speech at the Monument National, April 27, 1902. From *French-Canadian Nationalism* (1969), edited by Ramsay Cook.

National unity must be based on provincial autonomy, and provincial autonomy cannot be assured unless a strong feeling of national unity exists throughout Canada.

> N.W. ROWELL, lawyer and royal commissioner, in the *Report of the Royal Commission on Dominion-Provincial Relations* (1940), book II, section G, commonly called the Rowell-Sirois Report.

On the day when every French Canadian, wherever he may be in the country, enjoys the same advantages and the same privileges as his English-speaking compatriot, the last obstacle to the unity of the country will have disappeared.

> GÉRARD FILION, editor of *Le Devoir*, in *Saturday Night*, Nov. 24, 1954.

Canada has no cultural unity, no linguistic unity, no religious unity, no economic unity, no geographic unity. All it has is unity.

> KENNETH BOULDING, professor of economics at the University of Michigan, addressing a group of Toronto students in Nov. 1957.

I've had a long and public love affair with Canada. It represents something of unique value. It is dedicated to the idea of unity without uniformity.

> SAMUEL FREEDMAN, justice of the Manitoba Court of Appeal and chancellor of the University of Manitoba, quoted by Gerald Clark in *Canada: The Uneasy Neighbour* (1965).

University
See COLLEGES AND UNIVERSITIES.

Vancouver

To describe the beauties of this region will, on some future occasion, be a very grateful task to the pen of a skilled panegyrist. The serenity of the climate, the innumerable pleasing landscapes, and the abundant fertility that unassisted nature puts forth, requires only to be enriched by the industry of man with villages, mansions, cottages, and other buildings to render it the most lovely country that can be imagined; whilst the labour of the inhabitants would be amply rewarded, in the bounties which nature seems ready to bestow on cultivation.

> CAPTAIN GEORGE VANCOUVER, British navigator, a description of the area around Vancouver, in the spring of 1792, from *A Voyage of Discovery to the North Pacific Ocean and Round the World* (1798).

People from the prairies, who have made their pile, spend their declining years in Vancouver on the road to heaven.

> H.F. GADSBY, Toronto art critic, quoted in *Canadian Days* (1911).

Tyre and Sidon,—where are they?
Where is the trade of Carthage now?
Here in Vancouver on English Bay
With tomorrow's light on her brow!

> BLISS CARMAN, New Brunswick-born poet, from "Vancouver" (1922), in his *Selected Poems* (1954), edited by Lorne Pierce.

This seems to me the place to live.

> ELIZABETH THE QUEEN MOTHER, on her first visit to Vancouver, May 29, 1939.

It is a long way to Ottawa, but it is ten times as far from Ottawa to Vancouver.

> GERRY McGEER, former mayor of Vancouver, summoned to the Senate in 1945, quoted by Eric Nicol in *Vancouver* (1970).

Vancoozer: Canda's biggest oudoors port.

> DON HARRON, actor-writer, who created the crotchety farmer from Parry Sound, in *Charlie Farquharson's Jogfree of Canada* (1974).

Tawdry and romantic, bourgeois and raunchy at once, Vancouver is where the small ambitions flourish and the large dreams move furtively.

> DONALD CAMERON, writer and former academic, in *Weekend*, April 19, 1975.

Victoria Day
See also EMPIRE DAY.

Empire Day, the twenty-fourth of May.

> MRS. CLEMENTINA FESSENDEN, Hamilton school teacher and mother of Reginald Fessenden, had the idea in 1898 that a day should be set aside each year to commemorate the British Empire. She chose Queen Victoria's birthday, May 24, and within a few years that date was being observed throughout the British Empire.

The twenty-fourth of May
Is the Queen's Birthday;
If you don't give us a holiday,
We'll all run away.

> Traditional ball-bouncing rhyme, quoted by Sara Jeannette Duncan in *The Imperialist* (1904).

Vikings
See EXPLORATION.

Violence
See also SPORTS.

If they can't hit you, they can't hurt you.

> JIMMY McLARNIN, "Canada's most successful fighter," who retired in 1936 at the age of twenty-nine in Vancouver with half a million dollars, quoted by S.F. Wise and Douglas Fisher in *Canada's Sporting Heroes* (1974).

If you can't lick 'em in the alley, you can't beat 'em on the ice.

> CONN SMYTHE, Toronto hockey executive, in an interview with Trent Frayne in 1952. "I did not mean that you scare the other guy but that you show him there is no fear in you." Quoted by Bob Pennington in the Toronto *Star*, Oct. 1, 1973.

Nothing relaxes the boys like a good fight.

> FRANCIS "KING" CLANCY, former hockey

player and referee, quoted by Trent Frayne and Peter Gzowski in *Great Canadian Sports Stories* (1965).

My job is to win hockey games. If I have to bruise a few guys to do it, that's just too bad. I do what I think is necessary to win.

PUNCH IMLACH, hockey coach, quoted by Jack Batten in *The Inside Story of Conn Smythe's Hockey Dynasty* (1969).

Canada has never had a major civil war. After hockey, Canadians would probably have found it dull.

JIM BROSNAN, former major league American pitcher, quoted by Jack Batten in *Champions* (1971).

Without violence, there would be no such thing as hockey.

CLARENCE CAMPBELL, NHL president, at a hockey symposium, reported in the Toronto *Globe and Mail*, March 1, 1975.

Virtues and Vices
See also DRINKING; GOOD AND EVIL.

As far as I am concerned, I've gone through my life with one principle: Be to our faults a little blind, and to our virtues always kind.

SIR JOHN A. MACDONALD, prime minister, attributed by John G. Diefenbaker.

Some people make their virtues more unendurable than their vices.

PETER MCARTHUR, rural Ontario writer and columnist who died in 1924, in *The Best of Peter McArthur* (1967), edited by Alec Lucas.

No, thank you, I never indulge in any non-cooperative vices.

LISTER SINCLAIR, writer, when offered a cigarette in the early 1940s, quoted by Andrew Allan in *Andrew Allan* (1974).

As you get older virtue becomes easier.

LOUIS DUDEK, Montreal poet, in *Epigrams* (1975).

Vote
See also ELECTIONS; WOMEN AND THE LAW.

Another trouble is that if men start to vote, they will vote too much. Politics unsettles

men, and unsettled men mean unsettled bills—broken furniture, broken vows and—divorce . . . .

NELLIE L. MCCLUNG, suffragette leader, in an address ridiculing the manner of Sir Rodmond Roblin, premier of Manitoba, at the mock parliament in the Walker Theatre, Jan. 28, 1914, from *The Stream Runs Fast* (1945).

"No woman, idiot, lunatic, or criminal shall vote."

NELLIE L. MCCLUNG, writer and suffragette, cited this passage as appearing in the "Election Act of the Dominion of Canada" in *In Times Like These* (1915). The phrase does not appear in the *Revised Statutes of Canada, 1906*, which was not again revised until 1927.

Canadian women got the vote as a gift rather than as a reward.

CHARLOTTE WHITTON, outspoken woman mayor of Ottawa, "Is the Canadian Woman a Flop in Politics?" *Saturday Night*, Jan. 26, 1946.

Voyageur
See COUREUR DE BOIS.

War
See also CONSCRIPTION; WAR, CANADIANS AT; WAR OF 1812; WAR: WORLD WAR I (1914-1918); WAR: WORLD WAR II (1939-1945); WAR DEAD.

There is no such thing as an inevitable war. If war comes it will be from failure of human wisdom.

ANDREW BONAR LAW, New Brunswick-born prime minister of Great Britain who died in 1923, attributed.

Any war that is postponed is a war that may never be fought.

FLOYD S. CHALMERS, Toronto publisher, in "Britain's Bid for Peace," an address to the Canadian Club of Toronto, Oct. 24, 1938.

For permanent peace by the help of God, let us build more Friendships instead of Warships.

JACK MINER, pioneer naturalist, who banded wildlife at his famous bird sanctuary at Kingsville, Ontario, in *Wild Goose Jack* (1969).

In the future no one wins a war. It is true, there are degrees of loss, but no one wins.
> BROCK CHISHOLM, psychiatrist and first director-general of the World Health Organization, Geneva, in an address to the Empire Club of Canada in 1951.

Two world wars and ever-recurring economic crises are the modern equivalents of the Black Death.
> JOHN A. IRVING, philosopher, in *Science and Values* (1952).

Today, while Europe tilted, drying the Baltic,
I read of a battle between brothers in anguish,
A flag moved a mile.
> F.R. SCOTT, Montreal man-of-letters, from *Selected Poems* (1966).

Over the long run, it does not matter how small the probability of nuclear war is per unit time. It is mathematically demonstrable that, as time goes on, this probability approaches certainty.
> J.L. GRANATSTEIN, historian, in "A World without War?" *Visions 2020* (1970), edited by Stephen Clarkson.

Things done in wartime by men and women should not be marked down in a big book for posterity. Wartime is when no rules apply.
> BARRY BROADFOOT, interviewer, in *Six War Years: 1939-1945* (1974).

War, Canadians at
See also WAR.

Wish you to travel night and day. I want to show what the Canadian militia can do.
> SIR JOSEPH CARON, minister of Militia in Ottawa, in a telegram to the first detachment heading west to put down the Northwest Rebellion, March 31, 1885, quoted by Donald Creighton in *John A. Macdonald: The Old Chieftain* (1955).

Never let it be said the Canadians had let their guns be taken!

RICHARD E.W. TURNER, lieutenant in the Royal Canadian Dragoons, awarded the Victoria Cross for valour at Leliefontein, Union of South Africa, on Nov. 7, 1900, quoted by John Swettenham in *Valiant Men* (1973).

There has never been a war of Canadian origin, nor for a Canadian cause.
> WILLIAM ARTHUR DEACON, literary editor, in *My Vision of Canada* (1933).

It may be that the liberty of the nations still free will stand or fall with the liberty of Spain, and if the liberty of Spain falls it will fall not through the courage of its foes only but through the timidity of its friends.
> SALEM G. BLAND, Toronto minister who preached the social gospel, in *New Frontier*, Dec. 1936.

Madrid will be the tomb of fascism.
> NORMAN BETHUNE, Gravenhurst-born medical doctor and later hero of Mao's China, in a "Letter from Dr. Bethune," Madrid, Jan. 11, 1937, reprinted in the *Marxist Quarterly*, summer 1966.

Madrid is the centre of gravity of the world.
> NORMAN BETHUNE, medical doctor, in a letter written on Feb. 17, 1937, from *Bethune* (1973), by Roderick Stewart.

Canada is an unmilitary community. Warlike her people have often been forced to be; military they have never been.
> C.P. STACEY, military historian, the opening words of *Official History of the Canadian Army in the Second World War, Volume I* (1955).

. . . I submit, that although the Canadians are not a warlike people, they *are* a fighting people, none better.
> LESLIE F. HANNON, writer, in the foreword to *Canada at War* (1968).

If I had to choose a non-Israeli army to fight with, it would be the Canadian commandos, because they are all volunteers. Of course, I wouldn't want to spend my evenings with the Canadians. For that, I would choose the Italian commandos.
> MOSHE DAYAN, Israeli general, quoted by Peter C. Newman in "Israel" (1969), *Home Country* (1973).

Canada won its independence mostly by fighting against Germans.

F.R. SCOTT, Montreal man-of-letters, unpublished aphorism from his commonplace book, 1973.

"READY, AYE, READY"

If we were to be compelled to take part in all the wars of Great Britain, I have no hesitation in saying that I agree with my hon. friend that, sharing the burden, we should also share the responsibility. Under that condition of things, which does not exist, we should have the right to say to Great Britain: If you want us to help you, call us to your councils; if you want us to take part in wars let us share not only the burdens but the responsibilities and duties as well.

SIR WILFRID LAURIER, prime minister, referring to possible Canadian participation in the Boer War, in the House of Commons, March 13, 1900. "My hon. friend" was Henri Bourassa. "If you want us to help us, call us to your councils," became a catch-phrase of the period.

War is everywhere. When Britain is at war, Canada is at war; there is no distinction. If Great Britain, to which we are subject, is at war with any nation, Canada becomes liable to invasion, and so Canada is at war.

SIR WILFRID LAURIER, prime minister, in the House of Commons, Jan. 12, 1910.

It would be seen by the world that Canada, a daughter of Old England, intends to stand by her in this great conflict. When the call comes our answer goes at once, and it goes in the classical language of the British answer to the call of duty: "Ready, aye, ready."

SIR WILFRID LAURIER, leader of the Opposition, at the special war session, in the House of Commons, Aug. 19, 1914.

Let there be no dispute as to where I stand. When Britain's message came then Canada should have said: "Ready, aye ready; we stand by you." [Loud cheers] I hope the time has not gone by when that declaration can yet be made. If that declaration is made then I will be at the back of the Government.

ARTHUR MEIGHEN, leader of the Opposition, in an address to the Liberal–Conservative Business Men's Club, Toronto, Sept. 22, 1922, published the following day in the Toronto *Mail and Empire.* Meighen was referring to the British government's "invitation" to Canada to send troops to defend the neutrality of Chanak, which was threatened by Turkey. Prime Minister Mackenzie King withheld "a declaration of solidarity on the part of the Dominions."

War of 1812

See also ANNEXATION; BROCK, SIR ISAAC; SECORD, LAURA; WAR.

Inhabitants of Canada . . . . The army under my command, has invaded your country, and the standard of UNION now waves over the territory of Canada. To the peaceable unoffending inhabitant, it brings neither danger nor difficulty. I come to *find* enemies, not to *make* them, I come to protect, not to injure you.

GENERAL WILLIAM HULL, brigadier-general and commander of the Northwestern Army of the United States, issued his proclamation in Sandwich, Lower Canada, on July 12, 1812. Reproduced by Robert Christie in *A History of the Late Province of Lower Canada, Parliamentary and Political* (1854).

The acquisition of Canada this year, as far as the neighbourhood of Quebec, will be a mere matter of marching, and will give us experience for the attack of Halifax the next, and the final expulsion of England from the American continent.

THOMAS JEFFERSON, American statesman, in a letter to Colonel William Duane, Monticello, Aug. 4, 1812. From *The Writings of Thomas Jefferson* (1903), edited by Andrew A. Lipscomb.

As the *Chesapeake* appears now ready for sea, I request you will do me the favour to meet the *Shannon* with her and try the fortune of our respective flags. Choose your terms but let us meet.

SIR PHILIP BOWES VERE BROKE, captain of the H.M.S. *Shannon,* in a message to Captain James Lawrence of the U.S. *Chesapeake* in Boston harbour; Broke captured the American frigate after a fifteen-minute sea battle, June 1, 1813. Broke was seriously wounded and Lawrence killed.

Tell the men to fire faster and not to give up the ship; fight her till she sinks

> JAMES LAWRENCE, captain of the U.S. *Chesapeake* which was captured by "Brave Broke" of the H.M.S. *Shannon* after a fifteen-minute sea battle outside Boston Harbour, June 1, 1813. Lawrence's last command, "Don't give up the ship," became the motto of the U.S. Navy.

The *Chesapeake* so bold out of Boston as we're told
Came to take the British frigate neat and handy O,
And the people in the port all came out to see the sport
While their bands all played up Yankee Doodle Dandy O!

> First verse of "The *Chesapeake* and the *Shannon*," *Ballads and Sea-Songs from Nova Scotia* (1928), edited by Roy W. Mackenzie.

Can you tell me, Sir, the reason why the public buildings and library at Washington should be held more sacred than those at York?

> JOHN STRACHAN, influential Anglican minister, in a letter to Thomas Jefferson, written from York (later Toronto), Jan. 30, 1815. Reproduced by William F. Coggin in *1812; the War, and its Moral* (1864).

Very little is known about the War of 1812 because the Americans lost it.

> ERIC NICOL, Vancouver humorist, in *Say Uncle* (1961), illustrated by Peter Whalley.

War: World War I (1914-1918)
See also WAR.

Sentry: 'Alt, who goes there?
Reply: Scots Guards.
Sentry: Pass, Scots Guards.

Sentry: 'Alt, who goes there?
Reply: The Buffs.
Sentry: Pass, The Buffs.

Sentry: 'Alt, who goes there?

Reply: Mind your own God-damn business!
Sentry: Pass, Canadians.

> Quoted by Leslie F. Hannon in *Canada at War* (1968).

It's a long way to Tipperary, it's a long way to go;
It's a long way to Tipperary, to the sweetest girl I know!
Good-bye Piccadilly, farewell, Leicester Square,
It's a long, long way to Tipperary, but my heart's right there!

> HARRY WILLIAMS, Canadian lyricist, wrote the words to the popular marching song, "It's a Long Way to Tipperary," in 1908. The music was written by Jack Judge, a Britisher. The British army adopted it as a marching song in 1914. Tipperary is a town in Ireland.

Oh, Mademoiselle from Armentières, Parlez-vous,
Oh, Mademoiselle from Armentières, Parlez-vous,
She hasn't been kissed in forty years,
Hinky-dinky, par-lee-voo.

> GITZ RICE, Nova Scotian sergeant in the Canadian army, sat down at a little café in Armentières, a small French town near Lille, in 1915, and watched a chic barmaid serve drinks. He composed the words then and there of the world-famous "Mademoiselle from Armentières"; he performed his composition a few days later before the Fifth Battery, Montreal, stationed in France.

You have your orders, carry them out.

> LORD KITCHENER, British secretary of State for War, ordering Sir Sam Hughes, minister of Militia and Defence, to break up the First Canadian Division among British formations. Sir Sam's reply was: "I'll be damned if I will," after which he marched out. This meeting took place on Aug. 26, 1914. The First Canadian Division was never divided.

The soldier going down in the cause of freedom never dies—immortality is his.

> SIR SAM HUGHES, minister of Militia and Defence, in an address to the first contingent of Canadian troops at their departure from Valcartier, Quebec, Sept. 22, 1914, reproduced by R.C. Brown and M.E. Prang in *Confederation to 1949* (1966).

Those who have undertaken to bleed Canada white to uphold the forces of England and France in Europe tell us occasionally that our first line of defence is in Flanders. I say that our first line of defence is at Ottawa.

HENRI BOURASSA, French-Canadian nationalist, in *Le Devoir et la guerre* (1916), quoted by Joseph Levitt in *Henri Bourassa on Imperialism and Bi-culturalism, 1900-1918* (1970).

The Canadians played a part of such distinction that thenceforward they were marked out as storm troops; for the remainder of the war they were brought along to head the assault in one great battle after another. Whenever the Germans found the Canadian Corps coming into the line they prepared for the worst.

LLOYD GEORGE, prime minister of Great Britain, after the battles of the Somme, in 1916, quoted by G.F.G. Stanley in *Canada's Soldiers* (third ed., 1974).

It was Canada from the Atlantic to the Pacific on parade. I thought then, and I think today, that in those few minutes I witnessed the birth of a nation.

BRIGADIER-GENERAL ALEXANDER ROSS, at the Battle of Vimy Ridge, Easter Monday, 1917. Quoted by D.E. Macintyre in *Canada at Vimy* (1967).

Truly magnificent . . . the sight was awful and wonderful.

SIR ARTHUR CURRIE, general commanding the Canadian division, his entry for Easter Monday, April 9, 1917, concerning the Battle of Vimy Ridge. Reproduced in *Historical Documents of Canada: Volume V* (1972), edited by C.P. Stacey.

To those who will fall I say, "You will not die but step into immortality. Your mothers will not lament your fate but will be proud to have borne such sons. Your names will be revered for ever and ever by your grateful country, and God will take you unto Himself."

SIR ARTHUR CURRIE, general officer commanding the Canadian division, special order of the day on the eve of the final Battle of the Somme, March 27, 1918. Quoted by John D. Robins in *A Pocketful of Canada* (1946).

Take me to the rear, that my men might not see me suffer, not that I fear to suffer, but that I fear it might affect and discourage them.

JEAN BRILLIANT, lieutenant in the 22nd Canadian Infantry Battalion, was twice wounded but led his men to capture 150 enemy and fifteen machine guns on Aug. 8–9, 1918, during the Battle of Amiens, France. He died of a third set of wounds and was posthumously awarded the Victoria Cross "for most conspicuous bravery and outstanding devotion to duty." Brilliant's words were quoted by the premier of Quebec, Joseph-Adélard Godbout, in "Quebec and Pan-Canadian Unity," an address to the Empire Club of Canada, in 1940. Details of the action are described by George C. Machum in *Canada's V.C.'s* (1956).

Above them are being planted the maples of Canada, in the thought that her sons will rest the better in the shade of the trees they knew so well in life.

ARTHUR MEIGHEN, prime minister, address at the dedication of the Vimy Ridge Memorial, France, July 3, 1921.

When I first took command of the Canadian forces, someone said to me, "For goodness sake, never patronize the Canadians," to which I replied, "By Heaven, I would as soon patronize a wasp's nest."

LORD BYNG, an address soon after assuming duties as governor general, on Aug. 11, 1921.

War: World War II (1939-1945)
See also WAR.

The Dominion of Canada is part of the sisterhood of the British Empire. I give to you assurance that the people of the United States will not stand idly by if domination of Canadian soil is threatened by any other Empire. We can assure each other that this hemisphere, at least, shall remain a strong citadel wherein civilization can flourish unimpaired.

FRANKLIN DELANO ROOSEVELT, American president, upon receiving an honorary degree from Queen's University, Kingston, Aug. 18, 1938.

We're really mad now!

Caption to a cartoon depicting a Canadian soldier and a British bulldog, in a CNE program for 1940, reproduced by James Lorimer in *The Ex* (1973).

We will be with you to the end.
W.L. MACKENZIE KING, prime minister, at the conclusion of a stirring wartime address to the battle-weary Britons, Mansion House, London, 1941. Quoted by Ralph Allen in *Ordeal by Fire* (1961).

Oh, I have slipped the surly bonds of earth,
And danced the skies on laughter-silvered wings . . . .
JOHN GILLESPIE MAGEE, an American pilot who was only nineteen when he was killed in action with the RCAF, Dec. 11, 1941; from his poem "In High Flight."

We have not journeyed all this way across the centuries, across the oceans, across the mountains, across the prairies, because we are made of sugar candy.

*

. . . and France would have held her place as a nation in the councils of the allies, and not at the conference table of the victors.
But their generals misled them. When I warned them that Britain would fight on alone, whatever they did, their generals told their Prime Minister and his divided cabinet, "In three weeks England will have her neck wrung like a chicken." Some chicken! Some neck!
SIR WINSTON CHURCHILL, prime minister of Great Britain and wartime leader, in an address to a joint meeting of the Canadian Senate and the House of Commons, Dec. 30, 1941.

Very heavy casualties in men and ships. Did everything possible to get men off but in order to get any home had to come to sad decision to abandon remainder. This was joint decision by Force Commanders. Obviously operation completely lacked surprise.
MAJOR-GENERAL J.H. ROBERTS, in a message conveyed by pigeon to the First Canadian Corps Headquarters after the raid on Dieppe, Aug. 19, 1942. Reproduced by C.P. Stacey in *Official History of the Canadian Army in the Second World War: Volume I* (1955).

The Canadian Army is a dagger pointed at the heart of Berlin.
GENERAL A. G. L. MCNAUGHTON, general officer commanding-in-chief and "the Father of the Canadian Army," at a press conference in Washington, Oct. 1942. Quoted by John Swettenham in *McNaughton* (1968–69), who explains that, by Oct. 1943, when the Canadian Army was sent to Italy instead of to Germany, the "famous dagger had become more handle than blade."

The world's memory of Canadians in battle is a bright memory. The Canadians in World War I seemed to shine out of the blood and muck, the dreary panorama of trench warfare. They seemed to kill and die with a special dash of lavishness.
GENERAL A.G.L. MCNAUGHTON, "the father of the Canadian Army," general officer commanding-in-chief, observation made in 1943.

This was my brother
At Dieppe,
Quietly a hero
Who gave his life
Like a gift,
Withholding nothing.
MONA GOULD, west-coast poet, in "This Was My Brother," *Tasting the Earth* (1943).

I also inspected a bombed-out hospital in Luetzow Street. Several corpses were just being carried out—a touching picture. One of the nurses killed was an air-raid warden. It drives one mad to think that any old Canadian boor, who probably can't even find Europe on the globe, flies to Europe from his super-rich country which his people don't know how to exploit, and here bombards a continent with a crowded population. But let's hope we can soon deliver the proper reply . . . .
JOSEPH GOEBBELS, German propaganda minister, Feb.–March 1943, in *The Goebbels Diaries* (1948), edited and translated by Louis P. Lochner.

This war is so much like the last one, it's not even funny.
GENERAL H.D.G. CRERAR to Lieutenant-General E.L.M. Burns when the latter assumed command of the Fifth Canadian Armoured Division in Italy, Jan. 1944. Quoted by

E.L.M. Burns in *General Mud* (1970).

This is the second time in the lifetime of most of us that the Germans have forced war upon the world. It is the second time that Canadians have crossed the Atlantic, leaving the fishing boats of British Columbia and Nova Scotia, the farms on the prairies, and the villages and towns of Ontario, and, if it is not the last, I think we shall all have to bear a certain amount of responsibility.

GILBERT HARDING, well-known English television personality, in an address to the Empire Club of Canada in 1944.

They are upon us, the prophets, minor and major!
Madame Yolanda rubs the foggy crystal.
She peers, she ponders, the future does engage her;
She sees the *Fuehrer* purged by Nazi pistol.

A.M. KLEIN, Montreal poet, opening lines of "Psalm XXV," *Poems* (1944). These lines were published a year before Hitler shot himself with a "Nazi pistol."

Can you blame me if I call this fantastic?
Paris is free. Paris is happy again.
This is Matthew Halton of the CBC speaking from France.

MATTHEW HALTON, CBC Radio's overseas correspondent, in a historic broadcast, Aug. 26, 1944.

Canada proved herself there [on the vast Western Front], and it could never be the same Canada again, as her subsequent history has already shown. Vimy Ridge was followed by Passchendaele and Amiens, to mention only the highlights. Canada had found her consciousness, found herself, and found her secure place in the great world. There her title-deeds to the future were written.

JAN CHRISTIAN SMUTS, prime minister of the Union of South Africa, in the foreword to *Arthur Currie* (1950), by Hugh M. Urquhart.

I remember in the war in Italy, we would creep through the darkness of the hills on night advances. The Italian villagers that we encountered would whisper: "Are you English?" "No." "Are you American?" "No." "Then who are you?" "Canadians,"

we would reply. That seemed to puzzle them.

BARON TWEEDSMUIR, son of John Buchan, Lord Tweedsmuir, who was governor general from 1935 to 1940, in an address to the Empire Club of Canada in 1961.

War Dead
See also EPITAPHS.

AUX BRAVES
TO THE BRAVE

Inscription on the monument erected in the Parc du Monument des Braves in Quebec City in 1860, to commemorate those French and British soldiers who died at the Battle of Sainte-Foy in 1760.

They served till death—why not we?

SIR ARTHUR CURRIE, First World War general, words inscribed on the replica of the Cross of Sacrifice erected to mark his gravesite in Mount Royal Cemetery, Montreal, reproduced by Herbert Fairlie Wood and John Swettenham in *Silent Witness* (1974).

In Flanders fields the poppies blow
Between the crosses, row on row,
  That mark our place; and in the sky
  The larks, still bravely singing, fly
Scarce heard amid the guns below.

We are the Dead. Short days ago
We lived, felt dawn, saw sunset glow,
  Loved and were loved, and now we lie
    In Flanders fields.

Take up our quarrel with the foe:
To you from failing hands we throw
  The torch; be yours to hold it high.
  If ye break faith with us who die
We shall not sleep, though poppies grow
    In Flanders fields.

JOHN MCCRAE, Guelph-born major and First Brigade surgeon in the Canadian Field Artillery, wrote "In Flanders Fields" in the early morning of May 3, 1915, during the second battle of Ypres, Belgium. The poem was written out of his personal sorrow, for that night he had buried a young friend, Lieutenant Alexis Helmer. McCrae published his poem in *Punch* on Dec. 8, 1915. He died in France of double pneumonia on Jan. 28, 1918. "In Flanders Fields" was recited as part of the official Armistice Day program on Nov. 11, 1918, and has since become an integral part of all Remembrance Day ceremonies in Canada.

We giving all gained all.
Neither lament us nor praise.
Only in all things recall,
It is Fear, not Death that slays.
*
From little towns in a far land we came,
To save our honour and a world aflame.
By little towns in a far land we sleep;
And trust that world we won for you to keep!

> RUDYARD KIPLING, British man-of-letters, from "Epitaphs of the War: 1914-18." These are called "Two Canadian Memorials." The first was commissioned for use in Sudbury but never used; the second was commissioned by James W. Curran and used on the Sault Ste. Marie war memorial. Text taken from *Rudyard Kipling's Verse* (1940).

They are too near
To be great
But our children
Shall understand
When and how our
Fate was changed
And by whose hand

> RUDYARD KIPLING composed the stately inscription on the wall of the Memorial Chamber of the Peace Tower of the Parliament Buildings in Ottawa. It is a reference to those who fought and died in World War One and in all other wars.

A CANADIAN SOLDIER OF THE GREAT WAR KNOWN UNTO GOD

> RUDYARD KIPLING chose these words for the Imperial War Graves Commission, which came into existence in May of 1917, for headstones of unknown Canadian soldiers who died in the First World War.

THEIR NAME LIVETH FOR EVERMORE
LEUR NOM VIVRA A JAMAIS

> RUDYARD KIPLING chose these words from Ecclesiastes to appear on the Stone of Remembrance that acts as the centrepiece in many Commonwealth cemeteries for the dead of the First and Second World Wars. Reproduced by Herbert Fairlie Wood and John Swettenham in *Silent Witness* (1974).

Weather

Fair weather to you and snow to your heels.

> Newfoundland expression, quoted by L.E.F. English in *Historic Newfoundland* (1960).

Man wants but little here below zero.

> BOB EDWARDS, writer and publisher of the Calgary *Eye Opener*, Feb. 4, 1905.

Canadians love to sit in the dark trembling with fear at weather forecasts.

> ROBERT MORLEY, British actor, interviewed on CBC-TV, in 1972.

You don't own the land. In winter, the elements own it, and in summer the mosquitoes.

> DON CURRIE, Toronto business executive, on July 18, 1973.

West, The

See also PRAIRIES.

I am told that you can come in on the train in the morning and start ploughing in the afternoon. I am told that some in this new country are not content, but you know, ladies and gentlemen, some of us will not be content in heaven if we hear of a place farther west.

> SIR JOHN A. MACDONALD, prime minister, on his first visit to Brandon, Man., about 1881. Quoted by Beechan Trotter in *A Horseman and the West* (1925).

The Last Best West, beyond which one cannot dream of anything better.
*
The world's bread basket is western Canada.

> SIR CLIFFORD SIFTON, minister of the Interior from 1896 to 1905, slogans associated with his vigorous immigration policy.

Ask why the eagle soars in air
Or builds so high his craggy nest,
Ask why the fishes love the sea—
Then ask me why I love the West.

> JOHN D. HIGINBOTHAM, writer and pioneer, quoted this ditty in *When the West Was Young* (1933).

The history of the West is a chronicle of

voyages, a ceaseless ebb and flow from east to west and west to east of human beings in search of fur, buffalo, land, wealth, salvation. The quest never ends. Waves of people wash across the prairies and disappear, cast up on the island promontories of the island cities or wrecked at last on the beaches of Vancouver where they spend the last days of their lives gazing wistfully out to sea.

> HEATHER ROBERTSON, writer, *Grass Roots* (1973).

I think of western skies as one of the most beautiful things about the West, and the western horizons. The Westerner doesn't have a point of view. He has a vast panorama; he has such tremendous space around him.

> MARSHALL McLUHAN, media pundit, interviewed by Danny Finkleman in *Speaking of Winnipeg* (1974), edited by John Parr.

Wheat
See also FARMING.

Raise less hell and more wheat!

> SIR W.C. VAN HORNE, railroad builder, to a delegation of Manitoba farmers demanding lower freight rates. The line was earlier attributed to Mary Lease, a populist leader in Kansas in the 1880s.

Granary of the Empire.

> JAMES A. SMART, civil servant, chose this as the motto of the prairie section of a display of Canadian products at an exhibition in London, England, 1901, according to William Thomas Preston in *My Generation of Politics and Politicians* (1927).

In China rice is life. In Canada life is wheat. We should throw wheat on our brides.

> EMILY GOWAN MURPHY, feminist writer, in *Janey Canuck in the West* (1910).

I say to the minister, and I say to this Government: Trust the people; the heart of the Canadian people is as sound as our No. 1 Hard Manitoba wheat.

> ANDREW ROSS McMASTER, prairie M.P., in the House of Commons, June 24, 1919.

Why should I sell the Canadian farmers'

wheat?

> PIERRE ELLIOTT TRUDEAU, prime minister, at a Liberal party gathering in Manitoba, on Dec. 13, 1968.

Winners
See also SUCCESS.

You can't beat winning.

> JOHN BASSETT III, filmmaker and son of the publisher of the Toronto *Telegram*, quoted by John Gault in *Toronto Life*, Nov. 1965.

Doesn't everyone expect to win?

> NANCY GREENE, British Columbia-born skier who won an Olympic gold medal at Grenoble in 1968, quoted by Rod McKuen in *The Will To Win* (1971).

You don't play a game to lose. You go out and you give your best to win.

> BOBBY HULL, hockey's "golden jet," in the *Canadian*, Sept. 7, 1974.

You don't have to win the race to have done well in the race.

> PAUL MARTIN, on losing the Liberal leadership to Pierre Elliott Trudeau in 1968, in a television interview, July 14, 1975.

Winnipeg

So this is Winnipeg; I can tell it's not Paris.

> BOB EDWARDS, writer and publisher of the Calgary *Eye Opener* from 1902 to 1922, on arriving in Winnipeg, Sept. 12, 1894.

Winnipeg has Things in abundance, but has learned to put them beneath her feet, not on top of her mind, and so is older than many cities . . . . She is a little too modest.

> RUDYARD KIPLING, British man-of-letters in *Letters to the Family* (1908), reprinted in *Letters of Travel 1892–1913* (1920).

"Winnipeg!" the manager said in disbelief and derision. "How do they get there—by dog sled? What do they play in—an igloo?"

> RUTH HARVEY, famous actress who toured Canada, from her autobiography, *Curtain Time* (1949).

Boy Meets Girl in Winnipeg and Who

Cares?

> HUGH MACLENNAN, Montreal novelist, an essay title, from *Scotchman's Return and Other Essays* (1960).

This is the value of Winnipeg—you can still be a *Mensch*, which is a Jewish word for being a man, but it means more than that. It's very difficult to be a *Mensch* in a lot of places in the world today. But to be a man is to create, to bring changes about, to better the world and to maintain this inborn optimism that every human being has.

> JOHN HIRSCH, prominent director, interviewed by Danny Finkleman in *Speaking of Winnipeg* (1974), edited by John Parr.

People change, people come, people go, people die. But the Golden Boy is like Keats' Nightingale. Something so fixed it seems eternal, almost immortal.

> JACK LUDWIG, Winnipeg-born novelist, reacting to the gilt statue of a little boy atop the provincial Parliament buildings, in an interview with Terry Campbell in *Speaking of Winnipeg* (1974), edited by John Parr.

Winter
See SEASONS.

Wisdom
See also IDEAS.

The value of experience is not in seeing much, but in seeing wisely.

*

Look wise, say nothing, and grunt. Speech was given to conceal thought.

> SIR WILLIAM OSLER, world-famous physician and medical teacher, about 1900, in *Sir William Osler: Aphorisms from His Bedside Teachings and Writings* (1950), edited by W.B. Bean.

Some people might just as well be crazy for all the sense they have.

> BOB EDWARDS, writer and publisher of the Calgary *Eye Opener*, May 11, 1918.

Doubt is the beginning, not the end, of wisdom.

> GEORGE ILES, science writer, in *Canadian Stories* (1918).

There must somewhere have been an ancient Chinese philosopher who said, "The

summit of human wisdom is to know the exact shade of grey to wear on any particular occasion."

> SIR ROBERT WATSON-WATT, the radar pioneer who spent the postwar years in Thornhill, Ontario, in *Three Steps to Victory* (1957).

Wisdom is a variable possession. Every man is wise when pursued by a mad dog; fewer when pursued by a mad woman; only the wisest survive when attacked by a mad notion.

> ROBERTSON DAVIES, man-of-letters, in *Marchbanks' Almanack* (1967).

The day the child realizes that all adults are imperfect he becomes an adolescent; the day he forgives them, he becomes an adult; the day he forgives himself he becomes wise.

> ALDEN NOWLAN, poet and writer, in "Scratchings," *Between Tears and Laughter* (1971).

Wit
See HUMOUR.

Wolfe, James
See also CONQUEST OF 1759.

Mad is he? Then I hope he will bite some others of my generals.

> GEORGE II, king of Great Britain and Ireland, to the Duke of Newcastle in 1758, when the duke objected to the appointment of James Wolfe to command the expedition against Quebec. Quoted by Francis Parkman in *Montcalm and Wolfe* (1884), who observed: "Appointments made for merit, and not through routine and patronage, shocked the Duke of Newcastle, to whom a man like Wolfe was a hopeless enigma; and he told George II that Pitt's new general was mad."

Gentlemen, I would rather have written those lines than take Quebec tomorrow.

> MAJOR-GENERAL JAMES WOLFE, leader of the British forces at Quebec, the night before his famous assault of Sept. 12, 1759, recited Gray's "Elegy, Written in a Country Churchyard," and then made the above remark. Tradition has it that he lingered over the fourth line in the stanza below:

The boast of heraldry, the pomp of power,
  And all that beauty, all that wealth e'er gave,

Awaits alike th' inevitable hour:
The paths of glory lead but to the grave.
Eighteen hours later Wolfe was dead on the
Plains of Abraham. Quoted by Francis Park-
man in *Montcalm and Wolfe* (1884).

"There's no need," he answered; "it's all
over with me." A moment after, one of
them cried out: "They run; see how they
run!" "Who run?" Wolfe demanded, like a
man roused from sleep. "The enemy, sir.
Egad, they give way everywhere!" "Go,
one of you, to Colonel Burton," returned
the dying man; "tell him to march Webb's
regiment down to Charles River, to cut off
their retreat from the bridge." Then, turning on his side, he murmured, "Now, God
be praised, I will die in peace!" and in a
few moments his gallant soul had fled.
    JAMES WOLFE, the British commander, on be-
ing asked if he, then dying on the Plains of Abraham, needed a surgeon. From Francis Parkman in *Montcalm and Wolfe* (1884).

Here Died
WOLFE
Victorious
Sept. 13
1759
    Original inscription on Wolfe's Monument. A
memorial was erected in 1832 to mark the spot
where Wolfe fell on the Plains of Abraham,
the above inscription being added in 1849.
Someone effaced the inscription. When the
monument was replaced the word "victorious"
was found to be missing. *The Canadian Portrait
Gallery* (1880-81), by John Charles Dent.

He raiséd his head
Where the guns did rattle,
And to his aid he said,
    "How goes the battle?"
"Quebec is all our own,
They can't prevent it."
He said without a groan,
    "I die contented."
    Final verse of "Brave Wolfe" (1760s), from
Ballads and Sea-Songs of Newfoundland (1933),
edited by E.B. Greenleaf and G.Y. Mansfield.

In days of yore, from Britain's shore,
Wolfe, the dauntless hero, came,
And planted firm Britannia's flag
On Canada's fair domain.
    ALEXANDER MUIR, Toronto school teacher,

from "The Maple Leaf Forever," written in
1867.

Wolves
See also ANIMALS.

The story of Little Red Riding Hood has
laid an unreasoning fear on countless millions of human beings.
                    *
There are, of course, several things in Ontario that are more dangerous than wolves.
For instance, the step-ladder.
                    *
Any man that says he's been et by a wolf is
a liar.
    J.W. CURRAN, publisher of the Sault Ste. Ma-
rie *Daily Star*, in *Wolves Don't Bite* (1940). The
"et by a wolf" quote, which had quite a vogue,
Curran attributes to a hunter he calls "Old
Sam Martin."

Women
See also FEMINISM; MANKIND; MEN AND
WOMEN; WOMEN AND THE LAW.

"Women," added he, "were made for labour; one of them can carry, or haul, as
much as two men can do. They also pitch
our tents, make and mend our clothing,
keep us warm at night; and, in fact, there
is no such thing as travelling any consider-
able distance, or for any length of time, in
this country, without their assistance.
Women," said he again, "though they do
every thing, are maintained at trifling ex-
pence; for as they always stand cook, the
very licking of their fingers in scarce times,
is sufficient for their subsistence."
    SAMUEL HEARNE, Hudson's Bay Company ex-
plorer, in *A Journey from Prince of Wales's Fort in
Hudson's Bay, to the Northern Ocean* (1795). The
text is taken from *A Journey from Prince of
Wales's Fort* (1958), edited by Richard Glover.
The speaker is Matonabbee, Hearne's Chippe-
wyan guide, who had eight wives, all with him
on this trek across the Barren Lands in Oct.
1770.

The girls at *Montreal* are very much dis-
pleased that those at *Quebec* get husbands
sooner than they. The reason for this is,
that many young gentlemen who come
over from *France* with the ships, are capti-

vated by the ladies at *Quebec*, and marry them; but as these gentlemen seldom go up to *Montreal*, the girls there are not often so happy as those of the former place.

PETER KALM, Swedish-born traveller and botanist, in *Travels into North America* (1770-71), translated from the Swedish by J.R. Forster.

I have not often in my life met with contented and cheerful-minded women, but I never met with so many repining and discontented women as in Canada. I never met with *one* woman recently settled here, who considered herself happy in her new home and country: I *heard* of one, and doubtless there are others, but they are exceptions to the general rule.

ANNA JAMESON, British writer, in *Winter Studies and Summer Rambles in Canada* (1838).

Woman has had, from creation, distinctly defined duties, and until the power of education and influence is brought to bear upon these duties, and she has demonstrated her ability to do her own work well, she has no right to infringe on man's prerogative.

ADELAIDE HOODLESS, founder of the Federated Women's Institutes of Canada, in *Women Workers of Canada* (1902).

A nation cannot rise above the level of its homes, therefore, women must work and study together to raise our homes to the highest possible level.

ADELAIDE HOODLESS, early feminist, quoted by Ruth Howes in *The Clear Spirit* (1966), edited by Mary Quayle Innis.

Woman is a species of which every woman is a variety.

*

All women are rivals.

*

More women are wooed for their complexions than for their characters.

*

Widows rarely choose unwisely!

ARNOLD HAULTAIN, writer and aphorist who was Goldwin Smith's private secretary, in *Hints for Lovers* (1909).

Men continually study women, and know nothing about them. Women never study

men, and know all about them. [Oct. 15, 1910]

*

If a man understands one woman he should let it go at that. [Jan. 13, 1912]

*

A woman is more influenced by what she suspects than by what she knows. [Nov. 3, 1917]

*

If a girl has a pretty face, no man on earth can tell what kind of clothes she has on. [Oct. 5, 1918]

BOB EDWARDS, writer and publisher of the Calgary *Eye Opener* from 1902 to 1922.

It took the sea a thousand years,
A thousand years to trace
The granite features of this cliff,
In crag and scarp and base.

It took the sea an hour one night,
An hour of storm to place
The sculpture of these granite seams
Upon a woman's face.

E.J. PRATT, epic poet, from "Erosion" (1932), *The Collected Poems of E.J. Pratt* (second ed., 1958), edited by Northrop Frye.

Canada is destined to be one of the great nations of the world and Canadian women must be ready for citizenship. No nation ever rises higher than its women and that's why I must go on.

NELLIE MCCLUNG, pioneer feminist, in *The Stream Runs Fast* (1945).

We remain the most inert, in the consciousness or use of our power, of women in nations the world over.

CHARLOTTE WHITTON, first woman mayor of Ottawa, in "Women the World Over," *Chatelaine*, Sept. 1946.

Whatever women do they must do twice as well as men to be thought half so good . . . luckily, it's not difficult.

*

Call me anything you like, but don't call me a lady.

CHARLOTTE WHITTON, once described as "hell on wheels," characteristic remarks.

There are three sexes. Men and women and husbands' wives.

MADAME THÉRÈSE-FORGET CASGRAIN, former Quebec Cabinet minister, quoted by Lotta Dempsey in the Toronto *Star*, March 22, 1968.

It's marvellous being a woman in Toronto; you get to meet so many interesting women.

RICHARD J. NEEDHAM, Toronto columnist, in *A Friend in Needham, or a Writer's Notebook* (1969).

Some women are buried in coffins, but the majority are buried in bungalows.

RICHARD J. NEEDHAM, from "A Writer's Notebook," his column in the *Globe and Mail*, April 28, 1972.

Hustle grain, not women.

Wording on placards carried by feminists parading before Prime Minister Pierre Elliott Trudeau in Vancouver, Aug. 8, 1969.

Women take it for granted that it's a splendid achievement to have a sparkling toilet bowl.

DR. ESTHER GREENGLASS, Toronto academic, quoted by Carroll Allen in *Homemaker's Digest*, May-June 1972.

Woman is an oyster, with perils.

RAYMOND CANALE, Italian-born playwright living in Toronto, in 1975.

God may look after the working girl but he doesn't spoil her rotten.

BEVERLEY SLOPEN, Toronto writer, in *Maclean's*, Feb. 1975.

Asking why there are so few great women artists is like asking why there aren't any Eskimo tennis stars or Lithuanian jazz musicians.

MARYON KANTAROFF, sculptor, quoted in *Communiqué*, May 1975.

For generations, women have been relegated to the biological beat—bed, board, and babies.

LAURA SABIA, chairwoman of the Ontario Advisory Council on the Status of Women, quoted in 1975.

Women and the Law
See also ABORTION; VOTE; WOMEN.

If women keep on demanding a vote, cropping their hair, opposing us in the professions, wearing our coats, hats and shirts, and if men continue nursing babies, promoting female dress reform, and using curling tongs, first thing we know there will be a blurred line denoting a merging of the sexes. That would be a fine development in human anatomy with which to mark the close of the nineteenth century.

EDMUND E. SHEPPARD, founder and editor of *Saturday Night*, May 13, 1893.

There is one thing you have forgotten in your deliberations and that is justice to women. I hope that at your future meetings you will give more attention to the cause of women. That is all I have to say.

OLIVIA SMITH, an Englishwoman and militant suffragette, rose from the gallery and then made the above statement, as the lieutenant-governor was about to prorogue the Ontario legislature on March 19, 1910. She made a quick exit and was never heard from again. "Women's Work and the Public Policy in Canada," *The Canadian Annual Review of Public Affairs, 1910* (1911), edited by J. Castell Hopkins.

I am opposed by all the short-haired women and the long-haired men in the province.

SIR RODMOND P. ROBLIN, premier of Manitoba, criticizing the women's suffragette movement in 1912. According to Henry F. Woods in *American Sayings* (1945), the phrase "long-haired men and short-haired women" was fairly common in the United States in the 1920s.

What in the world do women want to vote for? Why do women want to mix in the hurly-burly of politics? My mother was the best woman in the world, and she certainly never wanted to vote!

SIR RODMOND P. ROBLIN, premier of Manitoba, when Nellie L. McClung was soliciting his support for the Winnipeg Political Equality League, Jan. 1914. Quoted by Nellie McClung in *The Stream Runs Fast* (1945).

If democracy is right, women should have it. If it isn't, men shouldn't.

MAY CLENDENAN, prairie feminist, in the *Grain Growers' Guide*, Feb. 24, 1915. Quoted by Catherine Lyle Cleverdon in *The Woman Suffrage Movement in Canada* (1950).

Heckler: Don't you wish you were a man?

Macphail: Yes. Don't you?

AGNES MACPHAIL, first woman elected to the House of Commons (1921–1940), a well-known riposte attributed to her, quoted by Margaret Stewart and Doris French in *Ask No Quarter* (1959).

Their Lordships are of opinion that the word "persons" in s. 24 does include women, and that women are eligible to be summoned to and become members of the Senate of Canada . . . .

Landmark decision in the "Persons" case, handed down by Lord Sankey, lord chancellor of the Privy Council of Great Britain, Oct. 18, 1929. The case is entitled "Henrietta Muir Edwards and Others *v.* Attorney-General for Canada (1929)." The five women behind this case were all from Alberta: Emily Murphy, Nellie McClung, Louise McKinney, Irene Parlby, Henrietta Edwards. *The Woman Suffrage Movement in Canada* (1950), by Catherine Lyle Cleverdon. *Historical Documents of Canada: Volume V* (1972), edited by C.P. Stacey.

Well, before the ladies sit here with us, I hope a new style of hats will have been introduced.

SIR THOMAS CHAPAIS, Quebec legislator and historian, on the third reading of the suffrage bill to give Quebec women the vote, April 25, 1940. Quoted by Catherine Lyle Cleverdon in *The Woman Suffrage Movement in Canada* (1950).

If there were enough women in Parliament, the health ministry would become more important than that of finance.

DR. GORDON BATES, director of the Health League of Canada, paraphrase of a remark made in 1941, quoted by Catherine Lyle Cleverdon in *The Woman Suffrage Movement in Canada* (1950).

Women's Liberation Movement

See FEMINISM; WOMEN.

Wonder

My Mary, there are no mysteries—only wonders.

JAMES EVANS, pioneer missionary, to his wife about 1846, quoted by Nan Shipley in *The James Evans Story* (1966).

In the wide awe and wisdom of the night
I saw the round world rolling on its way,
Beyond significance of depth or height,
Beyond the interchange of dark and day.

SIR CHARLES G.D. ROBERTS, poet and writer, opening lines of "In the Wide Awe and Wisdom of the Night" (1893), *Selected Poetry and Critical Prose* (1974), edited by W.J. Keith.

I shall not wonder more, then,
But I shall know.
Leaves change, and birds, flowers,
And after years are still the same.

RAYMOND KNISTER, poet, in "Change," *Collected Poems* (1949).

We grow to one world
Through enlargement of wonder.

F.R. SCOTT, Montreal man-of-letters, in "A Grain of Rice" (1954), from *Selected Poems* (1966).

Everything has its astonishing, wondrous aspect, if you bring a mind to it that's really your own.

ROBERTSON DAVIES, man-of-letters, in *World of Wonders* (1975).

Work

It is a good country for the honest, industrious artisan. It is a fine country for the poor labourer who, after a few years of hard toil, can sit down in his own log-house and look abroad on his own land and see his children well settled in life as independent freeholders. It is a grand country for the rich speculator who can afford to lay out a large sum in purchasing land in eligible situations; for if he have any judgment he will make a hundred per cent as interest for his money after waiting a few years. But it is a hard country for the poor gentleman whose habits have rendered him unfit for manual labour.

CATHARINE PARR TRAILL, pioneer author, a conversation between "a very fine lady" and "the son of a naval officer of some rank in the service busily employed in making an axe-handle out of a piece of rock-elm," in *The Backwoods of Canada* (1836).

Work! for the night is coming;
Work! through the morning hours;
Work! while the dew is sparkling;
Work! 'mid the springing flowers;
Work! while the day grows brighter,
Under the glowing sun;
Work! for the night is coming;
Night, when man's work is done.
ANNIE LOUISA (WALKER) COGHILL wrote the poem "The Night Cometh," on which the popular hymn "Work! For the Night Is Coming" is based. The poem was published anonymously in Montreal in a book of verses called *Leaves from the Backwoods* (1861). In her second book, *Oak and Maple* (1890), she expressed her surprise on finding her lyrics in Moody and Sankey's hymn-book.

Here's to the land of forests grand,
The land where labour's free;
Let others roam away from home,
Be this the land for me!
For here 'tis plain the heart and brain,
The very soul, grow vaster,
Where men are free as they should be,
And Jack's as good's his master.
ALEXANDER McLACHLAN, folk poet, final stanza of "Young Canada, or Jack's as Good's His Master," *The Emigrant, and Other Poems* (1861).

If you would meet your debts you must doff the broadcloth and don the overalls.
JOHN OLIVER, premier of British Columbia from 1918 to 1927, quoted by James Morton in *Honest John Oliver* (1933).

It is not within the power of the properly constructed human mind to be satisfied. Progress would cease if this were the case. The greatest joy of life is to accomplish. It is the getting, not the having. It is the giving, not the keeping. I am a firm believer in the theory that you can do or be anything that you wish in this world, within reason, if you are prepared to make the sacrifices, think and work hard enough and long enough.
SIR FREDERICK G. BANTING, medical researcher and discoverer of insulin, in an article in 1940, quoted by Lloyd Stevenson in *Sir Frederick Banting* (1946).

Paper has a genius for multiplication that

cannot be equalled anywhere else in nature.
HUGH L. KEENLEYSIDE, former External Affairs officer, to the board of Oxfam-Canada, Toronto, Sept. 24, 1972.

Work is what we have to do: play is what we like to do.
HANS SELYE, Montreal "stress" researcher, in the Toronto *Star*, Dec. 6, 1972.

There's no end, no end, to the big things that got to be done in Canada. But, damn it, you've got to work.
MARGARET "MA" MURRAY, pioneer newspaperwoman, on CBC-TV, June 3, 1975.

World

Taking things philosophically is easy if they don't concern you.
BOB EDWARDS, writer and publisher of the Calgary *Eye Opener*, April 3, 1915.

The world has drifted far from its old anchorage and no man can with certainty prophesy what the outcome will be.
SIR ROBERT BORDEN, prime minister, in his diary, Nov. 11, 1918, from *Robert Laird Borden* (1938), edited by Henry Borden.

One ending would be about as good as another for the fiasco of this world.
MAURICE HUTTON, educator, in an address to the Canadian Club of Toronto, Feb. 26, 1923.

We live in a damned wicked world, and the fewer we praise the better.
WILLIAM KIRBY, novelist and publisher of the Niagara *Mail*, quoted by Martin Burrell in *Betwixt Heaven and Charing Cross* (1928).

We must see the world as it is, if we are to have a world at all.
JAMES EAYRS, political scientist and author, in "Nuclear Dilemmas" (1960), *Northern Approaches* (1961).

The world around us is quite as senseless and unreadable as the *Encyclopaedia Britannica*. We have to make it up as we go along.
KILDARE DOBBS, Anglo-Irish author, in the introduction to *Reading the Time* (1968).

Worry

Without our cares our joys would be less lively.

CATHARINE PARR TRAILL, pioneer writer, in *Canadian Crusoes* (1850).

We spend our lives preparing for delights which don't come, and recovering from disasters which do.

RICHARD J. NEEDHAM, from "A Writer's Notebook," his column in the Toronto *Globe and Mail*, May 25, 1971.

Writers and Writing

See also LITERATURE; PLAYWRIGHTS.

Then hail to the chiefs of thought
  Who wield the mighty pen
That light may at last be brought
  To the darken'd souls of men,—
To the soldiers of the right,
  To the heroes of the true,—
Oh, ours were a sorry plight,
  Great conquerors, but for you!

ALEXANDER MCLACHLAN, folk poet, in the last stanza of "Heroes," *The Poetical Works* (1900), edited in 1974 by E. Margaret Fulton.

Style! I have no style. I merely wait till the mud settles.

GOLDWIN SMITH, British-born journalist, in May 1904, quoted by Arnold Haultain in *Goldwin Smith* (1913).

Personally, I would sooner have written *Alice in Wonderland* than the whole *Encyclopedia Britannica*.

STEPHEN LEACOCK, renowned writer and humorist, in *Sunshine Sketches of a Little Town* (1912).

You just jot down ideas as they occur to you. The jotting is simplicity itself—it is the occurring which is difficult.

STEPHEN LEACOCK, humorist and historian, attributed.

There are two kinds of writers: the one who tries to see the world out of his own eyes and the other one, the commercial writer, who tries to see the world out of the eyes of others.

*

There is only one trait that marks the writ-

er. He is always watching. It's a trick of mind and he is born with it.

MORLEY CALLAGHAN, Toronto writer and author, at the Canadian Writers' Conference, Queen's University, July 28–31, 1955, in "Novelist," *Writing in Canada* (1956), edited by George Whalley.

An editor is blessed with the talent of others.

ROBERT ZEND, Hungarian-born Toronto writer, in the 1960s.

A short time ago Morley Callaghan and I were talking typical writers' talk—about our current work, critics, publishers, other writers and what they were doing. Before we parted Callaghan said, "Being a Canadian writer is tough, isn't it?" I answered, "Well, it beats working in a pickle factory."

HUGH GARNER, Toronto writer, in "My First Hundred Years as a Writer," *Canadian Weekly*, Dec. 29, 1962.

The trouble with being a freelance writer is that if you take an extra half-hour for lunch, you think you are starving to death.

JOCK CARROLL, freelance writer, in 1965.

The Canadian Morley Callaghan, at one time well known in the United States, is today perhaps the most unjustly neglected novelist in the English-speaking world.
                                    *
The reviewer, at the end of this article, after trying to give an account of these books, is now wondering whether the primary reason for the current underestimation of Morley Callaghan may not be simply a general incapacity—apparently shared by his compatriots—for believing that a writer whose work may be mentioned without absurdity in association with Chekhov's and Turgenev's can possibly be functioning in Toronto.

EDMUND WILSON, American literary critic, in *O Canada* (1965).

Publication is a self-invasion of privacy.

MARSHALL MCLUHAN, media pundit, in *Counterblast* (1969).

It's easy to produce writers, but a public is much harder to come by.

MARSHALL MCLUHAN, media theorist, interviewed by Linda Sandler in *Miss Chatelaine*, Sept. 3, 1974.

Fundamentally, all writing is about the same thing: it's about dying, about the brief flicker of time we have here, and the frustrations that it creates.
MORDECAI RICHLER, Montreal novelist, quoted in *Time*, May 31, 1971.

It is not generally understood that most writing takes place away from the typewriter. When you finally approach the machine, it is really the beginning of the end. Nine-tenths of your work has already been done; it remains to put on paper what you have already created. It is this creative process that takes most of the time.
PIERRE BERTON, author and TV personality, in *Maclean's*, Oct. 7, 1971.

I think of an author as somebody who goes into the marketplace and puts down his rug and says, "I will tell you a story" and then passes the hat. And when he's taken up his collection, he tells his story, and just before the dénouement he passes the hat again. If it's worth anything, fine. If not, he ceases to be an author. He does not apply for a Canada Council grant.
ROBERTSON DAVIES, man-of-letters, in "The Master's Voice: The Table Talk of Robertson Davies," quoted by Peter C. Newman in *Maclean's*, Sept. 1972.

. . . the tested formula for becoming rich as an author is to write regularly to an uncle who is dying from a surfeit of oil wells.
ERIC NICOL, Vancouver humorist, in *One Man's Media—and How to Write for Them* (1973).

Every writer must eventually write his Ninth Symphony or give in to despair.
GABRIELLE ROY, Quebec novelist, in a letter of Aug. 1, 1973, quoted by Joan Hind-Smith in *Three Voices* (1975).

What we need is a Jewish-Canadian writer who's gay—or lesbian—named Ted, or Edwina, that would cover all the bases, eh?
MICHAEL HANLON, Toronto journalist, in Dec. 1974.

Youth
See also AGE.

Youth is the time for improvement.
THOMAS CHANDLER HALIBURTON, Nova Scotian satirist and judge, in *Sam Slick* (1836).

I wandered today to the hill, Maggie,
  To watch the scene below,
The creek and the creaking old mill, Maggie,
  As we used to long ago.
The green grove is gone from the hill,
  Maggie,
  Where first the daisies sprung,
The creeking old mill is still, Maggie,
  Since you and I were young.
GEORGE WASHINGTON JOHNSON, an Ontario schoolteacher, fell in love with a student, Maggie Clark, and wrote the love ballad, "When You and I Were Young," which he published in *Maple Leaves* (1864). Two years later an English composer living in Chicago, J.A. Butterfield, set the poem to music, and it became famous throughout the English-speaking world.

You realize that youth is not a vanished thing but something that dwells forever in the heart.
L.M. MONTGOMERY, author of *Anne of Green Gables* (1908), attributed.

Yukon Territory
See also GOLD RUSH.

This is the Law of the Yukon, that only the
  Strong shall thrive;
That surely the Weak shall perish, and
  only the Fit survive.
Dissolute, damned and despairful, crippled
  and palsied and slain,
This is the Will of the Yukon,—Lo, how
  she makes it plain!
ROBERT SERVICE, "the poet of the Yukon," in the final stanza of "The Law of the Yukon." From *The Spell of the Yukon and Other Verses* (1907); *The Complete Poems of Robert Service* (1944).

INDEX

The letter *a* or *b* after the page number indicates the left- or right-hand column of the page on which the complete quotation may be found.

Byron, Lord
a small drop of ink, 157a

C

Cable, Howard
beaver busy chewing, 19a

Cabot, John
terra primum vista, 155b

Cahan, Charles H.
a continuing Conservative, 60b
no reciproclty made in, 188a

Cahill, Jack
job of a journalist, 116a

Callaghan, Morley
of adventure in reading, 22b
new beauty, changing face, 31a
they'll discover it's Canadian, 152b
two kinds of writers, 237a
he is always watching, 237b

Callwood, June
no one for abortion, 10a
priorities discard children, 10a
reverence for life, 10a
maternal dislike, crippling, 142a

Cameron, Donald
Vancouver, dreams move, 221b

Camp, Dalton
Why Not?, 84a
world's finest whorehouse, 116a
politics, of irrelevancies, 177a

Campbell, Clarence
without violence, hockey, 222a

Campbell, William Wilfred
Vaster Britain, 35a
damned by too much government, 96a
along the line of smoky, 195b

Canale, Raymond
a man's heart melts, 100b
love, hours written, 130b
woman's sexual abandonment, 199a
woman is an oyster, 234a

Caouette, Réal
five years, bilingual, 21a
children of homosexual, 133b
important things, survival, 133b
what have you got to lose, 201a
don't have to understand, 201a

Capilano, Joe
we Indians have lost, 111b

Capone, Al
what street Canada on, 63b

Carleton, Sir Guy
populated to the end of time, 89b
nothing to fear, to hope, 89b
U.E., U.E.L., 130b

Carlyle, Thomas
shooting Niagara, 159a

Carmack, G.W.
I do, locate, claim, 94a

Carman, Bliss
success in silences, 16a
day to search for God, 93b
years or lives ago, 126a
greatest joy in nature, 153a
beautiful ships, long ago, 199a
tradition, persecutions, 214a
here in Vancouver on, 221a

Carnarvon, Lord
the term dominion, 71a

Caron, Sir Joesph
what the Canadian militia, 223a

Carpenter, Edmund
art in Aivilik, 16b
Eskimo sings of life, 79a
in Eskimo, anerca, soul, 174a

Carr, Emily
movement essence of being, 67a
years, little years, 78a
draw a line around think, 167b
forest, so full of silence, 200a

Carroll, Jock
being freelance writer, 237b

Carson, Johnny
Air Canada, good name, 17b

Carter, Kenneth
a buck is a buck, 85b

Cartier, Sir George-Etienne
call in de membres, 106b
an Englishman who speaks, 121b
O Canada, mon pays, 150a
Avant tout je suis, 150a

Cartier, Jacques
land God gave to Cain, 44b
ready way to Canada, 44b

Index

too much dignity in, 96a
virtuous nor contemptible, 124b

Herbert, A.P.
Labrador, old-age pension, 119b
Britain gave to Canada, 119b
all crafts except political, 156b

Herodotus
region excessively hard, 15a

Herridge, W.H.
purpose of life, economic, 74a

Herzberg, Gerhard
we support basic research, 195a

Hewitt, Foster
he shoots, he scores, 104b

Hiawatha
have a league of nations, 111a

Hiebert, Paul
the farmer is king, 83a

Higinbotham, John D.
why I love the West, 229b

Hill, Joe
where Fraser River flows, 219a

Hind, Henry Youle
paradise of fertility, 194b

Hind-Smith, Michael
our strong U.S. imports, 208a

Hindmarsh, Harry Comfort
world news is Canadian, 157b
punch in every paragraph, 157b

Hirsch, John
Winnipeg, be a mensch, 231a

Hitler, Adolf
how stupidly one managed, 172b

Hoffman, Abby
Olympics, vision of humanity, 165b

Hofsess, John
Canada's film culture, 85a
difficulty, word love, 130b

Hogg, Corporal C.
against sections 105 and, 192a

Hollander, Xaviera
more money vertically, 182a
Oshawa needs, brothel, 182a

every appeal except sex, 199a
never wanted to be a, 199a

Holloway, Stanley
no laughs or applause, 209b

Holton, Luther H.
John A. beats the devil, 131b

Honderich, Beland
need are more antidotes, 133a
nobody is bigger than, 158b

Hood, Hugh
Un-Canadianism, definition, 41b

Hoodless, Adelaide
for home and country, 105a
woman, distinctively defined, 233a
above level of its homes, 233a

Hope, Bob
a great town here if, 213a

Hopkins, J. Castell
only needs to be known, 214a

Hornby, Sir Edmund
Canadians, Turks, cash, 169b

Hornby, John
land of feast and famine, 162b

Horowitz, Gad
Red Tory, 176b
socialist, look southward, 202b

Horqarnaq
hard to speak the truth, 216b

Horton, A.L.
say it, shut up, sit down, 203a

Houde, Camillien
armaments, decorations, 59a
legend than into history, 102b
Montreal is wide-open, 141b
you know, your Majesty, 193a
to kick your balls off, 212b

Houston, James
arctic carvings, passionate, 79a

Howe, C.D.
sit in the House, 107a
who would stop us, 107a
what's a million, 107a
the taxpayer's pocket, 107a
I'm busier'n a whore, 107a
just give responsibilities, 107a

no time for frivolous, 161b

Laurence, Margaret
not yet totally alienated, 59b

Laurendeau, André
doubt that death is real, 67a
not so scrootchy, joual, 115a
joual instead of cheval, 115b
so the language will die, 115b
get the nigger-king, 184a
Canada, worth a royal, 192b

Laurier, Sir Wilfrid
Empire a galaxy of, 25b
France, political sentiment, 32a
Englishman, own opinions, 32a
never thinks of feelings, 32a
parallel, separate, 32a
England advance, recede, 34b
Canada first, last, always, 38b
going to ride that railway, 39b
traitor, jingoist, separatist, 40b
colony yet a nation, 52b
have opinions, sentiments, 89a
legislate against geography, 93a
difficult country to govern, 95b
not based on idealism, 108b
splendidly, dangerously isolated, 114a
eternal principles of justice, 116b
c'est fini, 123a
born on the banks of, 123b
British to the core, 123b
Laurier and the larger, 123b
excommunicated by the, 123b
follow my white plume, 124b
I have outlived Liberalism, 125a
marble to remain marble, 144a
Ottawa not a handsome, 166b
good principles organization, 172b
twentieth century belongs to, 217a
friendship, American, 220a
want us to help you, 224a
so Canada is at war, 224a
ready, aye, ready, 224a

Laut, Agnes
what is conservation 59a
the hereafter, Cree, 100b

Law, Andrew Bonar
if I am a great man, 101a
you are a curious fellow, 123a
I must follow them, 124a
if war comes it will, 222b

Lawrence, James
to give up the ship, 225a

Layton, Irving
bourgeoisie, revolutionary, 51b

death, beauty not in use, 67b
tell them they are free, 88a
envy the happiness of, 99a
idealist, cynic in the, 108b
Ireland is the Israel, 114a
Jew is neither a race, 115a
sing about life, understand, 126b
her devotion to literature, 127b
stopped being a misanthrope, 134b
Channukah lights, going out, 141b
nationalism, a snarl wrapped, 152a
poem is an Alka-Seltzer, 173a
happiest when I compose, 173a
as a mouth I serve, 173b
aphorism should be a burr, 185b
a dull people, rivers, 191a
Canadian, Socialist, 202b
time, small change of, 210b
leader worthy of assassination, 216a

Leacock, Stephen
advertising is arresting, 12a
old age better than death, 13a
believed in Santa Claus, 48a
Mariposa not real town, 48b
founding university, smoking, 52a
McGill, Queen's, Toronto, 52a
colonial status worn-out, 53a
detest life-insurance agents, 67a
apprehension from economists, 74b
political economy because, 74b
go into a bank, rattled, 85a
brambles, was history, 102b
rode madly off in all, 106a
humour, hyperbole, myosis, 108a
has no sense of humour, 108a
essence is human kindliness, 108a
contemplation, incongruities, 108a
English, Scotch, American, 121b
a great believer in luck, 131a
in love with a dimple, 135b
Ukrainians, battle of Trafalgar, 144b
prohibit the use of alcohol, 181b
to this retirement business, 189b
there be wheat, Saskatchewan, 194b
angels, no doubt, socialists, 202a
socialism, communism, bathroom, 202a
won't work in Heaven where, 202a
quit, quit at once, 205a
education has fitted me, 207a
Toronto, McGill University, 212b
have written *Alice in*, 237a
jot down ideas as they, 237a

Lead, Graham
war on poverty, Gaglardi, 177b

LeBlanc, Larry
a naked Anne Murray, 146a

Lee, Dennis

French Canada, Siberian, 89a
great library, necropolis, 125b
above all nations, humanity, 134a
common life, sentiments, 151b
Ottawa, sub-arctic lumber, 166b
rich by nature, poor, 172a
politics, noblest, meanest, 176b
always politics, 176b
really resolute quoter, 185b
for Conservatives to conserve, 188b
romantic age, science, 194b
I have no style, 237a

Smith, John
born man, died grocer, 78b

Smith, Olivia
justice to women, 234b

Smith, Ray
continent of Cape Breton, 163b

Smuts, Jan Christian
transformed the structure, 25b
title-deeds to the future, 228a

Smythe, Conn
lick'em in the alley, 221b

Snookum Jim
and I shot him, 63a

Soles, Paul
he who laughs, lasts, 108a

Souster, Raymond
a tree, in Sudbury, 215b

Sparshott, Francis
trivialities, emotional, 171b

Spicer, Keith
Westmount Rhodesians, 141b

Spraggett, Allan
too amazing to be true, 216b

Spry, Graham
without communication, society, 54a
defeated by large and, 76b
the State or the U.S., 186a

Stacey, C.P.
an unmilitary community, 223b

Stanfield, Robert L.
I represent help for, 76b
States has no place in, 181a
I speak too fast for, 197b

Starnes, Richard

indistinguishable, Americans, 37a

Steacie, E.W.
of a classical education, 75a
an efficient organization, 75b
academic atmosphere, science, 195a

Steele, James
loyal ally, exchanges, 80a

Steenman, L.F.
a little song of Cobalt, 138b

Stefansson, Vilhjalmur
unethical advertising, 12b
friendly Arctic, 15b
no prime minister exiled, 15b
agnosticism modest faith, 20b
Englishman sets foot on, 69b
their dreams of empire, 72a
would not appeal to fish, 86a
northward course of empire, 160a
have no remarkable future, 160a
Russians live North and, 160a
philosophers still arguing, 171b

Stegner, Wallace
prairie, land to mark, 178b

Stein, David Lewis
awaiting the next pogrom, 114b

Steinberg, Nathan
man goes without food, 86b

Stephen, George
stand fast, Craigellachie, 39b

Stephenson, Bette
psyches, their epididymis, 137b

Stevens, Geoffrey
Canadians, sense of absurd, 42a

Steward, Mary McIver
when the goals are known, 180a

Stewart, Andrew
Canadian content, 26b

Strachan, John
vote by ballot, ignorance, 76a
the law, the law, 123b
Washington, those at York, 225a

Straiton, John
advertising or Russia, 12b

Stratas, Teresa
don't call me Callas, 145b

artistic cult of the North, 160a
no CCF government will rest, 201b
between two managers, one, 201b
basis of socialism, ethical, 201b

Updike, John
great Victorian piles, 213b
British inns restored, 210b

Uvavnuk
great sea has set me, 100a

V

Vallières, Pierre
Confederation, financial, 57b
white nigger of America, 184b

Vancouver, Capt. George
beauties of this region, 221a

Van Horne, Sir W.C.
big things, no competition, 10b
building railroad, citizen, 39b
last spike, iron, 39b
done well in every way, 39b
future, as certain as, 92b
passes on Canadian Pacific, 170a
universal peace, either, 170b
sleep is only a habit, 200a
raise less hell, wheat, 230a

Vanier, Jean
all sick, all lonely, 129b
power with love, charity, 178a

Van Stolk, Mary
no lobbyists for children, 47a

Varley, F.H.
trouble, good for mankind, 215b

Vaudreuil-Cavagnal, Marquis de
Quebec is impregnable, 58a

Verchères, Madeleine de
fight to the death, 155a

Vickers, Jon
Canada is a great school, 145b

Victoria, Queen
unbroken chain from, 24a
shall form and be one, 71a

Viger, Denis-Benjamin
maple, king of our forests, 134b

Vigneault, Gilles
passport bilingual but, 21a

mon pays, ce n'est pas, 196a
my country, not a country, 196a

Viirlaid, Arved
man's spirit will grow, 108b

Vinci, Leonardo da
beaver eats testicles, 19a

Vizinczey, Stephen
dreams, be splendid, 72a
more power over ourselves, 177b
defeated know the secret, 179b

Vlastos, Gregory
life is human relatedness, 126a

Volkoff, Boris
nation's character, dances, 66b
dance good, it hurts, 66b

Voltaire
prefer peace to Canada, 58a
at war over a few acres of snow, 200a

W

Waddington, Miriam
scratch us, bleed history, 93b

Wales, Prince of
See Charles, Prince.

Walker, Thomas
behold the pope of, 45a

Wallace, Frederick William
wooden ships, iron men, 199a

Wallace, Joe
cough in Washington, 37a
panic, peace broke out, 170b
a politician's brother, 175a
American way of life, 220a

Wallace, W. Stewart
beginning was geography, 93a

Walters, Angus J.
vessel beat the *Bluenose*, 199b

Walz, Jay and Audrey
Laura Secord candy stores, 197a

Ward, Barbara
Canada, international nation, 33b

Warman, Cy
come to me, Sweet Marie, 129b